D1270473

You May Survive Armageddon into God's New World

"Before the day of Jehovah's anger come upon you. Seek ye Jehovah, all ye meek of the earth, that have kept his ordinances; seek righteousness, seek meekness: it may be ye will be hid in the day of Jehovah's anger."

—Zephaniah 2:2, 3, *American Standard Version.*

PUBLISHERS

WATCHTOWER BIBLE AND TRACT SOCIETY, INC.
INTERNATIONAL BIBLE STUDENTS ASSOCIATION
Brooklyn, New York, U.S.A.

1,750,000 Edition

DEDICATED

to the triumphant Kingdom of God,
for building up the hope
of all who want to live
in His incoming new world.

CONTENTS

CHAPTER   PAGE

1   Proclaiming the Good News 7

2   The Victorious Fighters at Armageddon . . 18

3   The Basis for Survival 31

4   The Universalness of the Conflict 51

5   Building the Armageddon-surviving Temple . 68

6   A·do·nay' Comes to His Temple 85

7   Shortening the Days for the Chosen Ones' Sake 107

8   Raising the Signal to All the Nations . . . 126

9   Separating the Peoples for Life or Destruction 159

10   Gathering the Great Crowd to the Temple . . 170

11   Gathering of the Nations to Armageddon . . 190

12   Executioners of the Divine Vengeance . . . 202

13   The Chief Executioner Takes a Wife . . . 218

14   The Flight to Safety 231

15   Fighting for Life Now as Jehovah's Witnesses 245

16   The "Desire of All Nations" Comes In . . . 260

17   Living Now in the New World Society . . . 273

18   Constructive, Lifesaving Activities 288

19   Benefits Flowing from the Temple 302

20   Awaiting the Attack by Gog of Magog . . . 315

21   The Universal War of Armageddon Breaks Out 331

22   God's New World After the Battle 348

23   Individual Decision Now for Surviving
Armageddon 362

List of 42 Types and Prophecies of the Earthly
Heirs of the New World 367

You May Survive Armageddon into God's New World

CHAPTER I

Proclaiming the Good News

SUNDAY afternoon, July 26, 1953, the sun shone brightly on the home of the permanent headquarters of the United Nations at New York city. On a marble wall that faces on the United Nations Plaza stood carved in large letters the words: "They shall beat their swords into plowshares, and their spears into pruning hooks. Nation shall not lift up sword against nation, neither shall they learn war any more."

[2] Those striking words had not originated with any of the framers of the United Nations. They are words far older that have echoed down through the previous twenty-six centuries from the lips of an ancient prophet of the Near East, Isaiah the Hebrew. The designers of the United Nations buildings had merely taken the words to themselves from the prophet's book found in that sacred volume known as The Holy Scriptures, The Holy

---

1, 2. (a) What words of Isaiah stand carved upon a wall of the United Nations structures in New York city, and for what reason? (b) Was it therefore from there that the good news was to be proclaimed to people from 97 lands Sunday, July 26, 1953?

Bible. Without authority they had copied them and carved them into the marble of the United Nations structures as symbolizing the United Nations' purposes "to maintain international peace and security: and . . . develop friendly relations among nations and to take other appropriate measures to strengthen universal peace." Halfway round the world, at Panmunjom, Korea, Monday, July 27, was already dawning, and that day representatives of the United Nations armies were preparing to sign with the Communist army representatives a truce to end the three-year-old Korean war that had come dangerously near to embroiling the nations in a third world war. However, it was not from this international organization's buildings there on the East River water front, between 42d Street and 48th Street, of New York city that the good news was to be proclaimed to representatives from ninety-seven lands this memorable Sunday afternoon.

[3] The number of visitors that afternoon to the United Nations buildings paled into insignificance in comparison with the tremendous throng gathered six air-line miles to the northwest at the world-famous sports stadium, the Yankee baseball park. There it was the eighth and last day of an international assembly that had changed Yankee Stadium from a popular sports arena into an assembly place for matters of far grander importance to all mankind. There that same Sunday morning at the climax of a speech on Haggai 2:7 those same words of the prophet Isaiah had rung out: "They shall forge their swords into ploughshares, and their spears into pruning-knives: nation shall not lift up sword against nation, neither shall they learn war any more."[*] The speaker applied them,

---

[*] Quoted from Isaiah, chapter 2, verse 4 (Da), in the 10:15 a.m. speech entitled "Filling the House with Glory."

---

3. How did those words of Isaiah happen to be applied at Yankee Stadium that Sunday morning?

not to the United Nations, but to a New World society.

[4] But now four o'clock in the afternoon had come. Never had there been seen at Yankee Stadium the sight that now greeted the eye, from the ground, from the spectator stands and from the airplane that wheeled above taking pictures. The baseball diamond had been transformed into a small paradise-like scene around the speaker's stand. The three-level spectator stands and the bleachers surrounding the playing field on every side were filled to the last seat. Outside the stadium vast overflow tents were filled with 25,240 persons anxious to hear by loud-speakers. But the crowd that turned out to hear the good news was too large; there was

—————
4. By 4 p.m. that Sunday afternoon how did Yankee Stadium come to be filled to overflowing with people?

not enough room in the tents and in the stadium stands. So a few minutes before the announced hour the gates were thrown open and thousands of men, women and children streamed in and onto the green playing field to seat themselves in well-ordered groups on the green grass to listen, swelling the crowd inside the stadium to 91,562 persons.

[5] Many other conventioners were listening elsewhere. At the assembly's "Trailer City" forty miles to the west in the neighboring state of New Jersey there was another record crowd of 49,027, to listen by direct wire connection with Yankee Stadium, making a total visible audience of 165,829. Besides that, by means of remote control, one of New York city's pioneer radio stations, WBBR, was daily broadcasting the convention's features over an area occupied by some fifteen million people, and it now stood ready to beam out to an uncountable invisible audience at their radio sets the good news to be proclaimed. Accountable for this record turnout was the tremendous advertising both before and during the convention—the millions of folders and handbills distributed, the thousands of window cards placed to view, the thousands of placards worn by information walkers on the city streets, the thousands of signs on the bumpers and sides of automobiles, and two placards in each and every subway car of New York's three subway systems.

[6] What was the good news to be proclaimed that brought together such a crowd on a hot July afternoon? It was the good news summed up in the intensely advertised subject, "After Armageddon —God's New World." The speaker was the presi-

5. How was the total visible audience raised to a record crowd of 165,829, how was an invisible audience served, and what was accountable for this record turnout?
6. What was the good news to be proclaimed that afternoon, and what opening words of the speaker drew applause?

dent of an organization represented in 143 lands at the time, far more lands than the sixty members of the United Nations. The speaker's very first words were applauded: "Armageddon will be the worst thing ever to hit the earth within the history of man. God's new world will be the best thing ever to come to distressed mankind and will never pass away." He went on: "For us to know that the best immediately follows the worst gives us courage to consider the subject of our discussion. . . . So if we have yet to endure Armageddon, it will be better for us to face it with understanding, in the hope of surviving and entering into a new world of God's making, a world altogether different from the one mankind has known now for thousands of years, to its sorrow. Armageddon will prove a great blessing in disguise."

⁷ Toward the close of his speech the speaker emphasized this "hope of surviving" by these words: "Just a while ago we said that the vast majority of the subjects of the new world's King will be people restored to life on earth by the resurrection of the dead. Why only the 'vast majority,' and not all? Because there is a great crowd of people of good will today living who will survive the world catastrophe of Armageddon and enter the world of new heavens and new earth without going down into the grave or ever afterward having the need to die and cease to exist. That means that Armageddon is so near at hand it will strike the generation now living." Then after an explanation came the encouragement to be among the Armageddon survivors: "Avoid perishing with this old world in the 'war of the great day of God the Almighty.' Get ready now to live AFTER ARMA-GEDDON in GOD'S NEW WORLD!" With these words the president of the Watch Tower Bible & Tract

_____

7. How was encouragement finally given to be Armageddon survivors, and after the speech what were all in the visible audience given?

Society closed his prepared speech to that 1953 international assembly of Jehovah's witnesses in Yankee Stadium, after which all the 165,829 in his visible audience were offered free printed copies of the speech.

[8] Never before in these twenty centuries of the so-called "Christian era" had there been such a stupendous witness on one occasion concerning this war with the ominous name Armageddon and concerning what it really means to mankind, especially the generation in which we are now living. With the passing of the years since then the warning witness regarding the real Armageddon has been greatly expanded world-wide. The seriousness of it deserves the greatest possible witness to all the nations. Its steady approach and its certainty to break forth at an unguarded hour for mankind inside this generation make it urgent that it be proclaimed on the greatest possible scale and that without letup.

[9] Faced with what the world faces from its own mad course, even men of this world take seriously their ideas of what Armageddon means and talk about it without embarrassment. Into the pages of the very *Congressional Record* of the United States Congress there have gone these words uttered on the Senate floor by the junior senator from the state of Vermont under date of March 9, 1954: "In very truth the world seems to be mobilizing for the great battle of Armageddon. Now is a crisis in the agelong warfare between God and the Devil for the souls of men." (Pages 2726-2727)

[10] Such men of this world, politicians, military

---

8. How did that witness concerning Armageddon compare with any previous, and why does it deserve the greatest possible witness?

9. How do even men of this world talk concerning Armageddon, according to their ideas of it?

10. How did this all-surpassing war come to be named, and how was its thieflike coming foretold by the greatest prophet ever on earth?

men and religious leaders, have not told the true facts about Armageddon, but have merely made the people familiar with the name as meaning something frightful that is stealing up on the human race. Long ago a prophet from heaven, the greatest prophet ever on earth, named this all-surpassing war and warned of its thieflike coming, in a revelation to his faithful follower, who wrote: "And I saw three unclean inspired expressions that looked like frogs come out of the mouth of the dragon and out of the mouth of the wild beast and out of the mouth of the false prophet. They are, in fact, expressions inspired by demons and perform signs, and they go forth to the kings of the entire inhabited earth, to gather them together to the war of the great day of God the Almighty. Look! I am coming as a thief. . . . And they gathered them together to the place that is called in Hebrew Har–Magedon [or, Armageddon]." That revelation was given in order to show "the things that must shortly take place."—Revelation 16:13-16; 1:1, NW.*

[11] That revelation having been given and written down about A.D. 96, it is now about nineteen centuries since the warning of the war was given by name, and we are at least that much nearer it. But the passing of all those centuries does not in itself argue that the surprise outbreak of Armageddon is near. Rather, the conditions and the events of the world in fulfillment of the great prophet's predictions, the noticeable going forth of the three unclean, froglike expressions inspired by the demons to the kings of the entire inhabited

---

* NW stands for the New World Translation of the Bible. See page 5 for the list of abbreviations of Bible translations used herein.

---

11. Aside from the passing of time since the warning, what makes it certain that the world catastrophe is not far off?

earth followed by the noticeable gathering of the
kings to a modern Armageddon, and the irrepres-
sible giving of a foretold witness concerning Armageddon on a globe-encircling scale, make it certain that this unequaled world catastrophe is not
far off. It is a time of all times to consider the
evidence at hand.

[12] This is not calamity-howling. The Holy Scriptures or Bible, which contains the warning and
description of the war of Armageddon, is not a
calamity-howling book. God's new world, which it
foretells as certain to follow Armageddon, is no
calamity. Armageddon will be a calamitous catastrophe, not for the winners, but for the losers. The
winners will enter God's new world. In this sense
those who examine into Armageddon need not
fear like those who dread a third world war and
for whom the terrible question is, "not who will
win a big war if ever there is one, but who will be
on hand—and in what condition—after such a
war is over?" All will lose, they fear, winner as
well as loser. But such is not the question and
conclusion for those who inform themselves on
the real Armageddon. They are assured that there
will be people on earth after the war of Armageddon, and they will be in a blessed condition.

[13] Ordinarily, for us to think of trouble is not
pleasant and we shrink from it. But the consideration of Armageddon, rightly understood, is inviting
and beneficial. No part of the earth will escape this
war. There will be no neutrals in this war; each
one will have to be on either the one side or the
other. Happy will those be who find themselves on
the winning side. Only those who favor and uphold
the winning side may have any hope of surviving
this greatest of all wars. It is possible now to know

12. For what reasons is this not calamity-howling?
13. What is it that invites us to a consideration of
Armageddon and of what follows it, and how do we
show ourselves wise concerning it?

the winning side and take one's stand in advance on it. And this is what invites us to a consideration of Armageddon and of God's new world that will follow it. That is why we are wise if we are thoughtful and consider the overwhelming evidence of the nearness of it. The proverbs of wisdom advise us against acting hastily without knowledge and taking a disastrous course: "It is not good for a man to be without knowledge, and he who makes haste with his feet misses his way. A prudent man sees danger and hides himself; but the simple go on, and suffer for it." (Proverbs 19:2; 22:3, *RS*) So do not consider this mere calamity-howling, scoff at it and go on in simplicity and suffer. "How long will scoffers delight in their scoffing and fools hate knowledge?" "A scoffer is punished." (Proverbs 1:22; 21:11, *RS*) Face the facts, understand them, and then choose the way of survival.

[14] The Bible is the only book on earth that tells us about the war of Armageddon and about God's new world to follow it. This is one of the many things that make the Bible the outstanding book among all the ancient books that are reputed to be sacred. We are under sheer necessity to go to the Bible if we want to know the truth about this important subject. Although its sixty-six books were completed almost nineteen hundred years ago, the Bible is not old-fashioned and out of date. It is of practical value today. It is far in advance of any other book on earth, no matter how recently written, and its prophecies that pierce into the future are actually history written in advance, so certain are they of being fulfilled. Its foreknowledge of the future, its sound rules for happy living, its view of life, its explanation of the cause of mankind's imperfect, dying condition and of the

14. For the truth about this important subject to what book are we under sheer necessity to go, and what proves that this book comes from a mind higher than that of its writers?

one remedy, and its showing us the road to salvation from this unsatisfying old world into a new world of endless life without torment of any kind, all this proves that the Holy Bible comes to us from a good and loving Mind far higher than that of the thirty-five or more men who were inspired to write its sixty-six books.

¹⁵ "Inspired to write"? Yes; for its very writers confessed that they did not write of their own accord. Peter, a writer of two books of the Holy Scriptures bearing his name, reminds us: "You know this first, that no prophecy of Scripture springs from any private release. For prophecy was at no time brought by man's will, but men spoke from God as they were borne along by holy spirit." (2 Peter 1:20, 21, *NW*) King David of the ancient nation of Israel, who wrote many prophetic songs or psalms, showed where and how he got his information, saying: "The spirit of Jehovah it was that spoke by me, and his word was upon my tongue. The God of Israel said, to me the Rock of Israel spoke." (2 Samuel 23:2, 3, *NW*) That is why the Holy Bible tells the truth and gives us information we can get from no other source. That is why it, above all other books, is worthy of our enjoyable study and of our fullest confidence. The more we know of it the more heartily we join in the confession to its great Author: "Your word is truth."—John 17:17, *NW*.

¹⁶ We need not be filled with fear, dread and horror as we take up an examination of Armageddon and what will follow. No matter how terrible that war will be, we can know its righteous purpose, and always we can let ring in our inner con-

---

15. Due to being written in what way does the Bible tell the truth and give us information we cannot get elsewhere?
16. Because of what special possibility for us need we not be filled with fear as we examine Armageddon and what follows it?

sciousness the cheering thought: "I may survive Armageddon into God's new world!" This thought is no self-deceiving dream. The same inspired Word that unerringly foretold many centuries ago the very situation that we face up to in this generation also drew many pictures, staged many prophetic dramas and presented many direct prophecies of the ones to be protected all through the war of Armageddon.

[17] It sharpens our interest to consider that unavoidable war from the standpoint of those who will live through it into the grandeurs of God's new world. In fact, it becomes an absorbing, delightsome, thrilling consideration for us. To share this delight with our readers, we hope in following pages to look into at least forty-two of these typical pictures, prophetic life-dramas and direct prophecies regarding the Armageddon survivors.* All these are very instructive and vital for us to consider now, for they show us in one way or another things that we should wisely do now in order to be of the favored class. "For all the things that were written aforetime were written for our instruction, that through our endurance and through the comfort from the Scriptures we might have hope." (Romans 15:4, *NW*) "Consequently, we have the prophetic word made more firm, and you are doing well in paying attention to it as to a lamp shining in a dark place, until day dawns and a daystar rises, in your hearts." (2 Peter 1:19, *NW*) For our part, we are thankful thus to carry forward the proclamation of the good news, in the hope that you, our reader, may be one of Armageddon's survivors, to enjoy forever God's new world afterward.

---

* See the list on pages 367, 368.

---

17. From whose standpoint does a considering of Armageddon sharpen our interest, and so what does the book hope to do, and why?

CHAPTER II

The Victorious Fighters at Armageddon

NO ONE can gain victory over an almighty fighter, nor can an almighty fighter ever lose. The prize of victory at Armageddon is so great, the issues that are to be fought out are so universal, that the war calls for the Almighty God of the universe himself to go into action. That explains why the war fought at Armageddon is Scripturally called "the war of the great day of God the Almighty." (Revelation 16:14, 16, *NW*) Those who are on his side can there say without national self-conceit, "God is with us."

[2] No one but the Almighty could take on a fight against all who array themselves against us and be certain to overcome all those that are against him. Against him there are now arraying themselves not only the "kings of the entire inhabited earth" but also the invisible demons who inspire the expressions that irresistibly gather all the earth's political rulers and their armies to the battlefield. That means also the great rebel against all divine authority, who is called the "ruler of the demons." Religious men contemptuously called him "Be·el'ze·bub," but his God-given names and titles are "the great dragon . . . the original serpent, the one called Devil and Satan, who is mis-

---

1. Why is Armageddon Scripturally called "the war of the great day of God the Almighty"?
2. Who will be arrayed against us and Him so that only the Almighty could take on the fight and overcome all such opponents?

18

leading the entire inhabited earth." (Matthew
9:34; 12:24-28 and Revelation 12:9, *NW*) He is
not merely the "ruler of the demons." He is even
the "ruler of this world," for which reason he
claims "all the kingdoms of the inhabited earth,"
and "the whole world is lying in the power of the
wicked one." (John 12:31; 14:30; Luke 4:5-7 and
1 John 5:19, *NW*) The seven great world powers taken note of in Bible history have all been
subject to his domination—Egypt, Assyria, Babylon, Medo-Persia, Greece, Rome and the British-
American imperial power, together with an eighth
world power that stems from the preceding seven,
namely, the present United Nations, successor to
the League of Nations. In his mighty position as
world ruler Satan the Devil can use his superhuman demons to maneuver the kings of the whole
inhabited earth onto his side and against Almighty
God.

³ Does the Almighty God have a name? Yes, and
at the showdown fight at Armageddon all men of
the nations will come to know the name of Him
against whom they are fighting. The prophetic
psalm prays to God, saying: "Let them be put to
shame and dismayed for ever; yea, let them be con-
founded and perish; that they may know that thou
alone, whose name is Jehovah, art the Most High
over all the earth." (Psalm 83:17, 18, *AS; Da; Yg;
Ro*) Jehovah comes out on top.

⁴ Armageddon will therefore be a battle of gods,
gods invisible and spiritual and persons among
men who are addressed as "gods" or divinities.
Besides being the "ruler of this world," Satan the
Devil is Scripturally called "the god of this system
of things." This means that those who are a part
of this world and who uphold this system of things

---

3. At Armageddon what will men of all the nations
come to know concerning the Almighty God?
4, 5. What scriptures show that Armageddon will be a
battle of gods, human as well as invisible spirit gods?

worship, in fact, Satan the Devil, regardless of how religiously they may deny this. (2 Corinthians 4:4, *NW;* Romans 6:16) The sacrifices that many tribes and nations offer to idols and images they really offer to the demons and to their ruler, Satan the Devil. Says an inspired writer on this: "I say that the things which the nations sacrifice they sacrifice to demons, and not to God, and I do not want you to become sharers with the demons." (1 Corinthians 10:20, *NW*) Besides demon gods, there are today men to whom are given the honors, praises, adulation and worship due only to the one living and true God. Recognizing that such are mighty ones among men, who claim to be sons of the Most High God, the inspired psalmist said: "I say, 'You are gods, sons of the Most High, all of you; nevertheless, you shall die like men, and fall like any prince.' "—Psalm 82:6, 7, *RS.*

⁵ Jesus Christ quoted this psalm to his enemies and said: "Is it not written in your Law, 'I said: You are gods'? If he called 'gods' those against whom the word of God came, and yet the Scripture cannot be nullified, do you say to me whom the Father sanctified and dispatched into the world, 'You blaspheme,' because I said, I am God's Son?" (John 10:34-36, *NW*) Different peoples may have their particular gods, but to the adherent of the Holy Bible Jehovah is the one Most High and Almighty God. "There is no God but one. For even though there are those who are called 'gods', whether in heaven or on earth, just as there are many 'gods' and many 'lords', there is actually to us one God the Father, out of whom all things are, and we for him, and there is one Lord, Jesus Christ, through whom all things are, and we through him." (1 Corinthians 8:4-6, *NW*) So at Armageddon Satan the Devil, the mighty "god of this system of things," with all his host of so-called "gods," will face Jehovah the Almighty God of the new world.

⁶ All the earth will be the scene of action. The more the astronomers with their mighty telescopes peer toward the outward reaches of our visible expanding universe, now reckoned to be about 4,800,000,000 years old,* the more our tiny planet earth shrinks in size by way of comparison; the more, too, its main inhabitant man shrinks in importance. How is it, then, that the Most High and Almighty God, who alone bears the name Jehovah, tangles with the mighty adversary Satan the Devil in battle with reference to our earth? It is not because earth or man upon it is so important, but because the chief issue of all, the issue of universal sovereignty, is tied in with this earth and must now be settled once and for all time. "Sovereignty" means more than supremacy. It means supreme and independent power in government and thus one's dominating all below as a sovereign lord. Jehovah God is the Creator of all things seen and unseen. The opening chapter of the Holy Bible says: "In the beginning God created the heavens and the earth," and then goes on to give us a day-by-day description of the ordering of our planet and of all life upon it, including man. (Genesis, chapter 1, *NW*) This earth and its inhabitants belong to Jehovah God. So his universal sovereignty rightly extends to earth also, by reason of his being Creator. He is the great Sovereign, *A·do·nay'* or "Lord" over all, including this earth, no matter how small it is.

⁷ By the way men and nations carry on they deny Jehovah's sovereignty over the earth. If they

---

* See the New York *Times* of February 26, 1955, page 17, last column.

6. Is it because of earth or man's importance that Jehovah tangles in battle with reference to our earth? And how does the matter of creation help us to see the reason for it?

7. Why is it at the earth that Jehovah's universal sovereignty must be vindicated, and so why will Armageddon outrank all previous battles?

could carry into reality their proposed space ships and land on other planets they would extend their defiance of His sovereignty there also. There is one creature that has no space ship and needs none and who has had entry into the heavens, into the very presence of God, and who has tried to stir up the defiance of Jehovah's sovereignty in all the heavens as well as in the earth. That rebellious creature is the "god of this system of things," Satan the Devil. It was here at the earth that he began his treason against the true and rightful Sovereign of the universe. Here he turned unfaithful to his trustworthy position in which the great Creator had placed him over man and he incited the first man and woman rebelliously to break the commandment of God as not being their Sovereign. His universal sovereignty having first been set in doubt here, and men and demons at this earth still challenging and defying the sovereignty of Jehovah, it is here that the chief issue must be put to rest and Jehovah's universal sovereignty be vindicated. The earth is now the "hot spot" of the universe, and the settling of the main question in dispute here will result in his vindication and glory and in the blessing of all men who take his side in the great controversy. The six-thousand-year-old issue will finally be settled at Armageddon, and that is why the battle there will outrank all previous battles.

⁸ Since the "whole world is lying in the power of the wicked one," practically all of mankind are lining up at Armageddon in opposition to the universal sovereignty of Jehovah God. Invisibly behind them are the legions of demons under their ruler, Satan the Devil. However, the Almighty God has had an invisible, heavenly, spiritual organiza-

---

8. Who in heaven will stand loyal and true to Jehovah's sovereignty at Armageddon, and what will the one in the foremost battle position there do to the "original serpent"?

tion that has stood loyal and true to him, just like a faithful, devoted wife. Jehovah God speaks of this inseparable organization as his "woman," his wife, who acknowledges and obeys him as Sovereign Lord. To demonstrate to all intelligent creation that he commands the love and unswerving allegiance of his wifely organization, yes, the allegiance of the chief and highest member of it, Jehovah has called into combined action with him in the war of Armageddon his first and most beloved Son, now known as Jesus Christ. At his right side in the battle the great Sovereign Lord Jehovah will fight: "The Lord [*A·do·nay'*] at thy right hand shall strike through kings in the day of his wrath." (Psalm 110:5) Assigning this Chief Member or Seed of his wifely organization to this foremost battle position at Armageddon, Jehovah said to the first rebel, "the original serpent," there in the garden of Eden almost six thousand years ago: "I shall put enmity between you and the woman and between your seed and her seed. He will bruise you in the head and you will bruise him in the heel." (Genesis 3:15, *NW*) In demonstration of his love and unwavering allegiance to the universal Sovereign, Jesus Christ as a heavenly Warrior will display his full enmity against the "original serpent" and his seed. He will bruise him in the head by a decisive victory over the enemy in vindication of Jehovah's universal sovereignty. Many battle survivors on earth will witness that glorious triumph.

⁹ Associated with the Son of God, the Seed of God's woman, in that issue-settling fight will be many angels. They will be a match for all the demons on the side of the "original serpent." This is made sure by a number of prophecies. Speaking of himself as "the Son of man," Jesus Christ prophe-

---

9. Who do the prophecies show will be associated with him in that issue-settling fight, and so why will Armageddon be a universal war?

sied of his coming into his heavenly kingdom and said: "When the Son of man arrives in his glory and all the angels with him, then he will sit down on his glorious throne." (Matthew 25:31, *NW*) In heaven he has always been known as "The Word of God," because of being God's Chief Spokesman. Therefore the following symbolic description of the forces of righteousness riding into battle applies to him and his angelic armies: "The name he is called is The Word of God. Also the armies that were in heaven were following him on white horses, and they were clothed in white, clean, fine linen. And out of his mouth there protrudes a sharp long sword, that he may smite the nations with it, and he will shepherd them with a rod of iron. He treads, too, the press of the wine of the anger of the wrath of God the Almighty. And upon his outer garment, even upon his thigh, he has a name written, King of kings and Lord of lords." (Revelation 19:11-16, *NW*) The taking part by Almighty God and his enthroned Son and the holy angels in the fight at Armageddon against rebellious spirit hosts will make Armageddon a universal war, involving heaven as well as earth. Never will there have been anything like it.

[10] There mankind will come to know Jesus Christ as they have not known him before. Christendom has no faith to look forward in the light of Bible prophecy but prefers to look back nineteen centuries and remember the Son of God as the self-sacrificing Jesus, yielding himself to be slaughtered like an unprotesting lamb. In the garden of Gethsemane, when he was being betrayed by one of his own twelve apostles, and when Peter struck with a sword in his defense against the soldiers, Jesus miraculously healed the wounded man and said to Peter: "Return your sword to its place, for

10. How was Jesus different in conduct nineteen hundred years ago from what he will be at Armageddon, and why?

all those who take the sword will perish by the sword. Or do you think that I cannot appeal to my Father to supply me at this moment more than twelve legions of angels? In that case, how would the Scriptures be fulfilled that it must take place this way?" (Matthew 26:48-54, *NW*) In order for the inspired prophecies to be fulfilled that foretold his sacrificial death, Jesus showed his unbreakable allegiance to Jehovah's universal sovereignty and his loving submission to the universal Sovereign's will. Thus he kept his integrity to his universal Sovereign down to the death, the shameful, painful death on a torture stake before the public eye at Calvary. His faithfulness until such a death in obedience to the divine will served as a vindication of Jehovah's universal sovereignty and showed His sovereignty to be the rightful thing to govern our lives. At the same time his death served as a means to give up his perfect human life as a repurchase price to buy back all obedient humans from the slavery of sin and its penalty death.

¹¹ But that was nineteen centuries ago. Now in order to fulfill other prophecies that foretold the future work he had to do, Jesus comes in royal heavenly glory, no more as a self-sacrificing Son of man, but as a mighty, unconquerable Fighter accompanied by many legions of angels, to rid the universe of all the enemies of Jehovah God and his universal sovereignty. Christendom may not expect to escape. All the hypocritical Christians in her will be executed along with all those who openly defy the universal sovereignty of the Most High God. Christendom does not like to think of God and Christ from the standpoint of divine justice, which requires that the enemy and the hypocrite be executed. She prefers to view God and

---

11. (a) But how does Jesus come now, and why that way? (b) Why may Christendom not expect to escape?

Christ his Son only from the standpoint of her favorite Bible verses: "For God so loved the world, that he gave his only begotten Son, that whosoever believeth in him should not perish, but have everlasting life. For God sent not his Son into the world to condemn the world; but that the world through him might be saved." (John 3:16, 17) But God is just even as he is loving, and his love does not overstep or set aside his justice. He must be just with himself as well as loving to undeserving sinners. "He cannot deny himself." (2 Timothy 2:13) He cannot be untrue to the eternal facts about himself. He cannot deny or ever renounce the fact that he is Sovereign of all the universe of which he is the Creator. He cannot let any of his creatures forever deny that all-important fact without finally being called to account for such willful denial.

[12] The all-transcending issue before all creation is the universal sovereignty of Jehovah the Most High and Almighty God. The foremost act of justice is to vindicate, to justify, his universal sovereignty before not only this earth but all the universe. That is overwhelmingly more important than the mere saving of earthly creatures who were justly condemned to death because of their imperfect, sinful condition. Jesus Christ loves Jehovah God more than man or any other creature, for the commandment to love God with everything we are and have is first and the commandment to love our neighbor as ourselves is second. (Matthew 22:35-40; Deuteronomy 6:5; Leviticus 19:18) Jesus Christ loves Jehovah God his heavenly Father. Although he knew he faced a cruel martyr's death here on earth he said to his loyal apostles: "In order for the world to know that I love the Father, I am even doing just the way the Father has given

---

12. What is the foremost act of justice, and how does Jesus show his love in connection with it?

me commandment to do." (John 14:31, *NW*) Jesus loves the vindication of his heavenly Father's universal sovereignty because that vindication is just and right and deserved; and Jehovah God has commanded Jesus Christ the Seed of His "woman" to be the Chief One in carrying out that vindication. Therefore the battle of Armageddon must come, although it means the greatest destruction of human life, for it is by this supreme conflict that the chief issue of all time will be forever settled, the universal sovereignty of Jehovah God the Creator and King of eternity.

[13] At that battle the once self-sacrificing Son of God must, out of his supreme love of God, play a different part, that of a Fighter bruising the original Serpent in the head and destroying the "kings of the entire inhabited earth" and all their patriotic backers. Then will occur the "revelation of the Lord Jesus from heaven with his powerful angels in a flaming fire, as he brings due punishment upon those who do not know God and those who do not obey the good news about our Lord Jesus. These very ones will pay the penalty of everlasting destruction from before the Lord and from the glory of his strength, at the time he comes to be glorified in connection with his holy ones." The fight at Armageddon will be righteous on the part of God and of Jesus Christ, even if it does mean the greatest tribulation since the world's beginning. "It is righteous on God's part to repay tribulation to those who make tribulation for you."—2 Thessalonians 1:6-10, *NW;* Matthew 24:21.

[14] Nineteen centuries ago God's love was so great that he gave his only-begotten Son that the

---

13. So what part does Jesus play at Armageddon, and why will it be a righteous war despite its being a tribulation?
14. Nineteen centuries ago how great was God's love for the world, and so what may he be expected to do at Armageddon for those he loves?

believers in him might not perish but have everlasting life. It was these believers that God loved so much as to make this unselfish provision for them, and at Armageddon Jehovah God by his Son Jesus Christ will fight for those he loves. Jehovah God has long been known as a Fighter. From the time that he fought to rescue the nation of Israel from slavery in ancient Egypt down till the religious leaders of Israel called for Jesus Christ to be killed on a torture stake outside Jerusalem, Jehovah loved that chosen people of his and he was their God. During those fifteen centuries he fought violently for the people of Israel out of love for them, so that his victories in war are recorded in these words: "Jehovah the God of Israel it was who was fighting for Israel." "They heard that Jehovah had fought against the enemies of Israel."—Joshua 10:42 and 2 Chronicles 20:29, *NW*.

[15] Sentimental Christian religionists pretend to recoil in horror and disgust at the historic fact of

---

15. How do sentimental Christian religionists blaspheme Jehovah respecting his ancient war record, but what kind of God do they show they worship when their nation gets involved in war with another nation?

Jehovah's fighting with such destruction to the enemies of his loved people. They call him a "tribal God," a "big bully," "cruel," "bloodthirsty" and "vengeful." They indulge in all such blasphemy of Jehovah God only till their political government and nation gets into war with another nation. Then what do these same Christian religionists do? Led by their clergymen, Catholic and Protestant, they pray to God that He should be with their armies and help them to  shed the blood and destroy the lives and property of their enemies to gain the victory, even though these national enemies are of the same religious faith, Catholic or Protestant. They will even offer such prayers to God after they have called in heathen armies and ungodly Communists to help them as allies to gain the victory. What kind of God is it that such war-mad Christian religionists then worship? And do they then look upon Jesus Christ as a warrior fighting at the head of their armies with weapons of wholesale destruction?

[16] Christendom's armies have fought for world

16. For what have Christendom's armies not fought, and why have God and Christ not taken part in Christendom's wars?

domination as regards the earth, but not for the universal sovereignty of Jehovah God. There is no inspired record that either Jehovah God of ancient Israel or Jesus Christ his Son has taken part in any of the wars of Christendom and fought for any of her nations. The prophetic Scriptures of the inspired Bible declare that Jehovah God and Jesus Christ his glorified Son have reserved their fighting for the field of Armageddon, when Satan the Devil and all his spirit demons and the kings of the entire inhabited earth and all their armies and peoples are unitedly challenging the universal sovereignty of Jehovah God and rejecting the kingdom of his Son Jesus Christ. Concerning that time the prophecy says: "Then shall Jehovah go forth, and fight against those nations, as when he fought in the day of battle. And Jehovah shall be King over all the earth: in that day shall Jehovah be one, and his name one." (Zechariah 14:3, 9, *AS*) Past wars of man have settled nothing, but Armageddon will settle the biggest issue before all creatures in heaven and earth, universal sovereignty, and that in favor of Jehovah. Then the new world, in which His will is to be done everywhere, will follow.

¹⁷ In the face of all this, do not miss the point that is vital for you. Your frail life, sinful as it is, is as nothing compared with justifying Jehovah God to his rightful place in the universe. At Armageddon your life will count for nothing if you are against His sovereignty over all creation. If you want to survive that most terrific war of all time you must love Jehovah's universal sovereignty, just as his Son Jesus Christ does; you must uphold it and proclaim it and remain true to it at all costs until it is vindicated. Only then may you survive Armageddon, receiving this consideration from the victorious Fighters there.

17. In view of universal sovereignty's being foremost, what vital point must we not miss?

CHAPTER III

The Basis for Survival

NOT just to live through the coming universal war and to die afterward, but to continue living afterward in God's new world—that is the solidly based opportunity set before people of this generation. That means that many will not die off the face of this earth. They will keep living to enjoy the earth in a paradise condition forever. This earth has had many generations of humankind live upon it; and the inspired saying has been true: "A generation goes, and a generation comes, but the earth remains for ever." (Ecclesiastes 1:4, *RS*) Here the generations have been literal, and so the "earth" here meant is also literal. Many of the present generation of mankind may have the privilege of remaining on earth as long as the earth remains—forever. Up till now the reason for the coming and going of generation after generation has been a death to which all the race of man has been condemned. Wars have killed off countless multitudes, but those surviving the violence and hardships of such wars have sooner or later fallen victim to the inescapable condemnation resting upon all men and have died. They have had to die, without exception. So the basis for any to [...]geddon and to enjoy living on a [...]arth forever must be the removing [...]he condemnation of death that has [...]human life till now.

[...] solidly based opportunity set before [...]eneration, and what is the basis for [...]?

31

[2] Animals lower than man do not have the life value of man. The Creator did not make them to live forever. (2 Peter 2:12) Man was created to live forever as a man on earth. This was why Jehovah created the first man in human perfection, in God's image and according to His likeness, and put him in a perfect garden spot, a paradise. There food supplies grew in their perfection to keep man going in perfect condition forever. If after a test man proved himself worthy of God's justifying him to the right to live in this earthly paradise forever, man was to be granted the privilege to "put his hand out and actually take fruit also of the tree of life and eat and live forever." (Genesis 3:22, NW) That the man might have satisfying companionship and raise a family to fill the entire earth with perfect, uncondemned children, Jehovah God gave the man a perfect wife, made of the man's perfect flesh and bone. (Genesis 1:26-28; 2:18-25) God made no mention to the man of dying, except if the perfect man acted against Jehovah's sovereignty over man's life and did so by the simple act of eating of one fruit prohibited at that time, the fruit of the "tree of the knowledge of good and bad." Eating from that tree before the Creator lifted the prohibition was to be punished with death at God's hand. (Genesis 2:15-17, NW) The test upon the perfect man was that of perfect submission to the universal sovereignty of his Creator, in even the smallest thing, submitting out of perfect love to his heavenly Father, the God whom he imaged as a "son of God."—Luke 3:38.

[3] Now rebellion against Jehovah's universal sovereignty broke out, not first on earth among man-

2. For how long was perfect man created to live, and what was the test upon him shown to be?
3. How did Jehovah name the first rebel against his universal sovereignty, and how is his sentence against the rebels vindicated?

kind, but in heaven among invisible sons of God. To name the spirit son of God properly who led off in this rebellion the Sovereign of the universe called him by the new name "Satan," which means "resister" or "opposer." To mark the way by which Satan proceeded to lead mankind to rebel with him, Jehovah God gave Satan the title "the Devil," which means "the Slanderer" or "the False Accuser." He also called him "the original serpent," because of the use Satan made of the serpent in paradise to slander God or falsely accuse him. (Revelation 12:9, 13-17; 20:2, *NW*) God told the first man Adam he would die if he ate from the forbidden tree of the knowledge of good and bad. Satan the Devil by means of the serpent told Adam's wife: "You positively will not die. For God knows that in the very day of your eating from it your eyes are bound to be opened and you are bound to be like God, knowing good and bad." (Genesis 3:1-5, *NW*) Satan thus brought reproach upon God's name by saying that God was a liar, unable to carry out the penalty for breaking his law, and was afraid of having Adam and Eve become like God, able to decide for themselves what is good and bad, right and wrong. God now pronounced the sentence of death upon the three rebels. In vindication of Jehovah's sovereignty and of the truth of his law, Adam and Eve did die, Adam at the age of 930 years, Eve at an unstated age. Satan the Devil will also die everlastingly, about seven thousand years after his rebellion, after God's purpose in letting him live that long has been served.—Genesis 5:1-5; Hebrews 2:14; Revelation 20:7-11, 14, 15.

⁴ In pronouncing sentence upon Satan, the original Serpent, Jehovah set his own beloved, only-

---

4. In pronouncing sentence upon Satan, the original Serpent, what arrangements did Jehovah make, and what had to be done to fulfill the prophecy?

begotten Son against the great Serpent, and the heavenly organization of holy angels under his beloved Son against the future organization of the great Serpent. Jehovah spoke of his heavenly organization as a fruitful woman and said to the original Serpent or Deceiver: "Because you have done this thing, you are the cursed one . . . And I shall put enmity between you and the woman and between your seed and her seed. He will bruise you in the head and you will bruise him in the heel." (Genesis 3:14, 15, *NW*) For this prophecy to be fulfilled, the heavenly Son of God had to come forth from God's woman (or universal organization) and be born as a perfect baby on earth. His heavenly Father had to perform the miracle of transferring his Son's life from the spirit realm of God's universal organization to the egg cell in the womb of a virgin maiden who was a descendant of King David. (Isaiah 7:14; Matthew 1:22, 23) To be bruised in the heel, God's Son as a perfect man had to suffer death at the hands of Satan the Devil, but only temporarily. To bruise the original Serpent in the head and destroy him thus, it became necessary for the Son of God to undergo another miracle of God by being resurrected or raised from the dead, not as a man to live again on earth, but as a divine, immortal, spirit Son of God to live again in the invisible heavens where the original Serpent, Satan the Devil, was living. —1 Peter 3:18, *RS;* also *NW; Ro; AT; Mo.*

[5] By not taking back human life Jesus the Son of God sacrificed that perfect humanity that he had enjoyed on earth for thirty-three years and a half. He could now use the value of his sacrifice for the benefit of human creatures who wanted to become perfect sons of God on earth as Adam had

5. By not taking back human life what was Jesus able to do, and what is the bruiser of his heel also called at Leviticus 16:8?

been in the paradise of Eden. Thus he was to be able to rescue the human race and also bruise the original Serpent. "Therefore, since the 'young children' are sharers of blood and flesh, he also similarly partook of the same things, that through his death he might destroy the one having the means to cause death, that is, the Devil, and might emancipate all those who for fear of death were subject to slavery all through their lives." "The Devil has been sinning from when he began. For this purpose the Son of God was made manifest, namely, to break up the works of the Devil." (Hebrews 2:14, 15 and 1 John 3:8, *NW*) As a bruiser of the heel of this Seed of God's "woman" the Devil is also called "A·za'zel," which is understood to mean "powerful against God."—Leviticus 16:8, 10, 26, *NW; AT; Mo; RS; Ro.*

⁶ God called his Son Jesus Christ to this course of sacrifice on earth and thus made him his High Priest. "So, too, the Christ did not glorify himself by becoming a high priest, but was glorified by him who spoke with reference to him: 'You are my Son; today I have become your Father.' Just as he says also in another place: 'You are a priest forever after the likeness of Melchizedek.' " "Seeing, therefore, that we have a great high priest who has passed through the heavens, Jesus the Son of God, let us hold onto our confessing of him." (Hebrews 5:5, 6; 4:14, *NW*) He was to act as God's High Priest in behalf of mankind, for it was a human sacrifice, himself as a perfect man, that Jesus Christ offered up to God.

⁷ This was necessary because God is just. For sin and its penalty death to be canceled, he requires a corresponding ransom or price of release. All mankind find themselves sinful and therefore

---

6. Who made Jesus Christ a high priest, how, and to act in whose behalf?
7. Why are all mankind now in sin, and for its penalty to be canceled what did God's justice require?

under God's condemnation of death. The true reason for this is stated in these inspired words: "Thy first father sinned, and thy teachers [interpreters] have transgressed against me." Our first human father was Adam, not when he was perfect in the paradise of Eden but after he had sinned and was driven out under sentence of death. "Through one man sin entered into the world and death through sin, and thus death spread to all men because they had all sinned—. For . . . death ruled as king from Adam." (Isaiah 43:27, *AS;* Romans 5:12-14, *NW*) Mankind could not inherit perfect life from sinful Adam through his sinful wife Eve. It therefore became necessary for the perfect Son of God on earth to surrender his sinless human life in behalf of Adam's descendants. This was in satisfaction of God's just law: "You must give soul for soul, eye for eye, tooth for tooth, hand for hand, foot for foot, branding for branding, wound for wound, blow for blow."—Exodus 21:23-25, *NW*.

[8] Jesus was born a Jew or Hebrew, a member of the ancient nation of Israel. As such he was a descendant of God's friend, Abraham the Hebrew, to whom God said: "I shall bless you and I will make your name great; and prove yourself a blessing. And . . . all the families of the ground will certainly bless themselves by means of you." "By means of your seed all nations of the earth will certainly bless themselves due to the fact that you have listened to my voice." (Genesis 12:2, 3; 22:18, *NW*) But Jesus Christ is God's High Priest, not for just the Jews or Israelite nation, but for all mankind who are to bless themselves by means of him as the promised Seed of Abraham. (Galatians 3:8, 16) The Jews or Israelite nation had their priestly family, of whom Aaron the brother of the

---

8. How was Jesus born as a descendant of faithful Abraham, and how was he, in spite of his birth in the tribe of Judah, to be like ancient Melchizedek?

prophet Moses was made the first Israelite high priest. The male members of Aaron's family, his sons, were made underpriests. Aaron was of the tribe of Levi, and all the male members of the tribe of Levi were made sacred servants of the priestly family of Aaron. Aaron offered sacrifices for the nation of Israel; and these sacrifices consisted of clean, acceptable animals. However, Jesus was born, not in the tribe of Levi or in the family of Aaron, but in the tribe of Judah and in the family of King David. So Jesus was born to be, not a priest for the nation of Israel, but a king; and God his Father also called him to be a high priest for all mankind. Jesus was therefore to be a King-Priest, like ancient Melchizedek. He did not offer up animal sacrifices, but offered up his perfect human life on earth.—Hebrews 7:14-27; Psalm 110:4, *AT; Mo.*

⁹ In sacrificing himself, however, Jesus was typified or prefigured by Aaron the high priest of Israel. For more than fifteen centuries Jehovah God dealt with the nation of Israel and used them to make types of things to come in the future. A type is a prefiguring symbol, that is, a symbol that prefigures or pictures beforehand something that is to occur in reality in the future. The Old Hebrew Scriptures set out many types, but the Christian Scriptures written in Greek set out the fulfillment of many of such types. The fulfillment of the type is called the *antitype.*

¹⁰ Types foreshadowed things to come. For that reason a type is sometimes spoken of as a shadow, and the antitype as the reality that was foreshadowed. Thus Aaron the Israelite high priest was a type. Jesus Christ whom Aaron typified was the

9. In what way was Jesus typified by high priest Aaron, and what is a type and what an antitype?
10. How can a type also be called a shadow, and what nation did Jehovah use to make many shadows or types, and why?

antitype. In other words, Aaron as sacrificing high priest foreshadowed Jesus the Son of God who sacrificed himself. That Jehovah God used the nation of Israel to provide many types or shadows is stated in these words respecting Israel: "Now these things became our examples [or, types], for us not to be persons desiring injurious things, . . . Now these things went on befalling them as examples [or, for a typical purpose] and they were written for a warning to us upon whom the accomplished ends of the systems of things have arrived." (1 Corinthians 10:6, 11, *NW*, marginal reading) Also, concerning the Law that God gave to Israel and the animal sacrifices that Aaron offered up, it is written: "Since the Law has a shadow of the good things to come, but not the very substance of the things, men can never with the same sacrifices from year to year which they offer continually make those who approach perfect." (Hebrews 10:1, *NW*) Hence the perfect human sacrifice of Jesus was necessary to make those who approached Jehovah God through Jesus Christ perfect.

[11] Looking at Israel as a typical nation, we note that Jesus' sacrifice for all mankind was pictured on the yearly "day of atonement" or Yōm Kippurim of Israel, on the tenth day of their seventh month, Tishri or Ethanim. (Leviticus 23:26-32) "Atonement" here means simply "covering" or "exchange." The thing exchanged or taken instead of another thing must exactly cover that other thing or correspond with it or duplicate it. The English word "atonement" is drawn from the expression "at one" and must be understood with the Bible meaning. That is, the thing which makes satisfaction for another thing that has been lost or

---

11. How was Jesus' sacrifice typified on Israel's day of atonement, and what is the Bible meaning of atonement?

forfeited must be "at one" with that other thing, covering it, coinciding with it or being exactly equivalent to it. This meaning shows what must be required of the sin offering that the High Priest Jesus Christ had to offer: It must correspond perfectly with the thing for which it atones or makes just satisfaction; it must neither overlap nor come short but must measure equal. The human life that Jesus Christ laid down in sacrifice must be exactly equal to that life which Adam forfeited for all his offspring: it must be a perfect human life, no more, no less. It must be a "corresponding ransom." This is just what Jesus gave, not for just the Israelites only but for men of all kinds. "For there is one God, and one mediator between God and men, a man Christ Jesus, who gave himself a corresponding ransom for all—this is what is to be witnessed to at its own particular times." (1 Timothy 2:5, 6, *NW*) This corresponding ransom was pictured or typified by the sin offering offered on the day of atonement.

[12] Now aside from the tribe of Levi with its priestly family of Aaron, Israel was divided up into twelve tribes, of which the tribe of Judah was the royal tribe or tribe with the promise of kingship. On the day of atonement the male members of the tribe of Levi served in connection with the sacred tabernacle or temple of God, but the other twelve tribes of Israel gathered to the east of the sacred tabernacle or temple, where its entrance was located. In this position the twelve tribes of Israel typified, in their self-affliction or abstaining from work, all those repentant, obedient ones of mankind who will gain everlasting life on earth by means of the sin offering of the great High Priest Jesus Christ. Included among such ones will be a

---

12. On the day of atonement whom did the twelve tribes of Israel typify, and whom did the special tribe of Levi typify?

numberless crowd of survivors of the war of Armageddon, who must, as it were, 'wash their robes of identification and make them white in the blood of Jesus' sacrifice.' However, the tribe of Levi, which was taken out from all the original tribes of Israel to serve at the tabernacle or temple, pictured Jehovah's High Priest Jesus Christ and those special followers of Christ whom God calls to sacrifice their earthly existence forever that they may enjoy heavenly life with Christ in the everlasting kingdom of God above. God's Word reveals them to be only 144,000 in number under the High Priest Jesus Christ, "the Lamb of God." "These were purchased from among mankind as a firstfruits to God and to the Lamb."—Revelation 14:1-5, NW.

¹³ These 144,000 antitypical Levites will attain to heavenly life by a resurrection from the dead, not as creatures of blood and flesh, which they sacrificed, but as immortal spirit creatures like their great High Priest. (1 Corinthians 15:44-54) They serve in a priestly way with Jesus Christ in behalf of mankind. So they are the first ones to benefit directly from Jesus' sin offering, in order to be in a position to serve God in behalf of the rest of mankind. The rest of repentant, obedient mankind benefit afterward from the sin offering of Jehovah's great High Priest. This is shown in the order of events on the ancient typical day of atonement.

¹⁴ A full description of Israel's day of atonement may be read in the sixteenth chapter of the book of Leviticus. The daylight hours of the day of atonement that were occupied by the offering up

---

13. How will the 144,000 antitypical Levites serve, and when do they receive the benefit from Jesus' sacrifice, and why then?
14. What was the antitypical day of atonement, and from when to when do the benefits of it continue to be applied? To last how long?

of the sin offering pictured the period of time from when Jesus presented himself as a human sacrifice and was anointed with holy spirit as Jehovah's High Priest, namely, autumn, A.D. 29, till he died as a martyr and was buried and was raised from the dead and ascended into the heavens into the presence of God to present to him the value of his human sacrifice, A.D. 33, spring. The applying of the benefits of his sin offering extends from then until the end of his reign over mankind for a thousand years after the battle of Armageddon. In the ancient type the benefits of the sin offering of the day of atonement lasted only for a year, until the following day of atonement. Christ's sin offering benefits forever.

¹⁵ On the typical atonement day Aaron the high priest foreshadowed Jesus Christ, the great High Priest who was sworn into office by Jehovah God himself. (Psalm 110:4; Hebrews 5:4-10; 7:15-28) Aaron was anointed with holy anointing oil to be high priest. Jesus as his antitype was begotten by God's spirit immediately after his baptism in the Jordan River to be a spiritual Son of God and then he was anointed with the holy spirit by his heavenly Father and God, to be a priest forever like Melchizedek of old. To make atonement for all Israel, Aaron sacrificed two animals, the bull of the sin offering and the goat of the sin offering. Although two animal sacrifices, they typified the one human sacrifice of Jesus Christ but viewed from two different standpoints. In proof of this Hebrews 9:11-14 (*NW*) states: "When Christ came as a high priest of the good things that have come to pass through the greater and more perfect tent not made with hands, that is, not of this crea-

---

15. On atonement day whom did the anointed high priest Aaron foreshadow, and what did the sin-offering bull and the sin-offering goat typify?

tion, he entered, no, not with the blood of goats and of young bulls, but with his own blood, once for all time into the holy place and obtained an everlasting release for us. For if the blood of goats and of bulls . . . sanctifies to the extent of cleanness of the flesh, how much more will the blood of the Christ, who through an everlasting spirit offered himself without blemish to God, cleanse our consciences from dead works that we may render sacred service to the living God?"

[16] The sacred tabernacle or tent was divided into two compartments, and in the second or rear compartment there was placed the gold-covered ark of the covenant. This chest contained the law of the covenant that God made through the prophet Moses with the nation of Israel. As a cover for the Ark there was a solid gold lid, on top of which were two golden cherubs facing toward each other with their outstretched wings. "In a cloud I shall appear over the cover," said Jehovah God to Moses. That cloud represented the invisible presence of Jehovah God in that innermost room, so that the innermost room or Most Holy symbolized heaven itself, God's dwelling place. "For Christ entered, not into a holy place made with hands which is a copy of the reality, but into heaven itself, now to appear before the person of God for us." (Leviticus 16:2 and Hebrews 9:24, NW) On the atonement day the blood of the two animals sacrificed as a sin offering was taken into the innermost room or Most Holy and sprinkled toward and before the cherub-mounted lid or cover. Likewise Jesus Christ the antitypical High Priest presented the value of his sacrifice to God when he ascended to heaven forty days after his resurrection from the dead.

---

16. What did the Most Holy of the tabernacle typify, and what was presented there as foreshadowed on Israel's atonement day?

[17] The typical high priest Aaron, being a sinful descendant from Adam, could not offer himself in sacrifice for anybody but had to include himself under the benefit of the animal that he sacrificed as a sin offering. "Aaron must present the bull of the sin offering, which is for himself, and he must make an atonement in behalf of himself and his house. . . . and he must slaughter the bull of the sin offering, which is for himself." (Leviticus 16:6, 11, *NW*) Aaron's house, for which he made atonement, meant not only his own household but also the entire tribe of Levi to which his household belonged. Since Aaron typified Jesus Christ and the entire tribe of Levi typified the 144,000 priestly ones under the High Priest Jesus Christ, the bull of the sin offering pictured Jesus' human sacrifice in its sin-atoning benefits for these 144,000 Christian fellow sacrificers. These have no part in the sin offering; that is, they have no part in providing the ransom sacrifice.

[18] Before Aaron entered into the Most Holy with the bull's blood he took a gold fire holder in and put special incense upon the fire before the cloud of Jehovah's presence, that the smoke of the incense might "overspread the Ark cover, which is upon the Testimony, that he may not die." (Leviticus 16:12, 13, *NW*) This unusual fragrant incense paved the way for Aaron to bring in safely the bull's blood. It pictured Jesus' faithful course here on earth, coupled with the fire of his zeal and sustained by sincere prayers of praise and petition to God. (On this, note Hebrews 5:7, 8; Luke 1:9, 10; Psalm 141:2 and Revelation 8:3, 4.) Jesus kept his faithfulness and integrity toward his universal

---

17. For whom did Aaron make an atonement with the sin-offering bull, and so what specially did that bull picture?
18. Before taking the bull's blood into the Most Holy what did Aaron burn there, and why? And what did this typify?

Sovereign amid the trials in this world and all the while praised Jehovah God and prayed his help. This was as a most pleasing, divinely prescribed incense to God. It proved Jesus Christ worthy of being saved out of death by a resurrection that he might ascend into God's presence and offer the value of the human sacrifice, which he had kept unspoiled.

[19] Why was the bull offered for Aaron's house and its blood sprinkled before the Ark cover in the Most Holy first? This was to typify that the value of Jesus' human blood is used or applied first for the sake of the 144,000 faithful believers and followers, that they may be cleansed from their sins due to Adam and be justified by God and thus be able to be accepted by God in sacrifice of everything earthly. This paves the way for God to give them life as his spiritual sons and make them underpriests under his great High Priest Jesus. This benefit has been going to them since the day of Pentecost, A.D. 33. It will continue toward them, even after Armageddon, until they lay down their earthly lives and are resurrected to life in the heavens with Christ.

[20] After sprinkling the bull's blood in the Most Holy, Aaron came out and gave his attention to the goat for Jehovah. Before the sacrificing began, this goat for Jehovah had been selected from two goats that were presented before Jehovah. Both goats were exactly alike in their sound, unblemished condition, but the goat for Jehovah was selected by drawing lots. The other goat became the goat for A·za'zel, that is, for the one "powerful against God," Satan the Devil, the original Serpent, who was to bruise the Seed of God's woman

---

19. To typify what fact was the bull sacrificed and its blood sprinkled first, and how long will this benefit go to the beneficiaries?

20. After the bull, to what animal did Aaron give attention, and for whom was it used?

at the heel. For whom was the goat of the sin offering to be used? For all the rest of the people of Israel, the twelve tribes who had furnished the two goats. "Next he must slaughter the goat of the sin offering, which is for the people, and he must bring its blood inside the curtain and do with its blood the same as he did with the bull's blood, and he must spatter it toward the cover and before the cover."—Leviticus 16:15, *NW*.

²¹ The goat of the sin offering therefore pictured the one sacrifice of Jesus but from the standpoint of benefiting all those of mankind who gain eternal life on the paradise earth in God's new world. It is this sacrifice of the antitypical goat of the sin offering that lays the basis for an unnumbered crowd of this present generation to survive Armageddon and live on endlessly in the new world without ever dying and going into the grave and needing a resurrection. The fact that the blood of Jehovah's goat was sprinkled last shows that the benefits of Jesus' sacrifice are extended to believing, obedient mankind after the 144,000 typified by Aaron's house have profited from the value of Jesus' sacrifice, the antitypical bull. An innumerable crowd of believing earthlings are already beginning to enjoy benefits from Jesus' blood now before Armageddon, but his blood will be applied in heaven in behalf of the twelve tribes of antitypical Israel immediately after that "war of the great day of God the Almighty." The benefits will continue to be poured out upon these antitypical twelve tribes, dead as well as living, during Christ's millennial reign.

²² Aaron having made the prescribed use of the

21. What did the sin-offering goat typify specially, and who are already beginning to enjoy benefits from it? Upon all whom will its benefits be poured out, and when?

22. After disposing of the blood, to which animal did Aaron next turn his attention, and what did the treatment of it typify?

blood of the bull and the goat, he now turned his attention to the other goat, still alive, the goat for A·za'zel. "And Aaron must lay both his hands upon the head of the live goat and confess over it all the iniquities of the sons of Israel and all their transgressions in all their sins and he must put them upon the head of the goat and send it away by the hand of a ready man into the wilderness. And the goat must carry upon itself all their iniquities into a desert land, and he must send the goat away into the wilderness." (Leviticus 16:20-22, *NW*) This live goat for A·za'zel also pictured Jesus Christ, but from the viewpoint of his being the one bearing away the sins of those for whom he died sacrificially, under great test at the hands of Satan the Devil, the real A·za'zel. The man that led the live goat away symbolized God's holy spirit under the power of which Jesus moved and acted upon earth. Remember how Jesus, "full of holy spirit, turned away from the Jordan, and he was led about by the spirit in the wilderness for forty days, while being tempted by the Devil." (Luke 4:1, 2, *NW*) The sins he bears away forever, contrary to the wishes of A·za'zel, are the sins mankind have inherited from the sinner Adam which they repentantly confess before God with faith in Jesus Christ the High Priest.

[23] Thus the live goat for A·za'zel was disposed of, but what was done with the carcasses of the bull and the goat of the sin offering? The divine instruction was: "He will make the fat of the sin offering smoke upon the altar." (Leviticus 16:25, *NW*) Jehovah always claimed the fat of a sacrifice and the Israelites were not permitted to eat it. Jehovah likewise claimed the strength, zeal and devotion of his self-sacrificing, sin-atoning Son, and Jesus rendered these up to God as a

---

23. What was done with the fat of the bull and goat of the sin offering, to typify what?

sweet savor to him.—Leviticus 4:31; 3:16; Deuteronomy 6:5.

²⁴ The remainder of the carcasses of the bull and the goat of the sin offering was now taken away from the court of the tabernacle and brought

24. What was done with the remainder of the carcasses of the bull and goat of the sin offering, to typify what?

outside the camp of the Israelites. "And they must burn their skins and their flesh and their dung in the fire." (Leviticus 16:27, *NW*) In the antitype Jesus Christ did not take his flesh and bones, his human body, into the Most Holy or "heaven itself," but he suffered fiery persecution in the flesh until he laid down his humanity in its perfection. He took the *value* of his human life, pictured by the blood, into heaven to present to God for believers on earth. (1 Corinthians 15:50) Due to the enmity of the original Serpent, who was to bruise him in the heel, he was considered as an outcast, rejected by those pretending to be God's people, and he was put to a violent death in public disgrace, as a vile stench in the nostrils of self-righteous religious society. He was persecuted, misrepresented and reproached, and he was condemned to death as a blasphemer and lawbreaker by his false accusers and was executed outside the gates of the holy city of Jerusalem.

[25] Jesus' faithful followers are called upon to bear the same reproaches that he did. In this light of this typical picture it is written to his faithful followers: "The bodies of those animals whose blood is taken into the holy place by the high priest for sin are burned up outside the camp. Hence Jesus also, that he might sanctify the people with his own blood, suffered outside the gate. Let us, then, go forth to him outside the camp, bearing the reproach he bore, for we do not have here a city that continues, but we are earnestly seeking the one to come. Through him let us always offer to God a sacrifice of praise, that is, the fruit of lips which make public decla-

---

25. Outside where are Jesus' faithful followers called upon to bear his reproach, and how did the city outside the gates of which he suffered prove to be no continuing one?

ration to his name." (Hebrews 13:11-15, *NW*)
The city of Jerusalem outside the gate of which
Jesus was hanged upon a torture stake till dead
in a national rejection of him did not prove to be
a "city that continues." Thirty-seven years later,
or A.D. 70, it was destroyed at the hands of
pagans in the greatest time of trouble that ever
befell a city, 1,100,000 Jews dying within it inside a few months and 97,000 being led away captive into all nations.

²⁶ The "city" to come, which the 144,000 priestly
followers of Jesus Christ have been seeking, is
the heavenly Jerusalem, the kingdom of God
under his great King Priest, Jesus Christ. (Revelation 21:2, 9-27) It will be the Government
of the new world, and through it the cleansing,
ransoming, reconciling benefits of Jesus' atonement sacrifice will flow to the antitypical twelve
tribes of Israel. (Matthew 19:28, *NW*) Hundreds
of thousands of these are already having a fore-
taste of these blessings now in their association
with the remnant or still remaining ones of the
antitypical tribe of Levi, the antitypical house of
Aaron, who are bearing Christ's reproach and yet
offering to God a sacrifice of praise, using their
lips in making public declaration of His name.
Those increasing hundreds of thousands know
that only the people who now accept the sin offering of Jehovah's great High Priest, Jesus Christ,
may hope to live through the greatest trouble
ever to be recorded in human history. For his
sin offering is the only basis for anyone's surviving the destruction during that time and living
on into the new world. There in that new world
the value of Christ's sin offering will be applied
in mankind's behalf.

26. What is the "city" to come that Jesus' priestly
followers are seeking, and for what attitude toward
the sin offering may any hope to live through Armageddon? Why?

CHAPTER IV

The Universalness of the Conflict

IF WE have the Scripturally based hope of surviving the coming universal conflict, "the war of the great day of God the Almighty," we do not grow stiff with terror at the thought of this unavoidable war nor refuse to face the facts about it. Concerning those who fear and obey the Almighty God, Jehovah, it is written: "He shall not be afraid of evil tidings: his heart is fixed, trusting in Jehovah." (Psalm 112:7, *AS*) The confidence of such ones is expressed in these words: "God is our refuge and strength, a very present help in trouble. Therefore will we not fear, though the earth do change, and though the mountains be shaken into the heart of the seas; though the waters thereof roar and be troubled, though the mountains tremble with the swelling thereof." (Psalm 46:1-3, *AS*) The universal conflict will result in the "end of the world," that is, the end of this present system of things of which Satan the Devil is the god and ruler. But since the earth will survive the conflict, there will be human and animal creatures that will survive with it. Trusting Jehovah regarding this conflict, we enjoy freedom from fear.

² In the universal conflict of Armageddon the

---

1. By having what Scripturally based hope shall we not be terrified at the thought of Armageddon, and how will any survive since it means the "end of the world"?
2. What nations will be included among those that will perish at Armageddon, and why such ones?

nations of this world will perish forever, including the so-called "Christian nations" of Christendom. "Come near, ye nations, to hear; and hearken, ye peoples: let the earth hear, and all its fulness; the world, and all that cometh forth of it. For the wrath of Jehovah is against all the nations, and [his] fury against all their armies: he hath devoted them to destruction, he hath delivered them to the slaughter. And their slain shall be cast out, and their stink shall come up from their carcases, and the mountains shall be melted with their blood. And all the host of the heavens shall be dissolved, and the heavens shall be rolled together as a scroll; and all their host shall fade away, as a leaf fadeth from off the vine, and as the withered [fruit] from the fig-tree." (Isaiah 34:1-4, *Da*) Christendom pretends to be made up of God's people, but she is really made up of those who do not live up to God's Book, the Holy Scriptures, but who go in the ways of the pagan nations. Christendom is hypocritical in her pretense of being Christian: "Isaiah aptly prophesied about you hypocrites, as it is written: 'This people honor me with their lips, but their hearts are far removed from me. It is in vain that they pay respect to me, because they teach as doctrines commands of men.' Letting go the commandment of God you observe the tradition of men." (Mark 7:6-8, *NW*) God hates hypocrites, for hypocrites bring reproach upon his name and oppose his universal sovereignty. Logically, God hates Christendom. Soon he will destroy her with the rest of the world.—Proverbs 6:12-19.

[3] Backsliding or apostate Christendom was foreshadowed by the ancient rebellious nation of Israel, whose capital city was Jerusalem. Jehovah

---

3, 4. (a) By whom was backsliding or apostate Christendom foreshadowed? (b) Regardless of what provisions and advantages did the nation of Israel fall away, and how so?

God had chosen them as his people because they were the descendants of his friend Abraham through faithful Isaac and Jacob. He had delivered their entire nation out of slavery in the land of Egypt and brought them into the land he promised to Abraham centuries before. On the way there he gave them a God-made law through his prophet Moses and brought them into a covenant with himself on the basis of that divine law. He took the city of Jerusalem out of the hands of its pagan occupiers and put it in the possession of faithful King David. Then Jehovah put his name on the city by having Solomon, the son and successor of King David, build a magnificent temple there to take the place of the sacred tabernacle or tent that Moses had built in the wilderness of Arabia. At this temple the priests of the family of Aaron, assisted by the Levites, carried forward the worship of the Almighty God Jehovah for the entire nation of Israel. To encourage them to be correct and faithful in their worship of him he sent his prophets to act as his spokesmen to them and to write the Holy Scriptures.

⁴ Regardless of all those provisions, helps and advantages the nation of Israel fell away. They mixed pagan idolatrous worship in with their form of worshiping Jehovah, polluted his temple and even killed his prophets whom he sent to warn the Israelites and set them straight. They became religious hypocrites such as the prophet Isaiah described them to be. In this course ancient Israel typified modern Christendom.

⁵ Any open-minded examination of Christendom in the light of the Bible, which she claims as her Book, will prove she is practicing an adulterated, degraded form of Christianity, not the pure Bible

5. What about Christendom shows she was typified by hypocritical Israel, and according to what divine rule is her destruction certain at Armageddon?

kind of Christianity, not the real imitation of
Jesus Christ. She claims to be in relationship with
Almighty God, not by the law covenant of ancient
Israel, but by the new covenant that Jesus Christ
mediated between Jehovah God and his congregation, the true Christian church. Christendom
claims to be the spiritual house of God or temple,
applying to herself the words addressed to the
true congregation of Christ's anointed followers:
"Do you not know that you people are God's temple and that the spirit of God dwells in you? If
anyone destroys the temple of God, God will destroy him; for the temple of God is holy, which
temple you people are." (1 Corinthians 3:16, 17,
NW) By bringing pagan doctrines and practices
into her organization, which she claims to be the
temple of God, and by persecuting those whose
lives and teachings show they are members of
that spiritual temple, Christendom has in effect
been engaged in destroying Jehovah God's temple.
There is only one possible outcome of this: God
will destroy Christendom. Her certain destruction
at Armageddon was typified by Israel's.

⁶ The first destruction of the ancient Jerusalem
and its polluted temple came at the hands of the
Babylonian armies under Emperor Nebuchadnezzar in the year 607 B.C. About fifty years before the city's destruction Jehovah raised up his
prophet Zephaniah and inspired him by holy spirit
to say:

⁷ "I will utterly consume all things from off the
face of the ground, saith Jehovah. . . . I will
stretch out my hand upon Judah, and upon
all the inhabitants of Jerusalem; and I will cut
off the remnant of [the false god] Baal from this
place, and the name of the Chemarim [foreign-
god priests] with the priests; and them that wor-

6, 7. When and by whom did Jerusalem's first destruction come, and fifty years before that what did Jehovah
inspire Zephaniah to prophesy?

ship the host of heaven upon the housetops; and them that worship, that swear to Jehovah and swear by [the false god] Malcam; and them that are turned back from following Jehovah; and those that have not sought Jehovah, nor inquired after him. . . . The great day of Jehovah is near, it is near and hasteth greatly, even the voice of the day of Jehovah; the mighty man crieth there bitterly. That day is a day of wrath, a day of trouble and distress, a day of wasteness and desolation, a day of darkness and gloominess, a day of clouds and thick darkness, a day of the trumpet and alarm, against the fortified cities, and against the high battlements. And I will bring distress upon men, that they shall walk like blind men, because they have sinned against Jehovah; and their blood shall be poured out as dust, and their flesh as dung. Neither their silver nor their gold shall be able to deliver them in the day of Jehovah's wrath; but the whole land shall be devoured by the fire of his jealousy: for he will make an end, yea, a terrible end, of all them that dwell in the land." —Zephaniah 1:1-18, *AS*.

[8] Likewise the antitypical unfaithful Jerusalem, hypocritical Christendom, will be destroyed. That will mean that the end of this world or system of things has begun. She stands first to be destroyed in the oncoming universal war in the great "day of Jehovah," and all the silver and gold of the Vatican and of all the big businessmen of Christendom will be unable to ransom her from total annihilation at the hands of Jehovah and his Christ. That Christendom's destruction is the first part of the end of this entire system of things is shown by the fact that, after describing ancient Jerusalem's destruction, the prophet Zephaniah goes on to foretell the destruction of neighboring

---

[8]. What will Christendom's destruction mean, and how was this fact shown by the order of Zephaniah's prophecies?

heathen nations, Philistia, Moab, Ammon, Ethiopia (and hence also Egypt) and Assyria with its capital Nineveh. (Zephaniah 2:4-15) This fact is also proved by the prophet Jeremiah, who was a contemporary of the prophet Zephaniah, and who actually saw the first Jerusalem destroyed in 607 B.C.

⁹ Likening the destruction that he was going to make worldly nations drink to a highly intoxicating potion in a wine cup, God told Jeremiah prophetically to pass this cup to all the nations and force them to drink of it. Who was made to drink of it first? Listen, as Jeremiah prophetically passing the cup says: "Then took I the cup at Jehovah's hand, and made all the nations to drink, unto whom Jehovah had sent me: to wit, Jerusalem, and the cities of Judah." Ah, Jerusalem with its temple was first in line for destruction, after which the cup of divine wrath was passed to Egypt, Uz, Philistia, Edom, Moab, Ammon, Phoenicia, Dedan, Tema, Buz, Arabia, Zimri, Elam (Persia), Media and "all the kingdoms of the world, which are upon the face of the earth: and the king of Sheshach [Babylon] shall drink after them."—Jeremiah 25:15-26, *AS*.

¹⁰ It is true that Christendom is most guilty of all the world because of her hypocrisy and her claim to be the city or institution that is called by God's name and so she justly deserves destruction at the hands of the God whom she has defamed. But the rest of the nations of this world need not think that they will escape destruction because of being less guilty. They are guilty as being a part of this wicked world or system of

---

9. How did Jeremiah also show this same fact prophetically?
10. Why should not the rest of the worldly nations think they will escape because of being less guilty than Christendom, and how does Jeremiah show they must be destroyed?

things of which Satan the Devil is the god and ruler. All worshipers and slaves of Satan the original Serpent must be destroyed, as they deserve to be. To those nations outside Christendom, who are now rising in rebellion against her yoke, Jeremiah's prophecy says: "Thus saith Jehovah of hosts, the God of Israel: Drink, and be drunken, and vomit, and fall, and rise no more, because of the sword that I will send among you. And it shall be, if they refuse to take the cup from thy hand to drink, then shalt thou [Jeremiah] say unto them, Thus saith Jehovah of hosts: Ye shall certainly drink." For what reason? "For behold, I begin to bring evil on the city that is called by my name [the antitypical apostate Jerusalem, Christendom], and should ye be altogether unpunished? Ye shall not be unpunished; for I call for a sword upon all the inhabitants of the earth, saith Jehovah of hosts."—Jeremiah 25:27-29, Da.

¹¹ Then to show that the "war of the great day of God the Almighty" will be a universal conflict sucking all the nations down to their everlasting destruction, the same prophecy continues: "The noise shall come to the end of the earth: for Jehovah hath a controversy with the nations, he entereth into judgment with all flesh; as for the wicked, he will give them up to the sword, saith Jehovah. Thus saith Jehovah of hosts: Behold, evil shall go forth from nation to nation, and a great storm shall be raised up from the uttermost parts of the earth. And the slain of Jehovah shall [be] at that day from [one] end of the earth even unto the [other] end of the earth: they shall not be lamented, neither gathered, nor buried; they shall be dung upon the face of the ground. Howl, ye shepherds [political and religious rulers and leaders], and cry; and wallow yourselves [in the

---

11. Then how does Jeremiah show that Armageddon will be a universal conflict sucking all nations down to destruction?

dust], noble ones of the flock: for the days of your slaughter [for you to be slaughtered] are accomplished, and I will disperse you; and ye shall fall like a precious vessel. And refuge shall perish from the shepherds, and escape from the noble ones of the flock."—Jeremiah 25:31-36, *Da.*

[12] For anyone to find safe refuge and to escape with his life amid such global destruction will be a most difficult thing beyond the power of any and all modern scientists to provide. Yet there will be survivors. Not that *we* say so, but that Jehovah of hosts himself says so. You may be among them. How? Jehovah, who is interested in the salvation of his true people, tells us how. After warning of the destruction to come upon unfaithful Jerusalem and her realm of Judah in the day of his wrath, Jehovah addresses himself to the nation that was weak in its worship of him and divided in its devotion between him and false gods, and he says: "Collect yourselves and gather together, O nation without shame, before the decree bring forth, [before] the day pass away as chaff, before the fierce anger of Jehovah come upon you, before the day of Jehovah's anger come upon you. Seek Jehovah, all ye meek of the land, who have performed his ordinance; seek right-eousness, seek meekness: it may be ye shall be hid in the day of Jehovah's anger."—Zephaniah 2:1-3, *Da;* see also *RS; AT; Mo.*

[13] Jerusalem, with all her Israelite adherents in the land of Judah, proved to be a nation without shame before God. The modern counterpart of

---

12. Despite its being beyond the power of scientists to provide, how does Jehovah say through Zephaniah that some may find safe refuge and escape with their lives?
13. (a) How has Christendom, like her ancient type, proved to be a shameless "nation"? (b) By what course were some in Judah and Jerusalem hidden and safe guarded, and who were among them?

that ancient nation, namely, Christendom, has likewise proved to be a shameless "nation" before Jehovah God and his Christ, and to this day she has not repented of her hypocritical, selfish, unchristian course that has resulted in two world wars since 1914 and now threatens a third one. But there were meek ones in the ancient city of Jerusalem and in Judah who were striving to carry out his ordinance by keeping right relations with him and his worship. These could not turn aside the doom of the shameless nation of apostate Israelites, yet they could pursue a course of action that resulted in their being hidden and safeguarded in that wrathful day when the whole land would be devoured by the fire of Jehovah's jealousy. That course was to seek Jehovah: "The name of Jehovah is a strong tower; the righteous runneth into it, and is safe." (Proverbs 18:10, *AS*) That meant seeking Jehovah's righteousness and giving up trying to justify oneself; it meant seeking meekness by being submissive to His judgment and lowlily accepting his correction and discipline and reforming oneself in accord with his will. In ancient Israel such seekers of Jehovah and of his righteousness and of meekness were hidden in the day when his fiery, destructive anger was poured out upon unfaithful Jerusalem and Judah and all the surrounding nations. Such survivors of that day of divine anger that then brought an end to those conditions picture those who will be hidden and carried through alive in the coming universal war of Armageddon, in the "great day of God the Almighty." Among such ancient survivors there were the prophet Jeremiah, Ebedmelech and the Rechabites. Whom do they picture?

[14] In the reign of the same king during whose

----

14. Despite what experiences did the prophet Jeremiah survive Jerusalem's first fall and also bear witness in Egypt?

reign Zephaniah prophesied, Jeremiah began to prophesy, exactly forty years before Jerusalem was first destroyed in 607 B.C. When he started prophesying under the spirit of Jehovah, Jerusalem was unchangeably doomed, and Jeremiah was inspired to prophesy of her certain destruction by the armies of Babylon under Emperor Nebuchadnezzar. He urged the people of the doomed country to go out peaceably and submissively to the foretold conqueror, the king of Babylon, and in that way escape the terrible hardship of the siege and destruction of the rebellious, corrupted, oppressive city of Jerusalem. For faithfully and uncompromisingly preaching the word of Jehovah to the shameless nation he was threatened with death. He was accused of sedition and thrown into prison. He was moved from one place of detention to another. Although forced finally to live on bare bread and water during the terrible famine of the besieged city, he survived its fall and desolation. He was taken out of prison at the conquering king's orders and was left to his own free choice as to where he would go. When eight hundred and thirty-two were carried off captive to Babylon, Jeremiah was left behind with some poor Jews who were left in the land. In the seventh Jewish month of that year these people took him with them down into Egypt. Even down there he continued to be a faithful witness of Jehovah, proclaiming the inescapable vengeance of God against the faithless, disobedient ones of the shameless nation.

[15] Jeremiah, whose name means "Jehovah is high," was a priest of the family of Aaron as well as prophet and writer of parts of the Bible. He is included among those ancient witnesses of Jehovah beginning with the first martyr Abel and who are mentioned in Hebrews, chapter eleven,

---

15. Whom did Jeremiah typify, and why properly so?

who "received their trial by mockings and scourgings, indeed, more than that, by bonds and prisons." (Verse 36, *NW*) As such Jeremiah typified those of Jehovah's witnesses of today who belong to the priestly 144,000 followers of Christ. These today are comparatively few in number. They are a mere remnant of this entire "body of Christ," the anointed congregation of which Jesus Christ is Head and High Priest. "He is the head of the body, the congregation." To this congregation it is said: "Now you are Christ's body, and members individually."—Colossians 1:18 and 1 Corinthians 12:27, *NW*.

¹⁶ The entire congregation of 144,000 under Jesus Christ have been Christian witnesses of Jehovah. The remnant of them today still in the flesh on earth must imitate Jeremiah's course. They must uphold the universal sovereignty of Jehovah and the purity of his worship; they must declare the day of his vengeance against antitypical Jerusalem, Christendom, and all the rest of the world. They must also advise the people to do as they have done: seek Jehovah and his righteousness and meekness, and put themselves on the side of his great Servant and King, Jesus Christ, if they want to be hidden and kept alive during Armageddon. Jehovah God is particularly interested in preserving this Christian remnant clear through the destruction of Christendom and of all this world into the godly new world. Even though now, as in Jeremiah's case, they have to endure hardships, opposition, false charges of sedition and communism, threats of death, and bonds and imprisonment, Jehovah will hide and preserve them through Armageddon, as he preserved Jeremiah through the first destruction of Jerusalem in 607 B.C.

---

16. How must they imitate Jeremiah, and, in turn, what will Jehovah do for them?

¹⁷ Jeremiah's friend, Ebed-melech, also survived Jerusalem's destruction. He was no Israelite or Jew. He was a foreigner, an Ethiopian, and a eunuch in the palace of Jerusalem's last king of David's line, Zedekiah. Some of the king's princes accused Jeremiah of obstructing the war against the enemy and doing "fifth column" work of disloyalty inside the besieged capital city and being a security risk, and they begged for his death. With the king's consent they lowered Jeremiah to the miry bottom of the dungeon or pit in the court of the guard, there to die without food in the mire. Ebed-melech heard of this wicked action of shameless Israelites and protested to King Zedekiah: "My lord the king, these men have done evil in all that they have done to Jeremiah the prophet, whom they have cast into the dungeon; and he is like to die in the place where he is, because of the famine; for there is no more bread in the city." At the king's command Ebed-melech took thirty men with him to the dungeon, let down ropes with rags for under Jeremiah's armpits and drew him up out of the miry dungeon. After that Jeremiah remained in the court of the guard until the city was captured by the besieging Babylonian armies. So Ebed-melech's action worked toward Jeremiah's survival.—Jeremiah 38:1-28, *AS*.

¹⁸ Ebed-melech thus sought Jehovah and his righteousness and meekness, and this worked to his own survival, although his action made bitter enemies for him. While Jeremiah was still imprisoned in the court of the guard, Jehovah's word came to him, saying: "Go and speak to Ebedmelech the Ethiopian, saying, Thus saith Jehovah of hosts, the God of Israel: Behold, I will bring my words upon this city for evil, and not for good,

---

17. Who was Ebed-melech, and what action of his does the Bible record?
18. What promise did Jehovah give him through Jeremiah?

and they shall come to pass before thy face in that day. And I will deliver thee in that day, saith Jehovah; and thou shalt not be given into the hand of the men of whom thou art afraid; for I will certainly save thee, and thou shalt not fall by the sword, but thou shalt have thy life for a prey; for thou hast put thy confidence in me, saith Jehovah."—Jeremiah 39:15-18, *Da.*

[19] A precious promise this, that there shall be others besides the Jeremiah class, the remnant, who will witness the destruction of antitypical Jerusalem, Christendom, at Armageddon and be delivered from their enemies there and survive the end of this doomed world. They are not members of the 144,000 or priestly class, not spiritual Israelites who have been "enrolled in the heavens," and so their destiny is not a heavenly one with Christ. But they put their confidence in the God of the spiritual Israelites, Jehovah. They are of that great crowd of Armageddon survivors with an earthly destiny in the new world. They see the injustices done to the anointed, priestly remnant of Christ's body by persons in power in Christendom and the attempt that is made upon the remnant's life to stop their preaching of Jehovah's message concerning this world and the only hope of salvation. At the risk of making enemies and exposing themselves to danger for their own lives, they protest. Then they use their position and influence and secure help and bring relief to the remnant in their danger of being killed.

[20] Just as the name of the typical Ebed-melech means "King's servant," so these are servants of the universal Sovereign Jehovah God and of his anointed King Jesus Christ. This class will

---

19. To whom today is this a promise, and how do these imitate Ebed-melech's course?
20. How is Ebed-melech's name fitting for them, and how will the promise be fulfilled toward them?

enter into the war of Armageddon, but they may take to heart the divine promise to Ebed-melech, really spoken and recorded for their benefit and comfort today. Jehovah will hide and save them, not only through the first part of the universal conflict, Christendom's destruction, but clear through it into his new world.

[21] Obedience to Jehovah God leads now to survival through Armageddon. This fact was illustrated by the Réchabites, who also were not Israelites. They were called Réchabites because they descended from Jonadab the son of Réchab. Since the Réchabites were Midianites of the tribe of Ken'ites (coppersmiths), Jonadab was related to Hobab, the brother-in-law of the prophet Moses. Their forefather Jonadab was a friend of Jehu, whom Jehovah by his prophet had anointed to be king over the ten northern tribes of Israel that he might execute the apostate Israelites who worshiped the demon god Baal. It was this tribal chief Jonadab that commanded his tribe, the Réchabites, not to drink wine and not to live in houses or engage in agriculture, but to continue living as nomads in tents, thus leading a sober, simple life, free from self-indulgence, and living as strangers in the land. For over 890 years, or since the days of Hobab, they had lived in among the Israelites, under Israel's theocratic form of government and in harmony with their worship of Jehovah, at the same time carrying out the commandments of their tribal chief Jonadab the son of Réchab. They feared Jehovah God.

[22] About 620-618 B.C., or during the last three years of the reign of King Jehoiakim, the Récha-

---

21. Who were the Rechabites, what were their family connections, and what did their forefather command them to do?
22. How did the Rechabites come to live in Jerusalem's houses, to what test did Jehovah subject them by Jeremiah, and how did Jehovah use the result of the test?

bites took up living in the houses of Jerusalem.
This was only because the Chaldeans or Babylonian armies under Nebuchadnezzar had come
against Jerusalem and made King Jehoiakim
tributary to Babylon. For safety against the army
of the Chaldeans and the army of the allied
Syrians the Réchabites were living at Jerusalem
like city people. But were they breaking their
forefather Jonadab's command respecting wine?
For the purpose of showing proper obedience to
a father, Jehovah had the Réchabites put to the
test. He had his prophet-priest Jeremiah bring
the Réchabites into the temple at Jerusalem and
there set cups of wine before them and tell them
to drink. However, the Réchabites faithfully refused out of respectful obedience to their forefather Jonadab. At this Jehovah was pleased and
he used this demonstration of unswerving obedience to an earthly father to show up the ungodly disobedience of the Israelites to the Creator
and universal Sovereign Jehovah. Said Jehovah to
the Israelites:

²³ "I have spoken unto you, rising early and
speaking, and ye have not hearkened unto me.
And I have sent unto you all my servants the
prophets, rising early and sending, saying, Return
ye now every man from his evil way, and amend
your doings, and go not after other gods to serve
them; and ye shall dwell in the land that I have
given to you and to your fathers: but ye have not
inclined your ears nor hearkened unto me. Yea,
the sons of Jonadab the son of Réchab have performed the commandment of their father which
he commanded them, but this people hath not
hearkened unto me; therefore thus saith Jehovah
the God of hosts, the God of Israel: Behold, I will
bring upon Judah and upon all the inhabitants
of Jerusalem all the evil that I have pronounced

---

23. After the test of the Rechabites, what did Jehovah
say through Jeremiah to the Israelites?

against them, because I have spoken unto them, but they have not hearkened, and I have called unto them, but they have not answered." About eleven years later the desolation did come upon Jerusalem and Judah and the land was rid of all its human inhabitants.—Jeremiah 35:1-18, *Da.*

[24] Jehovah gave a rewarding promise which has powerful prophetic meaning for today. After the test he inspired Jeremiah to say to the house of the Réchabites: "Thus saith Jehovah of hosts, the God of Israel: Because ye have obeyed the commandment of Jonadab your father, and kept all his injunctions, and have done according unto all that he hath commanded you; therefore thus saith Jehovah of hosts, the God of Israel, There shall not fail to Jonadab the son of Réchab a man to stand before me, for ever." (Jeremiah 35:18, 19, *Da*) The obedient Réchabites were therefore not wiped out at the destruction of Jerusalem in 607 B.C. They continued to have representatives of their tribe to stand with acceptance before Jehovah. Likely, in due time after Pentecost A.D. 33, some of them became Christians.

[25] In these final days of the antitypical disobedient Jerusalem and Judah, namely, Christendom, the situation presents the same features. Since A.D. 1919 in particular Jehovah has been sending his mouthpieces, the Christian witnesses of Jehovah; but Christendom, which claims to be in relationship with God by the new covenant, refuses to take Jehovah's witnesses seriously and to turn to God's Word and obey his commandments like his children. So Christendom's religious system will be destroyed at the universal war and her people will be moved out of existence. But

---

24. What promise did Jehovah give to the Rechabites, and how was it fulfilled?
25. How has Christendom been like the disobedient Israelites, but how have some been like the Rechabites, and what promise is now called to their attention?

there are those today like the Jonadab Réchabites: they are in the same class as those pictured
by Ebed-melech the Ethiopian. Although not
members of the remnant of the 144,000 priestly
followers of Christ, they do fear Jehovah and they
dedicate themselves to him through Jesus Christ,
the King of the New Jerusalem. They associate
themselves unbreakably with that remnant of
spiritual Israelites and worship the same God
with them and live and work under the same
theocratic rule with them. Thus they live like
strangers alienated from the world to which they
once belonged, and they live soberly, sensibly and
simply, abstaining from indulgence in the ways
of this selfish world. Their obedience stands out
in greatest contrast with the stubborn, proud disobedience of Christendom. By his anointed,
priestly witnesses Jehovah now calls to their
attention his promise and purpose to spare them
through Armageddon and to keep their kind always standing acceptably before him on earth in
the new world. In reward for their obedience they
will not perish with Christendom.

²⁶ Thus, in spite of the universalness of the war
of Armageddon, Jehovah will preserve all through
it those who meet his approval, the modern-day
antitypical Réchabites or the Ebed-melech class
and the anointed remnant of his witnesses like
the prophet-priest Jeremiah.

---

26. Thus, in spite of the universalness of Armageddon's
war, whom will Jehovah preserve through it?

CHAPTER V

Building the
Armageddon-surviving Temple

THE first temple to Jehovah, built on Mount Moriah in Jerusalem, was demolished with the entire city in 607 B.C., to the shock and surprise of the hypocritical worshipers in it. Not even the previous portable structure of worship, the tabernacle that Moses had built in the wilderness at the foot of the mountain of God, was carried to the land of captivity, Babylon, that the deported Jews might there carry on a form of worship of Jehovah. The temple to Jehovah that was built by the restored captives during the next century and later altered and enlarged by King Herod was likewise destroyed hundreds of years later, in the year 70 of the so-called "Christian era."

² Did that prove the worship of Jehovah to be wrong? No! Did it result in destroying the worship of Jehovah as the only living and true God? Not in the least! It only served to make the facts concerning the true and right worship of the Most High God appear more vivid and forceful. It only gave emphasis to the truism spoken by the Christian witness of Jehovah, the apostle Paul: "The God that made the world and all the things in it, being, as this One is, Lord of heaven and earth, does not dwell in handmade temples, neither is

1. What happened to the first temple built on Mount Moriah at Jerusalem and also to that built by the remnant restored from Babylon?
2. Did that destroy Jehovah's worship, and what did it prove respecting his worship?

68

he attended to by human hands as if he needed anything, because he himself gives to all persons life and breath and all things. And he made out of one man every nation of men, to dwell upon the entire surface of the earth, and he decreed the appointed seasons and the set limits of the dwelling of men, for them to seek God, if they might grope for him and really find him, although, in fact, he is not far off from each one of us."—Acts 17:24-27, NW.

[3] When Jehovah God created the perfect man Adam and put him in the paradise of Eden, he did not provide a material temple nor did he command Adam to build a temple of wood or stone there. He talked out of the invisible with Adam in no material religious building. Down to the global flood in Noah's day there was no temple on earth to God. Jehovah did not command his first faithful witness Abel to build a temple for him to offer animal sacrifices there. He did not command his prophet Enoch to do so. Noah he commanded to build an ark, not a temple, in order to survive the flood. There is no Scriptural record that a material temple to Jehovah was destroyed in that flood, nor did Noah build one during his 350 years after it. In the days of Noah's son Shem, Melchizedek was the "priest of the Most High" but built no temple to Jehovah in the city of Salem of which he was king; and Abraham did not go to any temple there to offer tithes to Jehovah through his priest Melchizedek. He offered the tenth of all the spoils of his God-given victory directly to the king-priest Melchizedek.—Genesis 14:18-20.

[4] Abraham's son Isaac and his grandson Jacob

---

3. From Adam to Melchizedek, to whom Abraham paid tithes, what can be said about a temple to Jehovah God?
4. From Abraham's son Isaac to Israel's deliverance from Egypt, what can be said about a temple to Jehovah God?

did not worship the Most High God Almighty in any man-made temple. Nor did Jacob's twelve sons and their families do so. For two hundred and fifteen years the twelve families of Jacob or Israel lived as temporary residents in the land of Egypt with its temples to its many false gods, and there they became the "twelve tribes of Israel." (Genesis 46:2-27; 49:28) At the end of those years, in 1513 B.C., Jehovah delivered the twelve tribes of Israel from the land of Egypt, where the ruler Pharaoh had forced them into slavery. By a miracle Jehovah brought his chosen people through the Red Sea and into the Arabian wilderness of Sinai to the foot of Mount Horeb, and there he organized them as a nation and gave them his theocratic law.

[5] Through the prophet Moses as a go-between or mediator the twelve tribes of Israel entered into a covenant with Jehovah to keep this law that required them to worship him as the only living and true God, the Sovereign of the universe, the King of eternity. It was while Moses was alone on top of the mountain, conversing with Jehovah's angel, that Jehovah gave Moses his law for Israel and commanded him to build a tabernacle or tent for carrying on the worship of Jehovah as God. He also chose Moses' brother Aaron to be the first high priest at this tabernacle and the sons of Aaron to be the underpriests; and since Moses and Aaron both belonged to the tribe of Levi, Jehovah chose all the other males of the tribe of Levi to be the servants or assistants of the Aaronic priesthood at the tabernacle or tent of meeting. This tabernacle had two compartments, the first called The Holy and the second or innermost or rear compartment called The Most Holy or Holy of Holies. In the Most Holy the ark of the covenant

---

5. Who was Jehovah's mediator there, what arrangements for worship did Jehovah there command to be established, and how was Jehovah's presence then represented?

containing the law of the covenant was placed; and above the lid or cover of this golden ark with its two golden cherubs on top facing each other the presence of Jehovah in the Most Holy was represented by the only light in it, the miraculous light called "the She·ki'nah light."

⁶ But was not Jehovah God at disagreement with himself in commanding this religious tabernacle or tent to be constructed for his worship when, in fact, he dwells in the highest heavens and not in temples made with human hands? No; for he had the sacred tabernacle made and religious ceremonies carried on in and about it for typical or pictorial purposes. They were types or symbols prefiguring greater realities and foreshadowing better things to come. For example, high priest Aaron prefigured or foreshadowed Jehovah's everlasting High Priest Jesus Christ. Aaron and the sons succeeding him as high priest of Israel were the type; Jesus Christ who sacrificed his perfect humanity for mankind is the antitype, the antitypical High Priest, serving in the antitypical tabernacle. Thus the Most Holy of the tabernacle was the type; heaven itself where God resides among the living cherubs is the antitype, the reality. In discussing these very things the inspired Christian apostle talks about Jesus as now an immortal priest and says:

⁷ "Now as to the things being discussed this is the main point: We have such a high priest as this, and he has sat down at the right hand of the throne of the majesty in the heavens, a public servant of the holy place and of the true tent, which Jehovah set up, and not man. For every high priest is appointed to offer both gifts and

---

6. Why was Jehovah at no disagreement with himself in commanding this tabernacle to be built for his worship?

7, 8. In discussing the typicalness of the tabernacle, what does the writer of Hebrews (8:1 to 10:1) say?

sacrifices; wherefore it was necessary for this one also to have something to offer. If, now, he were upon earth, he would not be a priest [for Jesus Christ was not of the tribe of Levi or of the priestly family of Aaron], there being men [Aaronic priests] who offer the gifts according to the Law, but which men are rendering sacred service in a typical representation and a shadow of the heavenly things; just as Moses, when about to make the complete tent, was given the divine command: For says he, 'See that you make all things according to the pattern that was shown you in the mountain.' But now Jesus has obtained a more excellent public service, so that he is also the mediator of a correspondingly better covenant, which has been legally established upon better promises."

[8] "For its part, then, the former covenant used to have ordinances of sacred service and its holy place upon this earth. For there was constructed a first tent compartment in which were the lampstand and also the table and the display of the loaves; and it is called 'the Holy Place'. But behind the second curtain was the tent compartment called 'the Most Holy'. This had a golden censer and the ark of the covenant overlaid all around with gold, in which were the golden jar having the manna and the rod of Aaron that budded and the tablets of the covenant, but up above it were the glorious cherubim overshadowing the mercy seat. . . . Therefore it was necessary that the typical representations of the things in the heavens should be cleansed by these means, but the heavenly things themselves with sacrifices that are better than such sacrifices. For Christ entered, not into a holy place made with hands which is a copy of the reality, but into heaven itself, now to appear before the person of God for us." "The Law has a shadow of the good things to come, but not the very substance of the things."—Hebrews 8:1-6; 9:1-5, 23, 24; 10:1, NW.

[9] That tabernacle, constructed during the first year of the Israelites in the wilderness after coming out of Egypt, was a costly, glorious structure, being valued now at more than two million dollars. Erected on the first day of their second year in the wilderness, in the spring of 1512 B.C., that tabernacle served the Israelites well during their travels through the wilderness until they reached the Promised Land of Palestine. But being only a typical copy and not the reality, being only the shadow and not the substance, it could not last. It must make way for the substantial real thing foreshadowed or prefigured, which is lasting and has to do with Jesus Christ.

[10] So the tabernacle served its valuable, typical purpose less than five hundred years. It did not survive the destruction of the city of Jerusalem and the desolation of the land of Judah in the year 607 B.C. But in passing out of use the tabernacle was not at once succeeded by the Christian reality. It was, rather, replaced by a more durable structure, the magnificent temple built by King Solomon on Mount Moriah in Jerusalem, the gold with which the king covered the Most Holy of the temple alone being valued at six hundred talents, or $26,496,000. King David, Solomon's father, had wanted to build such a temple to the Most High God but was not privileged to do so because he had been a warrior and had shed much blood in fighting theocratic battles for Jehovah. Solomon, whose name means "Peaceable," was so disposed.

[11] Work on the temple was begun in 1034 B.C., in the four hundred and eightieth year after the

---

9. When was that tabernacle erected, and why could it not last despite its costliness?
10. How long did the tabernacle serve its typical purpose, and how was it not at once succeeded by the Christian reality?
11. How long was Solomon's temple in building, how did it compare with the tabernacle in measurements, and how was it built at its site?

tabernacle was built by Moses in the wilderness, and it took seven and a half years to build. Concerning this the divine Record states: "It came about in the four hundred and eightieth year after the sons of Israel came out from the land of Egypt, in the fourth year, in the month of Ziv, that is, the second month, after Solomon became king over Israel, that he proceeded to build the house to Jehovah." Whereas the tabernacle had been thirty cubits long, ten cubits wide and ten cubits high, "the house that King Solomon built to Jehovah was sixty cubits in its length and twenty in its width and thirty cubits in its height." The Most Holy of the tabernacle had been a perfect cube ten cubits each way. As for Solomon's temple, "the innermost room in the interior of the house he prepared inside, to put there the ark of the covenant of Jehovah. And the innermost room was twenty cubits in length and twenty cubits in width and twenty cubits in its height." It was thus eight times as great in cubic space. The work on the temple was done quietly at its site. "As for the house, while it was being built, it was of quarry stone already completed that it was built, and, as for hammers and axes or any tools of iron, they were not heard in the house while it was being built."—1 Kings 6:1, 2, 19, 20, 7; 2 Chronicles 3:1-3, 8, *NW*.

[12] Some time before King David died he abdicated the throne in favor of his beloved son Solomon. So until David died, it was for Solomon a time of accession to the throne, an accession year. His first regnal year began in the spring of 1037 B.C., the first day of the first Jewish month Nisan or Abib. His fourth regnal year began on the first day of Nisan in 1034 B.C., and on the second day of the second month (Ziv) of that year he began to build the temple, laying the foundation for it. The work

12. In what year of his reign did Solomon begin building the temple, and in what year did he complete it?

was first completed seven years, six months and a few days later, some days into the eighth month of Solomon's eleventh regnal year. "In the fourth year the house of Jehovah had its foundation laid, in the lunar month of Ziv, and in the eleventh year, in the lunar month of Bul, that is, the eighth month, the house was finished as regards all its details and all its plan, so that he was seven years [roughly speaking] at building it."—1 Kings 6:37, 38, *NW.*

[13] However, Solomon dedicated the temple just before the day of atonement and the seven-day feast of booths or ingathering in the seventh lunar month, the month Ethanim. Hence, if he dedicated it in the same lunar year in which he finished it, then, to get ahead of the rainy eighth month, Bul, he dedicated the temple one month prior to its completion, and the fourteen-day celebration that he held necessarily delayed its completion. But in view of all the arrangements and preparations that would have to be made for the dedication and subsequent celebrations, it is likely that Solomon waited eleven months, until the seventh month of the following year, to dedicate the fully completed temple. The record is not definite as to this. After telling of the finishing of the work of the temple, it says: "At that time Solomon proceeded to call together the older men of Israel, all the heads of the tribes, the chieftains of the fathers, of the sons of Israel, to King Solomon at Jerusalem, to bring up the ark of the covenant of Jehovah out of the city of David, that is to say, Zion. And all the men of Israel came assembling to King Solomon in the lunar month of Ethanim in the festival, that is, the seventh month. So all the older men of Israel came, and the priests began to carry the Ark. . . . Then the priests brought in the ark of the

13. When did Solomon dedicate the temple, and what was then brought into the innermost room, and how?

covenant of Jehovah to its place, to the innermost room of the house, the Most Holy, . . . There was nothing in the Ark but the two stone tablets which Moses had deposited there in Horeb, when Jehovah had covenanted with the sons of Israel while they were coming out from the land of Egypt." —1 Kings 8:1-9; 2 Chronicles 5:1-10, *NW.*

[14] The seven-day festival of booths or ingathering began on the fifteenth day of the seventh month (Ethanim) and continued till the twenty-first day, and on the eighth day from the start of the festival, that is, on the twenty-second day of the month, there was a solemn assembly.* The following day, the twenty-third day, was the day of departure. But on the tenth day of the month, five days ahead of the feast of booths, there was the celebration of the annual day of atonement. Now regarding the celebration of these events following the inauguration of the temple we read:

[15] "Then Solomon sanctified the middle of the courtyard that was before the house of Jehovah, because there he rendered up the burnt offerings and the fat pieces of the communion offerings, for the copper altar that Solomon had made was itself not able to contain the burnt offering and the grain offering and the fat pieces. And Solomon proceeded to hold the festival [of booths] at that time for seven days, and all Israel with him, a very great congregation from as far as Ha'math down to the torrent valley of Egypt. But on the eighth day they held a solemn assembly, because the inauguration of the altar they had held for seven days and the festival for seven days. And on the

---

* See the book *"The Truth Shall Make You Free"*, pages 9, 10.

14. What sacred celebrations took place in the seventh Jewish month?
15. At the inauguration what did Solomon sanctify in order to accommodate all the sacrifices, and what festival did he and the people celebrate after inaugurating the altar?

twenty-third day of the seventh month he sent the people away to their homes joyful and feeling good at heart over the goodness that Jehovah had performed toward David and toward Solomon and toward Israel his people." (2 Chronicles 7:7-10, *NW;* 1 Kings 8:64-66) Since the "inauguration of the altar" occupied the seven days before the festival of ingathering, the first day of the inauguration must have been the eighth day of the seventh month, or two days preceding the day of atonement.

¹⁶ On the inaugural day Jehovah gave miraculous signs to show he had accepted the temple as a typical place of worship and the typical sacrifices that began to be offered there. This was after the priests had taken the ark of the covenant into the Most Holy. "And it came about when the priests came out from the sanctuary . . . that as soon as the trumpeters and the singers were as one in causing one sound to be heard in praising and thanking Jehovah, and as soon as they lifted up the sound with the trumpets and with the cymbals and with the instruments of song and with praising Jehovah, 'for he is good, for to everlasting is his loving-kindness,' the house itself was filled with a cloud, the very house of Jehovah, and the priests were not able to stand to minister because of the cloud, for the glory of Jehovah filled the house of The [true] God." Then Solomon blessed the assembled people and offered a long prayer, in which he recognized that this temple was only a symbol or type, saying: "But will God truly dwell with mankind upon the earth? Look! heaven, yes, the heaven of the heavens themselves, cannot contain you; how much less, then, this house that I have built?" In his prayer he included a prayer for foreigners from distant lands who would come

---

16. On the inaugural day how did Jehovah give miraculous signs to show he accepted the temple and its typical sacrifices?

to worship at the temple. "Now as soon as Solomon finished praying, the fire itself came down from the heavens and proceeded to consume the burnt offering and the sacrifices, and Jehovah's glory itself filled the house. And the priests were unable to enter into the house of Jehovah because Jehovah's glory had filled the house of Jehovah. And all the sons of Israel were spectators when the fire came down and the glory of Jehovah was upon the house, and they immediately bowed low with their faces to the earth upon the pavement and prostrated themselves and thanked Jehovah, 'for he is good, for his loving-kindness is forever.' " —2 Chronicles 5:11-14; 6:18, 32, 33; 7:1-3, *NW*.

¹⁷ That glorious temple on Mount Moriah in Jerusalem was approved at its inauguration and Jehovah God put his exclusive name upon it, but only for the typical purposes that it was to serve. (Acts 7:47-50) For that reason it could not last, but must give way to the better things to come, the antitypical realities. It could not survive, and it did not survive. After the apostate worshipers polluted it, it was destroyed at the first destruction of Jerusalem by the Babylonians in 607 B.C. But this did no damage to the coming antitypical realities. After seventy years of desolation of the temple site the remnant of devoted Jews restored from captivity in Babylon began to rebuild the temple on Mount Moriah. This temple, improved by King Herod of Judea, was the temple at which Jesus Christ worshiped. But it was no more enduring than Solomon's temple. As the prophet Jeremiah had foretold the destruction of Solomon's temple, so Jesus Christ foretold the destruction of King Herod's temple by the Roman legions A.D. 70. True to Jesus' prophecy, that temple did not survive when Jerusalem was razed to the

17. Why could not that temple last, and the one that succeeded it on Mount Moriah? So what happened to those temples in fulfillment of prophecy?

ground a second time, and this is of most solemn import for Christendom in these critical days. —Matthew 24:1-3, 15, 16.

THE ANTITYPICAL ENDURING TEMPLE

[18] Quite meaningfully that perishable temple has never been rebuilt, nor will it ever be. Why? Because the antitypical, imperishable temple is now under construction and nears completion. Under Jehovah God, Jesus Christ is the Builder of this real, enduring temple. He is the antitypical Solomon, yes, he is "something more than Solomon." (Matthew 12:42, *NW*) The temple that he builds is not a material one on Mount Moriah in Jerusalem, where now the mosque "The Dome of the Rock" stands. It is a heavenly or spiritual temple, and he himself is its Foundation Cornerstone laid by Jehovah God. As such he is the embodiment of Jehovah's temple.

[19] Jesus had this in mind when he first cast out men who were making the temple at Jerusalem a house of merchandise and said to the protesting Jews: "Break down this temple, and in three days I will raise it up." The Jews thought he meant Herod's temple, but the apostle John explains Jesus' words and says: "But he was talking about the temple of his body. When, though, he was raised up from the dead, his disciples called to mind that he used to say this, and they believed the Scripture and the saying that Jesus said." (John 2:13-22, *NW*) It was the Almighty God Jehovah who raised up his Son on the third day. The dead Jesus could not raise himself up from the grave. But he foretold to those Jews that he, as the embodiment or foundation of God's spiritual

18. Why will the temple never be rebuilt on Mount Moriah?
19. To fulfill his own words at the temple, how did Jesus raise up in three days the temple that the Jews broke down?

temple, would be raised to life on the third day. (Revelation 21:22) In that sense Jesus prophetically 'raised up in three days the temple that the Jews had broken down' by killing him.—Compare Jeremiah 1:9, 10; Ezekiel 43:3.

[20] Jehovah's temple, which was typified by Solomon's temple in its original purity, consists of more than Jesus alone. It includes his congregation of 144,000 spiritual members, the spiritual body of which Jesus Christ is the Head. Referring to himself as the temple Foundation, he said: "On this rock-mass I will build my congregation, and the gates of Ha'des will not overpower it." (Matthew 16:18, *NW*) The apostle Peter himself also points to Jesus as the living rock-foundation upon which the congregation of living stones is built up, when he says to these sanctified Christians:

[21] "Coming to him as to a living stone, rejected, it is true, by men, but chosen, precious, with God, you yourselves also as living stones are being built up a spiritual house for the purpose of a holy priesthood, to offer up spiritual sacrifices acceptable to God through Jesus Christ. For it is contained in Scripture: 'Look! I am laying in Zion a stone, chosen, a foundation cornerstone, precious; and he that rests his faith on it will by no means come to disappointment.' It is to you, therefore, that he is precious, because you are believers; but to those not believing, 'the identical stone that the builders rejected has become the chief cornerstone,' and 'a stone of stumbling and a rock-mass of offense'."—1 Peter 2:4-8, *NW*.

[22] The Jews who rejected Jesus as the Foundation Cornerstone and killed him could not keep him dead, but Jehovah God raised him up from

---

20, 21. (a) Of what does Jehovah's temple, typified by Solomon's temple, consist? (b) Who is its living rock-foundation, and how does Peter point this out?
22. How do the gates of Ha'des not overpower the congregation built on the rock-mass?

Ha'des to immortal heavenly life. It is therefore
manifest that the antitypical temple of God has an
enduring foundation and the gates of Ha'des, that
is, the gates of mankind's common grave, cannot
overpower the congregation and cause it to perish
or keep it from being built up to survive forever.

²³ Christ's twelve apostles, who were Christian
prophets, might serve as a secondary foundation
to the congregation of 144,000, but Jesus Christ
himself remains always as the basic rock-mass for
the entire spiritual temple of God. The 144,000
sanctified Christians are told this in these words:
"You have been built up upon the foundation of
the apostles and prophets, while Christ Jesus himself is the foundation cornerstone. In union with
him the whole building, being harmoniously joined
together, is growing into a holy temple for Jehovah. In union with him you, too, are being built
up together into a place for God to inhabit by
spirit." (Ephesians 2:20-22, NW) God's congregation built upon the rock-mass Jesus Christ are not
a temple for idol worship but a temple for the one
living and true God to dwell in by his spirit or active force. "What agreement does God's temple
have with idols? For we are the temple of the living God; just as God said: 'I shall reside among
them and walk among them, and I shall be their
God, and they will be my people.' " (2 Corinthians
6:16, NW) The congregation of 144,000 members
rest upon the heavenly Foundation Cornerstone,
Jesus Christ, "rooted and being built up in him,"
but they are also his body, of which he is the Head:

²⁴ "Just as the body is one thing but has many
members, and all the members of that body, although being many, are one body, so also is the
Christ. For truly by one spirit we were all baptized

23, 24. (a) To this temple what do the twelve apostles
serve as, and why is it not a temple for idol worship?
(b) Besides the basic rock-foundation, what else is
Jesus to the temple class, as stated by scriptures?

into one body, whether Jews or Greeks, whether slaves or free, and we were all made to drink one spirit. Now you are Christ's body, and members individually. And God has set the respective ones in the congregation." (1 Corinthians 12:12, 13, 27, 28, *NW*) "He also subjected all things under his feet, and made him head over all things to the congregation, which is his body." (Ephesians 1:22, 23, *NW*) "He is the head of the body, the congregation. He is the beginning, the firstborn from the dead, that he might become the one who is first in all things."—Colossians 1:18, *NW*.

²⁵ By pouring down the holy spirit from heaven upon his apostles and other disciples at Jerusalem during the festival of Pentecost, A.D. 33, Jesus Christ as the antitypical Solomon began constructing the spiritual temple upon himself as the rock-mass. That was very timely, for the material temple that was still standing on Mount Moriah in Jerusalem was doomed to everlasting destruction within the next thirty-seven years. (Acts 2:1 to 3:1, *NW*) When the city of Jerusalem was wiped out by the Romans under General Titus A.D. 70 with a destruction unparalleled till then, the polluted, commercialized temple was rifled and put to the torch and not one of its stones was left there upon another and not thrown down. Jehovah God had abandoned that misused religious house. He was now dwelling by his holy spirit in Jesus Christ and in the other living members of his real, antitypical, spiritual temple. No longer could it be said of that typical house, "My name will prove to be there," but God's holy name was transferred and put upon the Christian spiritual temple and the members of its congregation became henceforth the true witnesses of Jehovah, the "people

25. (a) When did the antitypical Solomon begin building the spiritual temple, and why was this very timely? (b) Why was Jehovah's worship not made impossible by destroying Jerusalem's temple A.D. 70?

for his name." (1 Kings 8:29, *NW;* 2 Chronicles 33:7; Acts 15:14) For this reason the worship of Jehovah was not made impossible by the destroying of earthly Jerusalem's temple. His pure worship with spirit and truth continued on in his spiritual temple that was being built by the antitypical Solomon, Jesus Christ.

[26] That spiritual temple survived the horrible destruction of Jerusalem in the year 70. That temple is now near its completion, the last of its "living stones" being yet under preparation on earth for being built into the temple in heaven. As its living stones are blessed with divine, immortal life in heaven, it is an imperishable temple. It will therefore survive Armageddon, triumphant over all false, idolatrous religious temples, yes, hypocritical Christianity. Faithless, antichristian Jerusalem pictured or typified modern Christendom in these last days. The consuming trouble that came upon typical Jerusalem A.D. 70 prophetically dramatized the everlasting destruction that will visit Christendom in the first part of the war of Armageddon. Jerusalem's defiled temple went down back there. Christendom's temple, a religious system of hundreds of confused, pretending Christian sects and cults, will go down first in the throes of Armageddon. It is already doomed, together with all the rest of this world's systems, and all the worshipers in that polluted temple of Christendom will perish with it. The real temple of Jehovah's worship is destined to stand eternally as the habitation of his spirit. It will gloriously survive Armageddon, and his worship will be carried on there in purity by an increasing multitude of everlasting worshipers.

---

26. Why is the spiritual temple imperishable, and what did the experiences of the two temples at Jerusalem's destruction A.D. 70 picture?

CHAPTER VI

A·do·nay' Comes to His Temple

BEFORE all false religion is destroyed in the war of Armageddon a noteworthy event suddenly takes place at God's true temple. Over four hundred years before the Christian era God foretold it by his prophet Malachi in these words: "Behold, I send my messenger, and he shall prepare the way before me; and the Lord whom ye seek will suddenly come to his temple, and the Angel of the covenant, whom ye delight in: behold, he cometh, saith Jehovah of hosts."—Malachi 3:1, *Da;* also *Nácar-Colunga,* Spanish.*

² The fulfillment of this prophecy was to take place at a time when most of those who professed to serve God at his temple, even those claiming to be priests, would worship him only formally. They would have an inward contempt for his worship, offering and approving defective sacrifices, neglecting the required support of his worship, preferring worldly connections to true relationship with God's organization, doubting whether there

---

* *An American Translation* renders Malachi 3:1: " 'Behold, I will send forth my messenger, and he shall prepare the way before me! And suddenly to his temple shall come the Lord whom you are seeking! And the messenger of the covenant in whom you delight—behold, he comes,' says the LORD [Jehovah] of hosts." The following Bible versions read similarly: Leeser, Soncino, American Baptist, *English;* Kautzsch, Elberfelder, Menge, *German;* Segond, L'École Biblique de Jérusalem, *French;* Bover-Cantera, *Spanish;* United Bible Societies, *Brazilian.*

---

1. What event did Malachi foretell to take place before all false religion is destroyed at Armageddon?
2. When was the fulfillment of this prophecy to take place, and what was to result from the Lord's coming to his temple?

would be any divine punishment for the wicked, and feeling that it did not pay to keep God's ways and commandments literally, worshiping him with spirit and truth. Unexpectedly the Lord would come to his temple, and this would result in purifying God's true people and their teachings and practices and in revealing who are the true worshipers of God and who are the hypocritical and what are the rewards to each class of worshipers. This important event becomes of serious concern to all of us, particularly the people of Christendom, when the facts of the day combine to show that the Lord has come to his temple and is present there.

³ At once the questions arise, When did the Lord come to his temple? Who is this Lord? Who is the messenger sent to prepare the way before Jehovah? Who is the Angel or messenger of the covenant, and of what covenant? There are inspired Scriptures and genuine facts of history to help us in getting at the correct answers. And it is startling to note that there was a first or minor fulfillment of the prophecy nineteen centuries ago and there is a second or major and complete fulfillment in our century.

⁴ As regards the first fulfillment, we have this inspired record identifying who the messenger was that was sent to prepare the way before Jehovah: "The beginning of the good news about Jesus Christ: Just as it is written in Isaiah the prophet, '(Here I am, sending forth my messenger before you, to prepare your way;) a voice of a man crying out in the wilderness, "Prepare the way of Jehovah, make his roads straight," ' John the baptizer turned up in the wilderness, preaching baptism of

---

3. What questions at once arise, and how are we helped in getting at the correct answers?
4. As shown by Mark and Jesus, who was the messenger sent to prepare the way before Jehovah in the first fulfillment?

those repenting for forgiveness of sins." (Mark 1:1-4, *NW*) The inspired writer Mark combines here the prophecies of Malachi 3:1 and Isaiah 40:3 and applies them to John, the son of an Aaronic priest. This John was the forerunner of Jesus and baptized him in the Jordan River, about twenty miles to the east of Jerusalem. Jesus Christ himself identified John the Baptist as the messenger of Malachi 3:1. Concerning John who was then in jail for his faithfulness Jesus said: "This is he concerning whom it is written, 'Here I am, sending forth my messenger before you, to prepare your way ahead of you!' Truly I say to you people, Among those born of women there has not been raised up a greater than John the Baptist; but a person that is a lesser one in the kingdom of the heavens is greater than he is. From the days of John the Baptist until now the kingdom of the heavens is the goal toward which men press, and those pressing forward are seizing it. For all, the Prophets and the Law, prophesied until John." —Matthew 11:10-15, *NW;* Luke 7:27, 28.

⁵ Who, then, was "the Lord" that came to "his temple" suddenly or unexpectedly? It was the One to whom the temple belongs, he who speaks of it as "his temple," Jehovah of hosts. It is not the temple of any creature. The temple at Jerusalem was always spoken of as the "temple of Jehovah" and as the "house of God," "the house of Jehovah." God spoke of it as "my house" and put his own name "Jehovah" upon it; and Jesus Christ his Son spoke of it as "my Father's house."*

⁶ In the Hebrew the word *A·dōn'* translated "Lord" means "master." At Malachi 3:1 a special

---

* 2 Chronicles 26: 16 and Jeremiah 7: 10, 4, *AS;* Ezra 1: 7, *Da;* Isaiah 56: 7; 1 Kings 9: 3, 7; John 2:16.

---

5. Who, then, is "the Lord" that comes to his temple?
6. How, by the Hebrew expression for "the Lord," is it proved that the Lord who comes is Jehovah? So what warning is given?

form of the Hebrew word occurs, *ha-A·dōn'*, namely, the word *A·dōn'* with the article *ha* ("the") before it. In the Hebrew text this expression *ha-A·dōn'* occurs only eight times. At Exodus 23: 17 and 34:23 the expression "the Lord Jehovah" occurs twice; and at Isaiah 1:24; 3:1; 10: 16, 33; 19:4 the expression "the Lord, Jehovah of hosts" occurs five times. (*Da*) In these seven cases of the expression *ha-A·dōn'* it unmistakably applies to Jehovah, and at Malachi 3:1* there is no exception; it applies to Jehovah, who is the master of "his temple" to which he comes. In harmony with this fact the warning is given: "Jehovah is in his holy temple. Let all the earth keep silence before him!" (Habakkuk 2:20, *Da*) "Jehovah is in his holy temple; Jehovah, his throne is in heaven; his eyes behold, his eyelids try, the children of men." —Psalm 11:4, *AS*.

⁷ It is Jehovah who sends his messenger ahead to prepare the way before Him; and it is Jehovah, "the Lord," the Great Master, who comes to his own temple for judgment purposes. Isaiah caught a vision that was prophetic of the time when Jehovah had come to his temple to judge his people. Isaiah describes the vision in these words: "In the year of the death of king Uzziah, I saw the Lord sitting upon a throne, high and lifted up; and his train filled the temple. Seraphim were standing above him: each had six wings; with twain he covered his face, and with twain he covered his feet, and with twain he flew. And one called to the other and said, Holy, holy, holy is Jehovah of hosts; the whole earth is full of his

---

* In the Greek *Septuagint Version* (*LXX*), instead of "the Lord," it uses the word *Ky'ri·os* without the definite article. This is the regular Greek equivalent for "Jehovah."

---

7. What vision did Isaiah have that was prophetic of when Jehovah had come to his temple to judge? And what Hebrew word did he use that is here translated "the Lord"?

glory! And the foundations of the thresholds shook at the voice of him that cried, and the house was filled with smoke. And I said, Woe unto me! for I am undone; for I am a man of unclean lips, and I dwell in the midst of a people of unclean lips: for mine eyes have seen the King, Jehovah of hosts." (Isaiah 6:1-5, *Da*) Here it is the Hebrew word *A·do·nay'* that is translated "the Lord." *A·do·nay'* is the plural of excellence of the word *a·dōn'*, but the more ancient plural ending *ay* is attached instead of *im*.

⁸ In the traditional Hebrew text *A·do·nay'* occurs over 300 times and in all cases it applies to Jehovah God. For example, Job 28:28 (*Da*) reads: "Lo, the fear of the Lord [*A·do·nay'*], that is wisdom." (Also Isaiah 8:5-7) The expression *A·do·nay' Jehovah* occurs 276 times, the expression *Jehovah A·do·nay'* once (Habakkuk 3:19, *Da*), and *"A·do·nay' Jehovah* of hosts" 19 times. Moreover, there are 134 cases in the traditional Hebrew text where *A·do·nay'* should properly read *Jehovah*, for the Jewish *Sopherim* or copyists changed the original text from *Jehovah* to read *A·do·nay'* in their traditional text. In Isaiah's vision *A·do·nay'* means Jehovah* as the Great or Most Excellent Lord; for Isaiah, after beholding *A·do·nay'* on the throne in the temple, cries out: "Mine eyes have seen the King, Jehovah of hosts." Thus it was *A·do·nay'* that came to his temple to judge.

⁹ Now since in the first fulfillment of the

---

* At Isaiah 6:1 about 100 Hebrew manuscripts read *Jehovah* instead of *A·do·nay'*. In fact, this is one of the 134 places where the Hebrew Sopherim changed "Jehovah" to *A·do·nay'* so that Isaiah should not say he saw Jehovah.

---

8. From what use of *A·do·nay'* in the Hebrew Bible do we know that *A·do·nay'* in Isaiah 6:1 means Jehovah?
9, 10. (a) In Malachi 3:1, with whom has it been the custom to identify the "Angel [or, messenger] of the covenant"? (b) Who is the "Angel of the covenant," and of what covenant?

prophecy John the Baptist was the messenger that prepared the way, and the Lord who came to his temple was Jehovah God, the question is, Who, then, was the "Angel [or, messenger] of the covenant," who was to come and in whom Jehovah's people delighted? The usual custom has been to interpret the "Angel of the covenant" as meaning the same as "the Lord" who comes to his temple. However, it is Scripturally clear that the "Angel of the covenant" and "the Lord" are two different individuals. Jesus Christ repeatedly stated that he came to earth not of his own accord but that his heavenly Father Jehovah had sent him; and John the Baptist was the messenger who was sent about six months ahead of Jesus to prepare Jehovah's way, to get the Jews ready for the coming of the "Angel of the covenant."

[10] John's father said at his circumcision: "As for you, young child, you will be called a prophet of the Most High, for you will pioneer before Jehovah to make his ways ready, to give knowledge of salvation to his people by forgiveness of their sins, because of the tender compassion of our God." (Luke 1:59, 76-78, NW) Unquestionably, then, Jehovah's "Angel [or, messenger] of the covenant" is Jesus, anointed with holy spirit after his baptism in the Jordan. Hence Jesus also had to come to Jehovah's temple, and to do so as Jehovah's representative or Angel. The covenant of which he is the Angel or messenger is not the law covenant, which God made with the Israelites through Moses, but a covenant 430 years older than that. It is the covenant that God made with Abraham their forefather, saying: "I shall make a great nation out of you and I shall bless you and I will make your name great; and prove yourself a blessing. And . . . all the families of the ground will certainly bless themselves by means of you." —Genesis 12:2, 3, NW.

¹¹ The fact that "the Lord" and the "Angel of the covenant" are two, namely, Jehovah God and Jesus Christ, agrees with the features of Isaiah's vision at the temple. After Isaiah underwent a cleansing there at the temple he said: "And I heard the voice of the Lord [A·do·nay'] saying, Whom shall I send, and who will go for us? And I said, Here am I; send me." (Isaiah 6:8, Da) The Lord's saying, "Who will go for us?" indicates that he was speaking for at least another besides himself. That other person was his Angel of the covenant who was representing A·do·nay' Jehovah there at the temple. For the mortal man Isaiah could not look upon the face of God himself and keep living; as Jehovah God told the prophet Moses: "You are not able to see my face, because no man may see me and yet live." (Exodus 33:20, NW) Also the apostle John shows that Jehovah's Angel of the covenant was there acting for God at the temple when he says this about the Jews' refusing to believe in Jesus: "The reason why they were not able to believe is that again Isaiah said: 'He has blinded their eyes and he has made their hearts hard, that they should not see with their eyes and get the thought with their hearts and turn around and I should heal them.' Isaiah said these things because he saw his glory, and he spoke about him."—John 12:39-41, NW; Isaiah 6:8-10.

¹² In the first fulfillment of Malachi's prophecy nineteen hundred years ago did the Lord's "Angel of the covenant" come to the temple at Jerusalem? Yes, not as a mere worshiper of the Lord Jehovah, but as a judicial messenger; and the Lord Jehovah was accompanying him by his holy spirit and was coming to the temple representatively by means of

11. How does this fact agree with A·do·nay"s saying to Isaiah at the temple, "Who will go for us?"
12, 13. What was the difference between Jesus' coming to the temple at Jerusalem A.D. 30 and A.D. 33?

his messenger or Angel. True, Jesus Christ did come to the literal temple in the spring of A.D. 30, during the first Jewish passover celebration after he had been baptized in water and anointed with the holy spirit. At that time he did drive the commercial salesmen and the greedy moneychangers out of the temple, saying: "Take these things away from here! Stop making the house of my Father a house of merchandise!"—John 2:13-16, *NW*.

[13] But at that time Jesus did not offer himself to them at the temple as the anointed King of Jehovah's people, for he was just beginning his public work of bearing witness to the truth and he had yet three years to go. In the year 33 he came again to the temple, this time presenting himself as their God-given King, the Son of King David and the Offspring of Abraham by means of whom all the nations of the earth would certainly bless themselves. (Genesis 22:15-18, *NW*) He came riding in kingly fashion upon the colt of an ass, while at the same time his disciples were waving palm branches and shouting: "Save, we pray, the Son of David! Blessed is he that comes in Jehovah's name! Save him, we pray, in the heights above!" "Blessed is the coming kingdom of our father David!" "Blessed is the One coming as the King in Jehovah's name! Peace in heaven, and glory in the heights above!" The city of Jerusalem was figuratively spoken of as the "daughter of Zion," and Jesus' royal ride into her was in fulfillment of Zechariah's prophecy: "Have no fear, daughter of Zion. Look! your king is coming, seated upon an ass's colt." —Matthew 21:7-9; Mark 11:9, 10; Luke 19:38 and John 12:12-16, *NW*.

[14] That was appropriately the tenth day of the first Jewish lunar month, Nisan, and after en-

---

14. At this latter coming to the temple how did the religious leaders act toward Jesus, and what did he do there?

tering Jerusalem according to the prophetic description Jesus went to the temple. The Jewish rulers did not there welcome him as the Messiah, the Christ, the Angel of the covenant in whom they professed to take a delight. Partly out of fear of the Roman government over them and more because of their own selfish ambitions and

prejudices, the priests, Levites, lawyers, scribes, Pharisees and Sadducees refused to accept him and anoint him as Messiah the Prince. They carried forward their plot to kill him. So all that Jesus did there at the temple the afternoon of that day was to look around upon all things. The next morning he returned to Jerusalem and re-entered the temple. Then he acted in a judicial role for Jehovah and cleansed the temple as far as he could of its commercial crowd, saying: "Is it not written, 'My house will be called a house of prayer for all the nations'? But you have made it a cave of robbers." (Mark 11:11-18, *NW;* John 11:46-54) It is after the account of this that the apostle John makes his application of Isaiah's vision of *A·do·nay'* at the temple in his glory, pronouncing condemnation upon the religionists who had willfully blind eyes, heavily dull ears and thickly fatted hearts.—John 12:12-19, 36-43.

[15] The following day Jesus at Jerusalem pronounced terrible woes upon the religious hypocrites whom he exposed. He ended up addressing the murderous city of Jerusalem and saying to her inhabitants concerning their temple: "Look! your house is abandoned to you." Since they had willfully rejected the Lord's Angel of the covenant and had made the temple a cave of robbers and murderers, the Lord Jehovah had abandoned the temple. It was no more his house, but theirs, to perish with them. Accordingly, after being shown the grand buildings of the temple, Jesus pronounced its doom, saying: "By no means will a stone be left here upon a stone and not be thrown down." Later, when asked privately about the time for this, he tied the temple's destruction to his great prophecy on the complete end of this

---

15. Next day what did Jesus have to say regarding the temple, and with what did he connect his prophecy concerning it? Why?

world or system of things. By this he showed that
the temple's destruction back there was prophetic
of the destruction to come upon the antitypical
religious system at the end of Christendom and
of all the world at Armageddon.—Matthew 23:1 to
24:22, *NW*.

¹⁶ However, there was more to *A·do·nay"s*
coming to his temple than the foregoing. The Jews
did not really "seek" *A·do·nay'* or the Lord Jehovah, because they did not seek his Messenger
of the covenant by means of whom He came.
Only a faithful remnant showed they sought Him,
but the majority rejected Him. They had his Son
nailed to a tree till dead. When the Messenger of
the covenant on the tree made his final cry with
a loud voice and ceased to breathe, "look! the
curtain of the sanctuary [of the temple] was rent
in two, from top to bottom, and the earth quaked,
and the rock-masses were split." (Matthew 27:50,
51, *NW*) That was truly a visitation of *A·do·nay'*
Jehovah at the temple by means of his active
force or his spirit. It was indeed a time of judgment upon the Jews, a time of their being inspected, which they did not discern. (Luke 19:44,
NW) But *A·do·nay'* Jehovah judged his Messenger
of the covenant to be faithful and true. So on the
third day of his death the Lord Jehovah declared
him "righteous in spirit" by raising him from
the dead in the spirit, an immortal, heavenly,
spirit creature, never to die again. (1 Timothy
3:16, *NW*) "He being put to death in the flesh,
but being made alive in the spirit."—1 Peter 3:18,
NW; Romans 6:9.

¹⁷ To show himself alive to his faithful disciples,

---

16. (a) Did the Jews then show that they sought the
Lord Jehovah, and how did Jehovah himself make a
visitation at their temple? (b) How did Jehovah judge
his Messenger and show it?
17. Forty days later how did *A·do·nay'* Jehovah come to
his antitypical temple with a favorable judgment?

the resurrected Messenger of the covenant materialized in flesh on a number of occasions the same as heavenly angels had done on previous occasions. Thus he renewed the faith and hope of his disciples who were soon to become "living stones" in the spiritual temple of God. Forty days from his resurrection he ascended from the Mount of Olives into heaven and vanished from the sight of his onlooking disciples. (Acts 1:1-11) He returned to the presence of his heavenly Father, A·do·nay' Jehovah, and there Jehovah laid him as the Foundation Cornerstone of the spiritual temple on the heavenly Mount Zion. (Isaiah 28: 16; Romans 9:33; 1 Peter 2:4-7) By this action A·do·nay' Jehovah came to his temple, his antitypical temple, with a favorable judgment upon its chief "living stone," Jesus Christ.—Acts 7:56.

[18] On the day of the festival of Pentecost, or ten days after his ascension to heaven, the glorified Jesus Christ, the one greater than King Solomon the temple builder, began the preparatory building work on the spiritual temple of which he was the living Foundation Cornerstone. At that festival in Jerusalem Jehovah God by means of his holy spirit begot Jesus' disciples assembled in that city to make them his spiritual sons. Then through Jesus at his right hand in heaven Jehovah poured out his holy spirit upon these spiritual sons to form them into the first "living stones" of the spiritual temple of God, displacing the material temple in Jerusalem. As the apostle Peter declared on this very occasion: "This Jesus God resurrected, of which fact we are all witnesses. Therefore because he was exalted to the right hand of God and received the promised holy spirit from the Father, he has poured out this which you see and hear." (Acts 2:32, 33, NW) By thus

---

[18]. Ten days later how did the glorified Messenger come to the temple of Jehovah?

first turning his attention to the temple-building work, the glorified Messenger of the covenant came to the temple as the representative of A·do·nay′ Jehovah. This was in an initial or miniature fulfillment of Malachi 3:1.

[19] The above-described events, Jesus Christ's coming to A·do·nay′ Jehovah's temple and cleansing it, his death on the tree and the rending of the temple curtain in two, Jehovah's raising him from the dead and laying him as the Foundation Cornerstone in the heavenly Mount Zion, and his begetting of the first Jewish disciples of Jesus Christ and anointing them to be living temple stones, all these events took place one after the other in close succession. They all took place from the middle of the fourth year after Jesus the Messenger of the covenant had been baptized in water and been begotten and brought forth as a spiritual Son of God and been anointed with the holy spirit to be Jehovah's Priest after the likeness of Melchizedek, the ancient king-priest of the Most High God.

[20] Just as the typical temple with its animal sacrifices was abandoned by Jehovah God and the sacrifice and oblation there ceased to have further value, so a new, antitypical spiritual temple with a better high priest and a better and truly effective sacrifice came into being. This was three and a half years after Jesus' being begotten spiritually and anointed with the holy spirit. This was in the midst of the foretold 'seventieth week' of years. (Daniel 9:24-27)* Since the spiritual

---

* See the book *"This Means Everlasting Life"*, chapter VIII, pages 81-91.

19. Thus what temple events took place in close succession, and from what time then?
20. At what time was that according to Daniel 9:24-27, and why was that only a minor or miniature fulfillment of Malachi 3:1?

temple was only beginning back there and must yet be completed after centuries of preparing other living temple stones, it is plain that the fulfillment of Malachi 3:1 nineteen centuries ago was only a minor or miniature one. The major and final, complete fulfillment of the prophecy must come when the antitypical spiritual temple is being completed. Nicely the time relationship of the pertinent events back there helps us to determine the time of the prophecy's complete fulfillment down here.

THE FINAL COMING TO THE TEMPLE

²¹ The last book of the Bible, called The Revelation, written about A.D. 96, showed that there was to be a yet future inspection of the spiritual temple of God. It associates this and other startling events at the temple with the setting up of God's kingdom and the coming of his royal Son Jesus Christ into Kingdom authority. The apostle John, the writer of the Revelation, says:

²² "And a reed like a rod was given me as he said: 'Get up and measure the temple sanctuary of God and the altar and those worshiping in it. But as for the court that is outside the temple sanctuary, cast it clear out and do not measure it, because it has been given to the nations, and they will trample the holy city underfoot for forty-two months.' And the seventh angel blew his trumpet. And loud voices occurred in heaven saying: 'The kingdom of the world has become the kingdom of our Lord and of his Christ, and he will rule as king for ever and ever.' And the twenty-four persons of advanced age who were seated before God upon their thrones fell upon their faces and worshiped God, saying: 'We thank

---

21, 22. How does the last book of the Bible show there was to be a yet future inspection of the spiritual temple of God?

you, Jehovah God, the Almighty, the one who is
and who was, because you have taken your great
power and begun ruling as king. But the nations
became wrathful, and your own wrath came, and
the appointed time for the dead to be judged, and
to give their reward to your slaves the prophets
and to the holy ones and to those fearing your
name, the small and the great, and to bring to
ruin those ruining the earth.' And the temple
sanctuary of God that is in heaven was opened,
and the ark of his covenant was seen in his temple
sanctuary. And there occurred lightnings and voices and thunders and an earthquake and a great
hail. And a great sign was seen in heaven, a
woman arrayed with the sun, and the moon was
beneath her feet, and on her head was a crown
of twelve stars, and she was pregnant. And she
cries out in her pains and in her agony to give
birth. And she gave birth to a son, a male, who
is destined to shepherd all the nations with an
iron rod. And her child was caught away to God
and to his throne."—Revelation 11:1, 2, 15-19;
12:1, 2, 5, *NW*.

[23] Note that, after the announcement of Jehovah's taking his power and beginning to rule
as king, "the nations became wrathful." This
draws our attention to the year 1914 (A.D.).
Suddenly, contrary to all the arrangements for
global peace, World War I broke out, with finally
27 Allied Powers waging war against four Central
Powers. Apparently the nations became wrathful
over the issue of world domination, but really
they were wrathful against Jehovah God and his
Christ, the King-Priest Jesus. He had decreed that
the so-called "times of the Gentiles" or "the appointed times of the nations" should end in that
year 1914, about October 1. Their grant of power

---

23. In fulfillment of that prophecy, when did the nations 'become wrathful,' and why or against whom?

to rule the globe without the interference of God's kingdom began with the destruction of royal Jerusalem and her temple and the laying waste of her realm about October 1 in 607 B.C. The "appointed times" of the Gentile nations being limited to 2,520 years, their grant of power was due to expire A.D. 1914, about October 1. So their ruling the globe was due to be interfered with by God's kingdom at that time. That meant that God's kingdom was there due to begin by His taking his great power and beginning to reign. God's long-promised, long-prayed-for kingdom was there due to be born and begin regulating the earth from heaven. It was born, and the "kingdom of the world" became the kingdom of the Lord Jehovah and of his Christ, Jesus his King-Priest.

²⁴ From the womb of his symbolic woman enveloped in heavenly lights, namely, his heavenly angelic organization, Jehovah the heavenly Father brought forth his kingdom by bringing forth his anointed King-Priest Jesus Christ and elevating him to the active kingship in the throne at God's right hand. The entire devilish organization was unable to prevent it. The symbolic male child thus born was "destined to shepherd all the nations with an iron rod." So this kingdom of God by means of his Christ must begin interfering with the nations of Satan's world in order that God's will might come to pass also on earth the same as it does in heaven. (Matthew 6:9, 10, *NW*) Against the wrath of the nations Jehovah God matched his own wrath to be expressed through his King, to bring to ruin at the war of Armageddon those ruining the earth. The time for the resurrection also drew near, "the appointed time

---

24. (a) How was the Kingdom brought forth, and what was its destiny regarding the nations? (b) The time for what else drew near, requiring *A·do·nay"s* coming to the temple?

for the dead to be judged," and also the time for
God's temple sanctuary in heaven to be opened
and for the divine presence, symbolized by the
"ark of his covenant," to be discerned there. That
meant that A·do·nay' must come to His temple,
accompanied by the Angel or Messenger of the
covenant in whom the faithful worshipers delight.
When was this due to occur? When did it occur?

[25] Nineteen hundred years ago Jesus was baptized in the Jordan River by Jehovah's advance
messenger John, and Jehovah immediately pronounced him His approved spiritual Son, saying:
"This is my Son, the beloved, whom I have approved." At that same time the holy spirit or
active force was poured out upon Jesus anointing
him to be a royal priest like Melchizedek.
(Matthew 3:13-17, NW) That was about October
1, A.D. 29, the thirtieth anniversary of his human
birth. (Luke 3:21-23) Afterward for three years
and a half he acted as a witness of Jehovah and
proclaimed: "Look! the kingdom of God is in
your midst." Jesus, as the one whom Jehovah
anointed for the heavenly kingdom, was there in
the midst of his enemies, the Pharisees and others.
He instructed his disciples, when preaching, to
warn the enemy resisters: "Keep this in mind,
that the kingdom of God has come near." (Luke
17:20, 21; 10:10, 11, NW) Toward the end of
the three years and a half of preaching, witnessing and warning and preparing the future temple
stones, Jesus rode like a king into Jerusalem,
came to God's temple there, cleansed it and later
pronounced its doom. Several days later, Nisan
14, A.D. 33, or passover day, he poured out his
human soul in death as a sacrifice for mankind
and went to She'ol, the common grave of man-

---

25. (a) For three and a half years after his baptism,
as what did Jesus act and in the midst of whom?
(b) What temple events then took place, reaching a
climax at Pentecost?

kind. On the third day Almighty God's power resurrected him from death and the grave to become the heavenly Foundation Cornerstone of Jehovah's spiritual temple. The fiftieth day from then, or on Pentecost, God used him to pour out the holy spirit and bring forth "living stones" of the spiritual temple to be built upon him.—Acts 4:10-12; 2:32-36.

²⁶ Corresponding with Jesus' being begotten by God's spirit and his being anointed to be King-Priest is the birth of God's kingdom in 1914 by the crowning and throning of his anointed King-Priest Jesus Christ, at the end of the "appointed times of the nations." This heavenly kingdom had to begin ruling in the midst of its foes, amid the nations already raging in World War I. Despite this, God said: "Yet I have set my king upon my holy hill of Zion." And his "set" King then said: "I will tell of the decree: Jehovah said unto me, Thou art my son; this day have I begotten thee. Ask of me, and I will give thee the nations for thine inheritance, and the uttermost parts of the earth for thy possession. Thou shalt break them with a rod of iron; thou shalt dash them in pieces like a potter's vessel." (Psalm 2:1-9, *AS*) So in 1914 the installed King-Priest Jesus Christ was a newborn king, ruling amidst his enemies.

²⁷ Nineteen centuries ago, it was three years and a half after Jesus' baptism, spirit-begettal and anointing with holy spirit that he came to Jerusalem's typical temple a few days before the passover, offering himself as Zion's king. To

---

26. In this century, what corresponds with Jesus' being begotten after his baptism and then anointed to be Jehovah's King-Priest?
27. How do we now measure to ascertain when the coming to the temple occurred, how was that coming, and how was *A·do·nay"s* presence there pictured in the Revelation?

correspond with that back there, we measure three years and a half from October 1, 1914, when the glorified Jesus Christ became the newborn king of the new world. This brings us to passover season of 1918. The passover night that year was Tuesday, March 26. According to the time parallel, A·do·nay' must have come to his spiritual temple shortly before that passover date. Being a Spirit whom no man can see, A·do·nay''s coming was necessarily with the invisibility of a Spirit Person. His Messenger of the covenant being now also a divine immortal spirit, his coming to the spiritual temple in company with A·do·nay' was also necessarily spiritual and invisible to human eyes. A·do·nay''s presence at the spiritual temple was symbolized by the sight of the "ark of his covenant" in the opened temple sanctuary in heaven. Such a sight pictured something phenomenal, for the typical ark of the covenant had disappeared at the first destruction of Jerusalem in 607 B.C. and was never put back in the Most Holy of any rebuilt temple in Jerusalem. So the Ark's being seen in the temple sanctuary most impressively indicated that A·do·nay' Jehovah had come to his temple, accompanied by his Angel or Messenger of the covenant, his King-Priest Jesus Christ. Thus what had taken place in the invisible spirit realm unseen to our natural eyes in the spring of 1918 amidst the wrath of the warring nations was pictured to our eyes of understanding in The Revelation.

[28] The time when the symbolic ark was seen in the temple sanctuary was connected with the time, not only for God's wrath against the nations, but for the dead to be judged and rewarded according to their deserts. Nineteen centuries ago

---

28. When, therefore, did the resurrecting of the symbolic temple stones asleep in death take place, and when was the Foundation Cornerstone laid in Zion in a complete sense?

Jesus' resurrection occurred about six days after his coming to the temple and driving out the commercial defilers of it. In 1918 at the time of *A·do·nay"s* coming with his Messenger of the covenant to His temple there were a remnant of the "living stones" of the temple class still in the flesh on the earth, and they were expecting by human death and heavenly resurrection to be built into the heavenly temple for God to inhabit by his spirit. However, the vast majority of the 144,000 members of Christ's body who had been prepared here on earth for being made "living stones" in the heavenly temple had already died as humans and were sleeping in death, awaiting the setting up of God's kingdom and the coming of *A·do·nay'* to his temple. At the temple was where his Messenger of the covenant in whom they delighted was to appear or be manifested; they loved his appearing or manifestation. (1 Thessalonians 4:13-17; 2 Timothy 4:8, *NW*) It is reasonable to believe, therefore, that the resurrecting of these symbolic temple stones asleep in death took place shortly after the arrival of *A·do·nay'* and his Messenger of the covenant at the spiritual temple in the spring of 1918. They could now be joined to the Messenger Jesus Christ, whom Jehovah at that time laid as the Foundation Cornerstone of the spiritual temple on the heavenly Mount Zion in a final and complete sense, thus coming to his temple.—See paragraph 17; Isaiah 28:16.

²⁹ Remember, too, that on the fiftieth day from Jesus' own resurrection God's spirit was poured out upon the faithful Jewish remnant, Christ's disciples, making them part of the spiritual temple. Similarly, after *A·do·nay"s* coming with his Messenger of the covenant to the spiritual temple

---

29. On the fiftieth day from Jesus' resurrection what development took place regarding the spiritual temple, and so what was due to follow the coming to the temple in 1918?

in the spring of 1918 there was due to follow an outpouring of God's spirit upon the faithful remnant still in the flesh on earth, to revive them in God's temple service and worship on earth. The facts show that so there was.

[30] As to time scheduling, this corresponds with the building of the typical temple by King Solomon. His father King David abdicated his throne in his old age, and Solomon began reigning before his father died. It is possible he began reigning in the fall of the year, around October 1, and that such year in the Jewish calendar was an accession year or year of accession to the throne. However, the *regnal* years of Israelite kings began counting from the first Jewish lunar month in the spring of the year, at Nisan 1. (2 Samuel 5:4, 5; 1 Chronicles 29:22) When, now, after Solomon became king did he start to build the material temple on Mount Moriah in Jerusalem? The inspired Record replies: "He started to build in the second month on the second [day], in the fourth year of his reign."—2 Chronicles 3:2, *NW;* 1 Kings 6:1.

[31] The second Jewish lunar month, called Ziv, began about the middle of our month April, so that the second day of the second lunar month, Ziv, in 1034 B.C., was about April 17, Gregorian time. So if Solomon's accession year began in the autumn of the year 1038 B.C., his starting to build the temple, his coming to the temple-construction work, was about three years and a half after his accession to the throne. However it is calculated, his starting the erection of the temple took place in his fourth year, just as it was in the fourth year after Jesus' anointing with God's

---

30. As to time scheduling, with the starting to build what does this correspond?
31. So about what date did Solomon come to the temple-construction work, how does this agree with events in Jesus' earthly life, and to what belief does it give a measure of support?

spirit to be King-Priest that he came as the Messenger of *A·do·nay'* to the rebuilt temple in Jerusalem. This timing of events in Solomon's day, therefore, gives a measure of support to the belief that *A·do·nay'* accompanied by his royal Messenger of the covenant came to the temple in the early spring of 1918. Modern events following this date give added proof to the correctness of this calculation.

³² According to Malachi's prophecy a period of severe judgment had to follow the coming of *A·do·nay'* and his Angel of the covenant to the temple. Upon it hinged the successful completion of the spiritual temple in heaven. The resurrecting of the temple stones from the sleep of death during *A·do·nay'*'s presence with his Angel or Messenger at the temple showed a favorable judgment of these temple stones. Thus this part of the temple was put in a place of security and upon a Foundation Cornerstone where it could never be destroyed at the "war of the great day of God the Almighty." It will survive Armageddon, to perpetuate Jehovah's worship throughout the universe, whereas Christendom's temple of confused religion will perish ingloriously as Jerusalem's temples did. That heavenly temple will be completed successfully by the glorifying of the faithful living temple stones yet in the flesh on the earth. For a time after *A·do·nay'* came to the temple in 1918 the position of this remnant of temple stones looked very perilous and their survival of Armageddon was seemingly a questionable matter. But now the survival of these members of Jehovah's temple class is made sure by his undeserved kindness. We now go on to learn how.

---

32. What was to follow *A·do·nay'* and his Angel's coming to the temple in 1918, and how did the completion of the spiritual temple hinge upon it?

CHAPTER VII

Shortening the Days
for the Chosen Ones' Sake

THE Foundation Cornerstone of God's spiritual temple is his High Priest, the King Jesus Christ. Because he was not born in the tribe of Levi and in the priestly family of Aaron, and because he offered his own perfect humanity as a better sacrifice than bulls, sheep and goats, the nation of Israel did not accept him as the only priest of God who could make real atonement for their sins and save them from death, the penalty for sin. Their very rejection and killing of him worked for his being sacrificed in support of Jehovah God's universal sovereignty and for the ransoming of believing, obedient men from sin and death. But because of Jesus' faithfulness, God did the opposite of what the nation of Israel did. He chose him, by his own oath swearing his Son into office as a royal Priest like Melchizedek. He made him a "living stone," the chief and all-necessary "living stone" in the spiritual temple of God's true worship. So he is Jehovah's precious Chosen One, Jehovah's Elect One. His true followers must come to him as such in order to become part of the true temple of worship: "Coming to him as to a living stone, rejected, it is true, by men, but chosen, precious, with God, you yourselves also as living stones are

---

1. As to the temple, how did the Jews' action and Jehovah's action toward Jesus differ, and how are his followers today thus like him?

107

being built up a spiritual house for the purpose of a holy priesthood, to offer up spiritual sacrifices acceptable to God through Jesus Christ." (1 Peter 2:4, 5, *NW*) Jesus' true followers are like him in being rejected by the religious systems of Christendom and of the world but in being chosen by Jehovah God for his temple class. They are his chosen ones or elect ones.

² The grand day approaches when all the 144,000 chosen "living stones" will be built up in heaven into a glorious temple upon the Foundation Cornerstone Jesus Christ. Today, after God has spent nineteen centuries in selecting and preparing these living temple stones for his "spiritual house," only a remnant of them is still alive in the flesh on the earth. These are the ones that have survived till the presence of the Lord Jesus at the temple as the Angel or Messenger of the covenant. Those who were asleep in death at his coming to the temple were raised in a spiritual, hence invisible, resurrection, to be united with him there at the temple.

³ In support of this the apostle Paul wrote for the information of the remnant today: "For this is what we tell you by Jehovah's word, that we the living who survive to the presence of the Lord shall in no way precede those who have fallen asleep in death, because the Lord himself will descend from heaven with a commanding call, with an archangel's voice and with God's trumpet, and those who are dead in union with Christ will rise first. Afterward we the living who are surviving will together with them be caught away in clouds to meet the Lord in the air; and thus we shall always be with the Lord." (1 Thessa-

---

2. How is it that today there is only a remnant of the temple's "living stones" alive on the earth?
3. However, how are the remnant in union with the Lord Jesus at the temple, and why is this vitally necessary for them?

lonians 4:15-17, *NW*) Now discerning in the light of the revealed Scriptures and of the fulfilled prophecies that the Lord Jesus is present at the temple of A·do·nay' Jehovah, the faithful remnant are, although still in a tabernacle of flesh, yet in union with him at the temple. They have been caught away from this world's system of things and been united with him in the worship and service of Jehovah God.* This is vitally necessary to their being spared during Armageddon and surviving that war, when the stones of Christendom's temples will go crashing down in ruin.

⁴ After Jesus predicted the destruction of Jerusalem's temple and his disciples asked him privately when such an astounding thing would occur, he uttered his inspired prophecy on the end of the present system of things. Christendom's temple or system of religion was typified by Jerusalem's temple, and so by prophesying about Jerusalem's temple Jesus associated the destruction of Christendom's religious organization and the end of this entire system of things together. We are now in the "time of the end" of Christendom and all the rest of this system of things. (Daniel 11:40; 12:4) It began in 1914 when the "appointed times of the nations" ended and the kingdom of God was set up in the heavens to dash all these nations to pieces at Armageddon and to usher in a new world or system of things. The correct timing of the start of the "time of the end" was proved by the raging of World War I in 1914, followed by all kinds of distress worldwide. This proved the infallible truth of Jesus' prophecy concerning this time: "Nation will rise

---

* See the book *"This Means Everlasting Life"*, pages 232-235.

---

4. How, in his prophecy, did Jesus associate the destruction of Christendom's religious organization with the world's end, and why are we now in its "time of the end"?

against nation and kingdom against kingdom, there will be earthquakes in one place after another, there will be food shortages. These are a beginning of pangs of distress."—Mark 13:8, *NW*.

[5] It was during this "beginning of pangs of distress" that the nations, particularly those of Christendom, brought great trouble upon the remnant of the temple class in an attempt to destroy the "spiritual house" of God. Because of such an attempt Christendom made her own coming destruction all the more deserved, as it is written: "Do you not know that you people are God's temple and that the spirit of God dwells in you? If anyone destroys the temple of God, God will destroy him; for the temple of God is holy, which temple you people are."—1 Corinthians 3:16, 17, *NW;* Ezra 6:11, 12.

[6] During the first world war of 1914-1918 the remnant of Jehovah's temple class came under a serious measure of God's disfavor. Jesus had predicted that his followers would then come under great persecution among all nations and there would even be difficulties and divisions within the organization of his own followers; and he added: "You will be objects of hatred by all people on account of my name. But he that has endured to the finish is the one that will be saved." (Mark 13:9-13, *NW*) The remnant, because of having themselves recently come out of Christendom's religious confusion, were still soiled religiously in a number of important respects. This fact resulted in the trials' proving to be quite hard upon them in those crucial years, and their spiritual weaknesses were shown up. Their course in this world

---

5. During the "beginning of pangs of distress," how did Christendom make her own destruction all the more deserved?
6. How did the remnant come under a serious measure of God's disfavor, and how might no flesh have survived Armageddon?

was not altogether true and in strict conformity to God's requirements. They were not carrying out an absolute neutrality toward this world and its conflicts and were not fully 'obeying God as ruler rather than men.' The fear of men both within their organization and without led them into a snare that threatened the loss of God's favor and his bringing destruction upon them together with all other flesh on earth in the great tribulation. (Proverbs 29:25) Had they been destroyed during this time of fear-inspired captivity to the world at war, there would have been no flesh to survive the battle of Armageddon.

⁷ The dangerousness of the situation was foretold by Jesus in these words: "Those days will be days of a tribulation such as has not occurred from the beginning of the creation which God created until that time and will not occur again. In fact, unless Jehovah had cut short the days, no flesh would be saved. But on account of the chosen ones that he has chosen he has cut short the days."—Mark 13:19, 20, NW.

⁸ Especially from the year 1925 on it has been appreciated how Jehovah God cut short the days of tribulation for the sake of his elect or chosen ones yet on earth.* The cutting short of those days is now taking place by causing a break in the tribulation between its commencement in heaven and its finish at earth in Armageddon. In 1914 Jehovah God, for the sake of vindicating his universal sovereignty, enthroned his King-Priest Jesus Christ at the close of the "appointed times of the nations" that year. He commanded

---

* See the article "For the Elect's Sake" in *The Watch Tower* of May 1, 1925.

---

7. In what words was the dangerousness of the situation foretold by Jesus?
8. (a) How have the days of tribulation been cut short for the sake of the chosen ones? (b) In 1914, after the enthronement of the King, what did the time come for?

him to rule in the midst of his enemies until Jehovah by him made all his enemies his footstool. (Psalm 110:1, 2, *AS*) That meant war, such a war as was implied in Jehovah's warning to Satan the Devil in the garden of Eden: "I shall put enmity between you and the woman and between your seed and her seed. He will bruise you in the head and you will bruise him in the heel." (Genesis 3:15, *NW*) In 1914 the time came for open hostilities between the enthroned King and the original Serpent, Satan the Devil, and all his seed in heaven and earth. What the Revelation foretold to take place on earth from that year forward has visibly taken place, and we may be absolutely sure that what The Revelation told to take place in the heavens at the same time has taken place, although invisibly to our eyes. The enthroned Jesus Christ is the "Angel [or, Messenger] of the covenant" and in heaven, both before his human birth and since his ascension to heaven, his name has been "Michael the archangel." He is the "great prince" who stands for the children of Jehovah's people and at whose standing up in power there comes a "time of trouble, such as never was since there was a nation even to that same time." (Jude 9; Daniel 12:1; Matthew 24:21, 22) Reporting Michael's fight, The Revelation says:

⁹ "She [that is, God's womanly organization in heaven] gave birth to a son, a male, who is destined to shepherd all the nations with an iron rod. And her child was caught away to God and to his throne. . . . And war broke out in heaven: Michael and his angels battled with the dragon, and the dragon and its angels battled but it did not prevail, neither was a place found for them any longer in heaven. So down the great dragon

---

9. In what descriptive words does The Revelation report Michael's fight and the outcome?

was hurled, the original serpent, the one called Devil and Satan, who is misleading the entire inhabited earth; he was hurled down to the earth, and his angels were hurled down with him. And I heard a loud voice in heaven say: 'Now have come to pass the salvation and the power and the kingdom of our God and the authority of his Christ, because the accuser of our brothers has been hurled down, who accuses them day and night before our God! And they conquered him because of the blood of the Lamb and because of the word of their witnessing, and they did not love their souls even despite the danger of death. On this account be glad, you heavens and you who reside in them! Woe for the earth and for the sea, because the Devil has come down to you, having great anger, knowing he has a short period of time.' Now when the dragon saw it was hurled down to the earth, it persecuted the woman that gave birth to the male child. . . . And the dragon grew wrathful at the woman, and went off to wage war with the remaining ones of her seed, who observe the commandments of God and have the work of bearing witness to Jesus."—Revelation 12:5-17, *NW*.

[10] That war in the invisible heavens meant great tribulation for Satan the Devil and his entire organization, heavenly and earthly, for it meant an unequaled defeat. For the first time in his thousands of years of existence Satan the Devil, together with his demon angels, had been excluded from the heavens, and that for all time to come. Even at the time when his visible organization on earth was destroyed by the global flood of Noah's day Satan the Devil had not been excluded from heaven, for he was reported as still

---

10. How did that war in heaven result in an unequaled defeat for Satan and his demons, and what effect has this had upon him?

having access to heaven in the days of patient Job centuries after the Flood. (Job 1:6 to 2:7) Now following the war in heaven that began at the King's enthronement in 1914 Satan the Devil has for the first time been hurled out of heaven, with no place any more up there for him and his demon angels. That humiliating defeat served notice upon him that it will not be long now before he is bruised in the head by the enthroned Seed of God's woman. The One whose heel he once bruised at Calvary outside Jerusalem now has him under his heel at this earth, of which Jehovah God says: "Heaven is my throne, and the earth is my footstool." (Isaiah 66:1, AS; Acts 7:48, 49, NW) Not strange, then, that he should be violently wrathful, determined to bring woe to the earth and sea and going off to "wage war with the remaining ones of [the woman's] seed, who observe the commandments of God and have the work of bearing witness to Jesus." Quite in agreement with this, too, was it that the worldly nations of whom Satan the Devil is ruler and god should be at one another's throats in the first global war for the domination of the earth.

[11] Jesus called the first world war, together with the earthquakes, food shortages and pestilences, all of which ran at the same time as the war in heaven, "the beginning of pangs of distress" for the present system of things. That indicated that the war in heaven and World War I and accompanying sorrows on earth were not all there was to be to the tribulation or trouble upon Satan's organization. There was more to follow at Armageddon, ending up with none of the wicked organization left alive on earth. But Jehovah God through his enthroned King did not follow up the hurling of Satan out of heaven by fighting the

11. On whose account did Jehovah God "cut short" the days of tribulation, and how?

battle of Armageddon immediately. He "cut short" the days of tribulation upon Satan's organization by causing a break in the hostilities, not by any agreed-upon armistice or "cease fire" with Satan the Devil, but for his own purposes in fulfillment of the prophecies. It was "on account of the chosen ones that he has chosen," that is, the remnant of his woman's seed who observe his commandments and have the work of witnessing to Jesus the enthroned King. So, at the hurling of Satan and his demon angels down to the earth the victorious, princely Archangel Michael did not at once seize Satan and his demons and bind them with a great chain for a thousand years and hurl them into the abyss, there shutting them up under a seal, to mislead the nations no more for a thousand years. To have gone that far with the invisible part of Satan's organization would have meant also the dashing of all the nations of earth to pieces and consequently 'no flesh would have been saved.' —Revelation 20:1-3, *NW*.

¹² To the contrary of this it was Jehovah's purpose to have survivors on earth of the battle of Armageddon, primarily the remnant of the seed of his "woman." Hence he cut short the days of tribulation by a halting of battle action on His part and he left Satan the Devil and his demon angels and the nations remain at his footstool, the earth, but only for a "short period of time" longer. Of course, this allowed time for Satan to send out his demons and gather the rulers and their armies to the field of Armageddon at the close of the "time of the end"; but at the same time it allowed Jehovah to have mercy upon his remnant yet in the flesh.

---

12. Whom, specially, did Jehovah want to survive Armageddon, and so what did his allowing Satan to remain a short time longer permit him to do toward them?

¹³ At the beginning of the year 1919 the remnant of the seed of God's woman, the remnant of living temple "stones," did need divine mercy. Because of yielding to the enemy pressure during the "beginning of pangs of distress" they had earned his displeasure and he had let them become captive to the enemy organization and be restrained from their free and open public witness work concerning God's kingdom by his enthroned King-Priest Jesus Christ. Leaders in the witness work were even then in a literal prison in the United States of America; and a reduced staff of workers had removed from the headquarters in Brooklyn, New York, to small quarters in Pittsburgh, Pennsylvania, continuing to publish the magazine *The Watch Tower and Herald of Christ's Presence*. Their connections with others of the remnant of witnesses throughout the earth had been badly broken up by World War I. Much of their literature was banned by warring governments. They were in a condition like that foretold in The Revelation, witnessing in a depressed condition, as though "dressed in sackcloth," during the course of World War I.

¹⁴ "And when they have finished their witnessing [thus in sackcloth], the wild beast [Satan's visible organization of nations] that ascends out of the abyss [the sea] will make war with them and conquer them and kill them. And their corpses will be on the broad way of the great city which is in a spiritual sense called Sodom and Egypt, where their Lord was also impaled. And some persons of the peoples and tribes and tongues and nations will look at their corpses for three and a half days, and they do not let their corpses be laid in a tomb. And those dwelling on the earth rejoice

---

13. Why did the remnant need divine mercy at the beginning of 1919?
14. When they finished their witnessing thus "in sackcloth," what took place as described by The Revelation?

over them and enjoy themselves, and they will send gifts to one another, because these two prophets tormented those dwelling on the earth." (Revelation 11:7-10; 13:1; Romans 10:7, *NW;* Deuteronomy 30:13) The witnesses to Christ's presence in his heavenly kingdom were thus shown to be hated internationally, and once their haters had them killed (as they thought), they did not want them remembered or resurrected from the death state, as pictured by refusing to "let their corpses be laid in a tomb."

¹⁵ Although Jehovah God was displeased with his faltering remnant on earth, he was not pleased either with the nations who, unitedly like Satan's beast, had risen up and killed their witness work in 1918. *A·do·nay'* Jehovah with His Messenger of the covenant had come to his temple in the spring of 1918, after which the faithful Christians whose preparation as temple stones had ended with their death were resurrected unseen to human eyes, because it was a spiritual resurrection, in a "spiritual body," to put them in their places in the heavenly temple. (1 Corinthians 15:42-44) In this way the judgment had started at the house of God with a favorable judgment rendered to the faithful ones of the temple class who had finished their earthly preparation. As it had been written: "It is the appointed time for the judgment to start with the house of God. Now if it starts first with us, what will the complete end be of those who are not obedient to the good news of God? 'And if the righteous man is being saved with difficulty, where will the ungodly man and the sinner make a showing?' " (1 Peter 4:17, 18, *NW*) However, with a remnant of the temple stones still on earth in the

---

15. How did the judgment at the temple start out with a favorable judgment, and for the heavenly temple to be completed what was necessary respecting the remnant on earth?

flesh, and that in a displeasing condition, the heavenly temple was still incomplete. It was necessary for the remnant to be brought to a finished state as temple stones, even if it meant their "being saved with difficulty," because of their then disapproved condition. This situation called for God's mercy, and he did exercise it because the remnant turned in repentance and called upon him.—Psalm 102:13-20.

[16] The beginning of 1919 found the remnant of anointed witnesses of Jehovah God lying like dead corpses "on the broad way of the great city which is in a spiritual sense called Sodom and Egypt, where their Lord was also impaled." More than thirty-four centuries previously Jehovah had delivered his Israelite people from captivity and abject slavery in ancient Egypt at passover season, and the passover lamb that they then killed and feasted upon before marching out free from Egypt typified the Lord Jesus Christ at his death on the tree outside Jerusalem. (Exodus, chapters twelve and thirteen; 1 Corinthians 5:7) Now, in 1919, Jehovah carried forward a greater deliverance of his faithful Christian witnesses, his spiritual Israelites. His Messenger of the covenant with Him at the temple served as a Greater Moses to lead them out. (Acts 3:20-26) From the temple Jehovah God had exercised his stupendous power by his Messenger Jesus Christ to raise the faithful temple members asleep in death to heavenly life with the Foundation Cornerstone of the temple. Now from his temple he would exercise his reviving power to restore his witnesses lying inactive in the broad street of spiritual Egypt to free and fearless action in his witness work among all nations. Beginning his judgment at the house of God, he rendered a

---

16. How did the beginning of 1919 find the remnant, and how did God render a merciful judgment to them?

merciful judgment to his repentant remnant of temple stones on earth. He energized them to lively activities in temple work, beginning with the spring of 1919. The Revelation says:

[17] "After the three and a half days [of lying like dead in the broad street of spiritual Egypt] spirit of life from God entered into them, and they stood upon their feet, and great fear fell upon those beholding them. And they heard a loud voice out of heaven say to them: 'Come on up here.' And they went up into heaven in the cloud, and their enemies beheld them. And in that hour a great earthquake occurred, and a tenth of the city fell, and seven thousand persons were killed by the earthquake, and the rest became terrified and gave glory to the God of heaven."—Revelation 11:11-13, *NW*.

[18] To the consternation of their international enemies Jehovah's remnant of anointed witnesses came to life in his service in 1919 solely by the deliverance of Jehovah God through his Greater Moses and by the power of his spirit or active force. They began freeing themselves from the binding restraints of the fear of men and they reorganized world-wide for the mighty witness work that they now learned lay ahead of them. In September of that year they held their first postwar general assembly at Cedar Point, Ohio, U.S.A. There the then president of the Watch Tower Bible & Tract Society addressed the convention on the significant subjects, "Blessed Are the Fearless" and "Announcing the Kingdom," and then a public audience of about 7,000 on "Hope for Distressed Humanity." To the continued publication of the magazine *The Watch Tower* there was to be added from that year on a new magazine

---

17. What followed, according to The Revelation?
18. How, in 1919, did the remnant come to life for Jehovah's future service?

entitled "The Golden Age," now known as "Awake!"

[19] The revived remnant gratefully responded to the commanding call from heaven, "Come on up here," and they entered into the witness work in union with Jehovah's Messenger at the heavenly temple. This elevating of them from the dust of inactivity to a part in Jehovah's lofty service distinct from this world (antitypical Egypt) was like having them ascend to heaven in the sight of their frightened enemies. The cloud of Jehovah's presence at his temple and of his favor and protection accompanied them. This corresponded with the apostle's prophecy concerning this remnant: "Those who are dead in union with Christ will rise first. Afterward we the living who are surviving will together with them be caught away in clouds to meet the Lord in the air; and thus we shall always be with the Lord." (1 Thessalonians 4:16, 17, *NW*) This reviving and exalting of the remnant of anointed witnesses stirred spiritual Egypt and shook her like a devastating earthquake, from which she has not recovered to this day. Unwillingly she had to acknowledge the power of Jehovah God in behalf of his witnesses.

[20] This has occurred during the "short period of time" by which Jehovah God has interrupted the days of tribulation upon Satan's organization. Armageddon, the "war of the great day of God the Almighty," lies yet ahead and will climax those days of tribulation, bringing destruction upon spiritual Egypt and abyssing its false god, Satan the Devil, and all his demon angels. Indeed, Jehovah God has cut short the days of tribulation

---

19. How did the remnant respond to the call from heaven, "Come on up here," and go up in the cloud, and with what effect upon spiritual Egypt?
20. During what period of time has this occurred, and with what yet ahead?

"on account of the chosen ones that he has chosen." Otherwise they would have been destroyed with spiritual Egypt and "no flesh would be saved."

²¹ For this life-giving mercy to them the remnant joyfully thanked God in fulfillment of the prophecy: "And there shall be a highway for the remnant of his people, that shall remain, from Assyria; like as there was for Israel in the day that he came up out of the land of Egypt. And in that day thou shalt say, I will give thanks unto thee, O Jehovah; for though thou wast angry with me, thine anger is turned away, and thou comfortest me. Behold, God is my salvation; I will trust, and will not be afraid: for Jehovah, even Jehovah, is my strength and song; and he is become my salvation. Therefore with joy shall ye draw water out of the wells of salvation." (Isaiah 11:16; 12:1-3, *AS*) Wrathfully the Dragon, Satan the Devil, has gone forth to make war with this remnant of the Seed of God's woman, but by their continuing faithfully in the witness work until the finish in obedience to God's commandments the remnant will be saved, finally being made part of the heavenly temple.

²² However, this spiritual remnant of living temple stones will not be the only ones on earth to be spared and carried alive through the oncoming battle of Armageddon. Jehovah's cutting short the days for the sake of the survival of his chosen or elect ones results mercifully in the preserving alive through that battle of an earthly class of people who are not "living stones" of God's "spiritual house." This earthly class of people who are

---

21. In fulfillment of what prophecy have the remnant thanked God for this life-giving mercy, and how will they finally be saved?
22. Will Jehovah's cutting short the days for the survival of his chosen ones result mercifully to others, and to what ancient typical rescue do we look for an answer?

not spiritual Israelites but who will survive Armageddon into the new world were typified amid the things that happened to the natural Israelites when Jehovah by his Angel and the prophet Moses rescued his people from captivity and slavery in Egypt in 1513 B.C.

[23] There were many non-Israelites in Egypt that sided with the Israelites because they worshiped the true God and had his promises. Indicative of this, Jehovah made these regulations concerning the celebration of the passover for the sake of having their first-born children and animals spared alive during the tenth and last plague upon Egypt: "This is the statute of the passover: No foreigner may eat of it. But where there is any slave man bought with money [thus becoming your property], you must circumcise him. Then first he may eat of it. And in case a temporary resident should reside for a while with you and he must celebrate the passover to Jehovah, let there be a circumcising of every male of his. First then he may come near to celebrate it, and he must become like a native of the land. But no uncircumcised man may eat of it. One law is to exist for the native and for the temporary resident who is residing for a while in your midst." (Exodus 12:43, 44, 48, 49, *NW*) Becoming circumcised, these bought slaves and temporary residents became proselytes to the faith of the natural Israelites and thus subjected themselves to those laws that were to apply equally to them and to the natural or native Israelites.

[24] Doubtless the Israelites during their long stay

---

23. How did God's law concerning the passover indicate there were many in Egypt that sided with the Israelites, and what did those complying with that law become?
24. (a) What did those who threw in their lot with the Israelites form, and what did they do when the Israelites marched out of Egypt? (b) Where are they last reported as being, and what does this show?

in Egypt had made many marriages with the Egyptians. There were also Egyptians themselves or other foreigners who chose to throw in their lot with the Israelites, especially in the light of the ten marvelous plagues that Jehovah brought upon the oppressive nation of Egypt, to demonstrate that he was the only true God and that the many gods of the Egyptians were false. (Leviticus 24:10) Such persons formed what was called a "mixed company," not purely Israelite. When Pharaoh the king of Egypt lost his first-born son in the tenth plague and finally yielded to Jehovah's demand that Pharaoh let the Israelites leave the country, this mixed company joined the Israelites in their march to freedom. The Record says: "The sons of Israel proceeded to depart from Rameses for Succoth, to the number of six hundred thousand able-bodied men on foot, besides little ones. And a vast mixed company also went up with them, as well as flocks and herds, a very numerous stock of animals." (Exodus 12:37, 38, *NW*) Did this mixed company go with them only as far as Succoth in Egypt? No; for more than a year later the mixed company were reported as being with the Israelites in the wilderness of the Arabian peninsula. Not favorably the Record says: "And the mixed crowd that was in the midst of them expressed selfish longing, and the sons of Israel too began to weep again and say: 'Who will give us meat to eat? How we remember the fish that we used to eat in Egypt for nothing, the cucumbers and the watermelons and the leeks and the onions and the garlic!' " (Numbers 11:4, 5, *NW*) Their presence in the wilderness means that they had completely left the land of Egypt, for the Red Sea separated Egypt from the Arabian peninsula.

²⁵ This fact also means that the mixed company

---

25. What did they therefore experience at the Red Sea, to make their escape from Egypt complete?

of non-Israelites had followed Moses and the Israelites as on dry land through the Red Sea, in striking contrast with the pursuing Egyptians upon whom the parted waters of the Red Sea closed in, destroying all those charioteers and horsemen and their horses. As the Israelites themselves marched through the sea, with the piled-up waters on their right hand and their left and with the cloud of God's presence overhead protecting them, they received a baptism, a symbolic baptism into Moses the prophet of Jehovah and their visible leader. Making this explanation, the apostle Paul writes: "Now I do not want you to be ignorant, brothers, that our forefathers were all under the cloud and all passed through the sea and all got baptized into Moses by means of the cloud and of the sea." (1 Corinthians 10:1, 2, NW) It was only by continuing to follow the Israelites and being baptized with them into Moses by means of the cloud and of the sea that the mixed company were saved from death in the Red Sea and made their escape from demon-controlled Egypt complete.

²⁶ Miraculously Jehovah destroyed the Egyptians' pursuit armies in the Red Sea after Moses, safe on the Arabian shore, stretched his hand out over the sea. That pictured God Almighty's war against his enemies, the antitypical Egyptians, to their complete annihilation at Armageddon. As Moses then described him in a victory song: "Jehovah is a manly person of war. Jehovah is his name. Pharaoh's chariots and his military forces he has cast into the sea, and the choice of his warriors have been sunk in the Red sea. . . . Your right hand, O Jehovah, is proving itself powerful in ability, your right hand, O Jehovah, can shatter an enemy. And in the abundance of your superiority you can throw down those who rise up against you; . . . Jehovah will rule as king forever and ever." (Exodus 15:3-18, *NW*) Moses there pictured Jehovah's Greater Prophet, the glorified Lord Jesus Christ, who leads all of Jehovah's witnesses safely through the battle of Armageddon without their fighting in it, to complete freedom in God's righteous new world.

²⁷ The mixed multitude's being saved along with the Israelites foreshadowed that not only will a remnant of the spiritual Israelites be preserved through Armageddon, but also a great crowd of persons who are not spiritual Israelites, who are not of the 144,000 members of the temple class of "living stones." To be spared and to pass through the Red Sea of Armageddon, this antitypical mixed company must imitate and keep with the remnant of spiritual Israelites and be baptized into the antitypical Moses, the Greater Moses, to follow him as Jehovah's Mouthpiece and Leader for us.

---

26. Jehovah's destroying the Egyptian armies in the Red Sea pictured what, and whom did Moses there picture?

27. What was foreshadowed by the mixed multitude's being saved along with the Israelites, and so what must the antitypical mixed company do?

CHAPTER VIII

Raising the Signal to All the Nations

EGYPT of ancient time was the first of seven world powers in the list that the Holy Bible makes. Being a part of this world or system of things, it was therefore used as a symbol of this world, because Egypt's real gods were Satan the Devil and his demons and Satan is the "ruler of this world" and the "god of this system of things." Because Egypt was thus used as a symbol of this world, this present wicked system of things is called 'spiritual Egypt' and its god and ruler was symbolized or typified by Pharaoh the king of Egypt. In fact, it was really to antitypical Pharaoh, Satan the Devil, that Jehovah addressed his remarks after pouring out his sixth plague upon the land of Egypt: "By now I could have thrust my hand out that I might strike you and your people with pestilence and that you might be effaced from the earth. But, in fact, for this cause I have kept you in existence, for the sake of showing you my power and in order to have my name declared in all the earth." (Exodus 9:15, 16, *NW*) By means of ten plagues upon her and by the destruction of her military hosts in the Red Sea under the eyes of Jehovah's people, Egypt was the first world power to realize the universal sovereignty of the Most High God Jehovah. But after Egypt had passed the peak of her power, Jehovah still kept Satan the Devil in existence for the sake

---

1. Of what were ancient Egypt and her Pharaoh symbols, and why was the antitypical Pharaoh kept in existence after Egypt passed the peak of her power?

126

of at last showing that wicked one the divine power at the battle of Armageddon, where the original Serpent, Satan the Devil, will be bruised in the head by the Seed of God's woman, the reigning King Jesus Christ.

2 In harmony with this purpose the righteous God Jehovah has permitted evil and wickedness to prevail and has allowed the god of this world to establish, all together, seven world powers in succession, followed by a combination world power, an eighth one. With all eight of these Jehovah's people have had much contact.

3 Because of its fierceness and cruelty Jehovah God in his Bible pictured Satan's visible organization as a wild beast that rises out of the sea or the great deep, the abyss. It is pictured as having ten horns on seven heads, the ten horns symbolizing the complete earthly power of this symbolic beast to push mankind around and control the earth. The seven heads of the beast symbolize the seven world powers that have dominated in their successive order over Satan's visible organization. These seven world powers the Bible and worldly history show to be (1) Egypt, (2) Assyria, (3) Babylon, (4) Medo-Persia, (5) Greece, (6) Rome and (7) the Anglo-American imperial power. The eighth world power is not symbolized as a head of this beast, because it "owes its existence to the seven," but it is the international alliance that was known, before World War II, as the League of Nations and, since World War II, as the United Nations. To the symbolic seven-headed wild beast Almighty God gave the opportunity to "wage war with the holy ones and conquer them, and author-

---

2. In harmony with this what has Jehovah permitted to prevail and what to be established?
3. How was Satan's visible organization pictured in The Revelation, what do its component parts picture, and what has been God's purpose in letting it abuse his holy ones?

ity was given it over every tribe and people and tongue and nation. . . . If anyone is for being led captive, he goes away led captive. If anyone practices killing with the sword, he must himself be killed with the sword. Here is where it means the endurance and faith of the holy ones." (Revelation 13:1-10; 17:3, 8-11, *NW*) God's purpose in letting the symbolic wild beast thus abuse his holy ones was in order to prove their integrity to him and to show to all creation that they submitted and stood loyal to his universal sovereignty, obeying God as ruler rather than men of this world.—Acts 5:29-32, *NW*.

⁴ The first head of the symbolic wild beast took Jehovah's chosen people, the twelve tribes of Israel, into captivity during their temporary residence in Egypt. But Jehovah rescued them from Egypt's jaws in the days of Moses, in 1513 B.C. The second head of the wild beast, Assyria, tried to take the entire people of Israel captive but succeeded in capturing and leading into exile only ten unfaithful tribes of that people. The third head of the wild beast, Babylon, overthrew Assyria by capturing its capital city Nineveh in 632 B.C. Afterward it blocked the resurging power of Egypt and moved against the remaining two tribes of Israel governed by Jerusalem. After besieging Jerusalem for eighteen months Nebuchadnezzar king of Babylon breached the city walls and captured the fleeing king in the summer of 607 B.C. About a month later Nebuchadnezzar razed to the ground the city and the temple that King Solomon had built. Besides the 3,023 Jews whom he had deported to Babylon eleven years earlier, Nebuchadnezzar now carried captive to Babylon 832 Jews, leaving many of the poorer Jews behind in their native land of Judah to take care of it. But

4. How did Egypt, Assyria and Babylon deal oppressively with Jehovah's people, and how and when was the land of Judah left completely desolate?

Jehovah God had decreed that the land of Judah and its capital Jerusalem should lie uninhabited by man and by domestic beast for seventy years. In harmony with this the poor of the land did not remain there but fled down to Egypt in fear two months later, so that in the seventh Jewish month of that year, or about October 1, 607 B.C., the land of Judah came to complete desolation.—Jeremiah 52:1-29.

⁵ By a miracle Jehovah God did not permit Nebuchadnezzar to move other people into the unoccupied land of Judah, nor did he let other peoples like the Samaritans move in to occupy it. People passing by the desolate land of Judah whistled at it in fear and dread as at a haunted place. Jehovah, in fulfillment of his prophecy, was keeping everybody out of it for seventy years. He was holding it in reserve for his faithful remnant of Jews whom he had promised to deliver from their Babylonish captivity and restore to their own God-given land. (Jeremiah 25:8-12; 29:10-14; 1 Kings 9:6-9, *NW*) This he did by turning the tables on Babylon. In 607 B.C. she had wrecked Jerusalem and its temple and had led the Jews off captive to Babylon; now she herself must be overthrown and be led off captive. This occurred in 539 B.C., when Jehovah brought against Babylon the fourth head of the wild beast, Medo-Persia, and delivered Babylon, despite her mightiness, into the hand of Darius the Mede and his nephew Cyrus the Persian. The fall of Babylon astonished the ancient world. But it was Jehovah's just punishment upon her for her sacrilegious violence against his own temple and chosen people, and it opened up the way for a faithful remnant of his people to return to their desolate-lying land of Judah.

---

5. How did Jehovah perform a miracle toward the land of Judah, and how did he punish Babylon for her violence against his temple and his chosen people?

⁶ Cyrus the Persian succeeded his uncle Darius as king of the fourth world power. In 537 B.C., in his first regnal year, Cyrus fulfilled the purpose for which Jehovah permitted him to overthrow Babylon and become king of the Medo-Persian world power. Ezra, an Aaronic priest and a Bible copyist, recorded this fulfillment of prophecy, saying: "And in the first year of Cyrus the king of Persia, that Jehovah's word from the mouth of Jeremiah might be accomplished, Jehovah roused the spirit of Cyrus the king of Persia so that he caused a cry to pass through all his realm, and also in writing, saying: 'This is what Cyrus the king of Persia has said, "All the kingdoms of the earth Jehovah the God of the heavens has given me and he himself has commissioned me to build him a house in Jerusalem, which is in Judah. Whoever there is among you of all his people, may his God prove to be with him. So let him go up to Jerusalem, which is in Judah, and rebuild the house of Jehovah the God of Israel—he is The [true] God —which was in Jerusalem. As for anyone that is left of all the places where he is temporarily residing, let the men of his place assist him with silver and with gold and with goods and with domestic animals along with the voluntary offering for the house of The [true] God, which was in Jerusalem."'" (Ezra 1:1-4, NW; 2 Chronicles 36: 20-23) The decree of Cyrus put the rebuilding of the house or temple of Jehovah as the chief purpose in releasing the captive Jews to return to their desolate homeland. The rebuilding of the temple on its original site in Jerusalem meant the restoration of the worship of Jehovah there. Babylon's idolatrous temples came low; Jehovah's temple came up.

---

6. How did Cyrus fulfill the purpose for which Jehovah let him overthrow Babylon, and what did Cyrus' decree put as the first purpose in releasing the captive Jews?

[7] A zealous remnant of the captive Jews in Babylonian territory responded to the grand privilege of returning to their theocratic land and restoring the worship of the one living and true God by engaging in temple rebuilding work in Jerusalem or Zion. For scores of years they had mourned, without Jehovah's temple, without a holy city, in the idolatrous land of Babylon, because they had offended their God. In that pagan land they had been marked by Satan the Devil for death; they were, so to speak, "the sons of death." But as Jehovah had heard the groaning of his people long before that in Egypt, so he heard their groaning in Babylon. He marked their repentance, and he heard their prayers for the foretold deliverance, that he might again make a glorious manifestation of himself in Jerusalem or Zion. He had pity, and he caused a new people to be created, a nation to be brought forth, upon the once desolate land of Judah and Jerusalem or Zion. (Isaiah 66:8) As the psalmist had prophetically sung of this:

[8] "So the nations shall fear the name of Jehovah, and all the kings of the earth thy glory: for Jehovah hath built up Zion; he hath appeared in his glory. He hath regarded the prayer of the destitute, and hath not despised their prayer. This shall be written for the generation to come; and a people which shall be created shall praise Jehovah. For he hath looked down from the height of his sanctuary; from heaven did Jehovah behold the earth; to hear the sighing of the prisoner; to loose those that are appointed to death; that men may declare the name of Jehovah in Zion, and his praise in Jerusalem; when the peoples are gathered together, and the kingdoms, to serve Jehovah." —Psalm 102:15-22, *AS*.

7, 8. (a) In Babylon what had been the experience of the remnant that responded to Cyrus' decree? (b) How did Jehovah then fulfill Psalm 102:15-22?

⁹ So it was that in 537 B.C. a remnant of faithful Jews under Zerubbabel their appointed governor and with Jeshua as their high priest left Babylon, tramped across the desert and four months later reached the beloved land and the ruins of Jerusalem. There were 42,360 Jews in all. By the seventh Jewish month in that year they were again located on the sites of their former cities, exactly seventy years after the decreed desolation of the land had begun. On the first day of that seventh month they assembled in Jerusalem at the temple site and established an altar to Jehovah on the proper altar location and then began sacrificing on it. But it was not until in the "second year of their coming to the house of The [true] God at Jerusalem, in the second month," that governor Zerubbabel and high priest Jeshua and their assistants set the builders to work and they laid the foundation for a new temple to Jehovah.

¹⁰ "When the builders laid the foundation of the temple of Jehovah, then the priests in official clothing, with the trumpets, and the Levites the sons of Asaph, with the cymbals, stood up to praise Jehovah according to the direction of David the [former] king of Israel. And they began to respond by praising and giving thanks to Jehovah, 'for he is good, for his loving-kindness toward Israel is to time indefinite.' As for all the people, they shouted with a loud shout in praising Jehovah over the laying of the foundation of the house of Jehovah." Many wept with emotion.—Ezra 2:64; 3:1-13, *NW*.

¹¹ According to the inspired rule stated at 1 Corinthians 10:6, 11, all this was typical. It fore-

---

9, 10. (a) So how did the desolation of Judah and Jerusalem come to an end? (b) How was Jehovah's worship restored there, and when and how was the rebuilding of the temple begun?
11. In that ancient prophetic drama what did Babylon typify, and whom did the Israelites typify?

shadowed a restoration of the true worship of the one living and true God Jehovah among his spiritual Israelites on the earth in this "time of the end" of the world. The various actors in that ancient prophetic drama were therefore figures of things to come. Babylon the third world power, which took Jehovah's people captive and held them as prisoners in a foreign, pagan land, was a type of Satan's world organization, for Satan was the god of ancient Babylon and King Nebuchadnezzar was a visible representative of his. The Israelites with whom Jehovah justly found fault typified the spiritual Israelites. A remnant of them are still alive on earth, in relationship with Jehovah God by the new covenant which was mediated by the Greater Moses, Jesus.

[12] What, then, did the destruction of Jerusalem and its temple, the deporting of the Israelites and the holding of them prisoner in an enemy land typify? This: In 1914 (A.D.) total war broke out between the nations of this Babylonish world of which Satan the Devil is the invisible ruler. Jehovah's people, the spiritual Israelites, are in this world, but they are not a part of this world. Because of their not staying strictly neutral amid this warring world but showing fear of men and submission to human decrees and arrangements that were contrary to the law of God, Jehovah was angered at his people. So he permitted them to be taken captive by this Babylonish world and he let their free worship of God according to his Word be broken up and interfered with. They were held prisoner, restrained from their proper conscientious worshiping of the Most High God through his High Priest Jesus Christ. Thus they were, in effect, taken from their proper theocratic place in the earth and deported to antitypical Babylon.

---

12. In the antitype, when, why and how were the remnant of spiritual Israelites taken into Babylonish captivity?

¹³ The "appointed times of the nations" began in 607 B.C. after the king of Babylon overturned the kingdom of the line of David and captured and deported its last human king, Zedekiah. In reverse fashion, those "appointed times of the nations" ended about October 1, 1914, when Jehovah restored the theocratic kingdom of the line of David by installing in the heavenly throne as King the glorified Jesus Christ, who on earth had been born as a descendant and royal heir of King David. (Matthew 1:1-18; 22:41, 42) In the war in heaven that then began, Jehovah by his King Jesus Christ hurled Satan the Devil and his demon angels out of heaven and down to the earth. This gaining the mastery over them and humbling and restraining them down to the earth must have been accomplished by the spring of 1918. It was then that A·do·nay' Jehovah and his Messenger of the covenant, Jesus Christ, came to the spiritual temple and began raising to a place in heaven the faithful Christians who had been prepared as temple stones and who had died prior to A·do·nay''s coming to the temple. Since the Devil is the invisible ruler and god of antitypical Babylon, this victory over him made Jehovah God and Jesus Christ comparable with the conquerors of ancient Babylon, Jehovah God being typified by Darius the Mede and Jesus Christ being typified by his nephew Cyrus the Persian. What now?

¹⁴ The rise of the ancient typical Cyrus and his part in the outworking of Jehovah's purpose had been foretold: "Thus saith Jehovah, . . . that saith of Cyrus, He is my shepherd, and shall perform all

---

13. When did the "appointed times of the nations" begin, when did they end, and how did Jehovah and Jesus Christ become comparable to Darius the Mede and Cyrus the Persian?
14. (a) How did Isaiah foretell the work of Cyrus? (b) To fulfill this prophecy why did more have to be done than raise the faithful Christians asleep in death?

my pleasure, even saying of Jerusalem, She shall be built; and of the temple, Thy foundation shall be laid. Thus saith Jehovah to his anointed, to Cyrus, whose right hand I have holden, to subdue nations before him, and I will loose the loins of kings; to open the doors before him, and the gates shall not be shut: I will go before thee, . . . that thou mayest know that it is I, Jehovah, who call thee by thy name, even the God of Israel. For Jacob my servant's sake, and Israel my chosen, I have called thee by thy name: I have surnamed thee, though thou hast not known me." (Isaiah 44:24 to 45:4, *AS*) This prophecy must finally be fulfilled in the greater King and Conqueror, the antitypical Cyrus, Jesus Christ. This must be by doing more than raising the faithful Christians then asleep in death to life and activity as "living stones" in the heavenly temple. It was down here on earth that, in an antitypical way during World War I, the symbolic Jerusalem and her temple had been destroyed and her remnant of spiritual Israelites taken captive and her theocratic land left desolate of worshipers by the modern-day Babylonians in the service of Satan the Devil. So it was here on earth that the Greater Cyrus, Christ the reigning King, must do something to restore Jehovah's worship at his spiritual temple.

[15] History does not lie. It bears witness to the physical fact that Babylon's Conqueror, the Warrior Jesus Christ, did do something in final, complete fulfillment of the ancient prophecy. What happened to the remnant of faithful Israelites back there in 537 B.C. was only a first or small-scale fulfillment of the prophecy. It in itself prefigured the final, major-scale fulfillment of the

---

15. (a) What happened to the Jewish remnant in 537 B.C. was what kind of fulfillment of prophecy? (b) When did the Greater Cyrus begin his role as temple builder on earth, and what unsightly place were the spiritual Israelites then like?

prophecy in our day. In 1919, the second year of his coming to the spiritual temple with A·do·nay', Jesus Christ began fulfilling the role of the Greater Cyrus as a temple builder on earth. He freed the captive remnant of "living stones" from the power of antitypical Babylon. In the spring of that year some of them, leading ones, were freed from literal imprisonment in antitypical Babylon. However, throughout the earth the spiritual Israelites in general began to cast off the restraining "fear of man" and to come out of Babylon's captivity and to undertake the temple work boldly in the fear of Jehovah. Their gaining this freedom was not from man or human governments. It was from the Greater Cyrus through the unfolding of the prophetic scriptures and the pouring out of God's spirit upon his loyal remnant. In antitypical Babylon, in captivity there, they had been like a deep depression, a valley, full of dry bones, disorganized, unsightly to the eye, dispirited, a vast graveyard not praising Jehovah God and not doing the work of bearing witness to the heavenly kingdom established in 1914.

[16] Ezekiel over two thousand years ago had a vision prophetic of them in that spiritually lifeless condition. Then Jehovah God, by means of his Greater Cyrus, Jesus Christ, poured out his energizing spirit upon them and gave them fresh spiritual strength, so that they became alive again in his service. He brought them out of their grave-like condition in antitypical Babylon and restored them to their own land, the realm of divine favor and spiritual freedom. "And ye shall know that I am Jehovah, when I have opened your graves, and caused you to come up out of your graves, O my people. And I will put my Spirit in you, and ye

---

16. How did Ezekiel picture their coming to life in God's service, and with what other vision does Ezekiel's correspond?

shall live, and I will place you in your own land: and ye shall know that I, Jehovah, have spoken it and performed it, saith Jehovah." (Ezekiel 37:1-14, *AS*) The fulfillment of this vision in 1919 corresponds with the fulfillment of John's vision described in Revelation 11:3-13.*

[17] So out through the gates of antitypical Babylon the thousands of Jehovah's spiritual remnant began streaming in the spring of 1919. They had one goal in view. That was the one which the Greater Cyrus, Jesus Christ the King, set before them: to return to Jehovah's theocratic organization and to the free and pure worship of him at his temple. Just as in 537 B.C. Zion or Jerusalem, with its temple, was the goal that beckoned the Jewish remnant out of Babylon to their own God-given land, so the antitypical Zion or Jerusalem, with its spiritual house of worship, stood up on high as a glorious signal beckoning to them to flee out of Babylon and come to Jehovah's theocratic organization and take up his temple work there. Jehovah by his Greater Cyrus had redeemed or delivered them for one purpose, that they might seek out the antitypical city of Jerusalem or Zion and "declare the name of Jehovah in Zion, and his praise in Jerusalem." That antitypical city was the Government of the reigning King, Jesus Christ, the earthly interests of which had been desolated during World War I. To it they had to assemble in loyal support and then to bear witness of it to others.

[18] In 537 B.C. the Jewish remnant had to or-

---

* See chapter VII, pages 119, 120.

---

17. In 537 B.C. what was the goal to which the remnant streamed out of Babylon, and what was the signal to which the spiritual remnant assembled out of antitypical Babylon?
18. As with the Jewish remnant in 537 B.C., what had to be done for the spiritual remnant to come to the beckoning Signal?

ganize themselves and then tramp for four months through the wilderness to come to the long-forsaken city of Zion or Jerusalem; the way had to be prepared for this redeemed people to make their return journey successful. In like manner in 1919 (A.D.) the way had to be prepared for Jehovah's redeemed remnant to assemble unitedly from the very ends of the earth, to seek first the now established kingdom of God, the beckoning Signal on the heavenly Mount Zion. The highway to their royal goal had to be cast up, graded up or banked up so as to make travel smooth and easy. All stones or causes of stumbling, such as false doctrines or untheocratic practices and arrangements, had to be cleared off the road. All this required time, but a good beginning of it was made in 1919 under the guidance of the Greater Cyrus and by the illumination of God's Word and with the revitalizing power of His spirit. The final and complete fulfillment of the Lord Jehovah's prophecy through Isaiah began coming true:

[19] "Pass through, pass through the gates, prepare the way of the people; grade up, grade up the highway, clear it of stones; raise a signal over the peoples. See! the LORD [Jehovah] has made proclamation to the end of the earth: 'Say to the daughter of Zion, "See! your salvation has come; see! his reward is with him, and his recompense before him." They shall be called, "The holy people, the redeemed of the LORD [Jehovah]"; and you shall be called, "Sought out, the city unforsaken." ' "—Isaiah 62:10-12, AT.

[20] On return to the antitypical city of God those first to arrive there had to "raise a signal over the peoples" that all others of the remnant of spirit-

19. The final and complete fulfillment of what prophecy of Isaiah then began coming true?
20. What did those first to arrive at the antitypical city of God have to do, and why?

ual Israel might see and know where to come for theocratic freedom and the pure worship of the one living and true God, the Lord Jehovah. That "signal" standing up gloriously on the heavenly Mount Zion is God's established kingdom, represented by his enthroned King Jesus Christ, the Greater Cyrus. He is the "Son of David," which David was the son of Jesse of Bethlehem.

[21] This identifying of the "signal" as being the reigning Son of David, the son of Jesse, is made infallibly certain for all Bible examiners by the words of the prophet Isaiah: "A shoot will spring from the stem of Jesse, and a sprout from his roots will bear fruit. And the spirit of the LORD [Jehovah] will rest upon him, . . . It shall come to pass on that day that the root of Jesse, who will be standing as a signal to the peoples—to him will the nations resort, and his resting-place will be glorious. On that day will the LORD [Jehovah] once more raise his hand to recover the remnant that remains of his people, from Assyria and from Egypt, . . . He will raise a signal to the nations, and will gather the outcasts of Israel; and the scattered daughters of Judah will he assemble from the four corners of the earth. Then the LORD [Jehovah] will dry up the tongue of the Sea of Egypt, with the glowing heat of his breath; and he will shake his hand over the River [the Euphrates River on which Babylon was situated], and will smite it into seven brooks [easily crossable], and will enable men to cross it with sandals. So there will be a highway from Assyria [territory of Babylon] for the remnant that remains of his people, as there was for Israel on the day that it went up from the land of Egypt."—Isaiah 11:1, 2, 10-12, 15, 16, AT.

---

21. How does Isaiah, chapter 11, infallibly identify the "signal" for us and show the remnant must be gathered to it?

[22] True to his word, the Almighty God began fulfilling this prophetic promise in a miniature way in 537 B.C. That was only a dramatic foreshadowing of the full-scale fulfillment of it beginning in the year 1919 (A.D.), in the fifth year of the established kingdom of God. That year it was unquestionably by the spirit of God that the then president of the Watch Tower Bible & Tract Society addressed the general convention of Jehovah's people at Cedar Point, Ohio, on Friday, September 5, and spoke on the subject, "Announcing the Kingdom." In that address he urged his hearers to reorganize for announcing the established kingdom, saying: "The organization that handled the Seventh Volume work* proved a wonderful success. Seven thousand of the friends were engaged in that special work. We are asking the classes everywhere to revive that organization and put it in proper form. . . . The door of opportunity is opening before you. Enter it quickly. Remember as you go forth in this work . . . you are an ambassador of the King of kings and Lord of lords, announcing to the people in this dignified manner the incoming of the Golden Age, the glorious kingdom of our Lord and Master, for which true Christians have hoped and prayed for many centuries." That these instructions for announcing God's kingdom might go to the ends of the earth to reach all the remnant, this convention address was published in the magazine *The Watch Tower* in its issue of September 15, 1919. Three years later in a

---

* The Seventh Volume work was the work of distributing by house-to-house calls the book entitled "The Finished Mystery," which was the seventh volume of the *Studies in the Scriptures*. It offered an explanation of the books of Revelation, Ezekiel and the Song of Solomon as then understood, and was published July 17, 1917.

22, 23. (a) As foreshadowed in 537 B.C., how was encouragement to raise the Signal given in 1919 (A.D.) at a general convention? (b) How was exhortation to do so given at the convention in 1922?

still larger international convention at the same place the same speaker, in demonstration of raising the Signal over the peoples, spoke on the Bible text, "The kingdom of heaven is at hand." (Matthew 4:17) In a grand climax he concluded this speech of September 8, 1922, saying:

[23] "Do you believe that the Lord is now in his temple, judging the nations of earth? Do you believe that the King of glory has begun his reign? [To this the convention roared, Yes!] Then back to the field, O ye sons of the most high God! Gird on your armor! Be sober, be vigilant, be active, be brave. Be faithful and true witnesses for the Lord. Go forward in the fight until every vestige of Babylon lies desolate. Herald the message far and wide. The world must know that Jehovah is God and that Jesus Christ is King of kings and Lord of lords. This is the day of all days. Behold, the King reigns! You are his publicity agents. Therefore advertise, advertise, advertise, the King and his kingdom."*

[24] In response to this ringing appeal the zealous members of the remnant joined in 'raising the Signal' as never before by more intensely advertising the King Jesus Christ and his kingdom. By this ever-expanding advertising work the royal Signal was made more prominent and more discernible to others who were yet in Babylon's world-wide prison and who needed to be gathered to the Signal as final members of the remnant. By 1932 there were about 30,000 of them assembled at the Signal. Although by then practically all the remnant of spiritual Israelites may have been de-

---

* See *The Watch Tower* of November 1, 1922, pages 332-337, for this convention discourse of September 8, 1922, by the then president, J. F. Rutherford.

---

24. How did the members of the remnant respond to this appeal, and what were all those afterward gathered obliged to do?

livered from Babylon and gathered to antitypical Zion, they were still under the obligation to raise the Signal, that is, to advertise the Kingdom.

[25] Jesus, in foretelling the evidence of the "time of the end" of this world, foretold this gathering of the remnant from all parts of the earth to God's kingdom after they spiritually discerned the King upon his heavenly throne. He said that, after the beginning of pangs of distress upon this world, "then the sign of the Son of man will appear in heaven, and then all the tribes of the earth will go to wailing and they will see the Son of man coming on the clouds of heaven with power and great glory. And he will send forth his angels with a great trumpet-sound and they will gather his chosen ones together from the four winds, from one extremity of the heavens to their other extremity." (Matthew 24:30, 31, *NW*) They were to be gathered, not for mere idleness or self-enjoyment of security, but for a united Signal-raising, a united witness to all nations concerning the established Kingdom. The command of Jesus Christ that applied to this "time of the end" rested upon them as temple workers: "This good news of the kingdom will be preached in all the inhabited earth for the purpose of a witness to all the nations, and then the accomplished end will come." (Matthew 24:14, *NW*) They had to preach, advertise. They did so.

MODERN NETHINIM (TEMPLE SLAVES)

[26] This gathering of Jehovah's remnant of chosen ones for a Kingdom witness to all the nations was what was prefigured by the releasing of the Jewish remnant from Babylon by King Cyrus' de-

---

25. How did Jesus foretell this gathering of the remnant, and for what purpose were they gathered?
26, 27. Besides the remnant of Israel, who also are reported by Ezra and Nehemiah as leaving Babylon with Zerubbabel and Jeshua?

cree and his authorizing them to return to Zion or Jerusalem and rebuild the temple of Jehovah, restoring the worship of the true God at its chosen center. But do not fail to note this: The remnant of 42,360 Israelites were not the only ones that left Babylon with governor Zerubbabel and high priest Jeshua to return and rebuild the temple at the holy city. There were thousands of non-Israelites who returned with them. Formerly they had dwelt with them in the land of Judah but were carried off into exile with them by the king of Babylon. Among these were the class called the Neth'i·nim, the name literally meaning "given ones." "And Judah itself was taken into exile at Babylon for their unfaithfulness. And the first inhabitants that were in their possession in their cities were the Israelites, the priests, the Levites and the Neth'i·nim [the given ones, *LXX*]." (1 Chronicles 9:1, 2, *NW*) Besides the Nethinim there were other non-Israelites, the slaves, the professional male and female singers and the descendants of the servants of King Solomon. In listing those who returned under King Cyrus' decree both Ezra and Nehemiah mention these non-Israelites.

[27] "All the Neth'i·nim and the sons of the servants of Solomon were three hundred and ninety-two. The entire congregation as one group was forty-two thousand three hundred and sixty, apart from their men slaves and their slave girls, these being seven thousand three hundred and thirty-seven, and they had two hundred male singers and female singers. And the priests and the Levites and some of the people, and the singers and the gatekeepers and the Neth'i·nim took up dwelling in their cities, and all Israel in their cities. When the seventh month [in 537 B.C.] arrived the sons of Israel were in [their] cities."—Ezra 2:43, 55, 58, 64, 65, 70; 3:1; also 6:21, 22, *NW*.

²⁸ Years later, in 468 B.C., in the seventh year of Artaxerxes the king of Persia, he commissioned Ezra the priest to go to Jerusalem to beautify Jehovah's house there and to stimulate his worship and to instruct the people in Jehovah's law. The Record informs us: "Consequently some of the sons of Israel and of the priests and the Levites and the singers and the gatekeepers and the Neth'-i·nim went up to Jerusalem in the seventh year of Artaxerxes the king." In his letter of commission to Ezra, King Artaxerxes showed respect for these Nethinim to the extent of freeing them from paying taxes: "As respects any of the priests and the Levites, the musicians, the doorkeepers, the Neth'-i·nim, and the workers of this house of God, no tax, tribute or toll is allowed to be imposed upon them."

²⁹ This was because of the Nethinim's part in carrying on the worship of the true God at his house upon which his name was called. In making this service visit to Jerusalem Ezra made certain that there were Nethinim in the group that accompanied him there, as he says: "Then I gave them a command concerning Id'do the head one in the place Ca·si·phi'a and I put in their mouth words to speak to Id'do [and] his brothers the Neth'i·nim in the place Ca·si·phi'a, to bring to us ministers for the house of our God. So they brought to us, according to the good hand of our God upon us, . . . from the Neth'i·nim, whom David and the princes gave to the service of the Levites, two hundred and twenty Neth'i·nim, all of whom had been designated by [their] names."—Ezra 7:7, 24; 8:17-20, *NW*.

28. Besides Israelites, who also came with Ezra to Jerusalem, and how did King Artaxerxes show respect for these?

29. Why was this respect shown? And whom did Ezra make certain to accompany him to Jerusalem?

[30] From this statement we see that the ancestors of these Nethinim had been given by David and the Israelite princes to the service of the Levites at the temple, evidently to do the work of drawing water and bringing in the wood. Such Nethinim doubtless included the Gibeonites, condemned Canaanites, who by a trick maneuvered judge Joshua and the princes of Israel into sparing them from destruction with all the rest of the Canaanites. Indignantly Joshua said to them: "Now you are cursed people [untouchables], and a slave's position and being gatherers of wood and drawers of water for the house of my God will never be cut off from you." So they became inseparably attached to Jehovah's house. "Accordingly Joshua constituted them on that day gatherers of wood and drawers of water for the assembly and for Jehovah's altar, down to this day, at the place that he should choose." (Joshua 9:22-27, *NW*) For this reason the Greek *Septuagint Version* (*LXX*) translates the title "Neth′i·nim" as "temple slaves" at Ezra 2:43, 58; 7:7, 24; 8:20.

[31] These Nethinim supported the restored remnant of Israel both in their worship at the rebuilt temple and in their special national vow to Jehovah God. In the twentieth year of the same King Artaxerxes of Persia, Nehemiah was made governor of Judah and he went to Jerusalem and rebuilt its walls. After celebrating the joyful festival of booths in the seventh month Nehemiah and other prominent leaders of the Jewish remnant entered into a special trustworthy arrangement with Jehovah God in order to hold themselves true to him and to keep themselves separate from the pagan

---

30. Whom did those Nethinim doubtless include, and for what reason? So how does the Greek *Septuagint* sometimes translate their title?
31. Not only in temple worship, but in what else did the Nethinim support the restored remnant, and to whom were they inseparable adherents?

peoples of surrounding lands. The Nethinim, as temple slaves of Jehovah, joined the rest of the remnant in backing up these majestic leaders of Israel in this arrangement. Of this it is written: "As for the rest of the people, the priests, the Levites, the gatekeepers, the singers, the Nethinim and everyone separating himself from the peoples of the lands to the law of The [true] God, their wives, their sons and their daughters, everyone having knowledge [and] understanding, they were adhering to their brothers, their majestic ones, and coming into [liability to] a curse and into an oath, to walk in the law of The [true] God, which had been given by the hand of Moses the servant of The [true] God, and to keep and to perform all the commandments of Jehovah our Lord and his judicial decisions and his regulations, and that we should not give our daughters to the peoples of the land and their daughters we should not take for our sons." (Nehemiah 9:38; 10:1, 9, 14, 28-30, *NW*) So down to the last mention of them in the Bible the Nethinim as well as descendants of the servants of Solomon were inseparable adherents to the remnant of the faithful Jews, Jehovah's ancient witnesses.—Nehemiah 11:3, 21, *NW*.

[32] The Nethinim, the slaves, the singers and the sons of the servants of Solomon, all non-Israelites, left the land of captivity and returned with the Israelite remnant to Jerusalem to engage in Jehovah's restored worship there. So is it right to think that today people of different nationalities who are not spiritual Israelites would associate themselves with the remnant of spiritual Israel and promote the worship of Jehovah God with them? Yes; for both the prophecies bear that out and also the physical facts of this "time of the end" do. For at least twelve years, from 1919 to

32. From 1919 to 1931 who, especially, forsook the antitypical Babylon, and who thereafter assembled around the Signal that they raised?

1931, the remnant's members were forsaking the antitypical Babylon of this world and coming over the prepared, stone-cleared highway to the free, theocratic organization of Jehovah and engaging in the restoration of Jehovah's worship as "living stones" of his spiritual temple. They assembled to the royal Signal on the heavenly Mount Zion, namely, God's kingdom as represented in his anointed, enthroned King, Jesus Christ. By obediently preaching the good news of the Kingdom set up A.D. 1914 to all the inhabited earth for a witness to all the nations, the assembled remnant raised the royal Signal over the peoples to the ends of the earth, that all might see it and receive a witness. Not all were converted at the sight of the Signal. Those, however, who yearned for a righteous, perfect government and for the pure worship of God at his true temple were gladdened by the Signal. They saw in it the hope of all mankind and the center of true worship. They acted on the witness that the remnant gave them. With their help and encouragement they left the state of Babylonish captivity and came to the Signal, the Kingdom, to assemble around it with the remnant.

³³ At first thousands, then tens of thousands, from all the nations that got the witness began flocking to the Signal; just as it had been foretold: "To him [the Signal to the peoples] will the nations resort." (Isaiah 11:10, *AT*) They, too, joined in raising it ever higher as the only Government of promise and hope. In 1955 already more than half a million of them had registered for a part in witnessing to the Kingdom Signal. They united with the spiritual remnant in worshiping Jehovah alone as God, gratefully and willingly becoming "temple slaves" in support of the remnant of "living stones" of the spiritual temple. By this action

---

33. What did these latter ones join in doing, and thus what did they make themselves in an antitypical way?

they made themselves or became modern-day, antitypical Nethinim, singers and sons of the servants of Solomon, loyally adhering to the remnant of spiritual Israelites. Jesus Christ, "the Son of David," as reigning King has given them to the remnant of his "royal priesthood" to be temple helpers. Thus they escape destruction.

THE SIGN OF JONAH TO MODERN NINEVITES

[34] This corresponds with the fulfillment of another prophetic drama in this "time of the end" when destruction impends over Christendom and all the rest of the world. Nineteen centuries ago, at the beginning of the time of the end for Jerusalem and her temple, Jesus Christ preached the kingdom of God. His religious opponents asked of him a sign from heaven to prove that he was the Messiah, the Christ, the Son of David, and that by him as the royal representative the kingdom of God was in among them. Jesus did not show them any miraculous clouds from heaven to fulfill the prophecy of Daniel 7:13, 14, but simply said: "A wicked and adulterous generation keeps on seeking for a sign, but no sign will be given it except the sign of Jonah the prophet. For just as Jonah was in the belly of the huge fish three days and three nights, so the Son of man will be in the heart of the earth three days and three nights. Men of Nineveh will rise up in the judgment with this generation and will condemn it; because they repented at what Jonah preached, but, look! something more than Jonah is here." (Matthew 12: 38-41; 16:1-4, NW) That sign of Jonah and the Ninevites was carried out in the time of the end of ancient Jerusalem; it is being carried out in a final and full-scale way in the present "time of the end"

---

34. What sign did Jesus say would be given to a wicked and adulterous generation, and so when was and is the time for this sign to be carried out?

of faithless Jerusalem's modern counterpart, Christendom.

35 The Ninevites were the inhabitants of Nineveh, the capital city of the second world power, Assyria. They were Gentiles, pagans, heathen, hence non-Israelites, and they were destined to afflict the Israelites greatly, threatening their destruction. On the other hand, Jonah was an Israelite and a prophet of Jehovah, and lived about the days of King Amaziah of Jerusalem. (2 Kings 14: 23-25) But for Jonah's prophesying, Assyria might not have become the second world power to oppress Jehovah's people. About 852 B.C., or seventy years before pagan Assyria began to make Israel feel its oppressive power, Jonah wrote the account of his experiences, detailing the sign. Jehovah commanded Jonah to leave the land of Israel and go to the Assyrian capital and prophesy against it. For imaginable reasons Jonah refused to do so. He went down to the Mediterranean seaport of Joppa and took a ship for Tarshish at the other end of the Mediterranean Sea, in what is now Spain. Jehovah miraculously raised a storm that threatened to wreck the ship. The sailors called on their false gods for rescue and threw overboard everything they could to lighten the ship. The ship's captain waked up the sleeping Jonah and asked him to cry also to his God.

36 Who was responsible for their dangerous state? The sailors superstitiously cast lots to find out. Jehovah guided the lot to fall upon his fugitive prophet. Under inquiry Jonah told them: "I am a Hebrew; and I fear Jehovah, the God of heaven, who hath made the sea and the dry land." Then the sailors became frightened when he explained

---

35. Who were the Ninevites, and in their days how did Jonah come to be in a storm at sea?
36. How was the one responsible for the storm found out, what action was taken, and what did those left in the ship do afterward?

how he was running away from his witness work
for Jehovah. Jonah told them they must get rid of
the one responsible for the tempest by throwing
him overboard. The sailors tried to avoid this by
rowing hard to get to land, but Jehovah's stormy
power was too much against them. At last in des-
peration they "cried unto Jehovah, and said, We
beseech thee, O Jehovah, we beseech thee, let us
not perish for this man's life, and lay not upon us
innocent blood; for thou, O Jehovah, hast done as
it pleased thee. So they took up Jonah, and cast
him forth into the sea; and the sea ceased from
its raging. Then the men feared Jehovah exceed-
ingly; and they offered a sacrifice unto Jehovah,
and made vows."—Jonah 1:1-16, AS.

³⁷ Certainly Jesus, in comparing himself with
Jonah, was not referring to Jonah's running away
and taking the ship for Tarshish in order to avoid
being Jehovah's witness to the Ninevites. Jesus
refused to be turned aside from bearing witness to
the truth but went submissively ahead to his martyrdom for the sake of vindicating the universal
sovereignty of his God and Father Jehovah. He
was like Jonah in unselfishly offering his own human life in behalf of storm-tossed mankind that
they might come to peaceful relations with Jehovah and worship Him as the great Peacemaker,
the Calmer of the storm who brings them to their
desired haven.—Psalm 107:23-31.

³⁸ Jesus was also like Jonah in the experience
that the prophet next had, for his plunge into the
raging sea did not spell his destruction. "Now, the
LORD [Jehovah] had assigned a great fish to swal-
low up Jonah; and Jonah was in the belly of the

---

37. Why was Jesus not likening himself to a runaway
prophet, but how was he like Jonah in the storm-tossed
ship?
38. How was Jesus like Jonah after this one was
thrown overboard, and to whom did Jesus give the
"sign of Jonah" directly? Why?

fish three days and three nights. Then the LORD [Jehovah] commanded the fish, and it vomited Jonah forth upon the dry land." (Jonah 1:17; 2:10, *AT*) For parts of three days the fish's belly was like a grave to Jonah, and on the third day God miraculously brought him out onto the dry land. Likewise, Jesus was in She'ol, the common grave of mankind, for parts of three days, Nisan 14-16, A.D. 33, and on the third day Jehovah raised him up from the dead to life as a divine spirit in heaven.* The resurrected Jesus did not appear to the sign-seeking, "wicked and adulterous genera- tion" of Jews to give them directly the sign of Jonah. By materializations in flesh and bones he appeared only to his faithful disciples and com- missioned them to bear witness to the sign of the Greater Jonah that men might have full basis for putting faith in Jesus Christ as the one sent by God, as the one anointed with holy spirit to be the Messianic King of God's promised new world.

³⁹ At the festival of Pentecost, the fiftieth day from Jesus' resurrection, Peter amidst 119 fellow witnesses testified to a Jewish audience: "This Jesus God resurrected, of which fact we are all witnesses." And when addressing the first non- Jewish converts in the house of the Italian centu- rion Cornelius, Peter said: "God raised this One up on the third day and granted him to become visible, not to all the people, but to witnesses appointed beforehand by God, to us, who ate and drank with him after his rising from the dead. Also he ordered us to preach to the people and to give a thorough witness that this is the One decreed by God to be judge of the living and the

---

* See the article "The Firstfruits of Resurrection" in *The Watchtower*, issue of March 15, 1944, pages 86-92, paragraphs 17-41.

39. Who then testified concerning the sign of Jonah, and how did some acknowledge the sign?

dead. To him all the prophets bear witness, that every one putting faith in him gets forgiveness of sins through his name." (Acts 2:32; 10:40-43, *NW*) Only the honest-hearted, humble-minded among that "wicked and adulterous generation" in that time of the end acknowledged the sign, took it as convincing and put faith in Jesus Christ as God's anointed King.

⁴⁰ Not Jesus, but his small band of disciples of the Jewish remnant were the ones that fled from their duty to God when Jesus was betrayed; they were scattered like the sheep of a smitten shepherd and they entered into a deathlike inactivity as in the night "when no man can work." But by his appearances in life on his resurrection day they were infused with new life, and from the day of Pentecost forward they became bold witnesses concerning the sign of Jonah to the "wicked and adulterous generation," which was now left without an excuse for further unbelief. (John 9:4; Matthew 26:31, 32) So his faithful disciples, anointed with the holy spirit on and after Pentecost, were the ones that carried forward the fulfillment of Jonah in bearing witness to the Ninevites after being in the fish's belly for parts of three days. In this way Jesus' interpretation of Jonah's experience was fulfilled: "This generation is a wicked generation; it looks for a sign. But no sign will be given it except the sign of Jonah. For just as Jonah became a sign to the Ninevites, in the same way will the Son of man be also to this generation."—Luke 11:29, 30, 32, *NW*.

⁴¹ When Jonah was swallowed by the huge fish

---

40. How did Jesus' disciples come into the night "when no man can work," but who afterward carried forward the fulfillment of Jonah in witnessing to the Ninevites? **41, 42.** (a) How was Jonah unlike the Englishman Bartlett in the stomach of the sperm whale? (b) Unlike Bartlett, how did Jonah come out, and what did he proceed to do?

for safekeeping, he did not become like one James Bartley, whose experience demonstrated the perfect possibility of Jonah's experience. On February 1, 1891, Bartley's ship, the whaler "Star of the East," was off the Falkland Islands. When Bartley and a companion put out in a boat from the whaler and harpooned a sperm whale, the struck whale flicked over the boat with its tail. The two men disappeared. Afterward, when the whale was being cut up and its stomach was hoisted onto the deck, a movement was detected in the huge stomach. Cutting it open, they found the Englishman Bartley inside, unconscious. A dash of salt water revived him, but he was a raving maniac for two weeks after that. The third week he came back to normal, but his skin that had been acted on by the

whale's stomach juices always stayed blanched like parchment.* Unlike Bartley, the prophet Jonah retained his consciousness and prayed to Jehovah in his temple.

⁴² "Then Jonah prayed unto Jehovah his God out of the fish's belly. And he said, I called by reason of mine affliction unto Jehovah, and he answered me; out of the belly of She'ol [or, the grave common to mankind] cried I, and thou heardest my voice. . . . When my soul fainted within me, I remembered Jehovah; and my prayer came in unto thee, into thy holy temple. . . . I will pay that which I have vowed. Salvation is of Jehovah." Then, unlike Bartley's experience on the same day, the third day "Jehovah spake unto the fish, and it vomited out Jonah upon the dry land." Jonah did not come out a raving maniac, but in appreciation of his miraculous deliverance he proceeded to pay his vow to Jehovah his Savior and went to Nineveh to act as Jehovah's witness there.—Jonah 2:1-10, AS.

⁴³ Nineveh, capital of the rising world power of Assyria, was a "great city, in which there are more than a hundred and twenty thousand persons who do not know their right hand from their left, and also much cattle," and a walk through it required three days. (Jonah 4:11, RS) Jonah reached the city and went just one day's journey into it and began proclaiming: "Forty days more, and Nineveh shall be overthrown." Thus the Assyrian capital entered into a judgment time of forty days. In a way that shamed the hardhearted Israelites of Jonah's time and of Jesus and his apostles'

---

* Based on the account published in the *Journal des Debats,* by the French scientist M. de Parville, 1914. See Robert Ripley's book, *Believe It or Not!* volume 2 of 1950.

---

43. How did the Ninevites act toward Jonah's preaching, and what consideration did Jehovah show for their action?

time, the Ninevites believed Jonah and showed sorrow. The king of Nineveh decreed that people and animals should go on a fast, wear sackcloth, call upon God, and each one turn from his evil way and from whatever violence he had in hand. It might be that Jonah's God would show mercy to the heathen out of consideration for their repentance and find it unnecessary to destroy the city at the end of forty days. This is what happened. To show he had no real pleasure in the death of the wicked but preferred rather that they repent and change their life according to God's will, "God relented of the evil which he had said he would do unto them, and he did it not." (Jonah 3:4, 10, *AT*) The repentant Ninevites survived the time of judgment. Nineveh was not destroyed till over 200 years later.—Nahum, chapters 1 to 3.

[44] Ancient Nineveh was part of heathendom and pictured those not considered Christian today. Ancient Israel laid claim to being the chosen people of Jehovah and pictured modern Christendom. Contrary to its Christian claims, Christendom is wicked in its disobedience to God and is adulterous in its unclean friendly connections with the political and commercial elements of this world. (James 4:4) Particularly since A.D. 1914 this "wicked and adulterous generation" has stubbornly closed its eyes to the Biblical and historical evidence of the presence of Jehovah's anointed King in the Kingdom. It has kept asking for a "sign" according to its own peculiar religious ideas, such as for Jesus Christ to appear visibly to all human eyes with a flesh body bearing the marks of crucifixion and riding on a cloud accompanied by hosts of visible angels. No such unreasonable, unscriptural sign of Christ's presence in

---

44. In contrast with antitypical Nineveh, how has Christendom been a wicked and adulterous generation asking for a sign, and, instead of their sign, what sign has been given her?

his kingdom has been given them since 1914, but the modern-day fulfillment of the "sign of Jonah the prophet" has been given them. How?

⁴⁵ During the world war that began A.D. 1914 Jehovah's remnant came short of their responsibilities to Jehovah to give a bold, uncompromising and sustained witness concerning the Kingdom and the approach of the "day of vengeance of our God." Because of their failure Jehovah God in his displeasure permitted them to be cast by the storm-tossed pilots and navigators of this world into the tempestuous sea of mankind. This looked like the end of the remnant, but Jehovah did not purpose matters that way. He let the delinquent remnant come under great restraint, under bans and restrictions in captivity to powers of this world, as in the belly of a huge fish. The remnant thought this meant She'ol, Ha'des or the common grave of mankind for them. In their captive state in antitypical Babylon they were like the valley of dry bones seen in Ezekiel's vision and like the corpses of God's witnesses lying in the broad street of spiritual Egypt seen in the revelation to the apostle John. (Ezekiel 37:1-14; Revelation 11:3-13) To Christendom and the antitypical Ninevites the remnant were as good as buried.

⁴⁶ As though from inside the gravelike belly of a huge fish, the remnant prayed repentantly to A·do·nay' Jehovah, who had now come to his temple in the spring of 1918 accompanied by his Angel or Messenger of the covenant. Jehovah at his temple heard their prayer and took steps for their salvation. He cut short the days of tribulation upon Satan's world organization for the sake

---

45. How, after 1914, did Jehovah's remnant come to be as in the belly of a huge fish?
46. How were the remnant brought up out of this condition, what did they proceed to do, and how did Christendom act toward this God-given "sign of Jonah"?

of this remnant of chosen ones. In the spring of
1919 he began bringing them up out of the fish's
belly of captivity and back to the land of the
living. They began to exercise their regained freedom and set themselves to pay their vow of obedience to Jehovah so as to carry out their commission of service from him, even if it meant going
to all nations like the Ninevites. From 1919 on
they began to raise up the glorious Kingdom
Signal over all peoples by carrying out the prophetic command given in Matthew 24:14 and
Mark 13:10. The "wicked and adulterous generation" of Christendom were startled at this recovery of Jehovah's remnant. Yet in their hard-
heartedness they refused to believe this God-given
"sign of Jonah" proving that God's kingdom had
been set up in the heavens in 1914 and that the
"time of the end" was upon this world. As with
the Jews in the days of Christ's apostles, this
generation will keep on in their willful disbelief
until everlasting destruction comes upon antitypical Jerusalem and Judea, namely, Christendom,
in the "war of the great day of God the Almighty."

[47] Anciently Jonah's proclamation inside the Assyrian capital of Nineveh was a message of God's
vengeance against the heathen or pagans. Today
Jehovah's remnant are anointed and commissioned, not only to preach good tidings about God's
established kingdom to the meek, brokenhearted,
captive and imprisoned people, but also to "proclaim . . . the day of vengeance of our God."
(Isaiah 61:1, 2, AS) At the proclamation of God's
coming vengeance at Armageddon the modern-
day Ninevites have repented and turned to Jehovah in hope that he will spare them. The religiously
self-righteous leaders and supporters of Christen-

---

47. What is it that Jehovah's remnant have preached
at which the modern-day Ninevites have taken action
different from that of Christendom?

dom have ignored the sign's meaning and rejected the preaching of the antitypical Jonah, and they hold fast to their unclean, adulterous relations with this doomed world.

[48] Today the great mass of people outside Jehovah's remnant are not spiritual Israelites, and spiritually they do not know their right hand from their left. The self-righteous pretending Christians of Christendom look down upon them as the self-righteous Israelites of Jonah's day did upon the Ninevites. But just as forecast in the prophetic drama of Jonah, it has been the antitypical Ninevites in this "time of the end" upon heathendom who have taken the course that has called forth Jehovah's pity. They have accepted the "sign of Jonah." They have not called the Jonah class "calamity howlers" but have repented at the warning that this heathenish world (including Christendom) is in its "time of the end" and the righteous vengeance of Jehovah God will be poured out upon it at Armageddon. They have lifted their eyes in faith to the Signal of God's kingdom raised aloft by his remnant. They have turned from their worldliness and come to Mount Zion, assembling to God's kingdom and taking up his pure and undefiled worship there. They may draw comfort from the fact that destruction did not come upon the ancient Ninevites at the end of the forty-days' time limit, because God had accepted their repentance and change of course. Destruction finally came upon backsliding Nineveh, as it will come shortly upon this unreformed world. But those today who have repented at the preaching of the antitypical Jonah will be spared during the destruction at Armageddon and survive into God's new world.

---

48. How have the modern-day Ninevites called forth Jehovah's pity, and from what fact about ancient Nineveh may they draw comfort?

CHAPTER IX

Separating the Peoples for Life or Destruction

SURVIVING the universal war of Armageddon into God's new world will not be our experience without our intelligently choosing between life and destruction. To choose understandingly one must know first which path of conduct leads to life and which path to destruction. Today there are only the two outlooks. This is not the case because now the means of warfare have become so deadly that mankind must either keep the peace, never letting a "cold war" between nations get hot, or else fight and bring on the ruin of civilization. No; but it is the case because Jehovah's theocratic government by Jesus Christ has been established in the heavens and it must rule the universe. The vital choice that determines life or destruction is not between democracy and communism; choosing either one still leaves us a part of this world. The choice is between God's kingdom by Christ and Satan's world, of which both communism and democracy are a part. Jehovah God's universal sovereignty is the chief question in dispute before heaven and earth, and his kingdom by Christ is what will prove God the rightful universal sovereign; his kingdom by Christ will vindicate his universal sovereignty. It is therefore over the

---

1. To choose understandingly between life and destruction now what must one know, and over what question are all peoples being separated to the right or to the left?

159

question of God's kingdom that all peoples today are being separated, to the right or to the left. It is a separation of them for life or for destruction, for the choice of God's kingdom results in eternal life, the choice of this world in destruction.

² The separation of all peoples for life or for destruction is now in progress in this "time of the end." Jesus Christ foretold that this would be so in his prophecy on the evidence of his invisible presence or *parousía* and the consummation of this system of things. He included several parables or illustrations in his prophecy, the last one of which describes this separation of the peoples over the Kingdom issue. In it he said: "When the Son of man arrives in his glory and all the angels with him, then he will sit down on his glorious throne. And all the nations will be gathered before him, and he will separate people one from another, just as a shepherd separates the sheep from the goats. And he will put the sheep on his right hand, but the goats on his left." (Matthew 25:31, 32, *NW*) This separation of people from one another does not take place in a 24-hour day, nor does it take place during the thousand-year reign of Christ after Armageddon. It takes place during this "time of the end" and specifically after A·do·nay' Jehovah comes to his temple accompanied by his Messenger of the covenant, for it is at the house of God or temple that judgment must begin. It is the judgment of Jehovah's Messenger Jesus Christ at the temple that separates people of the nations to the right or to the left.

³ By the parabolic expression "the Son of man"

---

2. In what prophecy did Jesus foretell this separating of the people, and how, and when specifically does the separating take place?
3. In Jesus' parable the sitting of the Son of man upon his glorious throne pictures the fulfillment of what prophecy of Daniel, and who are the "saints" to whom the kingdom is given?

Jesus Christ meant himself, and when he sits down
on his glorious throne it means he has come and
is present in his kingdom. Over five centuries before the Christian era Daniel had a prophetic
dream of this: "I beheld till thrones were placed,
and one that was ancient of days did sit: his rai-
ment was white as snow, and the hair of his head
like pure wool; his throne was fiery flames, and
the wheels thereof burning fire. I saw in the night-
visions, and, behold, there came with the clouds
of heaven one like unto a son of man, and he came
even to the ancient of days, and they brought him
near before him. And there was given him dominion, and glory, and a kingdom, that all the peoples,
nations, and languages should serve him: his dominion is an everlasting dominion, which shall not
pass away, and his kingdom that which shall not
be destroyed. And the kingdom and the dominion,
and the greatness of the kingdoms under the whole
heaven, shall be given to the people of the saints of
the Most High: his kingdom is an everlasting kingdom, and all dominions shall serve and obey him."
(Daniel 7:9, 13, 14, 27, AS) The "saints" or sanctified ones are the anointed followers of the Son
of man, Jesus Christ, and the 144,000 of them are
to reign with him in his heavenly kingdom. It was
after he came with A·do·nay' Jehovah to his temple in the spring of 1918 that he began judging and
raised his saintly followers, asleep in death, to life
in his heavenly kingdom as his royal joint heirs.
—Revelation 11:15-18.

⁴ The "saints" or sanctified ones are the spiritual brothers of Jesus Christ, for they are all begotten by the spirit of the same heavenly Father
to spiritual life in the heavens. Jesus Christ the
only-begotten Son of God is Jehovah's Chief Agent

---

4. Whose spiritual brothers are these saints, and why
is he not ashamed to call them brothers? So through
what test does he help the remnant to pass?

in their gaining the heavenly salvation. By his own sufferings for righteousness he showed them that they too must suffer innocently to have a part in the vindicating of Jehovah's universal sovereignty. "For it was fitting for the one for whose sake all things are and through whom all things are, in bringing many sons to glory, to make the Chief Agent of their salvation perfect through sufferings. For both he who is sanctifying and those who are being sanctified all stem from one, and for this cause he is not ashamed to call them 'brothers', as he says: 'I will declare your name to my brothers; in the midst of a congregation I will praise you with song.' For in that he himself has suffered when being put to the test, he is able to come to the aid of those who are being put to the test." (Hebrews 2:10-12, 18, *NW*) The remnant of these 144,000 saints are still alive in the flesh on earth, and they are being aided in passing through the test of their integrity to Jehovah's universal sovereignty by their oldest spiritual brother, Jesus Christ, at the temple. It is only by passing through the test successfully that God can bring them as his spiritual sons to the heavenly glory for which they are now being sanctified. They must conquer the world by their faith.

⁵ On account of this remnant of those chosen for the Kingdom Jehovah God cut short the days of tribulation on Satan's organization in 1918. (Matthew 24:21, 22) They had proved faulty during the trials of World War I and had been led into Babylonish captivity. In 1919 he set them free that he might put them to the test in the great witness that had to be given to the Kingdom before this "time of the end" closed and complete destruction came upon this world. Taking part in this wit-

---

5. For what purpose were the remnant of these saints set free in 1919, and how have they met the test that this meant for them?

ness work in all the inhabited earth would bring a severe test to them, for it would mean suffering many disagreeable things, hunger, thirst, nakedness, sickness, homelessness and imprisonment, not to speak of death in many cases. History of the remnant of these spiritual brothers of Christ since 1919 verifies that in preaching the good news of the Kingdom for a witness to all nations they have been tested by such sufferings as to their obedience to Jehovah as his witnesses. But never amid all their sufferings in all nations have they let the glorious Signal of the Kingdom fall. They have kept it upraised over all peoples that lovers of theocratic government might assemble to it.

⁶ In connection with these things that the remnant of Christ's brothers have been suffering, the peoples of all the nations have themselves been tested to determine whether they should be separated to the right or to the left of the Shepherd King Jesus Christ. Never should anyone think that Jesus does not care what happens to his remnant of spiritual brothers on the earth. He feels with them; he suffers with them; he takes what is done to them as being done to himself. He said to them: "He that receives you receives me also, and he that receives me receives him also that sent me forth." (Matthew 10:40, *NW*) This is because they are "ambassadors substituting for Christ." (2 Corinthians 5:20, *NW*) Jesus Christ the King, attended by all his angels, makes it clear that the separating of the peoples is according to the way they treat his ambassadors, his spiritual brothers. It will be useless, when the separating work is complete and the execution of judgment is due, for anyone to say: "Well, if we had actually seen you with our physical eyes and known it was you, we

───────

6. As shown by the parable, the separating of the people is according to what conduct on their part, and why? And will they be excused for not having to do with Jesus personally?

should have acted differently." The religious Jews of Jesus' day saw him, heard him and touched him, but that did not make them act differently; they killed him because he was Jehovah's Sent One, his Ambassador, and as such faithfully delivered God's message to them. They did not like God's Ambassador because they did not like God's message by him.

⁷ When the separation of the sheeplike people to the right and the goatlike people to the left is complete and the time for judgment to be executed is due at Armageddon, how does the Judge Jesus Christ emphasize this fact? "Then the king will say to those on his right: 'Come, you who have my Father's blessing, inherit the kingdom prepared for you from the world's foundation. For I became hungry and you gave me something to eat, I got thirsty and you gave me something to drink. I was a stranger and you received me hospitably; naked, and you clothed me. I fell sick and you looked after me. I was in prison and you came to me." The sheeplike ones who are thus to be ushered into earthly blessings under the Kingdom that God has prepared to rule over them now show that they do not see Jesus Christ on his throne directly with their literal eyes, but that his presence or *parousia* is invisible and he is only visibly represented by his remnant of brothers, his ambassadors on the earth in this time of the end. "Then the righteous ones will answer him with the words: 'Lord, when did we see you hungry and feed you, or thirsty, and give you something to drink? When did we see you a stranger and receive you hospitably, or naked, and clothe you? When did we see you sick or in prison and go to you?'" It was only indirectly, through his rem-

---

7. At the time of executing judgment how does the Judge Jesus emphasize that fact, and how do the sheep show they do not see the King on his throne literally?

nant of spiritual brothers. "And in reply the king will say to them: 'Truly I say to you, To the extent that you did it to one of the least of these my brothers, you did it to me.' " They loved the good news these brothers of his brought them.

⁸ There are no blessings on earth under God's kingdom for the goatlike people at the King's left to inherit. Their eternal portion is the same as that for Satan the Devil and his demon angels, fiery destruction beyond all rescue. "Then he will say, in turn, to those on his left: 'Be on your way from me, you who have been cursed, into the everlasting fire prepared for the Devil and his angels. For I became hungry, but you gave me nothing to eat, and I got thirsty, but you gave me nothing to drink. I was a stranger, but you did not receive me hospitably; naked, but you did not clothe me; sick and in prison, but you did not look after me.' " That these goats will include Christendom, which has the boldness to address Jesus as "Lord" although she does not slave for him or copy his example, Jesus now shows, saying: "Then they also will answer with the words: 'Lord, when did we see you hungry or thirsty or a stranger or naked or sick or in prison and did not minister to you?' " But Christendom will not be able to plead she has done many charitable works and, if she had seen Jesus in such a plight with her literal eyes, she would have included him in her charitable works. "Then he will answer them with the words: 'Truly I say to you, To the extent that you did not do it to one of these least ones, you did not do it to me.' "

⁹ Christendom will yet hear these stinging words of condemnation unveiling her hypocrisy spoken

---

8. What is the eternal portion for the goatlike ones to the left, and how is Christendom shown to be included among the goats?
9. Despite her charitable works, how has Christendom treated the least of the King's brothers, and with what words will he reject her?

to her at Armageddon. She loudly boasts of her charitable works, parades them before the public eye and takes up collections of millions of dollars, aside from the bingo gambling racket, to draw support of such charities from others. But it is a historical fact, undeniably backed up by the records in the courts of law, that she has had no charity for the remnant of Christ's brothers, even the least of them. She has not given them any comfort or support in their ambassadorial work of preaching the good news of God's established kingdom for a witness to all the nations and begging the sheeplike people: "Become reconciled to God." She has been the stiffest opposer and the most rabid persecutor of the remnant of Christ's spiritual brothers who are heirs of the heavenly kingdom. Pleading that Jesus Christ on his glorious throne has been invisible in this "time of the end" will not excuse her mistreatment of his least brothers on earth. She knows what the glorified Jesus said to Saul of Tarsus on his way to Damascus: "Saul, Saul, why are you persecuting me? . . . I am Jesus, whom you are persecuting." And Jesus had been invisible to Saul when this persecutor was abusing Jesus' followers. (Acts 9:1-5, *NW*) So the enthroned King will reject goatlike Christendom with the words that he gave in warning in his sermon on the mountain: "I never knew you at all. Get away from me, you workers of lawlessness." (Matthew 7:21-23, *NW*) She will meet an end like the Devil's.

[10] We are living in the "time of the end" when Jesus' prophetic parable is being enacted by living people on the earth. Which part are we acting on the stage of world action? To which side of the King are we being separated? Jesus' parable or

---

10. How can we tell whether we are being separated for life in God's new world or not, and what is the everlasting cutting-off (*kólasis*) for the goatlike people?

illustration helps us to know for certain by examining whether we are acting like sheep or like goats. From that we can determine whether we are being separated for life in God's new world or for destruction, for Jesus ended the parable and prophecy, after telling of the goats, saying: "And these will depart into everlasting cutting-off, but the righteous ones into everlasting life." (Matthew 25:31-46, *NW*) That everlasting cutting-off or *kólasis* for the goatlike people is the same as the "everlasting fire prepared for the Devil and his angels." It is not a death inherited by being born from Adam, but it is a death inflicted because of becoming a son of the Devil, a part of the seed of the original Serpent. Revelation 20:10, 14; 21:8 interprets it to be "the second death," the "everlasting destruction" with which the Lord Jesus will execute them at the battle of Armageddon when he is revealed from heaven in flaming fire of destruction to his goatlike foes.—2 Thessalonians 1:7-9, *NW*.

[11] The sheeplike ones go into an exactly opposite reward: "the righteous ones into everlasting life." This judgment of the King being enforced at the time of the universal war of Armageddon, it means that these sheeplike ones will live through the war and witness the everlasting destruction of the goatlike ones and then enter upon the opportunities for everlasting life in the new world.

[12] Jesus' parable or illustration foretells that, like a shepherd, he would separate such sheeplike righteous persons from the doomed goats and would put them to the side of his favor, the right side. Though not expressly stated in the parable,

---

11. Into what reward will the righteous ones go, and what will this mean for them at Armageddon?
12. (a) Being gathered to the King's right side, the sheeplike righteous persons are gathered into company with whom? (b) So what does Jesus call them, and will he be through gathering all such at Armageddon?

that right side is also where the spiritual remnant, "the least of these my brothers," are. So by the time that the judging and separating is complete and the outbreak of Armageddon is due all these sheeplike righteous people will have been gathered to the King's right side into company with the remnant of his spiritual brothers to whom they have rendered their good deeds, doing them as though they were doing them directly to the Shepherd King, Jesus Christ himself. Because they are not part of the "little flock" of Kingdom heirs to whom the heavenly Father has approved of giving the Kingdom, Jesus spoke of them as his "other sheep" in his parable of the Right Shepherd. After telling how he would shepherd the little flock of the Kingdom fold, he looks down to the time of the present-day remnant of his Kingdom sheep and says: "I have other sheep, which are not of this fold; those also I must bring, and they will listen to my voice, and they will become one flock, one shepherd." (John 10:16, *NW*) The great droves of other sheep whom the Right Shepherd Jesus Christ gathers into company with the remnant at his right side before Armageddon are merely the first of all the other sheep for whom he surrendered his soul, laying down his human life. After Armageddon he will gather all the rest of these other sheep, starting the gathering work then by the resurrection of all of them that are in their graves.—John 5:28, 29.

¹³ This time of separating the people of all the nations that are gathered before Christ's throne by the preaching of the good news of the Kingdom is the blessed time for the gathering of the sheep under divine favor and protection. Jehovah God, of course, is the great Shepherd. (Psalm 23:1, *AS*) He is chiefly responsible for the gathering of the

13. Who is chiefly responsible for the gathering of the sheep, and since when? And how has he used the gathered ones?

sheep since 1919, after he came to his temple with his Messenger of the covenant, the Right Shepherd. The first sheep he began gathering were the remnant of the Kingdom class, Christ's spiritual brothers, who had been scattered in the cloudy and dark day of World War I. Then he used these re-gathered ones themselves to engage in shepherding activities by going out with the Kingdom message and searching for the "other sheep" and bringing them in and feeding them with spiritual food.

[14] All these sheep of both classes he has now made one co-operative company or flock, all being heirs of life in the new world. He has delivered them from the false, greedy, oppressive shepherds of Christendom's religious and political systems and has placed them under the tender care of a shepherd who loved them all so much as to lay down his earthly life for them, Jesus Christ, the Son of David the shepherd. Jehovah has faithfully done as he long ago said: "I will set up one shepherd over them, and he shall feed them, even my servant David; he shall feed them, and he shall be their shepherd. And I, Jehovah, will be their God, and my servant David prince among them; I, Jehovah, have spoken it. And ye my sheep, the sheep of my pasture, are men, and I am your God, saith the Lord Jehovah."—Ezekiel 34:11, 12, 23, 24, 31, AS.

---

14. What has Jehovah done as to both classes of sheep, and how has he done as he said at Ezekiel, chapter 34?

CHAPTER X

Gathering the Great Crowd to the Temple

SINCE A.D. 1918, when *A.do.nay'* Jehovah with his Angel of the covenant came to his spiritual temple,* we have, as it were, been living in the calm center or "eye of the hurricane," the period of lull before the final resumption of the destructive whirling stormwind. The universal war of Armageddon is likened to a death-dealing tempest or windstorm, in Jeremiah 23:19; 25:32, and it will bring to a culmination the days of tribulation upon the Devil's organization, its invisible heavens and its visible earth or human part. Jehovah God, in full command of his angelic battle forces, is holding that destructive war in check, although, while he does so, wickedness and violence continue to mount in the earth. Not that he is in sympathy or in alliance with the doers of wickedness, but he tolerates with much long-suffering the human vessels that are made fit for destruction, in order that in the meantime he may have mercy upon those "vessels" that he is preparing for heavenly glory, for a place in his heavenly temple. He has cut short the days of tribulation upon Satan's organization on account of these chosen ones, these "living stones" for his heavenly

---

* See Chapter VI, entitled *"A.do.nay'* Comes to His Temple," page 85.

1. Since 1918, in what have we been living, figuratively speaking, and what has God's further toleration of the wicked permitted him to do for his chosen ones?

temple. He has an important work with them and for them on earth before the storm resumes and Armageddon strikes.—Romans 9:22-26; Mark 13:20.

2 This key fact is portrayed in sign language in chapter seven of the Revelation, written down by the apostle John about twenty-five years after the Romans destroyed Jerusalem and its temple A.D. 70. What he there describes referred to the future, the "time of the end," when the final trouble threatened and worldly men would "keep saying to the mountains and to the rock-masses: 'Fall over us and hide us from the face of the one seated on the throne and from the wrath of the Lamb, because the great day of their wrath has come, and who is able to stand?'" (Revelation 6:14-17, *NW*) John describes invisible actors behind the scenes and helps us to understand why Armageddon's windstorm has not yet struck, as he writes: "After this I saw four angels standing upon the four extremities of the earth, holding tight the four winds of the earth, that no wind might blow upon the earth or upon the sea or upon any tree. And I saw another angel ascending from the sunrising, having a seal of the living God, and he cried with a loud voice to the four angels to whom it was granted to harm the earth and the sea, saying: 'Do not harm the earth or the sea or the trees, until after we have sealed the slaves of our God in their foreheads.' And I heard the number of those who were sealed, a hundred and forty-four thousand, sealed out of every tribe of the sons of Israel." Then John lists twelve thousand sealed out of twelve Israelite tribes, namely, Judah, Reuben, Gad, Asher, Naphtali, Manasseh, Simeon, Levi, Issachar, Zebulun, Joseph and Benjamin (but

---

2. How does the apostle John show in picture language at Revelation, chapter 7, why Armageddon's windstorm has not yet struck, and thus who and how many have been sealed?

not Dan and Ephraim), totaling 144,000 Israelites sealed.—Revelation 7:1-8, *NW.*

³ The angel whom John saw ascending from the east and having a seal of the living God Jehovah is the Angel of the covenant who accompanied *A·do·nay'* Jehovah to his temple in 1918. In ancient Israel the temple of Jerusalem faced the east and was entered from the east. Fittingly it is from that direction that the Angel with God's seal ascends. In the war in heaven, which resulted in hurling down Satan and his demons from there to the earth, the angels fought alongside the archangel, this special Angel of the covenant who has God's seal. As he comes to the temple he calls for a cutting short of the days of tribulation at the earth to which Satan the Devil has been hurled down with his demons. (Revelation 12:7-13) He, as the archangel, calls upon his fellow warrior angels to hold back the four winds from converging upon the earth and the sea to produce a harmful windstorm, as it were. The storm must be held back until he has finished his God-assigned work, of sealing 144,000 slaves of God in their foreheads, all Israelites.

⁴ Here the seal is a symbol of the holy spirit or active force of God. It is with the holy spirit that Jehovah God seals the 144,000 members of the temple class or congregation, and it is by his Angel of the covenant, Jesus Christ glorified, that he does the sealing with the holy spirit. From the day of Pentecost A.D. 33 God began the sealing work by means of this Angel. The apostle Peter was one of those sealed with the spirit that very day, and he revealed whom God used as his Angel to do the sealing, saying to the gathered multitude:

---

3. Who is the angel with the seal, why does he ascend from the east, what does he call for, and why?
4. What is the seal, and whom did the apostle Peter at Pentecost reveal to be the Angel whom God used to do the sealing?

"This Jesus God resurrected, of which fact we are all witnesses. Therefore because he was exalted to the right hand of God and received the promised holy spirit from the Father, he has poured out this which you see and hear," that is, this spirit that was accompanied by a rushing stiff breeze and tongues as of fire upon the sealed ones and that inspired them to speak in foreign languages.—Acts 2:1-4, 14, 32, 33, *NW*.

[5] Previously the assembled multitude of unconverted Jews had accused these disciples of Jesus of being slaves of Beelzebub the Devil; but now by seeing and hearing these evidences of the holy spirit poured out upon these disciples those Jews saw that they were sealed with the holy spirit as slaves of God. That was a fact now plain to the public eye beyond all mistaking or denial. The seal of the holy spirit was promised only to Jehovah's "men slaves" and "women slaves," according to Joel 2:28, 29. Those disciples together with Peter had that spirit poured out upon them, and this fact stamped them, sealed them, made them recognizable as "slaves of our God." It gave proof that the natural twelve tribes of Israel were now no longer the chosen people of God, no longer his "special property," his "own possession," his "congregation," but that these spirit-begotten believing disciples of Jesus Christ were now his "congregation," his spiritual Israel, and that they had reserved for them a heavenly "inheritance" as "heirs indeed of God, but joint heirs with Christ." (Exodus 19:5; Romans 8:15-17, *NW;* Galatians 6:15, 16) In support of this fact the apostle Paul wrote to the believers in the Christ at the city of Ephesus: "By means of him also, after you believed, you were sealed with the promised holy spirit,

---

5. (a) According to Joel 2:28, 29, by that spirit whose slaves were Christ's disciples stamped as being? (b) Of what was that spirit with which they were sealed a token in advance?

which is a token in advance of our inheritance, for the purpose of releasing by a ransom God's own possession, to his glorious praise. Also do not be grieving God's holy spirit, with which you have been sealed for a day of releasing by ransom." —Ephesians 1:13, 14; 4:30, *NW*.

⁶ Paul also showed that the congregation at the city of Corinth were likewise sealed with the spirit, when he wrote: "He who guarantees that you and we belong to Christ and he who has anointed us is God. He has also put his seal upon us and has given us the token of what is to come, that is, the spirit, in our hearts." (2 Corinthians 1:21, 22, *NW*) Paul had been a natural Jew of the tribe of Benjamin; those to whom he wrote at Ephesus and at Corinth were, for a large part, non-Israelites according to the flesh. (Ephesians 2:11-19; 1 Corinthians 6:9-11) Consequently, since natural Gentiles believing were sealed with God's holy spirit by Christ the same as natural believing Israelites, and since only 144,000 slaves of God are thus sealed in their foreheads, it is unavoidable to conclude that the 144,000 sealed symbolic Israelites of Revelation 7:4-8 are spiritual Israelites, members of the twelve tribes or complete organization of spiritual Israel, and that they include believing Gentiles or non-Israelites as well as believing Israelites, all being circumcised in their hearts, all being Jews inside rather than outside in the flesh. (Romans 2:28, 29) The sealing of the believing natural Israelites began at Pentecost, A.D. 33; the sealing of the believing Gentiles or non-Israelites began three and a half years later, A.D. 36, when the apostle Peter preached to the first Gentile converts at the home of Cornelius, the Italian cen-

---

6. (a) Of whom were the congregations of sealed ones at Ephesus and at Corinth made up according to the flesh? (b) Hence whom do the 144,000 at Revelation 7:4-8 include, and when did the sealing of each group begin?

turion stationed at Caesarea.—Acts 2:1-42; 10:1-48.

⁷ In 1918, when *A·do·nay'* Jehovah came with his Angel of the covenant to his temple, the sealing of the 144,000 was not yet complete. At the time there were a number of sealed ones, a remnant, lying in captivity in antitypical Babylon. Had the symbolic "four winds of the earth" not been held back at that time from blowing and battering this antitypical Babylon to pieces, this captive remnant of sealed ones would not have had a chance to flee out of it and 'no flesh would have been saved.' But by ordering the four angels to hold the winds back, the days of tribulation were cut short, an opportunity to flee was afforded (Revelation 18:1-4), and thus the remnant in the flesh could be saved for the sake of Jehovah's holy name. (Ezekiel 36:21-24, *AS*) Many who associated with the remnant and who claimed to be part of it fell out during the fiery trials of World War I and also because of urgent demands made upon them to carry forward the world-wide Kingdom witness during the postwar period. But this loss to the loyal remnant was offset.

⁸ During the postwar era, as its history down to 1932 shows, many thousands all over the earth heard the preaching of "this good news of the kingdom" and by it they caught sight of the royal Signal that God had raised up. They fled out of antitypical Babylon and assembled to the Kingdom Signal, never to forsake it. As loyal upholders of it they dedicated themselves unconditionally and unreservedly to *A·do·nay'* Jehovah at his temple,

---

7. If the symbolic "four winds" had not been held back in 1918, what would have been the case with the sealed ones?

8. During the postwar period how was the loss to the loyal remnant by the falling out of many during and after World War I offset, in a final fulfillment of Joel 2:28, 29?

dedicating themselves to him through his Angel
of the covenant, Jesus Christ. In undeserved kindness Jehovah chose them to become part of the
remnant of "living stones" for his heavenly temple, and in a final fulfillment of his prophecy at
Joel 2:28, 29, 32 he poured out his holy spirit upon
them, anointing them to his royal priesthood under the High Priest Jesus Christ. This meant that
Jehovah's Angel from the sunrising had sealed
them in their foreheads with the seal of the living
God to be his slaves. It meant that they had been
made spiritual Israelites, with the opportunity to
become members of the 144,000 making up the
twelve tribes of spiritual Israel, the seed of the
Abrahamic covenant in whom all the families of
the earth will bless themselves.—Genesis 12:3;
22:18; Galatians 3:16, 29.

⁹ They thus replaced the unfaithful ones that
had dropped out or been cast out. (Matthew 22:8-
14) They displayed the seal of the outpoured spirit
in their foreheads by laying up treasures in heav-
en, engaging in temple work, offering to God the
spiritual sacrifices of praise to his name, and keeping themselves without spot from the Babylonish
nations of this world. They are determined to keep
the seal of the living God in their foreheads, until
the four winds are let loose. The eastern Angel's
work of sealing them had to be done before Armageddon. Jehovah's Angel of the covenant will not
fail in this sealing work.

¹⁰ However, a new thing was revealed to the
eyes of the remnant. They were not the only ones
to benefit from the holding back of the four winds

9. How did those who replaced the unfaithful display
the seal of the spirit in their foreheads?
10, 11. (a) What new thing was revealed to the remnant as to the benefit from the holding back of the
four winds? (b) In 1935 the remnant had an experience
corresponding with that of John in connection with
what vision?

that the days of tribulation might be cut short. There was to be a great crowd of others who were not spiritual Israelites, not members of the 144,-000. The twelve tribes of spiritual Israel being limited to the 144,000 sealed ones, then all other peoples on the earth today would be classified as Gentiles, non-Israelite nations, spiritually speaking. In the spring of 1935 the remnant of spiritual Israelites had the experience corresponding with that of the apostle John, who had a vision of the sealing of the 144,000 and then wrote:

[11] "After these things I saw, and, look! a great crowd, which no man was able to number, out of all nations and tribes and peoples and tongues, standing before the throne and before the Lamb, dressed in white robes, and there were palm branches in their hands. And they keep on crying with a loud voice, saying: 'Salvation we owe to our God, who is seated on the throne, and to the Lamb.' And all the angels were standing around the throne and the persons of advanced age and the four living creatures, and they fell upon their faces before the throne and worshiped God, saying: 'Amen! The blessing and the glory and the wisdom and the thanksgiving and the honor and the power and the strength be to our God for ever and ever. Amen.'" —Revelation 7:9-12, NW.

[12] It is significant that this great crowd stands before the throne on which God sits and before Jesus Christ, "the Lamb of God that takes away the sin of the world." (John 1:29, 36, NW) This position shows that they have seen the Signal upraised by the remnant over the peoples and they have gathered to it, that is, to the kingdom that God established in the heavens in 1914 by enthroning the Lamb Jesus Christ. That implies that

12. (a) What does the standing of this great crowd before the throne of God and before his Lamb indicate? (b) What does their attributing their salvation to God and the Lamb signify?

they recognize that Jehovah God is universal Sovereign, with the rightful power and authority to determine who should rule the earth at the close of the "appointed times of the nations" in 1914. They have learned that the nations, tribes and peoples out of which they have come are doomed to destruction at Armageddon, and so they have experienced a great salvation by having their eyes opened to see the Kingdom Signal and to gather to it as God's rightful government for all the earth. There is no salvation except from Jehovah: "Salvation belongeth unto Jehovah." (Psalm 3:8, *AS*) For the salvation of mankind he has established his kingdom, and by the sacrifice of his Lamb Jesus Christ he has provided for the ransoming of his subjects from sin and its penalty death. With good reason the great crowd turn away disappointed from man-made arrangements and say unashamed: "Salvation we owe to our God, who is seated on the throne, and to the Lamb." Thus they publicly bear witness to Jehovah and Christ.

¹³ In their symbolic white robes they are in a clean, acceptable appearance before the great King Jehovah God and his Lamb. The palm branches in their hand mark them, not as dead martyrs, but as living witnesses to God's kingdom in the hands of his Lamb. The palm branches carry the same meaning as when Jesus rode in kingly fashion into Jerusalem or Zion and went to the temple and cleansed it. As it is recorded: "The next day the great crowd that had come to the feast, on hearing that Jesus was coming to Jerusalem, took the branches of palm trees and went out to meet him. And they began to shout: 'Save, we pray you! Blessed is he that comes in Jehovah's name, even the king of Israel!' But when Jesus had found a

---

13. What does their being in white robes and with palm branches in their hands symbolize, and what does their cry about salvation show they become?

young ass, he sat on it, just as it is written: 'Have no fear, daughter of Zion. Look! your king is coming, seated upon an ass's colt.'" (John 12:12-15, *NW; ED*) Like that great crowd of Israelites expecting the Kingdom nineteen centuries ago, the "great crowd" foreseen in vision by the apostle John ascribe their salvation today to the universal Sovereign, Jehovah God, who in 1914 took his great power and began ruling as king toward this earth. They also hail his beloved Son, the Lamb, who has come into the kingdom to wield power in Jehovah's name and to save all who assemble to the Kingdom Signal. They gratefully acknowledge that by Jehovah's shortening of the days for his chosen ones' sake He has worked for their salvation also. Enthusiastically they become witnesses of Jehovah.

[14] With a united "Amen!" all the members of God's holy universal organization, his heavenly angels, back up the great crowd in their praising and witnessing to Jehovah, and they ascribe to God forever a perfect number of things, seven things, blessing, glory, wisdom, thanksgiving, honor, power and strength.

[15] For many years, specially from the October, 1879, issue of the magazine *Zion's Watch Tower and Herald of Christ's Presence,* the same question has been raised that was put to the apostle John: "These who are dressed in the white robes, who are they and where did they come from?" In 1935, or seventeen years after *A·do·nay'* Jehovah came with his Angel of the covenant to the temple and began cutting short the days of tribulation, the white-robed "great crowd" were first correctly

---

14. How do all members of God's universal organization back up the great crowd in praising Jehovah?
15. Since when, in particular, has there been a question as to the identity of the great crowd, but when and by what means was the true-to-fact answer given, similarly as to the apostle John?

identified. By then there were many thousands of them, the world over, that had assembled to the Kingdom Signal and that were standing here on earth in loyal allegiance before God's throne and before his Lamb. First in a convention at Washington, D.C., May 31, 1935, and later in the issues of August 1 and 15, 1935, of *The Watchtower*, in the serial article entitled "The Great Multitude," the true-to-fact answer as to their identity was given in fulfillment of this answer given to John: "These are the ones that come out of the great tribulation, and they have washed their robes and made them white in the blood of the Lamb. That is why they are before the throne of God, and they are rendering him sacred service day and night in his temple, and the one seated on the throne will spread his tent over them. They will hunger no more nor thirst any more, neither will the sun beat down upon them nor any scorching heat, because the Lamb who is in the midst of the throne will shepherd them, and will guide them to fountains of waters of life. And God will wipe out every tear from their eyes."—Revelation 7:13-17, *NW*.

¹⁶ From the inspired answer to John the "great crowd" must be sheep of the Lamb, Jesus Christ the Right Shepherd. They were not spiritual Israelites and hence they were not members of the "little flock" of 144,000 sheep to whom the heavenly Father has approved of giving the heavenly kingdom with the Lamb Jesus Christ. This great crowd is one that no man is able to number because God has not revealed the number as he has done concerning the little flock. The "great crowd" of sheeplike followers of the Lamb must be no others than "other sheep" whom the Right Shepherd long ago said he had to gather in due time. The great crowd are those of the "other sheep"

---

16. From the answer to John, of what general group is this great crowd, and when is it gathered?

whom he gathers after he comes to the temple and before the outbreak of the battle of Armageddon. This is made certain to our understanding by the statement: "These are the ones that come out of the great tribulation."

[17] This "great tribulation" is not persecution or martyrdom; it is the tribulation the climax of which comes when the four angels on the earth's four extremities release the four winds of the earth. It is the tribulation that Jesus said would mark this "time of the end" and that would be cut short because of its terribleness that some flesh might be saved. (Matthew 24:21, 22) During this interval in between the forepart and the final part of this tribulation, when the remnant of God's slaves are being sealed by his Angel in their foreheads, it is then that the "great crowd" come out. The vision of them is not a picture of after Armageddon but is one of the present time, particularly since 1931, before Armageddon.

[18] If they did not now wash their robes and make them white in the Lamb's blood before Armageddon, they would never get through that universal war alive and enter the new world. They do not get sealed in their foreheads with the seal of the living God the way the 144,000 spiritual Israelites do, but they do make themselves presentable to God on his throne, confessing faith in the blood of the Lamb Jesus Christ. On the basis of this faith they dedicate themselves to God through Christ. This does not make them "saints" or sanctified ones such as the twelve tribes of spiritual Israel, the "holy nation," are, but they do enjoy the forgiveness of their sins and are in God's sight righteous persons. Jesus' parable of the sheep and the

---

17. In what sense do they "come out of the great tribulation"?
18. Why is their washing their robes and whitening them in the Lamb's blood necessary before Armageddon, and so how does God favor them and view them?

goats speaks of them as the sheeplike "righteous ones" whom he puts at the right side of his throne. (Matthew 25:37, 46, *NW*) So they have favored recognition from God's throne.

[19] They are not chosen and sanctified to be "living stones" in God's spiritual temple, but they get in touch with the remnant of such temple stones and engage with them in the worship of Jehovah, who has come to his temple. Today finds hundreds of thousands of them "rendering him sacred service day and night in his temple." In doing so they fulfill the picture of the Nethinim, the non-Israelite temple slaves, who were the drawers of water and the gatherers of wood for the typical temple.* As the Nethinim were assistants at the typical temple in Jerusalem and returned with the remnant from captivity in Babylon, so now the "great crowd" come out of the antitypical Babylon and become assistants to the remnant of the "royal priesthood" at the temple.

[20] In connection with the typical temple at Jerusalem, King Solomon its builder was a type of "something more than Solomon," namely, Jesus Christ, the builder of Jehovah's spiritual temple. (Matthew 12:42, *NW*) Solomon's building operations would therefore be typical of things today having to do with the spiritual temple at which the "great crowd" serve God day and night. For Solomon's temple cedar timbers and juniper timbers were needed. A supply of such was to be found in Mount Lebanon under the jurisdiction of Hiram the king of Tyre, a faithful friend of Solo-

---

* See chapter VIII, pages 142-148.

19. In what do they engage with the remnant at the temple, and what picture of ancient temple slaves do they thus fulfill?
20, 21. (a) Why is it here fitting to refer to Solomon's building of the temple at Jerusalem? (b) How were many non-Israelites from outside as well as inside of Israel put to work in preparing for Solomon's temple?

mon's father David. Because the Phoenicians or Lebanese were such expert woodcutters, Solomon applied to King Hiram for cedar and juniper timbers for the proposed temple: "Now command that they cut for me cedars from Leb'a·non, and my servants themselves will prove to be with your servants, and the wages of your servants I shall give to you according to all that you may say, for you yourself well know that there is among us no one knowing how to cut trees like the Sidonians." So Solomon and Hiram entered into an agreement, Solomon to provide helpers from Israel and also wages to Hiram's woodcutters and Hiram to send out his woodsmen to the forest of Lebanon and to send the cut logs in rafts by the Mediterranean Sea south to the Israelite seaport of Joppa, from which Solomon had them transported to Jerusalem. Hiram also provided native stonecutters to quarry temple stones from the mountains. These worked with the burden bearers and stonecutters that King Solomon sent up.

21 "Accordingly the king commanded that they should quarry great stones, expensive stones, to lay the foundation of the house with hewn stones. So Solomon's builders and Hiram's builders and the Ge'bal·ites did the cutting and they kept preparing the timbers and the stones to build the house." For this purpose Solomon took advantage of the many thousands of non-Israelite sojourners or temporary residents in his realm. "Then Solomon took a count of all the men that were temporary residents, who were in the land of Israel, after the census that David his father had taken of them, and there came to be found a hundred and fifty-three thousand six hundred. So he made seventy thousand of them burden bearers and eighty thousand cutters in the mountain and three thousand six hundred overseers for keeping the people in service." (1 Kings 5:6-18 and 2 Chronicles 2:8-18, NW) There were thus many thousands of non-

Israelites, foreigners as well as temporary residents in Israel, that did work preparatory to building Jehovah's typical temple.*

[22] In Solomon's building program after finishing the temple he continued to use laborers conscripted from the non-Israelite temporary residents in his realm: "As for all the people that were left over of the Hit′tites and the Am′or·ites and the Per′iz·zites and the Hi′vites and the Jeb′u·sites, who were no part of Israel, from their sons that had been left behind them in the land, whom the sons of Israel had not exterminated, Sol′o·mon kept levying men for forced labor until this day. But there were none out of the sons of Israel that Sol′o·mon constituted slaves for his work, for they were war-

---

* Compare Ezra 3:6, 7, concerning the rebuilding of the typical temple at Jerusalem by the remnant restored from Babylon.

22. After the temple, whom did Solomon continue to use as laborers in his building program, and what does this typify?

riors and chiefs of his adjutants and chiefs of his charioteers and of his horsemen." (2 Chronicles 8:7-9, *NW*) This well typifies that there would be antitypical sojourners or temporary residents, who had been spared alive, whom the Son of David, the King greater than Solomon, would use as his willing slaves in the theocratic building program before the war of Armageddon.

²³ In comparing the type with the antitype, Solomon's conscripted non-Israelite builders and Hiram's foreign builders and the men of Ge′bal who cut down timbers and quarried stones for building Jehovah's temple picture those of the "great crowd" whom John saw rendering sacred service to Jehovah at his temple day and night. The temple service that this white-robed crowd with palm branches render in close unity with the remnant of spiritual Israelites is that of praising God's name and declaring his salvation through the Lamb Jesus Christ and raising aloft the Signal by advertising Jehovah's King, the Greater Solomon. Theirs is a continual service to God, day and night, keeping their robes white by a constant pursuit of righteousness and being ever on the watch to advance the worship of the one living and true God. In appreciation Jehovah spreads his tent of protection over them, and it will continue over them all through his war of Armageddon. Thus they will survive.

²⁴ In likening this "great crowd" to sheep under the tender care of God's Lamb, the apostle John drew upon language found in Isaiah, chapter 49: "They shall feed in the ways, and their pasture shall be on all bare hills. *They shall not hunger nor thirst, neither shall the heat nor sun smite them;*

23. (a) Thus whom do Solomon's conscripted builders and Hiram's foreign builders and the Gebalites picture? (b) What kind of service to God is theirs as to time? 24. In likening the great crowd to sheep, upon what prophecy of Isaiah did John draw as to expressions?

for he that hath mercy on them *will lead them, and by the springs of water will he guide them*. And I will make all my mountains a way, and my highways shall be raised up. Behold, these shall come from afar; and behold, these from the north and from the west; and these from the land of Sinim [in the south]. Shout, ye heavens; and be joyful, thou earth; and break forth into singing, ye mountains: for Jehovah hath comforted his people, and will have mercy upon his afflicted ones."—Isaiah 49:9-13, *Da*.

²⁵ But to know and feel the leading and shepherding of the Lamb who is in the midst of God's throne they must obey the command, "Go forth," and, "Shew yourselves." To begin with, these "other sheep" are prisoners of the spiritual "world-rulers of this darkness"; they are in the darkness of antitypical Babylon, which is in political and religious confusion and has no ray of hope and no light of Jehovah's favor, but only his condemnation. The members of the remnant of the 144,000 spiritual Israelites were once there themselves at the beginning of Babylon's "time of the end." But they answered the call of God through his written Word: "Get out of her, my people, if you do not want to share with her in her sins, and if you do not want to receive part of her plagues. For her sins have massed together clear up to heaven, and God has called her acts of injustice to mind." (Revelation 18:4, 5, *NW*) Jehovah God raised up his great Servant, the Greater Cyrus, Jesus Christ. This Conqueror of antitypical Babylon broke her power over the spiritual remnant and led them back to his free, enlightened theocratic organization, to engage in rebuilding Jehovah's temple,

---

25. (a) To know the shepherding by the Lamb, what command did the great crowd have to obey, and why? (b) How did the once-captive remnant come to be associated with the Greater Cyrus in proclaiming liberation to those yet in modern Babylon?

that is to say, restoring, building up and extending the pure worship of God. God accepted their repentance in this time of shortening the days, and it has been a "day of salvation" for them. Then Jehovah associated this restored remnant with his great Servant, the antitypical Cyrus, to proclaim liberty to the captives yet in modern Babylon and the opening of the prison to those yet bound there.

²⁶ That Jehovah raised up his Servant at the temple and then associated with him the delivered remnant, he shows, saying: "Thus saith Jehovah: In a time of acceptance have I answered thee, and in the day of salvation have I helped thee; and I will preserve thee, and give thee for a covenant [a guarantee, a pledge] of the people, to establish the land [of the theocratic organization], to cause to inherit the desolate heritages [desolate during the exile and captivity of Jehovah's people]; saying to the prisoners, Go forth; to them that are in darkness, Shew yourselves." (Isaiah 49:3, 5, 8, 9, *Da*) That the remnant come within the time for God's acceptance and within the day of salvation from the enemy, Jehovah inspired his apostle Paul to show by writing to his fellow Christians: "Working together with him, we also entreat you not to accept the undeserved kindness of God and miss its purpose. For he says: 'In an acceptable season I heard you, and in the day for salvation I came to your help.' Look! Now is the especially acceptable season. Look! Now is the day for salvation." (2 Corinthians 6:1, 2, *NW*) Enjoying that divine acceptance and partaking of the salvation of this day, the remnant must now act as a servant class, united with the Lamb, the great Servant, at the temple. They must call to the

---

26. (a) How does Paul's quotation from Isaiah 49 show that Jehovah raises up his Servant at the temple and now associates the delivered remnant with him? (b) So what must the remnant now do in behalf of the other sheep?

"other sheep" to go forth from Babylonish imprisonment. They must tell these bedarkened ones who are out of sight in places of restraint to show themselves as worshipers of the Almighty God, to reflect the light of his truth to still others.

²⁷ Particularly since 1931* Jehovah's great Servant, through his remnant on earth, has commanded the other sheep to go forth to freedom and to show themselves as supporters of God's kingdom, followers of his Lamb and sympathizers with the remnant in their preaching of "this good news of the kingdom" all over the earth. They must take their stand unashamed before God's kingdom. They must acknowledge his Lamb and wash their robes white and clean in the blood of his sacrifice, that they may be forgiven their sins in Babylon. They must enthusiastically take up the festal palm branches and hail God's anointed King, Jesus the Messiah. They must come to the temple of Jehovah's presence and there render him sacred service day and night, turning their backs on the worldly service of Babylon. Already hundreds of thousands of them have done this.

²⁸ In their case we see the divine promise being carried out. Their spiritual hunger and thirst are continually being satisfied by Jehovah's Right Shepherd. No longer does the sun of divine chastisement beat down upon them or the scorching heat of his fiery judgments broil them because of partaking in the sins of antitypical Babylon. They are a cleansed people, and the Lamb, Jehovah's great Servant, gives them the best shepherd's care even under the most unlikely circumstances, like

---

* See chapter XII, page 212, ¶15, ff.

27. Since when particularly has the command through the remnant gone forth, and in obedience what have hundreds of thousands already done?
28. How is the best shepherd's care being given to them, and why does Isaiah call upon heaven, earth and mountains to rejoice?

bare hills. He leads them to the life-giving water of Kingdom truth. They are a most grateful and happy people. By his provisions through his Shepherd, God has wiped every tear from their eyes, removing all causes for weeping over their spiritual state. From east, north, west and south he brings them, bringing them into co-operation with the remnant of "living stones" at the temple. No wonder Isaiah in prophesying over this called upon the heavens to sing, the earth to be joyful and the mountains to burst out in singing! It is no time for those on earth at the temple to weep, nor for the angels of heaven.

²⁹ Jesus long ago said at the house of Zacchaeus the publican or tax collector, who showed himself a "son of Abraham" by reforming in order to be a blessing to others: "This day salvation has come to this house, because he also is a son of Abraham. For the Son of man came to seek and to save what was lost." (Luke 19:9, 10, *NW;* Genesis 22:17, 18) The sheep of God's people were "what was lost"; hence Jesus said to his apostles, when sending them out to preach the Kingdom: "Go continually to the lost sheep of the house of Israel." (Matthew 10:6, *NW*) Now Jesus Christ at the temple sends out his sealed remnant to engage in pastoral work and seek the lost sheep, this numberless great crowd of other sheep. By now hundreds of thousands have been found and brought to the temple of worship. The pastoral work still goes on, being joined in by those other sheep already found and restored. A shepherd rejoices over finding and saving his lost sheep. So all those in the holy heavens and all those on earth in Jehovah's pastoral work rejoice at the rescue of the lost sheep from this Babylonish world, and they ascribe the power of this salvation to God by his Christ.—Luke 15:3-7.

---

29. What is now being found that has been lost, to cause great rejoicing in heaven and on earth?

CHAPTER XI

Gathering of the Nations to Armageddon

THE gathering of the nations to Armageddon is moving forward with rapidity. The question that faces each individual on earth is, On which side of the battle line-up shall I be found there, on the right side or the left? The present-day separating of the people of all nations as sheep and goats and the putting of the sheeplike individuals on the right hand of God's enthroned King leaves the nations themselves to be put on his left hand as goats. The goats as well as the sheep work out their destiny by the way in which they treat the remnant of the King's brothers, the remnant of the 144,000 spiritual Israelites. The reason why one's treatment of the remnant determines one's destiny is that the remnant have been anointed with Jehovah's spirit in these last days and are in line for a place on the heavenly throne with the King. Mistreatment of the remnant brings the greatest punishment, for it is an overt assault against the Kingdom. Respect for the anointed remnant brings the richest blessings from the Kingdom.

[2] The prophet Joel was inspired to foretell that

---

1. (a) During this gathering of nations to Armageddon what question faces each individual? (b) Why does one's treatment of the remnant determine one's destiny? 2. Joel foretold that God would pour out his spirit upon a remnant at what kind of time in human history, and how did the apostle Peter confirm this fact on Pentecost A.D. 33?

the pouring out of God's spirit upon the remnant would occur at a most crucial time in human history. Modern-day Christendom was typified by ancient Jerusalem and Judea. At a time when the Jews were under a judgment to determine the fate of Judea and Jerusalem and its temple, the holy spirit was poured out upon the Jewish remnant. On the day of Pentecost A.D. 33, when it was first poured out upon flesh of all kinds, the apostle Peter, a receiver of the spirit, publicly announced that this was a fulfillment of Joel's prophecy, saying: "This is what was said through the prophet Joel, ' "And in the last days," God says, "I shall pour some of my spirit out upon every kind of flesh, and your sons and your daughters will prophesy and your young men will see visions and your old men will dream dreams; and even upon my men slaves and upon my women slaves I will pour out some of my spirit in those days, and they will prophesy. And I will produce wonders in heaven above and signs on earth below, blood and fire and smoke mist; the sun will be turned into darkness and the moon into blood before the great and illustrious day of Jehovah arrives. And then anyone that calls upon the name of Jehovah will be saved." ' " And the prophet Joel fills out Peter's quotation of the prophecy by adding: "For in Mount Zion and in Jerusalem there shall be those that escape, as Jehovah hath said, and among the remnant those whom Jehovah doth call."—Acts 2:16-21, *NW;* Joel 2:28-32, *AS.*

³ Thirty-seven years after Peter quoted those words of Joel the city of Jerusalem with its gorgeous temple was destroyed for the second time. The remnant of Jews who had called upon Jehovah's name through faith in his Son Jesus Christ

---

3. What happened thirty-seven years after Peter quoted Joel, and why is that of solemn meaning to this generation since 1914?

escaped the frightful destruction upon earthly Jerusalem and Mount Zion at that climax of the "great and illustrious day of Jehovah." This is not without solemn meaning for this generation living since A.D. 1914. For what happened back there to literal Jerusalem and Judea was a prophetic pattern of what is to happen inside this generation to their modern counterparts, Christendom and her religious organization, in the opening phase of the "war of the great day of God the Almighty."

⁴ Proving that the larger and final fulfillment of Joel's prophecy is within this generation, the prophet follows up his words above with the further prophecy: "For behold, in those days, and in that time, when I shall turn again the captivity of Judah and Jerusalem, I will also gather all the nations, and will bring them down into the valley of Jehoshaphat, and I will enter into judgment with them there on account of my people and mine inheritance, Israel, whom they have scattered among the nations: and they have parted my land; and they have cast lots for my people." (Joel 3:1-3, *Da*) No such gathering of all the nations and bringing them down to the valley of Jehoshaphat to punish them for their mistreatment of Jehovah's people occurred back there in the days of Peter and his fellow apostles. That leaves Joel's prophecy concerning the outpouring of God's spirit and all related events to be fulfilled completely in all its details down here within this generation.

⁵ It is in these days since 1919 that Jehovah God has caused the remnant of the 144,000 spiritual

---

4. How do Joel's further words show that the prophecy has had to wait until this generation to be fulfilled completely?
5. So why is it in these days that Jehovah must bring the nations down to the valley of Jehoshaphat, and why to the valley of Jehoshaphat?

Israelites to return from their captivity in anti-typical Babylon. So it is in these same days that he must keep his word and gather and bring all the nations that have mistreated them down into the "valley of Jehoshaphat" and give them their deserved punishment. The expression "valley of Jehoshaphat" does not refer to the valley east of Jerusalem that has come to be called by that name. No, the expression is symbolic. Since a slaughter of the nations is to take place at this symbolic valley, Jehovah doubtless spoke of the "valley" in this way because of a slaughter of allied nations that astounded the world in the days of Jehoshaphat, king of Jerusalem.

⁶ The nations of Moab and Ammon and the mountainous region of Seir combined their military forces and marched up the western side of the Dead Sea to assault the realm of King Jehoshaphat. Before they got near to Jerusalem, King Jehoshaphat and the people marched out of the city to meet them, with Levitical singers at the head singing the praises of Jehovah. Jehovah's prophet had told them: "The battle is not yours but God's. . . . You will not need to fight in this instance. Take your position, stand still and see the salvation of Jehovah in your behalf." They did see the salvation that he gave. When the march and the singing began, Jehovah went into battle for them. He confused the nations of Moab and Ammon into ambushing their own ally, the army from the region of Seir, and annihilating them, after which He turned the Moabites and the Ammonites to the madness of fighting each other, down to the slaughter of the last man. —2 Chronicles 20:1-29, *NW*.

⁷ Bringing the modern nations down into the

---

6. What slaughter of allied nations did Jehovah cause in the days of King Jehoshaphat?
7. What does Jehovah's bringing the nations down to the symbolic valley of Jehoshaphat mean?

symbolic "valley of Jehoshaphat" means bringing them to the situation or state of affairs where Jehovah goes into battle against them and executes his judgment upon them by utterly destroying them, without Jehovah's witnesses on earth having any part in the violent fighting. The name "Jehoshaphat" fits the occasion very nicely, for it means "Jehovah is judge," or, "Jehovah-judged (that is, vindicated)."

[8] In view of the coming execution of divine judgment upon the nations at the symbolic valley, Joel's prophecy now hurls a challenge to the nations: "Proclaim this among the nations: prepare [sanctify] war, arouse the mighty men, let all the men of war draw near, let them come up. Beat your ploughshares into swords, and your pruning-knives into spears; let the weak say, I am strong. Haste ye and come, all ye nations round about, and gather yourselves together. Thither cause thy mighty ones to come down, O Jehovah. Let the nations rouse themselves, and come up to the valley of Jehoshaphat; for there will I sit to judge all the nations round about. Put in the sickle, for the harvest is ripe: come, get you down, for the press is full, the vats overflow; for their wickedness is great. Multitudes, multitudes in the valley of decision! For the day of Jehovah is at hand in the valley of decision. The sun and the moon shall be darkened, and the stars shall withdraw their shining. And Jehovah will roar from Zion, and utter his voice from Jerusalem; and the heavens and the earth shall shake: and Jehovah will be a shelter for his people, and the refuge of the children of Israel. And ye shall know that I, Jehovah, [am] your God, dwelling in Zion, my holy mountain; and Jerusalem shall be holy, and

---

8. In view of the coming execution of judgment what challenge does Joel's prophecy hurl to the nations, and by whom is this dramatic notice being served upon all nations today?

no strangers [non-Israelites] shall pass through her any more." (Joel 3:9-17, *Da,* margin) This is a serving of notice upon the enemy nations that they will unitedly fight against Jehovah God and his people but that they will not prevail. Like Joel who prophesied in Jehovah's name, Jehovah's witnesses of today are serving this dramatic notice upon all the nations of this world today.

⁹ In Joel's prophecy the "valley of Jehoshaphat" corresponds with what the apostle John calls the "place that is called in Hebrew Har–Magedon [or, Armageddon]," for each symbolic expression describes the one place to which the worldly nations are finally gathered. Jehovah God, although almighty, does not dictate and become responsible for the plans and policies of the governors of the nations. However, by establishing his kingdom by Christ in 1914 and by having it proclaimed worldwide by his witnesses he does maneuver the nations into gathering and coming to the state of worldly affairs where a violent fight is necessary, not a fight among nations, but a fight between Jehovah God and the nations. No matter how hostile the nations may be to one another, they unite their military, financial, political, religious, educational and social forces in one common cause and effort, to fight against the Kingdom heralded by Jehovah's witnesses everywhere for the purpose of a witness to all the nations. The United Nations, which is an organization of sixty nations to perpetuate them and this world, is simply a political expression of this common cause and effort. They could totally disarm and yet they would be against the universal Sovereign Jehovah God and his King Jesus Christ. The way they deal with the witnesses who are preaching the estab-

---

9. With what other battle place does the "valley of Jehoshaphat" correspond, and how can Jehovah be said to bring them down there? Yet how and against whom do the nations prepare their war?

lished Kingdom reveals their attitude toward God. By this sure means of judging, the facts show that theirs is a hostile attitude. (John 15:18-20) The nations religiously prepare or sanctify their warfare against Jehovah God in their own self-chosen way.

¹⁰ It is a time of judgment of the nations. Jehovah who sits as the Supreme Judge calls for the nations to appear in court and to account for the record they have made by their actions toward his kingdom and its preaching representatives on the earth. He is not afraid but is eager to have all of them come in their multitudes to the "valley of decision." He has decided in favor of their destruction, and the time for carrying out this decision must come within this generation. The international "vine of the earth" has grown long enough and produced its abundant crop of worldlings opposed to God's long-preached kingdom by Christ. Now that the harvesttime is at hand, that symbolic vine must be pitched into the "press of the wine of the anger of the wrath of God the Almighty" to be trodden down and all its grapes crushed. God's own enthroned King, "The Word of God," is the Fighter whom he has appointed to do the treading underfoot.—Revelation 19:11-16, *NW*.

¹¹ It is a vast globe-encircling "vine," but God's symbolic winepress is able to accommodate it all. The vats for receiving the juice squeezed out will overflow, "for their wickedness is great." But the result of the thorough treading that the King, the Word of God, will give the "vine of the earth" in the "valley of Jehoshaphat" will be a cause of

---

10. Why does Jehovah sit in judgment of the nations, and what does he decide concerning the "vine of the earth"?
11. What will result from the treading to Jehovah and all those on his side, and what will follow his roaring from Zion?

overflowing joy of heart to Jehovah God and his King and to all who have aligned themselves with the Kingdom. (Psalm 104:15; Judges 9:13) In that time there will be no light of favorable decision from heaven for the nations. From the midst of his universal organization Jehovah will utter his judicial decision in the form of a roaring war cry. It will be followed by a shaking of all parts of the Devil's organization, invisible and visible, to pieces, like solid visible matter being converted into invisible energy by the fission of the atoms.

¹² The fact that, in that terrible day, Jehovah will be a "shelter for his people and a refuge for the children of Israel" proves that there will be survivors on earth of the universal war of Armageddon and that they will be the remnant of his 144,000 spiritual Israelites and also all those who now call upon the name of Jehovah for salvation. It proves, too, that this remnant together with all others calling upon the divine name are the common target of attack by all the worldly nations, but that Jehovah God is on their side, for they visibly represent him. After this crushing defeat is dealt out to the combined nations there will never again be a conqueror, a stranger hostile to Jehovah and his people, that will pass through their visible organization again, breaking up their organization and leading them away captive to an enemy land.

¹³ True it is that the Almighty God challenges all the nations to come and he maneuvers them into coming against his people, but it is really the

---

12. What is proved by Jehovah's being then a "shelter" and "refuge" for his people, and in what way will not "strangers" pass through Jerusalem any more?
13, 14. (a) What really drives the nations to the situation that provokes the war of Armageddon? (b) In the Revelation how was the way prepared for Babylon's overthrow, and why did the vision associate the Euphrates River with Armageddon?

selfish desires of the nations and their falling victim to unseen demon powers that drives them to the situation that provokes the war of Armageddon. The apostle John saw that fact when he got a vision of the river Euphrates upon both sides of which the ancient city of Babylon, the third world power, was built. John saw the full bowl of God's anger poured out upon this defensive and commercially useful river, as a result of which Babylon's river had its waters dried up. By this the city was weakened defensively and the way was opened in the river bed for a march to victory over antitypical Babylon by the "kings from the rising of the sun," that is, Jehovah God the King of eternity and Jesus Christ his enthroned King. As regards all earthly kings, antitypical Babylon is the "great city that has a kingdom over the kings of the earth." It was in this connection that the apostle John received the vision of the gathering of all nations to Armageddon. It is true that the ancient mountain of Megiddo or Har–Maged-on was nowhere near the river Euphrates, but was hundreds of miles to the southwest in Palestine. But by thus associating the drying up of Babylon's river-defense with the gathering of earth's rulers to famous Armageddon the Revelation to John shows that the fall of antitypical Babylon is associated with the war at Armageddon. John writes:

¹⁴ "And the sixth one [of seven angels with seven bowls of the anger of God] poured out his bowl upon the great river Euphrates, and its water was dried up, that the way might be prepared for the kings from the rising of the sun. And I saw three unclean inspired expressions that looked like frogs come out of the mouth of the dragon and out of the mouth of the wild beast and out of the mouth of the false prophet. They are, in fact, expressions inspired by demons and

perform signs, and they go forth to the kings of the entire inhabited earth, to gather them together to the war of the great day of God the Almighty. . . . And they gathered them together to the place that is called in Hebrew Har–Magedon [or, Armageddon]."—Revelation 16:12-16; 17:18, *NW*.

¹⁵ What that vision shows is this: On the one hand, the "kings of the rising of the sun," Jehovah God and Jesus Christ, with their legions of holy angels, march against antitypical Babylon, as Darius the Mede and Cyrus the Persian marched against ancient Babylon. On the other hand, the kings or rulers of the entire inhabited earth march against God's visible organization, the symbolic Armageddon or mountain of Megiddo for a decisive fight, since the mountain of Megiddo was located in the land that Jehovah gave to his chosen people. The worldly kings or rulers march unitedly against their one target of attack under the influence of unclean, demon-inspired expressions that produce signs, such as the United Nations. These unclean, froglike expressions are inspired by the great ruler of the demons, Satan the Devil, the Dragon, and they are channeled by his demons through the symbolic "wild beast," the Devil's visible organization, and through his chief predictor, adviser and director of political matters in this time of the end, the Anglo-American imperial system.* These expressions issue from the mouth and picture what these powerful, world-dominating organizations have to say to the visible rulers. As a result there is a flood of propaganda flowing forth by all the means of communication and of imparting information, the speaking voice, the

---

* See the booklet *After Armageddon—God's New World,* page 10, ¶1, 2.

15. What two marches does that vision show, and by what influences are the kings of the earth being gathered to the war?

printed page, the motion pictures, the radio and television, the demonic purpose of which is to turn the entire inhabited earth against Jehovah God and his kingdom. It is accomplishing its purpose; the kings or rulers of the entire inhabited earth are being gathered together to war, not necessarily a third world war, but the "war of the great day of God the Almighty" at the place called Armageddon.

[16] The nations of Christendom or the nations holding to a western style of democracy need not think that at Armageddon they will be fighting for God by fighting against ungodly, political communism. No; they will there make common cause with the Communist powers against God the Almighty and his kingdom by Christ. They will *all* be for this divided old world against God's incoming new world. They will all together be under demonic influence instead of under the power of Jehovah's spirit poured out upon his remnant in these last days. They will all be found fighters against God because of interfering with God's work in the earth. As the Jewish lawyer Gamaliel said to those interfering with the work of Jesus' apostles: "Do not meddle with these men, but let them alone; (because, if this scheme and this work is from men, it will be overthrown; but if it is from God, you will not be able to overthrow them;) otherwise, you may perhaps be found fighters actually against God." (Acts 5:38, 39, *NW*) The world rulers have not heeded this religious advice. They have not acted upon the timely counsel of the psalmist, who, after telling of the dashing of all the nations to pieces by Jehovah's Son, the enthroned King, said: "Now therefore be wise, O ye kings: be instructed, ye judges of the

---

16. Why will the nations fighting communism not be fighting there for God, but contrary to what advice will they have marched there?

earth. Serve Jehovah with fear, and rejoice with trembling. Kiss the son, lest he be angry, and ye perish in the way, for his wrath will soon be kindled. Blessed are all they that take refuge in him." (Psalm 2:10-12, *AS*) So their cursed march goes on.

¹⁷ To march with the nations to Armageddon means to be led by unclean inspired expressions that come, not from God, but from his great adversary, the Dragon, Satan the Devil, who is the "god of this system of things." It means to be gathered with those who are fighters against God and his universal sovereignty. It means to answer God's challenge to arm oneself and come and fight against him at the valley of decision. To take such a course, God's warning Word says, means destruction at the hands of his executional forces.

¹⁸ Those who long for life in the glorious new world that God has promised and is about to bring in cannot afford to take such a course because it is popular and all the world is taking it. They will turn a deaf ear to the unclean, demon-inspired expressions that advocate war with the unconquerable God and will listen to the words that issue from the mouth of God. They will take their stand outspokenly for Jehovah's kingdom by Christ and will support those who are its ambassadors and preachers on earth. They will be gathered by Jehovah's King to his right side together with all his sheep to whom he has promised survival of the great judgment war against all nations into God's life-giving new world.

---

17. To march with the nations to Armageddon means what for the marchers?
18. However, what will those who long for life in the new world do? And to which side will they be gathered?

CHAPTER XII

Executioners of the Divine Vengeance

THE chief executioner of God's vengeance against all his enemies in heaven and earth is his enthroned King Jesus Christ. (2 Thessalonians 1:7-9) Jesus on earth as a fleshly descendant of King David was an expression of God's so great love, and Jesus' offering himself in sacrifice under a most cruel death was an expression of his own love for God and for those who are to gain life in the new world through his perfect sacrifice. But now Jesus Christ, resurrected from the dead as a divine spirit and exalted next to God himself in heaven, is no longer a *self-sacrificing* High Priest but has other duties that have to do with the carrying out of divine justice. Since A.D. 1914 he has become a *reigning* High Priest of God and must attend to Kingdom matters as well as to priestly matters. He has become God's chief executioner.

² As the principal executional officer of the Most High God, the reigning King Jesus Christ was prefigured by his earthly ancestor King David of Jerusalem. David was Israel's second king and succeeded Saul of Gibeah as king over all Israel in 1070 B.C. When David became king the Israelites had not yet taken over all the land that God had

1. Since 1914 what has Jesus Christ become, in contrast with what he was or did when he was on earth?
2. By what Israelite king was Jesus Christ prefigured as principal executional officer, and why fittingly by him?

202

promised to the nation of Israel, "from the river of Egypt to the great river, the river Eu·phra'tes," including the Jeb'u·sites. (Genesis 15:18-21, *NW*) The Israelites had not even taken complete possession of the city of Jerusalem, but the Jebusites continued to occupy part of it, particularly the citadel or stronghold Zion. Moved to action by the spirit of God to work for the vindication of Jehovah's word concerning the Promised Land, David promptly set himself to the task of subduing all the God-given territory. To start with, King David undertook the assault of the stronghold Zion and captured it and made it his capital. "And David took up dwelling in the stronghold, and it came to be called the city of David, and David began to build all around from the Mound and inward. Thus David went on getting greater and greater, and Jehovah the God of armies was with him."—2 Samuel 5:4-10, *NW*.

³ When the Philistines, the long-time enemies of the Israelites, heard that they had made David king, they organized their forces and moved against him. David left Jerusalem and came upon them at Baal-perazim. By a miracle of God David gained the victory over the Philistines. Still unconvinced of Jehovah's universal sovereignty, the Philistines later reorganized and came again against David. Under divine direction David came around the rear of them, and at the divine signal he went into action against them. "So David did just as The [true] God had commanded him and they went striking down the camp of the Phi·lis'tines from Gib'e·on to Ge'zer [a distance of more than ten miles]. And David's fame began to go out into all the lands and Jehovah himself put the dread of him upon all the nations." (1 Chronicles

---

3, 4. (a) What kind of warfare did David carry on against the Philistines and others in the God-promised land? (b) In proof of this, what disposal did he make of much of the spoils of war?

14:8-17, *NW*) After that King David went from victory to victory over the pagan or non-Israelite occupiers of territory that Jehovah had promised to Israel. His warfare was theocratic, for it was carried on according to Jehovah's will and purpose and under his direction. David ascribed his victories to Jehovah and dedicated much of the spoils of the war to him.

⁴ "These also King David sanctified [declared sacred] to Jehovah, together with the silver and the gold that he had sanctified from all the nations that he had subdued, from Syria and from Mo'ab and from the sons of Am'mon and from the Phi-lis'tines and from Am'a·lek and from the spoil of Had·ad·e'zer the son of Re'hob the king of Zo'bah. And David proceeded to make a name when he came back from striking down the E'dom·ites in the Valley of Salt—eighteen thousand. And he kept garrisons placed in E'dom. In all E'dom he placed garrisons, and all the E'dom·ites came to be servants of David, and Jehovah kept saving David wherever he went."—2 Samuel 8:1-15, *NW*.

⁵ David merely took over all the territory that he should rule according to God's decree. By his conquests under God the boundaries of the kingdom of Israel extended from the river or torrent valley of Egypt on the south to the great river Euphrates on the north and from the wilderness on the east to the Mediterranean Sea on the west. In subduing the enemies and taking over the domination of all the God-given land David was a picture of his most illustrious son, the King Jesus Christ enthroned in the heavens since 1914. There is no question about this, for Jehovah's victorious fighting against the Philistines was used as a prophetic picture of the battle of Armageddon.

---

5. By his conquests what territory did King David take over, and how do the Scriptures make certain that he pictured the King Jesus Christ in warfare?

(Isaiah 28:21) The Scriptures are plain spoken that at that coming universal war Jehovah God will fight to victory through the anointed Son of David, the reigning King Jesus Christ. That is why Jehovah has said to his enthroned Son: "Ask of me, and I will give thee the nations for thine inheritance, and the uttermost parts of the earth for thy possession. Thou shalt break them with a rod of iron; thou shalt dash them in pieces like a potter's vessel."—Psalm 2:1-9, *AS;* Acts 4:25-28.

⁶ Christ is to wield an earth-wide dominion, and Jehovah will no more fail to subdue all nations of the earth under the feet of this Son of David than he failed to do so in the Promised Land for King David. (Daniel 7:13, 14) Jehovah's war of Armageddon by his Chief Executioner Jesus Christ will bring about this subduing of all the worldly nations in their utter destruction. With Christ in the execution work will be associated the holy angels of heaven. "He is arrayed with an outer garment sprinkled with blood, and the name he is called is The Word of God. Also the armies that were in heaven were following him on white horses, and they were clothed in white, clean, fine linen."—Revelation 19:13, 14, *NW.*

⁷ King David foresaw that his promised Son and everlasting Heir would be the Chief Executioner of Jehovah God against all the enemies in heaven and in earth. He therefore addressed his Son prophetically as his Lord or Master, saying: "Jehovah said unto my Lord, Sit at my right hand, until I put thine enemies [as] footstool of thy feet. Jehovah shall send the sceptre of thy might out of Zion: rule in the midst of thine enemies. . . .

---

6. For Christ to wield an earth-wide dominion whom will Jehovah subdue by him, and who will be associated with Christ in this?
7. How did David prophetically address his Son and everlasting Heir, and how did this one become David's superior on Zion?

Jehovah hath sworn, and will not repent, Thou art priest for ever after the order of Melchisedek. The Lord [Jehovah]* at thy right hand will smite through kings in the day of his anger. He shall judge among the nations; he shall fill [all places] with dead bodies; he shall smite through the head over a great country." (Psalm 110:1-6, Da; Matthew 22:41-45) King David sat upon the "throne of Jehovah" on Mount Zion in Palestine. (1 Chronicles 29:23, AS) Jesus, the Son of David, was invited by Jehovah to sit upon his throne at his right hand in the heavens, hence on a heavenly Mount Zion. When? In 33 (A.D.), forty days after his resurrection from the dead, when Jesus ascended from the group of his disciples on the Mount of Olives into God's presence. (Revelation 3:21) This more exalted position made the Son of David superior to his ancestor, hence made him David's "Lord."

[8] However, as soon as Jesus sat down at his heavenly Father's right hand, Jehovah did not at once command him to rule in the midst of his enemies who had caused his death on earth. He told David's Son and Lord to wait until Jehovah made those enemies his footstool. Why? Because the "appointed times of the nations" had not yet run out. Obediently David's Son and Lord sat there as High Priest after the likeness of Melchizedek until those times did end in 1914. (Hebrews 10:13, NW) In that year Jesus Christ was installed to reign as king and began ruling with authority in the midst of all his enemies. But he did not begin

---

* This is one of the 134 places where the Jewish copyists or Sopherim changed the primitive Hebrew text to read A.do.nay' ("the Lord") instead of "Jehovah." Many Hebrew manuscripts still read "Jehovah" here.

8. Why did Jesus Christ not begin to execute his enemies as soon as he sat down at his Father's right hand, nor on becoming king in 1914, nor on coming to the temple in 1918?

to execute them in that year. He turned warrior like his enthroned ancestor King David and waged war against Satan the Devil and his demon angels in the heavens and hurled them down to the earth, where that original Serpent once had bruised him at the heel. In the spring of 1918 he came to the spiritual temple with A·do·nay' Jehovah for judgment work, but even then he did not begin to execute his enemies. Jehovah cut short the days of tribulation upon the enemy organization by not proceeding to an execution of the enemy then, but permitting the enemy to remain at the earth until the time for the "war of the great day of God the Almighty." Before the complete end of the enemy organization could come then at Armageddon, Jesus' prophecy had to be fulfilled that this good news of the kingdom established in 1914 would be preached in all the inhabited earth for a witness to all the nations.—Malachi 3:1; Matthew 24:14, 21, 22.

⁹ During this in-between period of divine long-suffering and tolerance A·do·nay' Jehovah begins judgment at the house of God, the temple, by his King and High Priest, Jesus Christ, as judge. (1 Peter 4:17) This means that judgment started with those who are obedient to the good news of God, namely, the remnant of the temple stones, the remnant of the 144,000 spiritual Israelites. In the judgment then started the remnant were offered the privilege of preaching the Kingdom good news for a witness to all nations. The faithful ones answered the call to Kingdom service and took up the witness work. Finding them faithfully striving to do God's will by serving the spiritual food of God's message to the spiritually hungry, the Lord Jesus entrusted to them his belongings on earth

---

9. In this in-between period with whom did the judging start, and how was a "faithful and discreet slave" appointed over all the King's belongings?

as to a "faithful and discreet slave." The remnant were thus judged to be the slave class whom Jesus foretold he would find when he came to the temple for judgment, saying: "Who really is the faithful and discreet slave whom his master appointed over his domestics to give them their food at the proper time? Happy is that slave if his master on arriving finds him doing so. Truly I say to you, He will appoint him over all his belongings." (Matthew 24:45-47, *NW*) In 1919 the "faithful and discreet slave" class began serving as one appointed by the Lord Jesus over all his belongings, or Kingdom interests on earth, to serve the spiritual food now due.

[10] However, there is a great religious organization operating under the name of Christ and claiming to be the "house of God." It is Christendom. In this time of judgment from the temple she, too, must come under judgment according to her claims. The judgment must show whether she is true to her claims, whether she is obedient to God's commands and is a true worshiper of him, and whether she is following in Jesus' footsteps, copying his example. Because Christendom has a sham Christianity and brings reproach upon the true Christianity, because she has merely a form of godliness but proves false to its power by being worldly the same as pagans, she is judged deserving of execution at Armageddon. The shadow of the slaughter weapons of Jehovah's executioners now falls across Christendom. How may any in her not of the remnant escape destruction?

[11] The prophet Ezekiel was given a vision of how

---

10. Why must Christendom also now come under judgment, and why is she judged deserving of execution at Armageddon?

11. When was Ezekiel given a vision of how many not of the "slave" class may be spared at Armageddon, and what conditions then at the temple were enough to make such kind sigh and cry in grief?

many who are not of the "faithful and discreet slave" class will be spared suffering annihilation with Christendom and her friend, the world. Ezekiel got the vision six years before Jerusalem and her temple were destroyed by the army of the king of Babylon and all the land of Judea was desolated in 607 B.C. Jerusalem and her realm were doomed to desolation by Jehovah's executioners because the Israelites had forsaken his pure worship. As Ezekiel himself was shown in the vision, they had set up an idolatrous image provocative of Jehovah's jealousy right there in the inner court of his temple at Jerusalem. They had even drawn pictures of unclean forms of lower animal life and idols upon the temple walls, and before these hateful pictures seventy of the Israelite elders could be seen standing, offering up incense to them. Women were even carrying on the rite of weeping for the Babylonian god Tammuz, another name for Babylon's founder Nimrod. Worse still, inside the inner court and at the very entry of the temple sanctuary of Jehovah there were twenty-five men with their backs toward the temple and their faces toward the east as they worshiped the sun in the heavens. What abominations to the true God, what reproach to his clean, holy name, what profanations of his sacred temple, what shameful attempt to mix the impure false religion with the true! It was enough to make anyone with a love for Jehovah God sigh and cry in sincere grief at such detestable religious practices committed inside his typical house. Little wonder that the land of Judah was filled with violence. Jehovah purposed to have no pity on them.—Ezekiel 8:1-18.

[12] Horrifying though the picture of conditions in Jerusalem's temple was, the view of what goes on today in the modern counterpart, Christen-

---

12. Why may Christendom not expect an end different from that of Jerusalem's, and how does Ezekiel's vision show whom Jehovah has called to prepare for action?

dom's house or system of religion, is no less shocking. With the Holy Bible at hand in millions of copies for their enlightenment and correction, Christendom's worshipers follow all sorts of pagan beliefs, practices, observances and idolatries, doing so under Christ's name and at what they call the house of God. Can Christendom expect an end different from that of ancient Jerusalem? No; for with greater knowledge open to her she is more reprehensible in God's sight. A calamitous end is certain and unavoidable for her, for God has called to his executioners to prepare for action, as in Ezekiel's vision: "Then he called aloud in my hearing, and said, 'Come forward, you officers [executioners, *Mo*] of the city, armed each with his weapon of destruction!' And lo! there came from the direction of the upper gate, facing the north, six men armed each with his weapon for slaughter, and in the midst of them another man clothed in linen, with a writer's inkhorn at his side. And they came and stood beside the bronze altar."—Ezekiel 9:1, 2, *AT*.

[13] The seven men that appeared in the vision picture Jehovah's devoted servants in this time of impending destruction for Christendom. The six armed men picture Jehovah's executional forces in the heavens, the holy angels under the leadership of the Chief Executioner, Jesus Christ. They are all invisible to human eyes, so that the destruction will come out of the invisible realm and be superhuman. The seventh man has no executioner's slaughter weapon in hand and takes no part in the slaughter work, but does do a lifesaving work by the use of his writer's inkhorn. Since this linen-clad writer proves faithful to the work assigned to him he pictures a visible class on

---

13. Who are pictured by the six armed men, and who is pictured by the man in linen with no weapon but a writer's inkhorn?

earth, the "faithful and discreet slave" class, the remnant of the spiritual Israelites who have been delivered from antitypical Babylon and been reinstated in Jehovah's service. Jesus Christ is their unseen head and they work in harmony with him in connection with Christendom's execution. The visible "slave" class and the unseen executional forces under Jesus Christ at the temple are pictured as a group of seven, a group perfect in proportions for the work at hand. Being symbolized as a linen-clad man with just a writer's inkhorn at his side, the spiritual remnant or "faithful and discreet slave" class are authorized to take no violent part in the battle of Armageddon. They will not fight there.

¹⁴ What, then, is the work of the "faithful and discreet slave" class? Ezekiel's vision furnishes the answer: "Now the glory of the God of Israel had gone up from the cherubim on which it rested to the threshold of the house. Then he called to the man clothed in linen, with the writer's inkhorn at his side, and said to him, 'Pass through the city—through Jerusalem—and set a mark upon the foreheads of the men who sigh and cry for all the abominations that are done in the midst of it.' " (Ezekiel 9:3, 4, AT) It was in the year 1931 that the meaning of this vision was correctly understood,* and it was then that the divine command to them could be acted on with understanding. So particularly since then the "faithful and discreet slave" class have gone up and down Jerusalem's modern antitype, Christendom, doing the marking work. As the man in linen was to use a pen and mark foreheads, evidently going from house to house, the marking work pictured a great

---

* See pages 94-116 of Volume 1 of the book *Vindication,* published by the Watch Tower Bible & Tract Society in 1931.

14. In the vision what was the work assigned to the man in linen, and when and how did this work begin to be fulfilled in reality?

Bible educational work to be carried on throughout doomed Christendom. It was a work with God's message in written or printed form as well as spoken form that would leave a mark of identification in that part of the body where slaves were anciently branded, most easily seen to all beholders, the forehead, where one's intelligence is located. It was a witness work, for in that same year of 1931 the remnant of spiritual Israelites, the "faithful and discreet slave" class, appreciated more fully the force of Jehovah's commission to them, "Ye are my witnesses, saith Jehovah, and my servant whom I have chosen; . . . ye are my witnesses, saith Jehovah, and I am God." (Isaiah 43:10-12, *AS*) So at their international convention in Columbus, Ohio, U.S.A., on Sunday, July 26, 1931, they embraced the name by which they have since been known, "Jehovah's witnesses." They have truly lived up to that honorable name as faithful Christians.

[15] Revelation 7:1-8 disclosed that the remnant

---

15. How does Revelation picture those who do the marking work and those who are marked, and why do the latter sigh and cry?

of God's slaves would be sealed in their foreheads with the seal of the living God as members of the twelve tribes of spiritual Israel. This sealed remnant is the "man in linen" of today that marks as with pen and ink the foreheads of those sighing and crying in Christendom. Who, now, are this latter class? They are those who become the other group that is also seen in Revelation, chapter 7, namely, the "great crowd" of sheeplike ones out from whose eyes God wipes every tear so that they no longer sigh and cry. They have a respect for God and a love of righteousness, for which reason they are grieved at all the abominable things that are said and committed in antitypical Jerusalem by those who claim to be Christians against the name and pure worship of the living and true God Jehovah. They sigh and cry at the detestable things that so-called Christians teach and do at what they call the "house of God," and they long to see God's worship purified, his house cleansed and his name honored. They appreciate the final catastrophe to which the religious abominations are destined to bring it, and they yearn for relief, for deliverance from captivity in their religious prison, the "synagogue of Satan." (Revelation 2:9; 3:9) To remain prisoners there means destruction for them with Christendom at the end of this world.

¹⁶ Ezekiel's prophecy shows God hears the sighing and crying of these "other sheep," and from the "threshold of the house" to which he has come for judgment he calls to the symbolic "man in linen," the "faithful and discreet slave" class, to go to all the homes of antitypical Jerusalem and find out who are the ones that sigh and cry at the religious abominations of hypocritical Christi-

---

16. With whose salvation were the "slave" class now to concern themselves, and how do the sheeplike ones react to the "slave" class in this work?

anity and to put a mark* on their foreheads. That meant for the spiritual remnant to concern themselves about others besides just the last remaining members of the "body of Christ," the remnant of the "little flock" to whom the heavenly Father has approved of giving the heavenly kingdom with Jesus Christ. The remnant must work for others also to gain salvation in the new world, and especially to be spared through Armageddon. So they were commanded to preach the lifesaving Kingdom message to all sighing and crying, again and again, until they became marked in their foreheads, as it were, openly identifiable as true, clean worshipers of Jehovah, as "other sheep" of his Right Shepherd Jesus Christ the King. Then these would take up palm branches and hail Jehovah's enthroned King the Lamb and would publicly declare their debt of salvation to Jehovah God and his glorified Lamb. To this end the sheeplike ones treat the "man in linen" class, the remnant of Christ's brothers, kindly, helpfully, favorably, and they gratefully submit to being marked. They are gathered to the right of the King's throne at the temple.

¹⁷ The goatlike stubbornly refuse to be marked, for they are not heartsick over the religious abominations and do not sigh or cry. They are gathered to the left of the King's judgment throne.

¹⁸ The marking work by the "man in linen" comes before the execution work by the six men

---

* The Hebrew word for "mark" is *taw*, the name given to the twenty-second and last letter in the Hebrew alphabet. Originally the letter *taw* was in the form of a cross, but that does not mean that the man in linen marked foreheads with a cross. The Hebrew word *taw* means "mark" or "sign," and that is what he marked on them. What form of sign or mark it was is not revealed.

---

17. To which side of the King are the goatlike gathered, and why?
18. When was the execution work to take place, and without regard for what was it to be done, and why?

with slaughter weapons. This makes clear the purpose of the marking. When the marking work is done, Jehovah at the temple speaks to the six executioners: "And to the others he said in my hearing, Go after him through the city, and smite: let not your eye spare, neither have pity. Slay utterly the old man, the young man, and the maiden, and little children, and women; but come not near any man upon whom is the mark; and begin at my sanctuary." (Ezekiel 9:5, 6, *Da*) None of the marked people were to be executed. Only the unmarked persons were to be slain, without regard to age or sex. Even children were not to be spared, for their unmarked parents or guardians were held responsible for them.

[19] In Ezekiel's day, in the terrible slaughter that mowed down the inhabitants of Jerusalem in 607 B.C., the Babylonian armies did not spare the children. (2 Chronicles 36:17; Psalm 137:8, 9; compare, too, Hosea 10:14; 13:16.) Also in the horrible destruction that came upon the rebuilt Jerusalem in apostolic days, A.D. 70, at the hand of the Roman legions, the little children and women suffered and died along with the men. In the approaching annihilation of Christendom at Armageddon Jehovah's heavenly executioners will destroy all the unmarked persons. Age and sex will call forth no mercy. This is something serious for parents of little children to consider.

[20] The apostle Peter declared: "It is the appointed time for the judgment to start with the house of God." (1 Peter 4:17, *NW*) Correspondingly, Jehovah's command to his executional forces is for them to begin at his profaned sanctuary.

---

19. How was this illustrated in 607 B.C. and in 70 (A.D.), and how will it be true at Armageddon?
20. Where did the executional forces begin, how was this illustrated with Jerusalem's priesthood in 607 B.C., and what fact does this point up respecting Armageddon?

"Then they began at the elders who were before the house. And he said unto them, Defile the house, and fill the courts with the slain: go forth. And they went forth, and smote in the city." (Ezekiel 9:6, 7, *Da*) Quite in keeping with this divine command and its symbolic execution, Se·rai'ah the chief priest and Zephaniah the second priest, under whose very eyes the detestable, defiling religious practices were carried on at the temple of Jerusalem, were specially selected at Jerusalem's fall in 607 B.C. and were brought to Nebuchadnezzar the king of Babylon at Riblah in the land of Hamath and were put to death by him there. (2 Kings 25: 18-21; Jeremiah 52:24-27) Divine judgment thus surely took notice first of the polluted temple and its most responsible priests and then expressed itself in a way that shocked religious sensibilities. This points up the surprising fact that at Armageddon the false, worldly, hypocritical religious element will be first to be executed, and Jesus Christ the Chief Executioner will not spare Christendom's religious structure and its exalted clergy just because they are thought to be Christian.

²¹ The slaughter weapons of the heavenly executioners will hack down untold numbers at the destruction of antitypical Jerusalem, but the "man in linen" class and the marked "other sheep" will not be touched. So many will be slaughtered that it will seem as if no one will finally escape; so it seemed to Ezekiel: "And it came to pass, while they were smiting, and I was left, that I fell upon my face, and cried, and said, Ah, Lord [*A·do·nay'*] Jehovah! wilt thou destroy all the remnant of Israel in thy pouring out of thy fury upon Jerusalem? And he said unto me, The iniquity of the house of Israel and Judah is exceeding great, and

---

21. But who will not be touched there despite the extensiveness of the slaughter, and for what will Christendom have to answer, justly?

the land is full of blood, and the city full of perverseness; for they say, Jehovah hath forsaken the earth, and Jehovah seeth not. And as for me also, mine eye shall not spare, neither will I have pity: I will recompense their way upon their head." (Ezekiel 9:8-10, *Da*) Christendom's land is full of perverseness and is more bloodstained than the rest of the earth. It is only justice that she answer for this. She will. After all these years of toleration and of warning to her Jehovah will show her no pity at the end of the system of things. He will bring the penalty of her own stubborn way upon her proud head.

²² The "faithful and discreet slave" class, the symbolic man in linen, will successfully finish their work before Armageddon's execution begins. "And behold, the man clothed with linen, who had the ink-horn by his side, reported the matter, saying, I have done as thou hast commanded me." (Ezekiel 9:11, *Da*) The report must be made at the temple to Jehovah, whose name this slave class bears. Because this class does as commanded and finishes the work, Jehovah does not let his executioners touch them, but they will survive Christendom's destruction. Neither will the executioners be allowed to come near to harm the "great crowd" of formerly sighing and crying ones with marked foreheads. They, too, will survive Christendom's destruction and pass alive through the rest of the "war of the great day of God the Almighty" into his clean, godly new world.

---

22. After doing as commanded, what does the 'man in linen' class do, and what will happen to them and the ones they have marked?

CHAPTER XIII

The Chief Executioner Takes a Wife

A N EVENT spreading happiness throughout
heaven and earth takes place during the
"time of the end" of this present wicked system of things. It is the marriage of the most deserving heavenly Son of God, the beloved Lord Jesus
Christ. He is God's Chief Executioner at the end of
this system, but that office casts no gruesome black-
ness upon his record or reputation nor any shadow upon his wife. It sheds glory upon him, for
as Chief Executioner he becomes the Chief Vindicator, Justifier or Upholder of the universal
sovereignty of the Most High God, Jehovah. The
happy event began to take place after he arrived
with A·do·nay' Jehovah at the spiritual temple
in the spring of 1918. This helps to explain why
God did not permit him to push on without a
break to the war of Armageddon after hurling
Satan and his demon angels out of heaven and
down to this earth. God cut short the days of
tribulation upon Satan's organization by calling
for a halt to further violent hostilities against
Satan's organization until the day and the hour
for the foretold war of Armageddon to be opened
up. God cut short the days of tribulation because
the bride of his beloved Vindicator and Son was
involved.—Mark 13:19, 20, *NW*.

---

1. What happy event takes place in this "time of the
end," from when on, and so why did God cut short the
days of tribulation?

² Jehovah the Father does not marry his Son to an angel or to angels. (Hebrews 2:14-17) He chooses the wife for his Son and unites him to a group of lovers whom he purchases from among mankind, the congregation of 144,000 faithful followers from among men on earth. (Revelation 14:1-5) By a resurrection from the dead he joins these with his Son in heaven in a union that corresponds with his own marriagelike relationship to his entire holy heavenly organization, his "woman," the "Jerusalem above." (Galatians 4: 26, 27, *NW;* Isaiah 54:1-6, *AS*) The Son got introduced to the first members of his prospective "bride" when he was here on earth as a man.

³ The espousal or making of the marriage engagement occurred nineteen centuries ago, seemingly quite a long marriage engagement. Some time after baptizing Jesus, John the Baptist announced Jesus Christ as the Bridegroom, when he said to inquiring Jews: "I am not the Christ, but, I have been sent forth in advance of that one. He that has the bride is the bridegroom. However, the friend of the bridegroom, when he stands and hears him, has a great deal of joy on account of the voice of the bridegroom. This, indeed, has been fulfilled as my joy." (John 3:28, 29, *NW*) Jesus himself gave a parable or illustration of a king that made a marriage for his son, and by it he pictured himself there as the marriageable Son of the eternal King, his heavenly Father. In his prophecy on the "time of the end" he gave another parable and likened his faithful remnant on earth to five discreet virgins that met the bridegroom with lighted lamps on his return from the wedding. So Jesus looked for-

2. To whom does Jehovah marry his Son, and how, and in what kind of relationship?
3. When did the espousal take place, how did John the Baptist announce the Bridegroom, and how did Jesus show he looked forward to the marriage?

ward joyfully to his coming marriage in heaven. (Matthew 22:1-3; 25:1-13, *NW*) The night before his cruel death on the torture stake he comforted his faithful apostles and assured them that he was going away to prepare a place for them in his Father's house above and that, if he went away for this purpose, he would come again and receive them home to himself that they might be where he would be. He then prayed to his Father that they might be with him to behold his heavenly glory.—John 14:1-3; 17:24, *NW*.

⁴ Saul of Tarsus became a member of the bride class and was called the apostle Paul. Describing the relationship between Christ and his congregation of 144,000 anointed followers, the apostle Paul writes: "Let wives be in subjection to their husbands as to the Lord, because a husband is the head of his wife as the Christ also is the head of the congregation, he being a savior of this body. In fact, as the congregation is in subjection to the Christ, so let wives also be to their husbands in everything. Husbands, continue loving your wives, just as the Christ also loved the congregation and delivered up himself for it, that he might sanctify it, cleansing it with the bath of water by means of the word, that he might present the congregation to himself in its splendor, not having a spot or a wrinkle or any of such things, but that it should be holy and without blemish. In this way husbands ought to be loving their wives as their own bodies. He who loves his wife loves himself, for no man ever hated his own flesh, but he feeds and cherishes it, as the Christ also does the congregation, because we are members of his body. 'For this reason a man will leave his father and mother and will stick to his wife, and the two will be one flesh.' This sacred secret is great. Now

4. With what words does the apostle Paul describe the relationship between Christ and his congregation to the Ephesian Christians?

I am speaking with respect to Christ and the congregation."—Ephesians 5:22-32, *NW*.

⁵ From this explanation of a great spiritual
mystery or sacred secret it is appreciated that
Jesus Christ delivered himself up or laid down
his human life for the future life of his bride class.
He could prove his love for her in no greater
way. The members of the bride are taken from
a sinful and dying race, and their rescue from
condemnation due to sin and from its penalty
death was first necessary. Jesus took care of this
life-necessity by offering his own perfect, sin-free
life for his prospective bride and for those who
would become his earthly children in the new
world. After this it is necessary for the members
of the bride to be patterned after Christ's image
to become a suitable marriage mate to him for
eternity. That is why it was God's will for them
to dedicate themselves wholly to him as Jesus did
and then be begotten by holy spirit to become
God's spiritual children, who might be heirs of
God and joint heirs with Jesus Christ in the heavenly kingdom. "As many as did receive him, to
them he gave authority to become God's children,
because they were exercising faith in his name;
and they were born not from blood or from a
fleshly will or from man's will, but from God."
(John 1:12, 13, *NW*) God foreordained the number of the bride class to be 144,000. By begetting
them according to his own will God called them
to the bride's hope. After finishing their earthly
course faithfully in imitation of their Bridegroom,
they are declared righteous or justified in spirit
by a resurrection to divine life in the spirit realm
and they are glorified with their Bridegroom.
—Romans 8:15-18, 28-30, *NW;* 1 Timothy 3:16.

---

5. According to that, for whom did Jesus lay down his
life, and how must the bride class become a suitable
marriage mate for him?

⁶ At her espousal, at being promised in marriage to the heavenly Bridegroom, the bride class is a virgin. She is properly so, for he is Jehovah's High Priest, and in the nation of Israel Jehovah ordained that the high priest, of Levite Aaron's family, could marry only a virgin. (Leviticus 21:10-15, *NW*) On earth during the period of betrothal or espousal the bride class must jealously guard its chastity, its spiritual virginity, not becoming wedded to earthly, human organizations that would claim her love and attention and subjection and turn her away from the hope of reigning with her Bridegroom in the heavens. To the Corinthians in danger of having their affections and hopes turned aside to another the apostle Paul wrote: "I am jealous over you with a godly jealousy, for I personally promised you in marriage to one husband that I might present you as a chaste virgin to the Christ. But I am afraid that somehow, as the serpent seduced Eve by its craftiness, your minds might be corrupted away from the sincerity and the chastity that are due the Christ. For, as it is, if someone comes and preaches a Jesus other than the one we preached, . . . you easily put up with him." (2 Corinthians 11:2-4, *NW*) Paul had preached that the true Bridegroom is the one and only Jesus Christ and the marriage promised in God's Word will be only to him as husband; the bride class cannot lead a loose life spiritually and become united on earth to another leader and expect in this corrupted, violated condition to be worthy to become the heavenly bride of God's glorified Son. Such a course of "friendship with the world" is spiritual adultery. It means "enmity with God" as well as with the Bridegroom Son of God. Such unchastity brings destruction. In ancient Israel God

6. In what proper condition must the espoused class keep itself, and what would a violation of this condition mean and lead to?

decreed that the engaged virgin who committed immorality should be killed.—James 4:4; Deuteronomy 22:23, 24.

[7] There are religious churches in Christendom that claim to be the bride of Christ. The facts about them belie their claim, for they have numbered far more than 144,000, the membership of the "body of Christ," and they are committing spiritual adultery with the political and commercial rulers of this world. The Bridegroom, who accompanied A·do·nay' Jehovah to the spiritual temple in 1918, judges them as adulteresses spiritually and condemns them to destruction with Christendom. Until he came invisibly to the temple, his true bridal congregation had been traveling for almost nineteen centuries to meet him, from Pentecost of A.D. 33 when the first Christian believers were begotten to spiritual life and called to become part of Christ's bride. Today there is merely a remnant of the bride class on earth. The majority of the bride class have never seen the Bridegroom, yet they love him victoriously over this world and keep their virgin chastity amid this world.—1 Peter 1:8.

[8] In this respect they are like Rebekah the grandniece of Abraham. When Abraham wanted a wife for his beloved son Isaac he did not pick one from the Canaanites among whom he was a temporary resident. He sent his household manager out of the country to his brother Nahor's household in upper Mesopotamia. Abraham's faithful servant went with ten camels and sufficient men to arrange a marriage contract with Abraham's flesh-and-blood relations and bring

---

7. (a) What do religious churches in Christendom claim to be, but how does the Bridegroom at the temple judge them? (b) How long have the espoused class been traveling to meet him?
8. How has this class thus been like Rebekah, Abraham's grandniece?

back a suitable woman for his son Isaac. On arriving at the city of Nahor the servant was instantly put in touch with Abraham's relations. By her conduct Rebekah recommended herself as the proper woman for Isaac. So the servant closed the contract for her to become his master's son's wife. Rebekah agreed to go with Abraham's servant without delay to become Isaac's wife. "At that they sent off Rebekah their sister and her nurse and Abraham's servant and his men. And they began to bless Rebekah . . . After that Rebekah and her lady attendants rose and they went riding on the camels and following the man." (Genesis 24:59-61, *NW*) They made a long journey southward into the Negeb of Palestine. From a distance Rebekah sighted Isaac walking alone in a field. Informed that it was her promised bridegroom, she took a headcloth and covered herself and with her nurse Deborah and other lady attendants she went to meet Isaac. The servant made the introductions and "after that Isaac brought her into the tent of Sarah his mother. Thus he took Rebekah and she became his wife, and he fell in love with her, and Isaac found comfort after the loss of his mother." (Genesis 24:62-67, *NW*) No clergyman officiated there.

⁹ Isaac, whom Abraham set himself to offer as a human sacrifice to God, was a type of Jesus the lamblike Son of God, who was offered in sacrifice that all the families and nations of the earth might bless themselves in him. (Genesis 22:1-18, *NW*) Abraham his father and the great ancestor of Jesus typified Jehovah God the heavenly Father. Abraham's aged servant whom he used as his agent pictures the active force or holy spirit of God by means of which Jehovah begets

---

9. In that prophetic drama whom do Isaac, Abraham, Abraham's aged servant, the ten camels, and Rebekah picture?

the bride class and brings them to their Bridegroom. The ten camels picture God's perfect and complete Word, by means of which he sustains the bride class and imparts to them spiritual gifts

and blessings. Rebekah typifies the bride of Christ, who are taken from this far country, the earth, to serve as his wife in heaven.

¹⁰ Rebekah's nurse was named Deborah and attended her marriage and waited upon her almost till Rebekah's death. (Genesis 35:8-19) Whom, then, do Deborah and the other lady attendants who journeyed with Rebekah to the meeting of her bridegroom typify? The "great crowd" of those symbolically "dressed in white robes," with "palm branches in their hands," who serve God day and night in his temple. They are those of the "other sheep" whom the Right Shepherd now gathers and makes one flock with the remnant of the "little flock." Deborah and the other lady attendants of Rebekah were more than mere bridesmaids of today, who are simply in a bride's train at the wedding, after which they return home. Deborah and the other lady attendants left the homeland the same as did Rebekah, never to return, that they might always attend upon her. Similarly, the "great crowd" of Jehovah's temple servants forsake this world completely and accompany the remnant of the bride class on earth until these finish their journey on earth and experience the "first resurrection" in order to be united personally with their spiritual Bridegroom at his Father's house in heaven.

¹¹ The marriage of his Son begins in the "time of the end" after Jehovah takes his great power to rule as king and lays authority upon his Son to rule at his right hand. This is manifest from John's description of the circumstances: "And I heard what was as a voice of a great crowd and as a sound of many waters and as a sound of

10. How were Deborah and the other lady attendants not mere "bridesmaids," and whom do they typify?
11. How does John describe the circumstances to show when the marriage of Jehovah's Son begins?

heavy thunders. They said: 'Praise Jah, you people, because Jehovah our God, the Almighty, has begun to rule as king. Let us rejoice and be overjoyed, and let us give him the glory, because the marriage of the Lamb has arrived and his wife has prepared herself. Yes, it has been granted to her to be arrayed in bright, clean, fine linen, for the fine linen stands for the righteous acts of the holy ones.' And he tells me: 'Write: Happy are those invited to the evening meal of the Lamb's marriage.' Also he tells me: 'These are the true sayings of God.'" After that the vision of the battle of Armageddon is given, and the Bridegroom, the King of kings and Lord of lords, is pictured as riding on a white horse with his heavenly hosts also on white horses dashing to victory over the gathered enemies.—Revelation 19:6-21, *NW*.

[12] Psalm 45 also associates the marriage of the King of kings and Lord of lords with the decisive war for the vindication of Jehovah's universal sovereignty. Overflowing with happiness, the psalmist sings: "I say what I have composed touching the king. . . . Gird thy sword upon [thy] thigh, O mighty one, [in] thy majesty and thy splendour; and [in] thy splendour ride prosperously, because of truth and meekness [and] righteousness: and thy right hand shall teach thee terrible things. Thine arrows are sharp —peoples fall under thee—in the heart of the king's enemies." (Psalm 45:1-5, *Da*) The following three verses of the psalm are applied at Hebrews 1:8, 9 to the Son of God, so that we know that it is the glorified Jesus Christ, equipped for the war of Armageddon, whom the psalmist addresses. After telling of the heavenly gladness that is appointed to the King, the psalmist turns

---

12. How does Psalm 45 associate the marriage with the war for vindicating Jehovah's universal sovereignty?

to his marriage and addresses himself to the bride: "Hearken, O daughter, and consider, and incline thine ear; forget also thine own people, and thy father's house: so will the king desire thy beauty; for he is thy lord; and reverence thou him. And the daughter of Tyre shall be there with a gift; the rich among the people shall entreat thy favor. The king's daughter within the palace is all glorious: her clothing is inwrought with gold. She shall be led unto the king in broidered work: the virgins her companions that follow her shall be brought unto thee. With gladness and rejoicing shall they be led: they shall enter into the king's palace."—Psalm 45:10-15, AS.

[13] The members of Christ's bride class have to pay attention to the divine invitation and consider it, counting the cost of responding to it. They are encouraged to incline their ear favorably to it, as Rebekah did to Abraham's invitation through his aged slave. The promised Bridegroom is in heaven and they are on earth, and to be joined to him above means to have less in mind her natural, earthly people, descendants of their first father Adam. For the most part the bride class have never seen the Bridegroom, but the psalmist assures that he is fairer than the sons of men. So if they look, not at visible earthly relationships, but at the unseen Bridegroom, the King will discern in them the beauty of faith and devotion and will desire them for his bride. They must recognize him as their lord or master and must give him corresponding reverence. The bride class is really a King's daughter, for all its members when invited or called are begotten by the holy spirit of the heavenly Father, the King of eternity. Poor they may appear in human eyes, but

---

13. How do the members of the bride have to treat the divine invitation and to consider the promised Bridegroom, and how do they form a king's daughter, well-clothed, virgin?

in Jehovah the King's eyes they are gloriously attired, as if in clothing inwrought with gleaming gold and broidered, hence rare and costly. They are clothed with the "righteous acts of the holy ones," which clothe them like bright, clean, fine linen. So the Bridegroom is not ashamed to receive them in their spotlessness of chaste spiritual virginity. They enter into ecstatic happiness, for they are "invited to the evening meal of the Lamb's marriage."—Revelation 19:8, 9; 20:6, *NW;* Ephesians 5:27.

[14] The majority of the members of the bride class have finished their earthly journey and have 'rendered their calling and choosing firm for themselves.' By the "first resurrection," which began for them after *A·do·nay'* Jehovah and his Messenger of the covenant came to the temple, they have been raised to heavenly life in the likeness of their Bridegroom and been united to him at the temple. (Romans 6:5) So there is boundless rejoicing in heaven, for the heavenly Father, for the Bridegroom and for the holy angels. On earth the remnant of the bride class must still travel on through this world, keeping a virgin's chastity. But as they approach the radiant day for their own union with him in his Father's presence, they have the strengthening, refreshing companionship of an increasing group of 'virgin companions,' just as Rebekah had the companionship of Deborah and other lady attendants on her camel ride to Isaac.

[15] These are the growing numbers of the "great crowd" whom the Right Shepherd gathers and leads to fountains of waters of life, making them

---

14. What is now the case with the majority of the bride class, but what must the remnant still do, yet not alone now?
15. Who are these 'virgin companions,' and how is it that with gladness and rejoicing they are brought and enter the palace?

one flock with his remnant. Unselfishly these "other sheep" rejoice at the approach of the culmination of the marriage of the Lamb and his wife, and they offer spiritual help to the remnant to prepare for the grand occasion. Just as John the Baptist rejoiced at introducing the first of the bride class to the Bridegroom Jesus Christ on earth, so these "other sheep" now rejoice and give thanks that they are privileged to see and enjoy companionship with at least the final members of the bride class. So it is that "with gladness and rejoicing" they are being led along with the bridal remnant. They are privileged to enter into the King's palace, not by being taken to heaven with the bride, but by being brought in their white robes and with their palm branches to the temple, there to render sacred service to God day and night.

16 To accompany the virgin bride, they, too, must prove themselves virgin pure spiritually while passing through this world, leaving it behind just as Rebekah's nurse Deborah and her other lady attendants left Mesopotamia behind. The Bridegroom Shepherd does not marry them —he has only one bride—but he loves these "other sheep," and he is interested in their welfare now and forever. For them, too, he laid down his human life. For their life as well as his bride's he will fight at the battle of Armageddon. Because of their sheeplike kindness to his bride, now represented by "the least of these my brothers," they are under the shadow of his right hand and he will safeguard them from the destructions of that universal war. With unspeakable joy the bridal remnant and the "great crowd" of their virgin companions will rejoice to survive Armageddon together.

---

16. How must they prove themselves virgin and companions of the bride, and why will they survive Armageddon?

CHAPTER XIV

The Flight to Safety

TO THE generation of Jews of his day Jesus said: "Here I am sending forth to you prophets and wise men and public instructors. Some of them you will kill and impale, and some of them you will scourge in your synagogues and persecute from city to city; that there may come upon you all the righteous blood spilled on earth from the blood of righteous Abel to the blood of Zechariah son of Barachiah, whom you murdered between the sanctuary and the altar. Truly I say to you, All these things will come upon this generation. Jerusalem, Jerusalem, the killer of the prophets and stoner of those sent forth to her." (Matthew 23:34-37, *NW*) Jerusalem had a blood-stained record, not for having engaged in theocratic warfare under God, but for having shed innocent blood and done many of God's prophets to death, even the Son of God being condemned to death there. (Luke 13:33, 34) Seven centuries earlier, in Jeremiah's day, Jehovah had commented on her bloodguilt: "Also on your skirts is found the lifeblood of guiltless poor; you did not find them breaking in. Yet in spite of all these things you say, 'I am innocent; surely his anger has turned from me.' Behold, I will bring you to judgment for saying, 'I have not sinned.' " (Jeremiah 2:34, 35, *RS*) He did, in 607 B.C., when the Babylonian executioners reddened their swords and spears with her blood at her appalling over-

---

1. How did Jesus and also Jeremiah call attention to Jerusalem's bloodguilt, and how did Jehovah bring her to judgment for it?

231

throw. In the summer of A.D. 70 Jerusalem came in for another blood bath in fulfillment of Jesus' words, the Roman executioners leading off 97,000 Jewish captives after leaving 1,100,000 dead in the ruined city.

² This is a solemn warning example for Christendom, the present-day counterpart of Jerusalem and her realm of Judah. From her beginning in the fourth century, in Constantine's day, blood unjustly shed has stained Christendom's record before God, who declared to Noah after the Flood: "Your blood of your souls shall I ask back. From the hand of every living creature shall I ask it back; and from the hand of man, from the hand of one who is his brother, shall I ask back the soul of man. Anyone shedding man's blood, by man will his own blood be shed, for in God's image he made man." That divine covenant concerning the sanctity of blood is everlasting. It still stands, like its symbol the rainbow. (Genesis 9:1-6, 12-16, *NW*) Christendom, not to mention the whole world, has a frightful blood debt to settle according to God's covenant concerning blood. Her thousands of wars, besides religious inquisitions and crusades, prior to 1914 have expended the lives of countless millions. Her two world wars since 1914, both of which started within her realm, were the most sanguinary of all; and the dreaded third world war promises to be the greatest spiller of blood, the most costly of all in human lives, because Christendom is now armed with atomic or nuclear weapons of mass destruction.

³ Those wars were not theocratic. Jehovah's

2. Why is that a solemn warning example to Christendom, and according to what covenant does she have a blood debt to settle?
3. What kind of wars were those, but why more is Christendom under bloodguilt that calls for a blood avenger?

spiritual Israelites have not fought in those wars, for their weapons of combat are spiritual, harmless to the flesh. Christendom stands under bloodguilt, not only because of those wars, but more so because of taking the lives of many of the spiritual Israelites, the holy ones of Jehovah God. Of Christendom in particular it can be said that she is "drunk with the blood of the holy ones and with the blood of the witnesses of Jesus." (Revelation 17:6, *NW*) This makes her only more like her ancient type, unfaithful Judah and Jerusalem. Armageddon draws near when the blood avenger brings her blood upon her.

⁴ All the people of Christendom who approve and uphold the record and traditions of Christendom have a society responsibility for her bloodguilt and have to face a settlement with God at Armageddon. They face destruction for their common guilt. Is there no way to fly to safety and survival? Yes; and in his laws to ancient Israel God provided a type of the way to flee to safety before his Avenger of blood strikes at Armageddon. This type was that of the "cities of refuge." These cities were provided, not for the willful murderer, but for the unintentional killer. "The cities must serve you as a refuge from the blood avenger, that the manslayer may not die until he stands before the assembly for judgment. . . . Three cities you will give on this side of the Jordan and three cities you will give in the land of Canaan. As cities of refuge they will serve. For the sons of Israel and for the temporary resident and for the settler in the midst of them these six cities will serve as a refuge, for anyone to flee there that fatally strikes a soul unintentionally." (Numbers 35:9-15, *NW*) The antitypical cities of refuge are therefore for

---

4. Who share a society responsibility with Christendom, and how was the way to flee from the Avenger of blood typified, and for whom?

those who go to make up the spiritual Israelites and for those who go to make up the "great crowd" of companions pictured by the non-Israelite temporary resident and the settler in ancient Israel.

[5] It would do no good for the willful murderer to flee to the nearest city of refuge. After he would be tried and his willful intent to kill was proved, he was to be expelled from the city and turned over to the hands of the blood avenger, the proper executioner. "And you must take no ransom for the soul of a murderer who is deserving to die, for without fail he should be put to death." (Numbers 35:16-21, 30, 31, NW) But if it was unexpectedly without hostility and not seeking another's injury that an Israelite or a non-Israelite killed someone, he could preserve his life by flight to the nearest city of refuge before he was overtaken by the pursuing avenger of blood. He now stood trial before the assembly. "Then the assembly must judge between the striker and the avenger of blood according to these judgments. And the assembly must deliver the manslayer out of the hand of the avenger of blood and the assembly must return him to his city of refuge to which he had fled, and he must dwell in it until the death of the high priest who was anointed with the holy oil." "It is then that the manslayer may return and he must enter into his city and into his house, into the city from which he had fled."—Numbers 35:22-25 and Joshua 20:1-9, NW.

[6] All six cities of refuge were given to the Levites, one of them being Hebron belonging to the Levite priests. So if a Levite or a priest killed anyone accidentally within such a city or its pas-

---

5. How did flight to a refuge city not benefit a willful murderer but benefit an unintentional killer?
6. How was a Levite or priest affected by killing unintentionally?

ture grounds, he had to remain in such a city. He lost the privilege of going up to the sacred tabernacle or to the temple at Jerusalem and performing his regular Levite or priestly duties there, until the high priest then active in office died.

⁷ Who, then, is the blood avenger or "go'el" before whom those having bloodguilt in the divine sight must flee? In typical Israel the blood avenger was the nearest male relative of the person killed. (2 Samuel 14:7-11) In fact, the word "go'el" came to mean "kinsman with the right to repurchase (or redeem)," such as Boaz was to the widowed Naomi and her daughter-in-law Ruth. (Ruth 2:20; 3:12, 13; 4:1-10, NW) At Armageddon Jehovah's Avenger of blood will be his Chief Executioner, his King Jesus Christ. Nineteen centuries ago he became a blood relative of all humankind by emptying himself of his heavenly glory and becoming perfect flesh; "who was produced out of a woman and who came to be under law." (John 1:14 and Galatians 4:4, NW) Jesus' perfect human life was equivalent to that which the first man Adam enjoyed in the paradise of Eden. He surrendered this sinless life in death as a sacrifice and, after his resurrection from death, he presented its value to God for the sake of Adam's dying descendants. He thus became mankind's Redeemer, hence our closest relative. At the same time his self-sacrifice proved him to be the acting High Priest, sworn into office by Jehovah God.

⁸ What, then, is the antitypical city of refuge? Since the manslayer was required to remain in the city of refuge until the acting high priest

---

7. Who is the blood avenger before whom to flee now, and how so?
8. What, then, is the antitypical city of refuge, how must the covenant violator proceed, and how did Saul's case illustrate this?

died, the antitypical city of refuge must be Jehovah's provision for protection from death for violating the divine covenant concerning the sanctity of blood by our coming and remaining under the benefits of the active service of his High Priest Jesus Christ. The covenant violator must seek God's forgiveness and cancellation of his sin through faith in the lifeblood of the High Priest. He must show his sincere repentance over having committed a violation by obediently remaining under this divine provision through Christ, trusting in the righteousness and the good offices of the High Priest. Here, then, is the only practical arrangement to which to flee for those inside Christendom and outside her who are sharing in bloodguilt before God's Avenger of blood. Remember the apostle Paul, who at first was Saul of Tarsus. As a fanatical Pharisee he persecuted the Christian congregation and had many put to death, violating the covenant concerning blood. "Nevertheless," he says, "I was shown mercy, because I was ignorant and acted with a lack of faith." That was why the Avenger of blood, the resurrected Jesus Christ, did not put him to death when he met him on the road to Damascus. Then Saul repented and rose, got baptized and washed away his sins by calling upon the name of the Lord Jesus Christ. (Acts 7:58; 8:1; 9:1-19; 22:4-16; 26:9-19; 1 Timothy 1:13-16, *NW*) Shielding from execution by the divine Avenger of blood lies only in taking a course like Paul's.

[9] Today bloodguilt rests heavily upon Christendom and upon all the world. Many persons, because they have not directly killed a man or directly gone to war, are unaware of their personal share in the guilt. Many have engaged in

---

9. Why are many, not directly killers, sharers in bloodguilt, and so who will not pass them by?

the persecution of Jehovah's witnesses that has
resulted in the death of many of these, some even
killing these witnesses of Jehovah and thinking
they were thus rendering sacred service to God.
(Matthew 24:9; John 16:2, NW) Just because a
priest or clergyman of Christendom has imparted
his blessing, some have felt authorized to kill
fellow men and to be without bloodguilt before
God. But coming under such priest or clergyman's
blessing was not a coming into the city of refuge
of Jehovah's High Priest Jesus Christ. Religious
and patriotic feelings do not excuse. Those with
such feelings who approve, aid and back up either
persons that directly commit bloodshed or propaganda and movements that lead to spilling of
innocent blood become like unintentional or acci-
dental killers in Israel. They are parties to the
crime and come under a society responsibility
or community responsibility that the God of justice cannot and does not pass by, neither his
Avenger of blood.—Deuteronomy 21:1-9, NW.

¹⁰ Many or all of the remnant of spiritual Israelites were under such a responsibility as unintentional killers before they took the course that
resulted in their being sealed as members of the
144,000. Whether Jehovah held those of the original remnant guilty as regards bloodshed for their
displeasing course during World War I, he must
be left to judge. At any rate, they have repented
of their shortcomings then and have fled to the
antitypical city of refuge under Jesus Christ. All
those who, since 1919, have become members of
the remnant or of the "great crowd" of antitypical "temporary residents" and "settlers" in
spiritual Israel have likewise had to escape unintentional bloodguilt by fleeing to the antitypical

---

10. Why have those of the remnant and those of the
"great crowd" been obliged to flee to the antitypical
refuge city, to abide there?

city of refuge to be safe from destruction at Armageddon. There all must abide under God's mercy through his acting High Priest.

[11] If an unintentional manslayer ventured outside his refuge city before the high priest's death, what? "But if the manslayer should at all go out of the boundary of his city of refuge to which he may flee, and the avenger of blood does find him outside the boundary of his city of refuge and the avenger of blood does slay the manslayer, he has no bloodguilt. For he ought to dwell in his city of refuge until the high priest's death and after the high priest's death the manslayer may return to the land of his possession." (Numbers 35:26-28, *NW*) Should those of the remnant of spiritual Israelites and those of the "great crowd" become self-reliant and leave the city of refuge by losing faith in the High Priest's sacrifice and trusting no more in its covering of sins, they expose themselves to destruction at Armageddon. There the divine Avenger of blood will suddenly come upon them and execute them, without any bloodguilt to himself but rather vindicating God's covenant concerning the sanctity of the blood of His creatures.

[12] Those of the remnant must keep within the antitypical city of refuge till they faithfully finish their course in death and forever sacrifice their human nature. Since Christ's sacrifice applies only to those having human nature, the High Priest dies, as it were, to them, in the sense that he no more needs to act in their behalf with the merit of his human sacrifice, for in the resurrection they are raised to spirit life with the "di-

---

11. What happened if an unintentional manslayer went outside the refuge city before the high priest's death, and how could this happen to any of the remnant or of the great crowd?
12. How long must the remnant keep within the antitypical refuge city, and how long the great crowd?

vine nature." (2 Peter 1:4) Those of the "great crowd" of antitypical "temporary residents" or "settlers" must "have washed their robes and made them white in the blood of the Lamb" before Armageddon and they must confine themselves to the antitypical city of refuge beyond Armageddon and to the end of the thousand-year reign of Christ. When they attain to human perfection by that time, Christ hands them over for the final test of their integrity by Satan's loosing and for the faithful to be justified by God himself to everlasting life in the endless world. Then his High Priest will, so to speak, die to them, for he will no more need to act in their behalf with the cleansing blood of his sacrifice.

[13] Jesus Christ, the Avenger of all human blood, now stands poised to execute all those of the earth under bloodguilt at Armageddon. "For see! the LORD [Jehovah] is coming out of his place, to punish the inhabitants of the world for their guilt; and the earth will uncover her blood, and will no more conceal her slain." (Isaiah 26:21, AT) There all mankind, Christendom and all, will be brought face to face with their joint responsibility for the blood of all those unrighteously slain, on a larger scale than Jerusalem and Jewry did A.D. 70. (Matthew 23:33-38) They will be made to pay the penalty. The earth must be cleansed of all such blood that has soaked it. The only way to flee to safety is to take the road that Jehovah's Word marks out to the antitypical city of refuge and to continue dwelling in it under benefit of the acting High Priest, Jesus Christ. There is no other way to survive Armageddon.

[14] Time grows shorter. In view of the threaten-

---

13. Where will the Avenger of all human blood execute the guilty, and why, and what is the way to survive the general execution?
14. Like whom is it now the course of wisdom to act without delay for preservation?

ing destruction it is the course of wisdom to act without delay, as did the Gibeonites of old. The Gibeonites were not Israelites, hence do not typify the spiritual Israelites. They were Canaanites who came under the curse that Noah pronounced upon their forefather Canaan. (Genesis 9:22-25; 10:15-19; 2 Samuel 21:2) The iniquity of the Amorites had come to completion, and the Israelites under Joshua, Moses' successor as leader, had crossed the Jordan River by a miracle and had entered the land of Canaan, the Promised Land. Jericho's walls had fallen flat before them, and they had reduced the city of Ai to a permanent mound of desolation. The Gibeonites realized that Jehovah was fighting for Israel and was using Joshua and the Israelites as his executioners in destroying the pagan inhabitants who had defiled the land with bloodshed and detestable idolatries.

¹⁵ The inhabitants of Gibeon, Chephirah, Beeroth and Kiriath-jearim now stood in line to be executed as pagan Canaanites. They did not want to die; they would rather enjoy life, even if as subjects of the Jehovah-fearing Israelites. They resorted to shrewdness to trick the Israelites into making a covenant with them to let them live. They sent ambassadors to Joshua at Gilgal near the Jordan River, and these pretended to come from a very distant land outside the territory whose inhabitants were condemned to extermination. Out of regard for the name of Jehovah they asked for a covenant to be made with them. Joshua and the Israelite princes accepted the seeming evidence that they offered to their claims; "at the mouth of Jehovah they did not inquire. And Joshua went to making peace with them and concluding a covenant with them to let them live, and so the chieftains of the assembly

---

15. By what procedure did the Gibeonites and their neighbors come to be put in a safe place?

swore to them." (Joshua 9:1-15, *NW*) This put the Gibeonites in a safe place.

¹⁶ Three days later the Israelites learned the truth, and they came upon their cities. The Israelites were held back from putting the inhabitants to the sword. The Israelite chieftains explained: "We for our part have sworn to them by Jehovah the God of Israel, and now we are not allowed to hurt them. This is what we shall do to them while letting them live, that no indignation may come upon us over the oath that we have sworn to them. . . . Let them live and let them become gatherers of wood and drawers of water for all the assembly, just as the chieftains have promised them." Joshua then informed the Gibeonites: "Now you are cursed people, and a slave's position and being gatherers of wood and drawers of water for the house of my God will never be cut off from you." Thus the Gibeonites became menial temple servants with thankfulness, grateful to be spared alive.—Joshua 9:16-27, *NW*.

¹⁷ Aptly the Gibeonites picture the "great crowd" not spiritual Israelites. Joshua, whose name is spelled "Jesus" in the Greek Septuagint Version of the Hebrew Scriptures, pictures the glorified Jesus Christ, Jehovah's Chief Executional Officer. He cannot be tricked, but he appreciates the desire and effort of the antitypical Gibeonites to live. The only way they can enter into an arrangement with him to spare them from execution is for them publicly to declare their faith in Jehovah as the true God and live as being no part of this world condemned to destruction. Then they have to submit to the service of the Greater Joshua, Jesus Christ, and become humble slaves of Jehovah, rendering sacred service to him

---

16. What was done with them when the Israelites learned the truth about them?
17 Whom do the Gibeonites typify, and how does it befall these like the Gibeonites?

at his spiritual temple under the guidance of the remnant of spiritual Israelites, the "faithful and discreet slave" class. Those who become antitypical Gibeonites quickly take advantage of the remaining time before Armageddon to fulfill these requirements, and they win the promise of being spared alive.

¹⁸ The spiritual Israelites may not despise this divine provision through the Greater Joshua for these antitypical Gibeonites to live and survive Armageddon. They must work for as many of these as possible to survive, more, not less, of them. Once the first Israelite king, Saul of Gibeah, transgressed upon the covenant and tried to blot the Gibeonites out of the land because they were not Israelites. The bloodguilt for this rested upon Saul's house even after he died in battle. So it became necessary for seven of his male descendants to be killed and hanged in order to wipe out the bloodguilt of Saul's family. This satisfied the Gibeonites. It met God's requirement and he stopped the famine in Israel.—2 Samuel 21:1-9.

¹⁹ Jehovah will avenge his modern-day antitypical Gibeonites if any spiritual Israelite should try to abuse his position and try to injure these temple servants instead of seek their welfare. Let those who try to destroy these antitypical Gibeonites be, not any of us, but the ungodly powers of this world. For trying to do so let them experience what five kings of the Amorites did who formed a league against the Gibeonites. They wanted to destroy the Gibeonites because they had come to peaceful terms with Joshua and Israel. They laid siege to Gibeon. The Gibeonites sent word to Joshua to come save them. Joshua made an all-night

---

18. How was King Saul's mistreatment of the Gibeonites settled for with his household? So how should spiritual Israelites act toward antitypical Gibeonites?

19. Who will avenge abused antitypical Gibeonites, and what non-Israelite kings should we avoid being like?

march to the rescue. Jehovah told him not to be afraid of the combined enemy.

20 When Joshua took the enemy by surprise, then Jehovah did his part. "Jehovah went throwing them into confusion before Israel, and they began to slay them with a great slaughter at Gibeon and went pursuing them by way of the ascent of Beth-ho'ron and slaying them as far as A·ze'kah and Mak·ke'dah. And it came about that while they were fleeing from before Israel and were on the descent of Beth-ho'ron Jehovah hurled great stones from the heavens upon them as far as A·ze'kah, and more got to die who died from the hailstones than those whom the sons of Israel killed with the sword." Then a great miracle took place, the natural mechanics of which have not been explained to this day. Joshua saw that the sun was about to set and the moon was coming up, and he wanted more daylight to pursue the enemy to their utter annihilation. "And he went on to say before the eyes of Israel: 'Sun, be motionless over Gib'e·on, and, moon, over the low plain of Ai'ja·lon.' Accordingly the sun kept motionless and the moon did stand still until the nation could take vengeance on its enemies. Is it not written in the book of Ja'shar? And the sun kept standing still in the middle of the heavens and did not hasten to set for about a whole day. And no day has proved to be like that one, either before it or after it, in that Jehovah listened to the voice of a man, for Jehovah it was who was fighting for Israel. After that Joshua and all Israel with him returned to the camp at Gil'gal."
—Joshua 10:1-15, *NW*.

21 The deliverance of the non-Israelite Gibeonites was one of the most spectacular rescues in

---

20. How did Jehovah then perform his part, even to 'listening to the voice of a man'?
21. By what act were the Gibeonites delivered, and of what is this a strong assurance respecting Armageddon?

all human history. A true "act of God" made it such. He performed his unusual act that it might serve as a type of his still greater act at the coming battle of Armageddon, when he will vindicate his own universal sovereignty and deliver his people from their enemies. In foresight he inspired his prophet Isaiah to write: "For Jehovah will rise up as on mount Perazim, he will be moved with anger as in the valley of Gibeon; that he may do his work, his strange work, and perform his act, his unwonted act. Now therefore be ye not scorners, lest your bonds be made strong; for I have heard from the Lord Jehovah of hosts a consumption, and [one] determined, upon the whole land." (Isaiah 28:21, 22, *Da*) While divine victory was given to Joshua and the Israelite armies at the battle of Gibeon, it must be kept in mind that it was the Gibeonites who were preserved and rescued there from their overwhelming enemies. No stronger assurance could there be than this that in the "war of the great day of God the Almighty," when he will perform his unusual act, it will be the present-day antitypical Gibeonites, the "great crowd" of temple servants, that will be preserved and delivered so as to survive the battle of Armageddon.

²² As for the enemies, there will be a thorough annihilation of them down to the last individual, but victory will crown the Greater Joshua, Jesus Christ the King, and all the spiritual Israelites who uphold his righteous execution of the enemies.

---

22. But what about the enemies then, and the antitypical Israelites?

CHAPTER XV

Fighting for Life Now as Jehovah's Witnesses

WHEN Jehovah God enthroned Jesus Christ as King on the heavenly Mount Zion A.D. 1914 and sent out the scepter of his might, he said to the new King: "Rule in the midst of thine enemies." (Psalm 110:1, 2, *Da*) This meant letting the enemy remain for the length of the "time of the end" to permit them to display whether they would peaceably submit to the new theocratic King, yield their national sovereignties to him and give up their ideas of world domination or not. During the more than forty years since the new King's installation the nations of earth, and particularly those that claim to be Christian, have proved that they are foes of the kingdom of Jehovah God by Jesus Christ. As a symbol of their purpose to hold control of the earth by their own means of preserving peace and security, the nations formed the international organization, the United Nations, in 1945, immediately after World War II. Outstandingly the clergy of Christendom have approved of this political successor to the defunct League of Nations and they pray and hold religious masses for it and trust in it to prevent the self-suicide of the nations. In complete contrast with this, Jehovah's witnesses have raised up the Signal of God's kingdom and have advertised it as the only world gov-

1. What shows that since 1914 Jesus Christ has had to rule in the midst of enemies, and why have Jehovah's witnesses been obliged to stand and fight for their lives?

ernment to which to pin mankind's hope. Down to the present moment they have done this by an ever mightier fulfillment of Jesus' prophecy concerning this time of the end: "This good news of the kingdom will be preached in all the inhabited earth for the purpose of a witness to all the nations, and then the accomplished end will come." (Matthew 24:14, *NW*) This has required Jehovah's witnesses on earth amidst their King's enemies to stand and fight incessantly for their lives.

[2] All this is simply in agreement with the typical picture in the Bible. Jesus Christ who reigns since 1914 is the Son of David and was typified by King David. From his days as a shepherd boy David was a fighter, engaging in combat not only with a lion and a bear but also with the Philistine giant named Goliath, whom David vanquished with a stone to the forehead from his shepherd sling that he swung in the name of Jehovah of armies. So David began fighting the "wars of Jehovah" in theocratic warfare. (1 Samuel 17:34-54; 25:28, *NW*) Saul the king of Israel came to be jealous of David's popularity and tried various ways to bring about his death. Finally he outlawed him. David fled for his life. King Saul persistently hunted him down, but without success. In all his fight for survival David never fought against King Saul, for Saul was anointed at Jehovah's command. David never dared to do Jehovah's anointed one harm, but waited upon Jehovah to remove the unfaithful king and make way for David to come to the throne of Israel.

[3] King Saul had a son named Jonathan, twenty-five to thirty years older than David. David's

---

2. How does their experience agree with that of David before becoming king?

3. What were Jonathan's attitude and conduct toward David?

exploits as a fighter of the wars of Jehovah awakened no jealousy in the heart of Jonathan the heir apparent to the throne. They only caused him to love David with a love that surpassed that of a man for a woman. He tried to shield David and aided in his escape to safety. He entered into a covenant with David for continuous peaceful relations between his own household and David's. Jonathan went to David in the wilderness and encouraged him, saying: "The hand of Saul my father will not find you and you yourself will be king over Israel and I myself shall become second to you." (1 Samuel 18:1-3; 23:16-18, *NW*) Jonathan did not begrudge David the throne of Israel, for he recognized him as Jehovah's anointed. He submitted to the theocratic decision.

[4] The persecutions upon David picture those upon the faithful anointed followers of Jesus Christ, the spiritual Israelites, and notably so in the "time of the end." David's lover Jonathan failed to come to the throne of Israel and pictures lovers of the Greater David, Jesus Christ, who do not come to the heavenly throne. In being so much older than David and in having fought the wars for Jehovah for more than twenty-five years before David, Jonathan may well picture that long line of witnesses of Jehovah before Christ, which extends all the way back to Abel the first martyr for Jehovah. All these witnesses entertained loving hopes for the coming of the Messiah or Christ. John the Baptist, the last of the pre-Christian witnesses, loved Jesus Christ, the Greater David, and was pleased to work for His increase. (Hebrews 11:1 to 12:2, *NW;* 1 Peter 1:10-12; John 3:27-30) That none of the pre-Christian witnesses will be in the heavenly throne with him, Jesus showed in his comment on John the Baptist: "Among those born of women there

---

4. Before meeting David, whom may Jonathan well picture?

has not been raised up a greater than John the Baptist; but a person that is a lesser one in the kingdom of the heavens is greater than he is." (Matthew 11:11, *NW*) These ancient witnesses gave proof of their faith in Jehovah and of their hope in his Messiah, just as Jonathan did before he met David, the anointed of Jehovah.

⁵ Again there has appeared a loving class like Jonathan since the coming of Jesus Christ to the temple and the sealing of the remnant of the 144,000 spiritual Israelites. Notably since 1932 they have been gathered together into association with the remnant. They have heard "this good news of the kingdom" and have set their affections upon the enthroned Jesus Christ as Jehovah's Anointed and as the rightful ruler of the new world. They love him as King and tender their unbreakable allegiance to him, following in His footsteps. They recognize that the spiritual remnant are the last members on earth of the "body of Christ" and that they are, what Jesus called them, "the least of these my brothers." So they do not let themselves be influenced by the hatred and persecution upon the remnant by the rulers of Christendom, typified by King Saul, David's persecutor. They express practical love for the remnant of the "body of Christ" by doing good to them, shielding them, helping them out of their difficulties, risking their lives for them, and aiding them in preaching the "good news of the kingdom."

⁶ They do not begrudge the remnant an exalted place with Jesus Christ in his heavenly throne, but recognize the theocratic arrangement and

---

5. Since Christ's coming to the temple and sealing his remnant, what loving class like Jonathan has appeared, and how have they been expressing their love?
6. How are they theocratic-minded, and what conduct of David toward Jonathan's house shows whether they will be spared?

are gratefully pleased to take a secondary place, remaining on earth under the kingdom of the new world. For this loving devotion Jesus the Greater David will spare them, seeing to it that they gain earthly life in the new world, just as King David spared Jonathan's offspring, not holding them guilty because of their family relationship to King Saul. Jonathan's descendants survived to at least ten generations after his son Me·phib'o·sheth. (2 Samuel 9:7, 8; 19:27-30; 1 Chronicles 8:34-40) Thus Jonathan, after he met David the giant killer, pictured the "great crowd" in white robes who hail Jehovah on his throne and his Lamb with palm branches.

⁷ King Saul and his oldest son Jonathan died in the battle of Mount Gilboa not far from Megiddo. The tribe of Judah then made David their king at the city of Hebron. About seven and a half years later he was anointed as king over all twelve tribes of Israel. Not long afterward he established his national capital at Jerusalem.

⁸ In the theocratic warfare that King David waged for subjugating all the Promised Land, he had valiant Israelite armies under courageous Jehovah-fearing commanders. (1 Chronicles 11: 10 to 12:39) Whom did these typify? The remnant of the spiritual Israelites on earth today since 1919, who are the joint heirs of the Greater David, the King Jesus Christ. The Kingdom is not earthly, but heavenly, spiritual. Correspondingly the remnant's warfare is not a warfare with earthly governments, with human armies, nor with earthly weapons of the flesh. "For," says the apostle Paul, "though we walk in the flesh, we do not wage warfare according to what we are in the flesh. For the weapons of our warfare

---

7. How did David become king, with his capital at Jerusalem?

8. Whom did King David's armies of Israelites typify, and how do these war?

are not fleshly, but powerful by God for overturning strongly entrenched things. For we are overturning reasonings and every lofty thing raised up against the knowledge of God, and we are bringing every thought into captivity to make it obedient to the Christ." (2 Corinthians 10:3-5, *NW*) Now, by preaching the "good news of the kingdom," the remnant are fighting the Devil's anti-Kingdom propaganda and are endeavoring to bring the thoughts of the sheeplike people into captivity to make their thoughts obedient to the reigning Christ.

⁹ In this fight in support of Christ's kingdom the remnant are bitterly opposed by the policy makers of this world, especially the religious rulers and guides like jealous King Saul. The remnant are subjected to intense persecution and world hatred. But they do not fight back with material weapons of the flesh, for they are not authorized by the great Theocrat Jehovah to fight with such. They know that the intent of such opposition and persecution is to make them quit preaching the good news and living for the new world. They know the ones who are invisibly behind all this antagonism and persecution and that the fight is really a spiritual fight with such invisible forces. They know they have to "stand firm against the machinations of the Devil; because we have a fight, not against blood and flesh, but against the [nonblood and flesh] governments, against the authorities, against the world-rulers of this darkness, against the wicked spirit forces in the heavenly places." (Ephesians 6:11, 12, *NW*) They know, too, that the Dragon, Satan the Devil, has been cast out of heaven down to the earth and that they, as the remnant of the royal seed of God's "woman," are the target of the

9. With what are the remnant fighting back the visible opposition, and against whom do they really have their fight?

Dragon's attack: "And the dragon grew wrathful at the woman, and went off to wage war with the remaining ones of her seed, who observe the commandments of God and have the work of bearing witness to Jesus." (Revelation 12:17, *NW*) It would be useless and untheocratic now to resort to worldly weapons of the flesh. On this account the remnant obey the inspired command to take up the "complete suit of armor from God." In this armor they are making a victorious fight for life as His witnesses.—Ephesians 6:13-18, *NW*.

¹⁰ The remnant are not now alone on earth in this fight, and the ancient type illustrated this fact. In the wars of ancient Israel there were engaged on their side not only the registered armies of natural Israel but also Jehovah-fearing foreigners of real devotion, and not mere mercenaries. The divine Record mentions with honor that in David's armies there were enlisted such foreigners as Uriah the Hittite; Zelek the Ammonite; Ithmah the Moabite; Ittai the Gittite, a Philistine of Gath, together with six hundred other Gittites; and also King David's special bodyguard known as the Cherethites and the Pelethites, who appear to have been non-Israelites. (2 Samuel 11:6-17; 23: 37-39; 1 Chronicles 11:26, 46; 2 Samuel 15:18, 19; 8:18; 20:7, 23; 1 Kings 1:38, 44; 1 Chronicles 18:17) They were sanctified for theocratic warfare the same as the Israelites.

¹¹ In whom do those non-Israelite theocratic warriors of ancient Israel find their antitype today? In the "great crowd" of those not spiritual Israelites whom the Right Shepherd, the Greater David, gathers to the side of the remnant of the "little flock." By lining up with the remnant they

---

10. Are the remnant now alone on earth in this fight, and how was it shown in the type of King David's armies?
11. In whom do such ancient non-Israelite warriors find their antitype today, and why?

make themselves also targets of the wrathful Dragon. They, too, have to engage in the theocratic war against him and his invisible spirit forces. They are valiant fighters, expert at using the same spiritual weapons that the remnant does. In the fight they keep unity with the remnant and unity in their own ranks. Together with the remnant they march forward under their invincible Leader and Commander, Jesus Christ the Greater David.

¹² Not being sealed spiritual Israelites or members of the "chosen race, a royal priesthood, a holy nation, a people for special possession," they are not "saints" or sanctified ones. (1 Peter 2:5, 9, *NW*) They are not part of the "ones chosen according to the foreknowledge of God the Father, with sanctification by the spirit," and in the new world they will not share in the heavenly "inheritance among all the sanctified ones." (1 Peter 1:1, 2 and Acts 20:32; 26:18, *NW*) They are not of that congregation of spiritual Israelites, "who have been sanctified in union with Christ Jesus, called to be holy ones [or, saints]." (1 Corinthians 1:2; 14:33, *NW*) However, since in ancient times wars were "sanctified" and those in the armies of Israel were sanctified for the theocratic warfare, the "great crowd" today who are not spiritual Israelites are only sanctified as theocratic warriors and as such they are required to measure up to the holy standards of the theocratic camp in order to engage in today's theocratic warfare. That is, they are sanctified for the warfare and must aid in keeping the camp of the theocratic warriors clean, unworldly, pleasing to God.—Jeremiah 51:27-29; Isaiah 13:1-4 and Joel 3:9, *AS*, marginal reading.

---

12. Though not spiritual Israelites, for what are they specially sanctified, and so what standards must they measure up to?

[13] Today Jehovah's witnesses are making a stand for their lives in the face of mounting opposition, international hatred and the world-wide threat to blot them out. This was foreshown in the prophetic drama of Mordecai and Esther, in the fifth century before Christ. Medo-Persia, the fourth world power, was dominating the earth, with 127 provinces from India on the east to Ethiopia on the southwest. In the preceding century a remnant of the Jews had gone back to Jerusalem, rebuilt the temple of Jehovah and restored his worship at the place where he had put his name. The province of Judah under Jerusalem was one of the 127 provinces of Persia, where Jews were to be found. Mordecai had not returned to Jerusalem, but he sat officially in the gate of King Ahasuerus at the imperial capital, Shushan the Castle. He had adopted his much younger cousin Hadassah, that is, Esther, for she was orphaned.

[14] Embarrassingly King Ahasuerus' authority was challenged by his wife Vashti. So he deprived her of her queenship. Later his counselors advised that he send commissioners throughout all the Persian empire and collect together at Shushan the Castle all the beautiful virgin young women to be given a beauty treatment and the one that pleased the king most should be made queen instead of Vashti. To this the king agreed. Esther was found to be a beautiful virgin and was brought from Mordecai's home to the king's house of the women for her twelve-months-long treatment. One after another the fully conditioned virgins were individually brought in for a visit with the king. In time Esther's turn came. She was brought in to the king's royal palace. He

---

13. In what prophetic drama in the Persian empire was it foreshown that Jehovah's witnesses would make a stand for their lives?
14. How did Esther come to be made queen of Persia?

came to love her more than all the other beautiful virgins. So he put the royal headdress upon her and made her queen instead of Vashti. But he did not know that she was a Jewess, for Mordecai had told her to keep quiet about it.

[15] Mordecai now uncovered a plot to kill the king. Through his cousin Esther he notified the king, the two conspirators were hanged on stakes, and the matter was recorded in the king's books for Mordecai's future rewarding. Then difficulty arose. The king advanced a certain Haman to be chief of all his princes. So now all the king's servants in the gate gave him the respect due his office by bowing low or prostrating themselves before him, all except Mordecai. Why not Mordecai? He knew that Haman was an Agagite, which meant that he was a royal Amalekite; and Jehovah had decreed that his people Israel should not honor the Amalekites, but should war against them to their extermination. (Exodus 17:8-15) King Saul the Benjaminite had displeased God for failing in this regard, and now would Mordecai, also a Benjaminite, come under divine disapproval? Mordecai's refusal to bow down or prostrate himself was a flat No to the question. Naturally Haman was incensed at Mordecai. When he learned that Mordecai was an Israelite or Jew, he saw an opportunity to kill off, not only Mordecai, but also all the hated Jews in all the 127 provinces of Persia, including Judah.

[16] It was the twelfth year of Ahasuerus' reign, and in the first month Haman had the Pur, or lot, cast before him to decide upon which day of which month he should order the Jews to be

---

15. How did Mordecai come in for future rewarding, but how did his faithfulness under trial bring Jews throughout the empire into peril of their lives?
16. How did Haman decide on the day for their extermination, how did he present his case before the king, and what was he then permitted to dictate?

exterminated. The lot or Pur fell, not in favor of an early extermination, but of a late one, on the thirteenth day of the twelfth and last month A·dar'. Haman now put his case before the king, painting up the Jews as seditious and a security risk: "There is one certain people scattered and separated among the peoples in all the jurisdictional districts of your realm, and their laws are different from all the people's, and the king's own laws they are not performing, and for the king it is not appropriate to let them alone." (Esther 3:8, *NW*) So Haman asked for a law to have them destroyed and offered to pay money into the king's treasury to finance the destroyers. The king then permitted Haman to dictate the law, not realizing he was decreeing the destruction of his own beloved Esther. The law was then published in Shushan the Castle and throughout all the realm.

[17] At the publication of the law Mordecai was grief-stricken. He advised Esther the queen of the danger to her as well as her people and appealed to her to appear before the king and plead for her people. To appear unbidden before the king could be punished with death. So Esther asked Mordecai to have all the Jews fast three days for her, she and her attendants doing so also: "Upon that I shall come in to the king, which is not according to the law, and in case I must perish, I must perish." (Esther 4:16, *NW*) But she did not perish. The third day when she went in uncalled, the king held out his golden scepter for her to be spared, and she touched the scepter's top. She then invited the king and his chief prince Haman to a banquet that day. At the banquet Esther asked that they come to a like banquet the next day, on which occasion she would make her urgent request known. Afterward Haman bragged

17. What did Mordecai advise Esther to do, what action did she take, and what was Haman then induced to do?

about it to his wife and friends and ordered a stake seventy-five feet high to be set up in his courtyard on which to hang Mordecai without delay.

¹⁸ That night, unexpectedly, the king decided that Mordecai should be honored for exposing the plot against his life. Next day when Haman came to the king to ask for Mordecai to be hanged, the king maneuvered Haman into having his own self, Haman! to do the public honors to Mordecai. After rendering these, to his own great inward chagrin and humiliation, Haman was taken to Esther's banquet. Here before Haman Esther asked the king for her life. Her people were decreed to be destroyed and this would be to the king's own damage, for she his queen was a Jewess. Asked who had engineered such a policy, Esther said: "The man, the adversary and enemy, is this bad Haman." Vainly Haman pleaded with Esther for his life; the king ordered him to be hanged on the stake he had set up for Mordecai.—Esther 7:6-10, *NW*.

¹⁹ King Ahasuerus then made Mordecai his prime minister. At Esther's request he permitted Mordecai and Esther to draw up a law to counteract Haman's law that still stood unchangeable, for the Jews in all the provinces to stand for their lives against all attackers on A·dar′ 13 and to kill them. When this fighting law was published in all 127 provinces it brought hope to the Jews and great joy. They prepared for the day. It came. Haman's law fell due. But so did Mordecai and Esther's, and the Jews stood for their lives. They slaughtered their enemies. In Shushan the Castle

---

18. How was Haman humiliated into doing public honors to Mordecai, how was he afterward exposed, and to what was he sentenced?
19. How was Haman's law counteracted, what did the Jews do on the day of peril, and by what festival did they begin commemorating the victory?

they had an extra day of slaughtering, and Haman's ten sons were killed and also hanged one above the other on the stake meant for Mordecai. The yearly commemoration of this victory of the remnant of Jews is the annual festival called Pu'rim or Lots, in reproach of Haman.

[20] No less so the remnant of spiritual Israelites have been misrepresented as seditious and a security risk to modern governments. Their extermination has been decreed by the modern-day Haman class, the religious leaders, whom Jehovah has decreed to be destroyed like antitypical Amalekites. In the drama King Ahasuerus (thought to be Xerxes the Great) pictured regal power as now wielded by Jesus Christ. His power permits such an attempt to be made upon the life of the remnant of spiritual Israelites under such false accusations, all for a test of the remnant's obedience to God and for an opportunity to show God's preserving power on their behalf. Mordecai the older representative of the Jews pictures the older part of the remnant who lived through World War I and who survived the fiery spiritual tests when the King Jesus Christ came to the temple A.D. 1918. Esther pictures those who became members of the remnant since 1919, the year of the remnant's reorganization; hence she typifies the spiritually younger part of the remnant. At the risk of life both parts act together as one for the sake of the common interest in the face of the common danger, as Mordecai and Esther did of old.

[21] The regal power in the hands of the King Jesus Christ, while permitting the remnant of

---

20. How have the spiritual Israelites been misrepresented by the Haman class, and who were pictured by King Ahasuerus, Mordecai and Esther?
21. What has the regal power in Christ's hands allowed the remnant to do, and how have they done this, and with what effect?

spiritual Jews to come under world-wide danger because of their obeying God's laws rather than man's laws, also allows for the remnant to stand for their lives against their foes. The fight is to preserve their spiritual lives as witnesses of Jehovah and preachers of his kingdom by Christ, and it must be fought with spiritual weapons, especially the "sword of the spirit, that is, God's word." (Ephesians 6:13-17, *NW*) In this fight, especially since 1931, the remnant have stood for their lives in God's "full suit of armor." They have never resorted to fleshly weapons; they have never used illegal means but have taken advantage of what the law allowed. With their spiritual weapons and the use of legal means they have killed many attackers, that is, the power and influence of enemies who have tried to kill them literally or work for their spiritual death by making them stop witnessing and worshiping Jehovah God. They still preach the "good news."

[22] Anciently, when God's power became manifest in favor of the Jewish remnant by the publication of Mordecai and Esther's counterlaw, something prophetic of our day happened: "Many of the peoples of the land were declaring themselves Jews [or, were Judaizing], for the dread of the Jews had fallen upon them." Also when the Jews turned the tables on the enemy on A·dar' 13, "not a man stood his ground before them, for the dread of them had fallen upon all the peoples. And all the princes of the jurisdictional districts and the satraps and the governors and the doers of the business that belonged to the king were assisting the Jews, for the dread of Mordecai had fallen upon them."—Esther 8:17; 9:1-3, *NW*, margin.

---

22. When Mordecai and Esther's counterlaw was published, what happened prophetic of our day?

[23] True to that ancient type many people not spiritual Israelites have been impressed both by God's provision for the remnant of spiritual Israelites to stand for their lives and by their actual fight by all God-given and legal means to preserve and exercise those things that mean spiritual life for them. The dread of God's power backing up the spiritual Jews has fallen upon them. As a result, a "great crowd," whose numbers keep growing as the fight goes on, have come over onto the side of the remnant and they, too, have become Jehovah's witnesses. They have dedicated their lives to the God of the witnesses and have joined forces with them. In thus declaring themselves fellow worshipers they have exposed themselves to the same danger as the remnant and have obligated themselves to stand with them for their spiritual lives and to fight on victoriously against the enemies of the new world.

[24] Even men in high worldly station who stand in dread of the righteous principles for which Jehovah's witnesses stand lend what official or judicial assistance they can in the fight. In doing so they act wisely in accord with the advice of Psalm 2:10-12. The antitypical Haman and his ten sons may be already dead and strung up, in that their malicious designs have been exposed and the effect of Haman's law has been killed and has worked for the enemy's own slaughter, but the fight must go on. Regal power in the hands of Jesus Christ, pictured by King Ahasuerus, fully approves of this fight. It will be extended till God's own executional fight at Armageddon. Then will come rest from the enemies. —2 Thessalonians 1:6-8.

23. True to that ancient type, who have been "declaring themselves Jews," and how, and with what obligation to themselves?
24. Also how have men in high worldly station acted, in accord with Psalm 2:10-12, and how long must the fight be extended?

CHAPTER XVI

The "Desire of All Nations" Comes In

IN THE spring of 1918 (A.D.) *A·do·nay'* Jehovah and his Messenger of the covenant came to the spiritual temple for judgment work. That was in fulfillment of the prophecy of Malachi 3:1. It was not at the same time a fulfillment of the prophecy of Haggai 2:6, 7: "For thus saith the LORD of hosts; Yet once, it is a little while, and I will shake the heavens, and the earth, and the sea, and the dry land; and I will shake all nations, and the desire [the desired] of all nations shall come: and I will fill this house with glory, saith the LORD of hosts." The "desire of all nations" here meant was not the Kingdom established in the heavens in 1914, neither was it the Messenger of the covenant, Jesus Christ the reigning King. In the original Hebrew language of the prophecy "the desire" refers to more than one person or thing. This is shown by the fact that the verb "come" of which "the desire of all nations" is the subject is in the plural number, not the singular number. So a suitable translation of the Hebrew text could read: "And they, the desire of all the nations, shall come in."

---

1. Why was not the fulfillment of Malachi 3:1 also a fulfillment of Haggai 2:6, 7, and why could not the "desire of all nations" refer to a single thing or person?

[2] Centuries before Christ, Greek-speaking Jews began translating the Hebrew Scriptures into common Greek and finally produced the Greek version known as the *Septuagint* (*LXX*). They took note of the collective sense of the Hebrew word for "desire" and so they made their translation read: "And the choice things [or, chosen things] of all the nations will come." (*LXX*, Falcon Wing Press) The modern Bible translations, Jewish, Catholic and Protestant, are almost all alike in bringing out the force of the Hebrew text in agreement with the Greek *Septuagint*. The *English Revised Version* of 1884 rendered it: "And the desirable things of all nations shall come." The *American Standard Version* of 1901, also the Hebrew *Leeser* version of 1905, the *Brazilian Version*, and the *Nácar-Colunga* version of 1948 used the expression "the precious things of all (the) nations." The Hebrew *Soncino* edition said: "the choicest things of all nations." *An American Translation*, the French *Lienart* and the *Crampon* translations said: "the treasures of all the nations." The French *Maredsous* translation said: "the riches of all the peoples."

[3] The French *L'Ecole Biblique de Jérusalem* and the German *Kautzsch* and other translations render the wording to show that in shaking the nations Jehovah has as one of his purposes the coming of such things. In agreement with this the *Revised Standard Version* of 1952 renders Haggai 2:7: "And I will shake all nations, so that the treasures of all nations shall come in, and I will fill this house with splendor, says the LORD of hosts." Moffatt's translation makes the verse read: "And

---

2. How did the ancient Greek *Septuagint Version* show the collective sense of the Hebrew word for "desire," and how have modern translations made renderings in agreement with the *Septuagint?*

3. How do other modern translations render the wording to show a purpose in Jehovah's shaking all nations?

shaking all nations till the treasures of all nations are brought hither and my House here filled with splendour (says the Lord of hosts)."

⁴ The house here referred to is Jehovah's house, his temple. The circumstances under which this prophecy was given through Haggai and which help us in properly understanding its fulfillment were these: In 537 B.C., under the decree of Cyrus King of Persia, the original remnant of the Jews left Babylon, the land of their captivity, and returned to their desolated homeland, Judah, to build another temple to Jehovah at its site on Mount Moriah in Jerusalem. They built an altar to Jehovah there and renewed his sacrifices and proceeded to lay the foundations of the new temple. Then the heathen opposers of the worship of Jehovah round about began to interfere and lodged false accusations against the temple builders with the Persian imperial government. Instead of pushing the unchangeable decree of Cyrus authorizing the temple building until they had finished it in obedience to imperial orders, the remnant grew frightened at the rulings of misguided lawmakers and laid off from building God's house. Till 520 B.C. the building of the temple lagged. Showing that their material prosperity rested upon their spiritual well-being, Jehovah did not bless them, for his name was not being exalted by their neglect of his house. His worship suffered and the spiritual interests of the Jewish remnant were injured.

⁵ Jehovah now raised up his prophets Haggai and Zechariah to remind the remnant of their obligations toward God's house and to encourage them to go ahead with building it in spite of enemy opposition. When the enemy renewed their

----

4. What is the "house" here referred to, and what circumstances led up to the giving of Haggai's prophecy?
5. How was the temple rebuilding renewed, and when was the temple finished?

protests, the temple builders appealed to their rights under God and under Cyrus' decree. When the enemy brought the matter before the imperial government, King Darius backed up the temple builders on the basis of Cyrus' unchangeable decree. Four years later (516 B.C.), "this house was finished on the third day of the month A·dar', which was in the sixth year of the reign of Darius the king."—Ezra 4:1 to 6:15; Haggai 1:1-15; 2:15-19.

⁶ It was about one month after the remnant under governor Zerubbabel and high priest Joshua had resumed building the temple that Haggai was inspired to utter the above prophecy. The new building under construction gave no promise of being anything to compare with Solomon's temple. Yet Jehovah could add a glory to it such as the former temple of Solomon never had. For the purpose of encouraging the temple builders he promised to do this: "The silver is mine, and the gold is mine, saith Jehovah of hosts. The latter glory of this house shall be greater than the former, saith Jehovah of hosts; and in this place will I give peace, saith Jehovah of hosts." (Haggai 2:8, 9, *AS*) Jehovah would make this come true by causing the desirable, precious, choicest things of all nations, their treasures, their riches, to come to his house.

⁷ This divine promise was not fulfilled in the temple built by governor Zerubbabel and high priest Joshua. Still the prophecy has not failed of fulfillment. In vindication of Jehovah's word it has been undergoing a surprising fulfillment since he came accompanied by his Messenger of the covenant to the spiritual temple in 1918 and afterward liberated the remnant of spiritual

---

6. Through Haggai, how did Jehovah promise to glorify this temple more than that built by Solomon?
7. Since when has the antitypical temple rebuilding work been going on, and in spite of what developments?

Israelites from antitypical Babylon by his Greater Cyrus, Jesus Christ. In 1919 the remnant began their reconstructive work corresponding to the temple activities of the ancient restored Jewish remnant in Jerusalem. Under incitement by the invisible Dragon, Satan the Devil, whom the Greater Cyrus has cast down to the earth, the opposition to the temple activities of the spiritual remnant has mounted. But in this "time of the end" the temple builders could not afford to let the construction work stop or lag. So they pushed on with the work in defiance of all the 'mischief that the religious enemies tried to frame by law.' (Psalm 94:20) By 1931 it appeared that the full remnant of "living stones" of the spiritual temple had been assembled into Jehovah's visible organization.

⁸ In 1931, too, the magazine *The Watch Tower* published a series of articles on the entire prophecy of Haggai. But in August of 1935, or sixteen years after the temple activities of the remnant began, *The Watchtower* published a series of articles on the "Great Multitude" of Revelation 7:9-17, disclosing that at the temple there were not only the restored remnant of spiritual Israelites but now also the first ones of a "great multitude" of persons not spiritual Israelites out of all nations, kindreds, peoples and tongues. In robes made white in the blood of the Lamb of God they also were serving God day and night in his temple and they also were under the loving care of his Shepherd King, Jesus Christ.

⁹ However, first in 1953, in the unparalleled in-

---

8. Through issues of August, 1935, of *The Watchtower,* what disclosure was made that has a bearing on the fulfillment of Haggai's prophecy?
9. When was it revealed that this "desire of all nations" to come in was this "great multitude"? How many had then come in, and how many heard this information directly?

ternational convention of Jehovah's witnesses at Yankee Stadium, New York city,* it was revealed that the "desire of all nations" that was to come in is this great multitude, this "great crowd" of worshipers of Jehovah who had become the companions of the spiritual remnant. Already that year more than 460,000 throughout the earth had come in and were filling Jehovah's house with glory by their presence and their loving service of Him. Scores of thousands of them from 97 nations, territories and islands were in the visible audience there at Yankee Stadium to hear this joy-inspiring information.

¹⁰ In glowing terms other prophecies bolster up this understanding of Haggai 2:7 as correct. After Jehovah spoke prophetically of the birth of the Kingdom A.D. 1914 and the comforting of his "woman," the "Jerusalem above," by restoring his remnant to become a nation in a newborn land, Jehovah said principally for his remnant today: "Rejoice ye with Jerusalem, and be glad for her, all ye that love her: rejoice for joy with her, all ye that mourn over her; that ye may suck and be satisfied with the breasts of her consolations; that ye may milk out, and be delighted with the abundance of her glory. For thus saith Jehovah, Behold, I will extend peace to her like a river, and the GLORY OF THE NATIONS like an overflowing stream: and ye shall suck thereof; ye shall be borne upon the side [like a cherished child], and shall be dandled upon the knees. As one whom his mother comforteth, so will I comfort you; and ye shall be comforted in Jerusalem. And ye shall see it, and your heart shall rejoice, and your bones shall flourish like the tender

---

* See chapter I, pages 8-11.

---

10. How does Isaiah 66:7-14 bolster up this understanding of Haggai's prophecy, and when did the remnant particularly rejoice at seeing this?

grass." (Isaiah 66:7-14, *AS*) In 1953 particularly the remnant of temple builders did see this with enlightened understanding, and they did rejoice as never before with their mother, the "Jerusalem above," Jehovah's universal organization.

[11] Back in 1918, as a result of the hostile action of war-delirious nations and revengeful religious clergymen of Christendom, the remnant of the children of the "Jerusalem above" were lying prostrate in the dust of the earth, captive, inactive, like the "two witnesses" of Revelation, chapter 11. But in the spring of 1919 the prophetic call addressed to their mother, Zion or the "Jerusalem above," began applying to them: "Arise, shine! for thy light is come, and the glory of Jehovah is risen upon thee. For behold, darkness shall cover the earth [down to which the Dragon Satan has been cast], and gross darkness the peoples; but Jehovah will arise upon thee, and his glory shall be seen on thee."

[12] That meant the glory of Jehovah's deliverance and restoration would rest upon his remnant of spiritual Israel and would make them the only light of the world. Their arising to bold and free activity and letting the light from Jehovah shine by preaching the good news of his established kingdom would have an effect upon the people of all nations: "And the nations shall walk by thy light, and kings by the brightness of thy rising. Lift up thine eyes round about, and see: all they gather themselves together, they come to thee: thy sons come from afar, and thy daughters [of the spiritual remnant] are carried upon thy side. Then thou shalt see, and shalt be brightened, and thy heart shall throb, and be enlarged;

---

11. In what condition were the remnant when the call of Isaiah 60:1, 2 began to apply to them?
12. What glory of Jehovah was to rest upon the remnant, and how were the nations to be affected by their letting the light shine?

for the abundance of the sea shall be turned unto thee, the WEALTH OF THE NATIONS shall come unto thee. A multitude of camels shall cover thee, young camels of Midian and Ephah; all they from Sheba shall come: they shall bring gold and incense; and they shall publish the praises of Jehovah. All the flocks of Kedar shall be gathered unto thee, the rams of Nebaioth shall serve thee; they shall come up with acceptance on mine altar, and I will beautify the house of my magnificence."

[13] In Isaiah's time the doves flew in such great flocks that they appeared like great white clouds that literally hid the sun from the eyes of earthlings. Prophetically referring to the flight of the innocent, harmless people of all nations and languages to the place Jehovah provides for his worship and for safety, the prophet voices his amazement at what has taken place observedly since A.D. 1931: "Who are these that come flying as a cloud, and as doves to their dove-cotes? For the isles shall await me [represented by my Kingdom preachers], and the ships of Tarshish [in the far west] first, to bring thy sons from afar, their silver and their gold with them, unto the name of Jehovah thy God, and to the Holy One of Israel, for he hath glorified thee. And the sons of the alien shall build up thy walls, and their kings shall minister unto thee. For in my wrath [A.D. 1914-1918] I smote thee, but in my favour have I had mercy on thee [from 1919 onward]. And thy gates shall stand open continually: (they shall not be shut day nor night,) that the WEALTH OF THE NATIONS may be brought unto thee, and that their kings may be led [to thee]. For the nation and the kingdom that will not serve thee shall perish; and those nations shall be utterly wasted. The glory of Lebanon shall come unto thee, the cypress, pine,

---

13. To what did Isaiah liken the flight of innocent, harmless people to Jehovah for safety, and since when has this observedly taken place?

and box-tree together, to beautify the place of my sanctuary [the temple]; and I will make the place of my feet [the temple] glorious. And the children of them that afflicted thee shall come bending unto thee; and all they that despised thee shall bow themselves down at the soles of thy feet; and they shall call thee The city of Jehovah, the Zion of the Holy One of Israel."—Isaiah 60:1-14, *Da*.

[14] How truly this prophecy has come to reality since 1931! Persons in official worldly positions and just ordinary citizens who under the impulse of religious prejudice, patriotic nationalism and ignorance of the truth despised and afflicted Jehovah's remnant of spiritual Israelites have since gotten their eyes opened and seen the glory of Jehovah upon them. In self-humiliation they have come to them, acknowledging that they are the visible organization of Jehovah, the Holy One of spiritual Israel. They have become active witnesses of Jehovah; this leads to their preservation during the universal war of Armageddon. The nations that hate the glory light of Jehovah and that refuse to lend themselves in support of his remnant, continuing to persecute them instead, will be utterly wiped out at Armageddon. World rulers do well to imitate the course of the queen whose faraway land Sheba is mentioned in Isaiah's prophecy. "Now the queen of She'ba was hearing the report about Solomon in connection with the name of Jehovah. So she came to test him with perplexing questions." Her test did not fail, and the visible proof of the report, including the glorious temple, overwhelmed her. "Look! I had not been told the half," she exclaimed. "May Jehovah your God come to be blessed, who has taken delight in you by putting you upon the

---

14. (a) Since 1931 how has this prophecy come true regarding the attitude and conduct of people high and low toward Jehovah's remnant? (b) What ancient queen do world rulers do well to imitate?

throne of Israel, because Jehovah loves Israel to time indefinite, so that he appointed you as king to render judicial decision and righteousness." —1 Kings 10:1-9, *NW*.

¹⁵ The queen of Sheba's visit to Solomon was typical and now takes on point in this generation by the force of Jesus' own words: "This generation is a wicked generation; it looks for a sign. . . . The queen of the south will be raised up in the judgment with the men of this generation and will condemn them; because she came from the ends of the earth to hear the wisdom of Solomon, but, look! something more than Solomon is here." (Luke 11:29, 31, *NW*) That "something more than Solomon" is Jesus Christ, the Son of David. He is now at the temple as the Messenger of the covenant, and the separation of the people of the nations as sheep and goats is going on before his judgment throne. Those in prominent, ruling positions in this world who balk at coming to Jehovah's temple to the Greater Solomon for the solution of all their problems are goats. The example of the far-traveling queen of Sheba who became a praiser of Jehovah rises up in this judgment day as a condemnation of them and they will be cut off forever at Armageddon. At the same time her example stands as a praiseworthy type of those of worldly prominence who turn from worldly human wisdom and seek "wisdom from above" through the Greater Solomon at the temple. Such become part of the "great crowd" of Jehovah's worshipers there.

¹⁶ Jehovah's great day keeps getting closer for

---

15. In what way is the queen of Sheba raised up in the judgment with this generation, and of whom is her example a praiseworthy type?

16, 17. (a) How has Jehovah's shaking of the nations since 1919 been having its effect? (b) So in agreement with Haggai 2:7 what prophecy of Isaiah do we see coming to reality?

him to shake the heavens and the earth of Satan's organization to pieces that Jehovah the God of Jacob or Israel may alone be exalted. He has already shaken all the nations, shaking them by the world-disturbing restoration of his spiritual remnant in 1919 and by the preaching of his witnesses in now more than 160 lands, territories and islands. The shaking is having its effect: the desirable ones, the choicest ones, the precious ones from the standpoint of Jehovah and his witnesses, keep coming in to fill his house with glory. There they experience what he promised to give at his house: "In this place will I give peace." (Haggai 2:7-9) Another wonderful prophecy thus takes on fulfillment. The "time of the end" is fast running out; we are indeed living in the "latter days" or "end of the days." Now we see in stark reality what Isaiah saw in bright vision:

[17] "And it shall come to pass in the end of days, [that] the mountain of Jehovah's house [typified by Mount Moriah] shall be established on the top of the mountains, and shall be lifted up above the hills; and all the nations shall flow unto it. And many peoples shall go and say, Come, and let us go up to the mountain of Jehovah, to the house of the God of Jacob; and he will teach us of his ways, and we will walk in his paths. For out of Zion shall go forth the law, and Jehovah's word from Jerusalem. And he shall judge among the nations, and shall reprove many peoples; and they shall forge their swords into ploughshares, and their spears into pruning-knives; nation shall not lift up sword against nation, neither shall they learn war any more. House of Jacob, come ye, and let us walk in the light of Jehovah."—Isaiah 2:1-5, *Da.*

[18] After ten years of functioning the United

---

18. Why has the United Nations to date failed to bring the fulfillment of Isaiah's words which it displays carved on one of its walls?

Nations has failed to bring to this divided world the fulfillment of Isaiah's words, which it displays carved on one of its walls facing on the United Nations Plaza, New York city.* Instead, the world shudders before the most menacing, nuclear armaments race between East and West. There is a reason for its failure. It is not on the "mountain of Jehovah"; it, with its meditation room, is not the "house of the God of Jacob." Seventy-six nations have flowed into it, but not to be taught of Jehovah's ways or to walk in his paths or to correct themselves according to his judgment and reproof. They go on learning war in the most fiendishly scientific way.

19 There is one place where Isaiah's prophecy now finds complete fulfillment before Armageddon has to smash the deadly armaments of warlike nations. That is where Isaiah foretold it would be, at Jehovah's house, where his witnesses worship him. His house tops all things in these crucial days. His worship is foremost, more vital than anything else, and is absolutely obligatory upon all who would survive Armageddon and live forever. To his clean, purifying worship the desirable, choicest, precious people of all the nations have flowed, and they invite and encourage others to come with them, by preaching the Kingdom message. There persons who formerly were bitterest enemies in the world's warfare, lifting up weapons like sword and spear against one another, meet and worship peacefully together, as loving brothers in the New World society. They were not forced to do this, nor did they wait to do this until scientists began warning that the invention of the hydrogen bomb, yes, super-superbombs,

---

* See chapter I, page 7.

---

19. At what one place does Isaiah's prophecy find complete fulfillment, how so, and since when?

272 YOU MAY SURVIVE ARMAGEDDON INTO GOD'S NEW WORLD

made death-dealing warfare inadvisable and obsolete as a sane means for settling international disputes. Especially since 1931, years before the atomic bomb was invented, they have done this because they have accepted Jehovah's reproof and word and law that have gone forth from his temple on the heavenly Mount Zion. He has taught them his ways through his Messenger at the temple, and they have lovingly and obediently chosen to walk in His paths.

[20] At Armageddon Jehovah will cause the human bomb to explode and the members of the United Nations and the peoples of all other nations will fight confusedly among themselves, every man's hand being against his neighbor, but the "great crowd" of worshipers at Jehovah's house will, in spite of their different nationalities, colors and tongues, keep the peace of his house, serving him unitedly, exalting him above all as they survive with his temple into the new world. At the blessed sight of the desire of all nations thus coming in, the remnant of spiritual Israel (or, Jacob) have every reason to say: "House of Jacob, come ye, and let us walk in the light of Jehovah."

---

20. At Armageddon how will the conduct of the "great crowd" differ from that of the people of the nations? So now what do the remnant of Israel or Jacob have every reason to say in exhortation?

CHAPTER XVII

Living Now in the New World Society

TO GAIN life in the new world of God's promise the life seeker has to begin now before the end of the old world to live according to the standards of the new world. The effort to meet this requirement now in this "time of the end" of the old world has resulted in the forming of a New World society. Such a thing as a New World society was first mentioned at the first international assembly of Jehovah's witnesses at Yankee Stadium, New York city, in the summer of 1950. Such a society actually exists. It is not incorporated according to the laws of any Old World nation, for its members are found all over the earth and not even the 60-member United Nations is in position to authorize or incorporate it. Yet it is a real society with a constantly growing membership. Its members live according to a common standard, Jehovah's Word or Bible, and act in unity, preaching the "good news of the kingdom" in the entire inhabited earth. They have a common worship, imitating Jesus Christ and his apostles, and they hold to common beliefs, meeting together regularly to build one another up on their "most holy faith" and to further their common, God-given work. They are organized, not democratically or communistically,

---

1. As a result of what has the New World society been formed, and how is it really a society and for the new world?

273

but theocratically, with Jehovah ruling from above as God and King and through his Son Jesus Christ as his "leader and commander to the peoples." (Isaiah 55:4) They are not working like the United Nations to perpetuate the doomed old world. They live for the new world that follows Armageddon, and they are preparing to live in it for its duration, forever. They try to live now as they must live then.

[2] A strengthening, impelling, joy-inspiring power to them is Jehovah's ancient promise through his prophet Isaiah: "For behold, I create new heavens and a new earth; and the former shall not be remembered, nor come into mind. But be ye glad and rejoice for ever in that which I create." (Isaiah 65:17, 18, *Da*) Seven centuries later the apostle John had this promise confirmed to him, for he wrote: "And I saw a new heaven and a new earth, for the former heaven and the former earth had passed away, and the sea is no more. And the one seated on the throne said: 'Look! I am making all things new.'"—Revelation 21:1, 5, *NW*.

[3] The apostle Peter gave still further Christian confirmation to Jehovah's promise through Isaiah. Symbolically describing the passing away of the present heavens and earth that make up Satan's world or system of things, Peter wrote in words that especially apply to true Christians today: "Jehovah is not slow respecting his promise, as some people consider slowness, but he is patient with you because he does not desire any to be destroyed but desires all to attain to repentance. Yet Jehovah's day will come as a thief, in which the heavens will pass away with a hissing noise, but the elements being intensely hot

---

2. What promise of Jehovah, as confirmed by him to the apostle John, is a power to this society?
3. How did Peter give still further Christian confirmation to Jehovah's promise through Isaiah?

will be dissolved, and the earth and the works in it will be discovered. Since all these things are thus to be dissolved, what sort of persons ought you to be in holy acts of conduct and deeds of godly devotion, awaiting and keeping close in mind the presence of the day of Jehovah, through which the heavens being on fire will be dissolved and the elements being intensely hot will melt! But there are new heavens and a new earth that we are awaiting according to his promise, and in these righteousness is to dwell. Hence, beloved ones, since you are awaiting these things, do your utmost to be found finally by him spotless and unblemished and in peace."—2 Peter 3:9-14, *NW*.

⁴ Those of the New World society, therefore, do not have a depressing outlook that stops all progress, stifles all righteous ambition and deadens all interest in what is going on. They are the greatest optimists for the future. They wisely do not waste time, effort and sentiment on trying to preserve the old world that is doomed and fast nearing destruction. They live under a continual sense of urgency, keeping close in mind the day of Jehovah's execution of the satanic heavens and earth and his replacing of these with righteous new heavens and a new earth, new heavenly ruling powers and a new organization of human society. They know God is not slow or dilly-dallying but will be unchangeably on time in carrying out his promise of a new world. So now, without any delay, they must take advantage of his patience, which he is still exercising, that some may have time to repent before his time is up and destruction overtakes all those who are part of the old world. Without loss of time and motion they do their utmost to co-operate with God in

4. Why do the New World society not have a depressing outlook, and how do they try to avoid being caught unawares by Jehovah's great day?

his lifesaving purpose. By continual watchfulness as to their right conduct and by constant activity in Jehovah's service they want to avoid being caught unawares by the great "day of Jehovah." They want to survive it under his approval into his new world.

⁵ Since eternal life is God's gift through Christ Jesus our Lord, the worship of the God of the new world must mark the New World society. The members must identify themselves as being undividedly for Jehovah and must therefore be his witnesses. The spiritual remnant must display the "seal of the living God" in their forehead. The "great crowd" who have joined the remnant in Jehovah's worship must display the mark in their forehead put there by the remnant, the symbolic 'man clothed in linen, with a writer's inkhorn by his side.' (Revelation 7:1-4; Ezekiel 9:1-4) All must, as it were, put on garments of identification as worshipers of the only living and true God and must show they are in heart accord with his purpose through Christ to destroy all worshipers of false gods at Armageddon. The vitalness of this part of New World living was typified in the relations of King Jehu and Jehonadab.

⁶ In the tenth century before Christ, Elisha the prophet sent and had general Jehu anointed to rule over the ten-tribe kingdom of Israel for a special purpose, to wipe out the descendants of the unfaithful King Ahab, who officially set up the worship of the pagan god Baal in Israel, and to overthrow Baal worship among Jehovah's chosen people. Jehu promptly set himself to carry out the divine commission. He not only exterminated

---

5. Whose worship must mark the New World society, and what garments of identification must they put on before Armageddon?
6. How did Jehu become king, how did he proceed with fulfilling his commission, and what typical figure then stepped upon the stage?

Ahab's wicked descendants but also rode his war chariot over the pagan promoter of Baal worship, Ahab's widow Jezebel. The sympathetic friends of Ahab's house who came from the kingdom of Judah also met with destruction at Jehu's executional sword. Here there steps upon the stage of action a figure typical of the "great crowd" of today, Jehonadab the son of Rechab, from whom the later Rechabites took instructions. (Jeremiah 35:1-11)* Jehu's executional program as Jehovah's anointed King had become well known to Jehonadab. Did he approve of it?

⁷ "As he was going along from there he got to encounter Je·hon'a·dab the son of Re'chab [coming] to meet him. When he blessed him, he [that is, Jehu] accordingly said to him: 'Is your heart upright with me, just as my own heart is with your heart?' To this Je·hon'a·dab said: 'It is.' 'If it is, do give me your hand.' So he gave him his hand. At that he made him get up into the chariot with him. Then he said: 'Do go along with me and look upon my toleration of no rivalry toward Jehovah.' And they kept him riding with him in his war chariot. Finally he came to Sa·mar'i·a [the capital city]. Now he went striking down all who were left over of A'hab's in Sa·mar'i·a until he had annihilated them, according to Jehovah's word that he had spoken to E·li'jah."—2 Kings 10:15-17, NW.

⁸ Jehonadab plainly said he was in heart harmony with King Jehu in his executional work in fulfillment of Jehovah's words against the house of Ahab by the prophet Elijah. He openly made known this fact by publicly riding alongside King

---

* See chapter IV, pages 64, ¶21, to 67, ¶26.

7, 8. (a) How did Jehonadab show he approved of Jehu's executional program? (b) Whom did King Jehu typify, and how does the antitypical Jehonadab go along with the antitypical Jehu?

Jehu in his chariot, thus going with Jehu to witness how he tolerated no rivalry in Israel between Baal and Jehovah. In this prophetic drama King Jehu typified the One whom Jehovah has anointed as his leading executional officer, his enthroned King Jesus Christ. The name "Jehu" means "Jehovah is He," not meaning that King Jehu was Jehovah himself but well suiting the king who championed Jehovah as being the true God. Jesus Christ is the antitypical Jehu and he is represented on earth by the remnant of the members of the "body of Christ," who proclaim Jehovah's judgments against the house or seed of the antitypical King Ahab, Satan the Devil. In 1932 the remnant became familiar with the antitypical Jehonadab.* Jehonadab was no Israelite but was a Midianite temporary resident in Israel who worshiped Jehovah. His name means "Jehovah is liberal (or, has impelled)." His descendants, the Rechabites of Jeremiah's day, typified the "great crowd" of Jehovah's worshipers not spiritual Israelites. Jehonadab their forefather typified the same group. The Jehonadab class of today give their right hand of co-operation to the remnant to show they are uprightly in heart accord with Jesus Christ in his executional work against the Devil's organization. They join with the remnant in 'declaring the day of vengeance of our God.' They publicly go along with the remnant as these show that they tolerate no rivalry toward Jehovah God in the New World society.

[9] In this connection, remember that the unfaithful ten-tribe kingdom of Israel under King Ahab

---

* See The Watchtower as of July 1 to August 1, 1932, presenting the series of three articles on "Jehovah's Executioner." Also see pages 77-87 of Volume 3 of the book Vindication, released on July 18, 1932, at Brooklyn, New York.

9. What did the unfaithful ten-tribe kingdom of Israel under King Ahab's house typify, and what worship will the Greater Jehu not tolerate in its antitype?

and his house pictured Christendom. She divides her worship between what she considers God and the unclean, materialistic god Baal, whom the antitypical Ahab, Satan the Devil, has introduced into Christendom. At the capital city, Samaria, King Ahab built an altar and temple to Baal. Did Jehu tolerate it as a rival to Jehovah's worship? No more than the Greater Jehu will tolerate modern Baalism in Christendom. "Further, Je'hu collected all the people together and said to them: 'A'hab, on the one hand, worshiped Ba'al a little. Je'hu, on the other hand, will worship him a great deal. So now call all the prophets of Ba'al, all his worshipers and all his priests to me. Do not let a single one be missing, because I have a great sacrifice for Ba'al. Anyone that is missing will not keep living.' As for Je'hu, he acted slyly, for the purpose of destroying the worshipers of Ba'al."

[10] From the ancient type it is made clear why the King Jesus Christ now ruling in the midst of his enemies still permits modern Baalism to go on in Christendom as well as in the rest of the world. It is to put men to the test, to let them prove whom they worship, Jehovah or Baal, and thus whether they deserve preservation or execution. "And Je'hu went on to say: 'Sanctify a solemn assembly for Ba'al.' Accordingly they proclaimed it. After that Je'hu sent through all Israel, so that all the worshipers of Ba'al came in. And not a single one was left over that did not come in. And they kept coming into the house of Ba'al, and the house of Ba'al came to be full from end to end. He now said to the one who was over the wardrobe: 'Bring out garments for all the worshipers of Ba'al.' So he brought the attire out for them. Then Je'hu entered with Je·hon'a·dab the son of Re'chab into

---

10. How does the ancient type show why the King Jesus Christ still lets modern Baalism go on in Christendom and the rest of the world?

the house of Ba'al. He now said to the worshipers of Ba'al: 'Search carefully and see that there may be here with you none of the worshipers of Jehovah, but only the worshipers of Ba'al.' Finally they came in to render up sacrifices and burnt offerings, and Je'hu himself stationed eighty men outside at his disposal and went on to say: 'As for the man that escapes from the men whom I am bringing into your hands, the one's soul will go for the other's soul.'"

[11] The antitypical Jehu of today will corner every one of the modern Baal worshipers by the time of Armageddon. He sees to it that all worshipers of Jehovah are gathered out into the New World society. That includes the Jehonadab class. Even though many claim to be Christians, the Greater Jehu forces all worshipers of Baal to don their garments of identification, proving they are at heart and in fact Baal worshipers, not worshipers of Jehovah. He forces this putting on of identification garments for his own guidance at execution time, and he does so by setting the vital issue of Jehovah's worship before mankind and then letting them show how they stand toward Jehovah's witnesses who promote His worship. When people oppose and persecute, they are allowed to do this as a way of putting on their garments of Baal worship. They thus mark themselves for sure execution. By Armageddon all will have marked themselves.

[12] When King Jehu had the Baal worshipers all bottled up by themselves and actually engaged in the false worship he ordered his executional forces into action. Not a Baal worshiper escaped them. Then they destroyed all the idolatrous furniture

---

11. How will the antitypical Jehu have cornered all worshipers of Baal by Armageddon, but where will Jehovah's worshipers be?
12. How did King Jehu then annihilate Baal out of Israel?

and lastly Baal's temple itself and made its location a public latrine. "Thus Je'hu annihilated Ba'al out of Israel."—2 Kings 10:18-28, *NW.*

¹³ Jehonadab witnessed the destruction of Baal worshipers and of Baalism out of Israel. His worship of Jehovah saved him from execution. So, too, in the immediate future. With all the worshipers of Jehovah's rival fully identified by the time of Armageddon, his anointed and commissioned King Jesus Christ will lead all his angelic executional forces into action and catch the false worshipers red-handed and will make no mistake in annihilating them down to the last man. None will survive Armageddon; neither will the temple of false religion. But the remnant of spiritual Israelites will, and the Jehonadab class will. In the New World society they now uncompromisingly render exclusive devotion to Jehovah as God. Together they will witness the complete execution of the false worshipers at Armageddon and will survive to carry forward Jehovah's pure worship in the new world.

¹⁴ Another picture of the relationship between the remnant and the Jehonadab class is to be found in the relations of Israel with Hobab. He was Moses' kinsman by marriage but a fleshly relative of Jehonadab. He was a Midianite temporary resident among the Israelites in the wilderness of Arabia. Moses had built the tabernacle of worship and inaugurated Jehovah's worship at it. The time came for the Israelites to move from the region of Mount Sinai toward the Promised Land of Canaan. Although Jehovah's cloud would go before the Israelites to lead them in the general direction

---

13. What saved Jehonadab from execution, and how will it be similar in the immediate future at Armageddon?
14. By what other typical figure was the relationship between the remnant and the Jehonadab class pictured, and what invitation and promise did Moses extend to him?

and to determine their stopping places, the eyes of a good scout could be used in searching out the local territory, its water supplies and its pasturage. Here Hobab would prove useful. "Then Moses said to Ho'bab the son of Reu'el the Mid'i·an·ite, the father-in-law of Moses: 'We are pulling away for the place about which Jehovah said, "I shall give it to you." Do come with us and we shall certainly do good to you, because Jehovah has spoken good concerning Israel.' But he said to him: 'I shall not go along, but I shall go to my own country and to my relatives.' At this he said: 'Please, do not abandon us, because for the reason that you well know where we may encamp in the wilderness you must serve as eyes for us. And it must occur that in case you should come with us, yes, it must occur that with what goodness Jehovah will kindly deal with us we in turn will kindly deal toward you.' So they went marching from the mountain of Jehovah."—Numbers 10:29-33, *NW;* Exodus 2:15-22.

[15] As typified by Hobab, the members of the "great crowd" come along with the remnant of spiritual Israelites through the wilderness of this "time of the end." The remnant invite them into the New World society, which Jehovah has promised to bless and preserve and usher into the new world toward which they are journeying. To do this, the members of the "great crowd" must cut their ties with their earthly country and worldly relatives. Yet they do it to be of assistance to Jehovah's remnant under the Greater Moses, Jesus Christ. They have served as "eyes" to the New World society, especially in going forth as missionaries and pioneer publishers of the Kingdom news to new lands and territories, to open them up

---

15. How does the antitypical Hobab come along with the remnant, and how does the remnant deal with them in turn?

for the extending of the New World society to those regions and establishing congregations of Jehovah's witnesses. Because they come along as loyal companions and tender their valuable services, the remnant does good to them, especially spiritually. The goodness with which Jehovah kindly deals with his remnant they share lovingly with the "great crowd" typified by Hobab.

¹⁶ Hobab later had a relative by the name of Heber the Kenite. Hobab was a Midianite of the tribe of Kenites. The Kenites came with Israel into the Promised Land and kept up their attachment with them by settling on the southern border of Judah, toward the wilderness to which the Kenites were adapted. (Judges 1:16; 1 Chronicles 2:55) Heber the Kenite, however, moved his family northward and settled near the city of refuge, Kedesh-Naphtali. (Joshua 20:1-7) "Incidentally He'ber the Ken'ite had separated from the Ken'ites, the sons of Ho'bab, whose son-in-law Moses was, and he had his tent pitched near the big tree in Za·a·nan'nim, which is at Ke'desh." (Judges 4:11, NW) While Heber was here an event took place that set a pattern of action that the "great crowd" of today must follow in the New World society before Armageddon.

¹⁷ After Israel settled in the Promised Land without a visible human king, Jehovah raised up judges to administer justice to them. Because of their falling away from Jehovah's worship Jehovah let the Israelites come under harsh oppression for twenty years by Jabin the king of Canaan, whose army chief was named Sisera. Then Jehovah used Deborah a prophetess to call Barak the

---

16. Where did Hobab's relative, Heber the Kenite, move to put his tent in a place of typical action?
17. How did a typical battle of Armageddon take place before the prophetess Deborah and Judge Barak, but for whom was the "crowning feat" reserved to be performed?

son of Abinoam, of the tribe of Naphtali, to serve as judge for the overthrow of the enemy and the deliverance of Israel. Barak, accompanied by the prophetess Deborah, gathered an army of ten thousand at the city of refuge Kedesh, and then went up to Mount Tabor, not quite fifteen miles northeast of Megiddo. Sisera now brought his nine hundred war chariots with iron scythes and his mighty army of footmen up against Barak. By a miraculous act Jehovah knocked the war chariots out of action and put the army of Sisera to rout. It was a typical battle of Armageddon. (Judges 5:19-23, *NW*) Barak and his ten thousand chased after the enemy and cut them down till none remained. That is, except one, Sisera. He got down off his chariot and fled on foot. In his case Deborah's prophecy to Barak had to come true: "The crowning feat will not become yours on the way that you are going, for it will be into the hand of a woman that Jehovah will sell Sis'e·ra." (Judges 4:8, 9, *NW*) To perform this crowning feat meant a test for the woman. How?

[18] "As for Sis'e·ra, he fled on foot to the tent of Ja'el the wife of He'ber the Ken'ite, for there was peace between Ja'bin the king of Ha'zor and the household of He'ber the Ken'ite. Then Ja'el came on out to meet Sis'e·ra and said to him: 'Turn this way, my lord, turn this way to me. Do not be afraid.' So he turned aside to her into the tent. Later she covered him with a blanket." At his request for water she gave him milk to drink. As he lay in her tent, violating the sanctity of a woman's tent, he told her to stand at the entrance and steer away any Israelite pursuer. The test of Jael was now on. Would she side with King Jabin with whom her husband Heber was at peace at the time and try to help his army chief to escape?

---

18. How was Jael the wife of Heber put to the test in connection with Sisera, but what action did she take?

Or would she show loyalty to Jehovah's people among whom she was a temporary resident? Would she aid in their deliverance? Sisera fell asleep. "And Ja'el the wife of He'ber proceeded to take a pin of the tent and to put the hammer into her hand. Then she went to him stealthily and drove the pin into his temples and beat it into the earth, while he was fast asleep and weary. So he died."—Judges 4:17-21, *NW*.

¹⁹ Had Jael tried to harbor an enemy it would have led to her execution as an ally of those who fell at Megiddo. Her courageous strike for Jehovah won his blessing in the victory song of Deborah and Barak: "Ja'el the wife of He'ber the Ken'ite will be most blessed among women, among women in the tent she will be most blessed. Water he asked, milk she gave; in the large banquet bowl of majestic ones she presented curdled milk. Her hand to the tent pin she then thrust out, and her right hand to the mallet of toilers. And she ham-

---

19. From what did Jael's strike for Jehovah safeguard her, and what blessing did it win for her?

mered Sis'e·ra, she pierced his head through, and she broke apart and cut up his temples. Between her feet he collapsed, he fell, he lay down; between her feet he collapsed, he fell; where he collapsed, there he fell overcome."—Judges 5:1, 24-27, *NW*.

20 Jael produced the strongest evidence that she was loyal to Jehovah's sovereignty over Israel and that she approved of his slaughter of the enemy by his executional forces. "Look! there was Ba'rak pursuing Sis'e·ra. Ja'el now came on out to meet him and said to him: 'Come and I shall show you the man you are looking for.' So in he went to her and, look! there was Sis'e·ra fallen dead, with the pin in his temples."—Judges 4:22, *NW*.

21 Judge Barak is listed as one of the pre-Christian witnesses of Jehovah. (Hebrews 11:32 to 12:2, *NW*) Deborah was also one. She pictured God's "woman," his universal organization of which Jesus Christ is the head member. Barak typified the Deliverer Jesus Christ, who has a remnant of members of "his body" still on the earth in these pre-Armageddon days. These ask and choose to act always under the direction and with the help of God's universal organization, the antitypical Deborah, in declaring the day of the vengeance of our God and proclaiming his judgments against the foes and oppressors of spiritual Israel. The oppressor, King Jabin, an accursed Canaanite, pictures Satan the Devil, the accursed original Serpent. Army chief Sisera pictures the visible agents, the ruling factors of this wicked system of things, whom Satan has used in oppressing Jehovah's remnant, the nucleus of the New World society. The battle fought at and near Megiddo pictured the battle of Armageddon, in

20. What evidence did Jael produce of her loyalty and backing?
21. Who were pictured by Deborah, Barak, King Jabin and army chief Sisera, and what was pictured by the battle near Megiddo?

which Jehovah will fight by his Chief Executioner, Jesus Christ, for the vindication of his universal sovereignty and for the rescue and relief of his witnesses.

²² Whom, then, does the non-Israelite woman Jael typify? The same as Hobab, the same as Jehonadab, the same as her other kinsmen the Rechabites. She typifies the "other sheep" who do good to the remnant of spiritual Israelites, the 'least of these Christ's brothers,' doing it the same as to him. This "great crowd" of his "other sheep" dwell as "temporary residents" in among the spiritual Israelites. No matter what the friendly ties of their close relatives may be to this old world, the Jael class cannot approve of the oppression of world rulers upon Jehovah's people. Their choice is to be loyal to the Greater Barak, Jesus Christ, and to the New World society of Jehovah's witnesses. They cannot harbor the enemy oppressors of Jehovah's remnant. They use their wisest strategy to hammer to death the influence, power and effect of the worldly ruling factors in their endeavors to oppress Jehovah's people and reproach His name. They must do this before Armageddon, not after when none of the enemy will remain. Even at the risk of their life they show their sympathy with the coming execution of Jehovah's foes. Even after Armageddon has begun and the organized forces of false religion have been overthrown, they will have to display stanch allegiance to the Greater Barak and loyalty to his remnant and proclaim with them Jehovah's judgments yet to be executed upon the enemies left, including the Devil himself. That way they will escape execution themselves and will continue to live in the New World society until its joyful entry into the "new earth" free from enemies.

---

22. Who was typified by Jael, and in what special respects?

CHAPTER XVIII

Constructive, Lifesaving Activities

THE members of the New World society are not a fanatical crowd of unrealistic people, impractical, idle dreamers, moved with false hopes. They are the greatest realists, facing the actual facts of this "time of the end" since 1914 and courageously putting the meaning on them that God's Book of prophecy puts on them. With trust in him they calmly look to the destruction of this unsuccessful world in the "war of the great day of God the Almighty." They are organizing now to go into action in the postwar period to do the enormous reconstruction work then. They do not try to hasten the destruction of this world by in any way subverting its political governments of any kind, and it is likewise contrary to God's will for them to engage in any violence during the battle of Armageddon. Christ's command to them is: "Pay back, therefore, Caesar's things to Caesar, but God's things to God." (Matthew 22:21, *NW*) They cannot save this doomed, not-worth-saving world from destruction by Almighty God, but in his most practical way they can try to save as many people as possible from that sudden destruction. Reasonably they cannot take part in any reconstruction of this old world but must let it fall to its destruction. Yet they are the most constructive people, specializing on constructive work the effects of which will pass through the

---

1. How are the New World society a most realistic people, life-benefiting and constructive in their work for lasting good?

288

demolition of this world and last forever. They work for the coming new world.

² The Sacred Scriptures foresaw the activities of the New World society in the time of the end. A historical picture of them is presented in the tenth man in the line of descent from Adam, Noah, and his family. Noah, too, lived in a time of the end, the end of the preflood world; and Jesus, in his prophecy, declared that the happenings of Noah's day were typical of things to happen in the time of the end of this postflood world. He said: "Heaven and earth will pass away, but my words will by no means pass away. Concerning that day and hour nobody knows, neither the angels of the heavens nor the Son, but only the Father. For just as the days of Noah were, so the presence of the Son of man will be. For as people were in those days before the flood, eating and drinking, marrying and giving in marriage, until the day that Noah entered into the ark; and they took no note until the flood came and swept them all away, so the presence of the Son of man will be. Keep on the watch, therefore, because you do not know on what day your Master is coming." (Matthew 24:35-39, 42, *NW*) From Noah any person seeking survival can learn what is practical now.

³ The violence and moral corruption of the world since A.D. 1914 find their correspondency in the like things of Noah's day. But Noah and his family were different; so must the members of the New World society be now. Noah leading his family walked with the true God; so must the New World society under Christ do today. Noah and his family were righteous in God's sight in his genera-

---

2. In whom is there given a picture of the New World society in doing what is practical now for survival?
3. How must the New World society be like Noah and his family morally and religiously?

tion; so must the members of the New World society be now. Noah was a "preacher of righteousness," an upbuilding, constructive preacher; so must the New World society preach what Jesus foretold they should preach, "this good news of the kingdom" for a witness.

⁴ Noah, at the command of God the supreme Architect and Builder, built a huge ark or chest to preserve human and animal life through the flood of which God warned. "By faith Noah, after being given divine warning of things not yet beheld, showed godly fear and constructed an ark for the saving of his household, and through this faith he condemned the world, and he became an heir of the righteousness which is according to faith." (Hebrews 11:7, NW) Noah's works of faith were different, being works of righteousness and of obedience to God. Thus by such works of faith he condemned the world for its wicked, faithless works. He showed that it deserved to perish, but that he and his household were worth preserving. Similarly through faith proved by their works of obedience to God the New World society condemns this world. It gives practical, visible proof that there is a better organization than this world and that this world deserves to perish but the New World society is the practical thing, worthy of being preserved and perpetuated.

⁵ Armageddon will not be a global flood, for God said there would be no repeating of such a flood. So the New World society does not build an ark for survival through Armageddon. The ark was typical of something greater, and Jesus Christ is the antitypical Noah who builds it. The apostle Peter refers to it in these words: "The patience of

4. How does the New World society, like Noah, condemn this world?
5. Of what was Noah's ark typical, and what baptism for salvation did Noah's family experience?

God was waiting in Noah's days, while the ark was being constructed, in which a few people, that is, eight souls, were carried safely through the water. That which corresponds to this [or, which thing as an antitype] is also now saving you, namely, baptism, (not the putting away of the filth of the flesh, but the request made to God for a good conscience,) through the resurrection of Jesus Christ. He is at God's right hand, for he went his way to heaven, and angels and authorities and powers were made subject to him." (1 Peter 3:20-22, *NW*, margin) The ark, therefore, typifies the new system of things that the resurrected, glorified Jesus builds. (Hebrews 1:2, *NW*) The seven human souls with Noah were not saved by being baptized in the flood the way the ancient world was, but were saved by being baptized into Noah in the ark, just as centuries later the Israelites and the "mixed crowd" with them were baptized into Moses by means of the Red Sea and the cloud of Jehovah overhead. (1 Corinthians 10:1, 2, *NW*)* Today the New World society is the organization of Jehovah's witnesses and it must get into the "ark," the new system of things that God builds through Jesus Christ.

⁶ The members of the organization or New World society must be baptized into the antitypical Noah, Jesus Christ, by being submerged into him as their Leader and Commander, to obey and copy him and to go where he goes. That results in the "good conscience" that they request from God. If they are baptized into him, then where he goes as the Head they will go as the body under him. Now they must keep close to him within the antitypical ark, the new system of things. As with the Israelites at crossing the Red Sea, which typified

---

* See chapter VII, pages 123, ¶25, to 125, ¶27.

---

6. What is the baptism of the New World society that now leads to salvation through Armageddon?

surviving Armageddon, so with the New World society at Armageddon: they will there in a special sense be baptized into the Greater Noah by means of the fiery baptism of Armageddon.

[7] Since A.D. 1914 Jesus Christ, "the Son of man," has been present in his kingdom. Since then we have been living in the "presence of the Son of man," when it is to be "just as the days of Noah were." As Noah typified the exalted Jesus, Noah's wife well typified the "bride, the Lamb's wife." On earth today she is represented by the remnant of the "bride" class, those who, like a "chaste virgin," are promised in marriage to the "one husband," the Christ. (Revelation 21:9; 19:7; 2 Corinthians 11:2, *NW*) The three sons of Noah, namely, Shem, Ham and Japheth, and their three wives typified those who are with the remnant of the "bride" class within the new system of things under Christ, namely, the "other sheep" whom the Right Shepherd has gathered and whom he has made "one flock" with the remnant under the one Shepherd. Through bringing the life-giving good news of the Kingdom to these "other sheep" and helping them into the way that leads to everlasting life the remnant of the "bride" class has mothered these "other sheep" and they have become the children-to-be of the "Everlasting Father" Jesus Christ.—John 10:16; 1 Corinthians 4:15; Isaiah 9:6, 7.

[8] During the time of the end of the ancient world Noah and the family of which he was the head were engaged in lifesaving activities to keep the human family and the family kinds of the many

---

7. Since when have we been living in the "presence of the Son of man," and who were typified by Noah, his wife, and his three sons and their wives?
8. How were Noah and his family engaged in life-saving activities, and how are Jehovah's witnesses likewise now engaged?

beasts and birds in existence for the future world. Likewise the organization of Jehovah's witnesses in the new system of things under Christ must be engaged in lifesaving activities. They are no part of this old world that is insanely preparing for a third world war of death-dealing power to practically all mankind; no, rather, that is bringing on its own violent death by fighting against Jehovah and his kingdom by Christ. By preaching the Kingdom news and warning of the approaching "day of vengeance of our God" they upbuild people in righteousness and help them to get into the only destruction-proof shelter for Armageddon, the new system of things with its baptism into the Greater Noah, Jesus Christ.

⁹ Nuclear scientists of today may doubt the possibility of mankind's surviving a world war with nuclear weapons, but Jehovah's witnesses with their "wisdom from above" know from that type of Noah's experience that Almighty God can preserve them through the world's end at Armageddon, and that this education of the people in the Bible and obeying the commandments of Jehovah God is the only scientific way that leads to preservation. "Certainly if God did not hold back from . . . punishing an ancient world, but kept Noah, a preacher of righteousness, safe with seven others when he brought a deluge upon a world of ungodly people; . . . Jehovah knows how to deliver people of godly devotion out of trial, but to reserve unrighteous people for the day of judgment to be cut off."—2 Peter 2:4-9, *NW*.

¹⁰ The old world's "time of the end" is the time

---

9. From the type of Noah's experience, what do Jehovah's witnesses know respecting preservation?
10. (a) The world's time of the end is a time of restoring whom? (b) Like whose restoration of old is it, and who was anointed to declare a restoration of a larger kind?

of the beginning of the "new heavens" for bringing in a completely new world. It is a time of founding the "new earth" by forming the New World society. It is a time of restoring those who were recently captives of the old world and in peril of being destroyed with it. (Isaiah 51:14-16) It is a time like that of the restoring of the captive Israelites from Babylon to their Palestine homeland that had lain desolate for seventy years, with its cities, even Jerusalem, in ruins and its fields and vineyards uncultivated, running wild. Much reconstruction work was then needed; the pure worship of Jehovah God needed to be started there anew by his legitimate Aaronic priests and their Levite ministers or assistants. To declare real restoration and to invite the liberty-loving, true worshipers to take advantage of it, Jehovah anointed his Son Jesus Christ with holy spirit that he might say: "The Spirit of the Lord Jehovah is upon me, because Jehovah hath anointed me to announce glad tidings unto the meek; he hath sent me to bind up the broken-hearted, to proclaim liberty to the captives, and opening of the prison to them that are bound; to proclaim the acceptable year of Jehovah, and the day of vengeance of our God; to comfort all that mourn; to appoint unto [the mourners of Zion], that beauty should be given unto them instead of ashes, the oil of joy instead of mourning, the garment of praise instead of the spirit of heaviness: that they might be called [oak trees] of righteousness, the planting of Jehovah, that he may be glorified."—Isaiah 61:1-3, *Da; AT.*

[11] During his first presence nineteen centuries ago the anointed Jesus did preach such a message

---

11. How did Jesus accomplish such a restoration work during his first presence, and how does he continue this restoration during his presence in the time of the end now?

and accomplish a joy-giving, life-bringing restoration work among Jews who mourned because of their religious captivity to Judaism with its law-transgressing traditions, its man-made commands and its religious oppressors. That restoration work continued on till Jehovah's "day of vengeance" came upon unfaithful Zion or Jerusalem A.D. 70 and the adherents of Judaism were scattered to the ends of the earth. A continuation of that restoration, but on a greater scale, has come in this "time of the end" during the "presence of the Son of man" in his heavenly throne. He has restored the remnant of spiritual Israelites from their religious captivity in antitypical Babylon, doing this by means of the spirit with which the remnant have been anointed and by means of the truth. As he said: "You will know the truth, and the truth will set you free." (John 8:32, NW) Instead of dry ashes, mourning and the spirit of heaviness, they have spiritual beauty, shine with the oil of joy, and wear the praises of God like a garment of identification. They droop no more, but have become like strong oaks producing righteous fruits, planted by Jehovah and therefore rooted and grounded in his organization, that they may serve to His glory, proving that he is God.

¹² Their earthly condition was specially desolated during World War I. But the reconstruction work in Jehovah's pure worship that the joyful, delivered remnant now do in it the prophecy concerning Jehovah's anointed goes on to describe symbolically thus: "And they shall build the old wastes, they shall raise up the former desolations, and they shall repair the waste cities, the places desolate from generation to generation."—Isaiah 61:4, Da.

---

12. What work do the remnant do in their formerly desolated earthly condition, and how did Isaiah 61:4 foretell this?

¹³ Since 1919 this has gone on. The spiritual remnant, the original part and those who have been added to them since 1919 and down to 1931, have done great spiritual reconstructive work, converting their once desolate-looking earthly estate into one that resembles the paradise of Eden. They have built up their citylike organizations, their congregations, and have fortified them spiritually before Armageddon. (Fortified cities will not be needed after Armageddon.) They have been comparatively few in number, in a hostile world. It is clear that, not by might nor by power but by Jehovah's spirit or active force, the prophecy has been fulfilled concerning them: "And the land that was desolate shall be tilled, whereas it was a desolation in the sight of all that passed by. And they shall say, This land that was desolate is become like the garden of Eden; and the waste and desolate and ruined cities are fortified and inhabited." (Ezekiel 36:34, 35, *AS*) This beautiful transformation becomes noticeable from the fact that the congregations of Jehovah's remnant grew not only in size but in number. Whereas in 1919 they had to employ outside factories to do all their printing of Bible literature, they had a number of their own factories by 1931 to do their own printing in and outside the United States of America. Whereas in 1919 they reorganized the work with about 14 branches outside America, there were 38 such branches in 1931, and the Watch Tower literature was published in a corresponding number of different languages.

¹⁴ However, the restored remnant were not to enjoy this spiritual paradise to themselves. Addressing the anointed remnant of spiritual

---

13. How have they transformed their once desolate-looking earthly estate and built fortified cities, and how was the growth to be noticed from 1919 to 1931?
14. Were they to enjoy this spiritual paradise to themselves, and how does Isaiah go on to say whether or not?

Israel, Isaiah's prophecy goes on to say: "And strangers shall stand and feed your flocks, and the sons of the alien shall be your ploughmen and your vine-dressers. But as for you, ye shall be called priests of Jehovah; it shall be said of you: Ministers of our God. Ye shall eat the wealth of the nations, and into their glory shall ye enter. Instead of your shame [ye shall have] double; instead of confusion they shall celebrate with joy their portion: therefore in their land they shall possess the double; everlasting joy shall be unto them. For I, Jehovah, love judgment, I hate robbery with wrong; and I will give their recompence in truth, and I will make an everlasting covenant with them. And their seed shall be known among the nations, and their offspring among the peoples: all that see them shall acknowledge them, that they are a seed that Jehovah hath blessed." —Isaiah 61:4-9, *Da*.

¹⁵ To natural Israelites, if strangers and sons of the alien fed their flocks and were their plowmen and vinedressers, it would be something remarkable. For the terms "strangers" and "sons of the alien" did not refer to such people in Israel as the temporary residents or immigrants or the Nethinim temple slaves or the non-Israelite singers or the servants of Solomon, but referred to those who came from outside the land, foreigners. When dedicating the temple on Mount Moriah in Jerusalem, King Solomon prayed for such in these words: "Also as to the foreigner who is no part of your people Israel and who actually comes from a distant land by reason of your name (for they shall hear of your great name and of your strong hand and of your stretched-out arm), and he

---

15. How was strangers and sons of the aliens' serving in these occupations something remarkable for Israel, and how did Solomon pray for such ones at the temple dedication?

actually comes and prays toward this house, may
you yourself hear from the heavens, your established place of dwelling, and you must do according to all that for which the foreigner calls to you,
in order that all the peoples of the earth may get
to know your name so as to fear you the same as
your people Israel do and so as to know that your
name itself has been called upon this house that I
have built." (1 Kings 8:41-43, *NW;* 2 Chronicles
6:32, 33) Thus the strangers or foreigners were
to be drawn to Israel because of Israel's worship
of the true God and because of his favor upon
Israel.

[16] The fulfillment of Isaiah's prophecy and the
answer to the temple prayer of Solomon, typical
of the One greater than he, Jesus Christ, are to be
seen distinctly since 1931. Of course, from February of 1918 on the anointed remnant preached the
message "Millions Now Living Will Never Die,"
but from 1931 on they turned their attention to
marking with the Kingdom truth the foreheads of
the people who were grieved over spiritual conditions in the world, especially in Christendom.
From house to house, from city to city, from nation to nation, they went doing the marking.
(Ezekiel 9:1-4) Jehovah blessed the work and
many marked "strangers" and "sons of the alien,"
that is, many not of the remnant of spiritual
Israel, came to Jehovah's visible organization in
its spiritual prosperity. They did not let persecutions or the breaking up of natural home ties prevent them from coming and associating with Jehovah's remnant. They recognized the remnant as
being "priests of Jehovah" and "ministers of our
God," that is to say, as being members of a "chosen
race, a royal priesthood, a holy nation, a people

---

16. Because of what work since 1931 have such "strangers" and "sons of the alien" come, and as what have
the remnant been recognized by them?

for special possession," so that with these it was
necessary to worship Jehovah as God. (1 Peter
2:9, *NW*) As time has gone on they have come
from all parts of the earth to form what the apostle
John saw in vision, "a great crowd, which no man
was able to number, out of all nations and tribes
and peoples and tongues, standing before the
throne [of Jehovah] and before the Lamb [Jesus
Christ]." And Jehovah has done what these have
called to him for at his temple.

¹⁷ The prophet Zechariah, who was raised up
with Haggai to encourage the Jewish remnant to
rebuild the temple, also foretold the coming of the
great crowd from all nations and their attaching
themselves to the remnant of spiritual Jews.
Zechariah encouraged the remnant to be a joyful,
glad and cheerful people and to love truth and
peace, and then added: "Thus saith Jehovah of
hosts: Yet again shall there come peoples, and the
inhabitants of many cities; and the inhabitants of
one city shall go to another, saying, Let us go
speedily to supplicate Jehovah, and to seek Jehovah of hosts: I will go also. And many peoples and
strong nations shall come to seek Jehovah of hosts
in Jerusalem, and to supplicate Jehovah. Thus
saith Jehovah of hosts: In those days shall ten
men take hold, out of all languages of the nations,
shall even take hold of the skirt of him that is a
Jew, saying, We will go with you [people]; for
we have heard [that] God is with you [people]."
(Zechariah 8:18-23, *Da*) Thus the great attraction
to strangers and sons of the alien of all nations is,
not the remnant of spiritual Jews in themselves,
but the God to whom they are priests and ministers and also the truth and peace with which God
has blessed them.

---

17. Who did Zechariah foretell would attach themselves
to spiritual Jews, and what is it really that attracts
these?

[18] These antitypical "strangers" and "sons of the alien" come to serve God with the remnant. They cannot become spiritual priests and ministers of Jehovah, for God has not called them to that spiritual service; but they become, as it were, feeders of the flock in the charge of the spiritual remnant and plowmen and vinedressers of theirs. The membership of the New World society has grown so, the congregations of Jehovah's witnesses have increased so, to over 14,500 throughout the earth by 1955, under 75 branch offices of the Watch Tower Bible & Tract Society, that it has become needful to make many of these strangers and aliens responsible servants with oversight of congregations in most cases. This has prominently been true since the publication of the article "Company Servant" in the issue of May 1, 1937, of *The Watchtower*. But all these strangers and aliens have engaged in a general pastoral work of hunting and finding the other sheep and feeding them spiritually and inviting them to come up to Jehovah's house and worship him. They have also done figurative plowing up of the ground for the scattering of the seed of the Word of God and done vinedressing for toning up the vine of the organization to produce fruits of righteousness to make God glad and make Jehovah-fearing men glad.

[19] The prophet Isaiah, after telling Zion or Jerusalem to arise and shine in Jehovah's glory, said to her: "And the sons of the alien shall build up thy walls, and their kings shall minister unto thee." (Isaiah 60:10, *Da*) When the Jewish remnant left Babylon in 537 B.C. and returned to Jerusalem to rebuild it and its temple, not only were there non-

---

18. How have these antitypical "strangers" and "sons of the alien" served as feeders of the flock and as plowmen and vinedressers, and particularly since when?
19. What case is there of "sons of the alien" engaged in building up the walls of ancient Jerusalem, and what has been the antitype of this in the time of the end now?

Israelite Nethinim or "temple slaves" that went along but also Gibeonites are listed with those returning: "the sons of Gib'e·on, ninety-five." (Nehemiah 7:25, 46-56, 60, *NW*) When governor Nehemiah came from Shushan in Persia to Jerusalem to repair or rebuild its walls, he assigned portions of the wall not only to the families of the Israelite inhabitants but also to the non-Israelite Gibeonites: "At their side Mel·a·ti'ah the Gib'e·on·ite and Ja'don the Me·ron'o·thite, men of Gib'e·on and Miz'pah, did repair work, for the throne of the governor beyond the River." (Nehemiah 3:7, *NW*) So in Israel's case there was a partial fulfillment of the prophecy that the sons of aliens should build up the walls of the city where Jehovah had placed his name. But in this time of the end of the old world it has been overwhelmingly true that antitypical "sons of aliens," those not of the remnant, have done fortification work in the New World society corresponding to the rebuilding of the walls of ancient Jerusalem.

[20] The constructive, lifesaving activities of the New World society continue to expand. The growing numbers of the "great crowd" work alongside the remnant and in support of them. All carry out the "one law" that is to "exist for the native and for the temporary resident," which law is: "Also in all the nations the good news has to be preached first."—Exodus 12:49 and Mark 13:10, *NW*.

---

20. So with whom does the "great crowd" now work, and what "one law" do all carry out together?

CHAPTER XIX

Benefits Flowing from the Temple

IT IS at the one spiritual temple of unified worship that the remnant of the "royal priesthood" and the "great crowd" serve the one living and true God. That has come about because of the life-bringing benefits that are flowing from the temple for all who desire to partake. True, "it is the appointed time for the judgment to start with the house of God," and in the spring of 1918 *A·do·nay'* Jehovah and his Angel or Messenger of the covenant came to the temple for the judgment proceedings and that meant a severe time to follow. But even this judgment has been of incalculable benefit, for it has resulted in a needed purification and straightening out of vital matters. The prophet Malachi, foretelling the coming of *A·do·nay'* and his Messenger to the temple, went on to describe the judgment work and the desirable results, saying: " 'Who can endure the day of his coming? And who can stand when he appears? For he shall be like a refiner's fire, and like fullers' soap. And he shall sit down as a refiner and cleanser of silver, and shall cleanse the sons of Levi. He shall purify them like gold and silver, so that they shall become for the LORD [Jehovah] men who bring him offerings in righteousness. Then the offering of Judah and Jerusalem shall be pleasing

---

1. (a) Where and because of what do the remnant and the "great crowd" carry on a unified worship? (b) What kind of time was to follow the coming of Jehovah and his Angel to the temple, but of what benefit did Malachi say this would be?

to the LORD [Jehovah], as in the days of old and
as in former years. Then I will draw near to you
for judgment, and I will be a swift witness against
the sorcerers and adulterers, and against those
who swear to falsehood; and against those who
oppress the hireling in his wages, the widow and
the orphan; and those who defraud the resident
alien, and do not fear me,' says the LORD [Jeho-
vah] of hosts."—Malachi 3:2-5, AT.

² When Jesus Christ, as Jehovah's Messenger,
came to the temple the question arose, Which pro-
fessing Christians will be able to endure the tests
of loyalty and zeal that will be applied? Who will
stand approved before him for his future service?
He himself was to be a great test to those claiming
to follow him; he himself would be like a gold and
silver refiner's fire and like a clothes cleaner's lye
or alkaline solution, which God would apply.
Would they show up like precious metal to Him,
purified by their acceptance of His Messenger Jesus Christ as the Foundation Cornerstone laid in
Zion, as Jehovah's enthroned King? Would their
garments of identification as Christians show up
clean by taking to themselves Jehovah's Messenger
as their Leader and Commander and as the one
to be copied? Those who accepted Jehovah's Messenger in the royal, spiritual offices with which
Jehovah clothed him were found precious and purified. Those not doing so did not endure the test,
could not stand approved and were rejected. (1 Peter 2:4-8; Isaiah 8:13-15, AS) They proved they
were not antitypical Levites and were disqualified
from serving as priests or ministering at Jehovah's
spiritual house. They were not offering right sacrifices.

---

2. At the coming of Jehovah's Messenger to the temple,
what main questions arose, and how was he himself
like a gold and silver refiner's fire and like a clothes
cleaner's solution?

³ Jehovah's Messenger also sat down at the temple like a refiner and cleanser of silver, and the ones to be cleansed first were the antitypical "sons of Levi." (In Israel the priests and the temple ministers were taken from the tribe of Levi. According to Numbers 3:40-51, they were taken by Jehovah in exchange for the first-born of Israel that had been spared alive on the passover night down in Egypt. They therefore typified the "congregation of the firstborn who have been enrolled in the heavens," mentioned in Hebrews 12:23 [NW]. The remnant are the last on earth of this congregation of the "firstborn" and are therefore antitypical "sons of Levi.") On coming to Jehovah's temple in 1918 his Messenger applied the fire to them, testing them by organization arrangements on their loyalty to Jehovah's organization rather than to human leaders, testing them by service instructions and provisions as to their zeal and devotion for Jehovah's worship and witness work, testing them by revealed truth as to their love of it. What a fiery time it was!

⁴ He called his professed followers and servants before him for an accounting. Those who proved to be an "evil slave" class indulging themselves and abusing the faithful slave class; those who proved to be a "wicked and sluggish slave" class, a "good-for-nothing slave" class, he deprived of service privileges in Jehovah's organization and threw them out. Those who proved to be a "faithful and discreet slave" class, a "good and faithful slave" class, like purified gold and silver, he retained in service. He entrusted them with more interests of Jehovah's worship and more Kingdom

---

3. Who are the antitypical "sons of Levi," and how did Jehovah's Messenger at the temple sit like a silver refiner and test them as by fire?
4. How did his accounting with his professed followers and servants turn out?

interests.—Matthew 24:45-51; 25:14-30 and Luke 12:42-48; 19:11-27, *NW.*

⁵ The beneficial result of this has been that the remnant of antitypical "sons of Levi" have become for Jehovah "men who bring him offerings in righteousness." They have a higher regard for his spiritual temple; they do not consider his altar to be a contemptible table on which any defective sacrifice can be laid; they have inspected carefully and tried to offer to him wholehearted sacrifices of praise and good works, doing service out of love and not for hire.—Malachi 1:6 to 2:9; Hebrews 13:15, 16; Philippians 4:18.

⁶ They have gradually been led to a theocratic form of organization, ruled from God on top. Their sacrifice of preaching the Kingdom news in all the inhabited earth has been offered with greater appreciation, devotion and efficiency, being participated in by all the antitypical "sons of Levi." Jehovah, the theocratic Ruler of the organization, has been a swift witness against those engaged in any spiritistic practices, those guilty of adultery physically or spiritually, those false to their vows to God, those unjust and oppressive toward others who are weak and helpless and entitled to wages, and those not giving the due to people like a "resident alien" in Israel, the "great crowd" from all nations. Against such spiritual Israelites Jehovah has caused an exposure and has either brought about their correction and purification or cast them out, disfellowshiped them. In consequence the spiritual offering to God by the purified remnant has become "pleasing to the LORD [Jehovah], as in the days of old and as in former years," as in the days of the primitive congregation in the

---

5, 6. (a) Of what beneficial result has this been to the antitypical "sons of Levi"? (b) Against whom has Jehovah at the temple been a swift witness? (c) How has the spiritual offering by the remnant now become, and what do noticers of this call them?

time of the "twelve apostles of the Lamb." So Jehovah has blessed his restored remnant with delightful spiritual prosperity. The "great crowd" in all nations have taken note of this and the prophecy goes into fulfillment: "And all nations shall call you blessed; for ye shall be a delightsome land, saith Jehovah of hosts."—Malachi 3:10-12, *Da*.

⁷ The life-bringing benefits that have flowed from the temple of pure worship the prophets liken to a stream of precious water of life. In speaking of the time of the remnant's restoration and of their spiritual prosperity the prophet Joel says: "And a fountain shall come forth from the house of Jehovah, and shall water the valley of Shittim." (Joel 3:18, *AS*) The place where, figuratively, only the shittah trees or acacias of the waste places or deserts would grow becomes well watered, more productive and lovely in appearance. Since the house of Jehovah, his temple, was in Jerusalem, the prophecy would thus be fulfilled: "It shall come to pass in that day, that living waters shall go out from Jerusalem; half of them toward the eastern sea, and half of them toward the western sea: in summer and in winter shall it be. And Jehovah shall be King over all the earth: in that day shall Jehovah be one, and his name one." (Zechariah 14:8, 9, *AS*) Thus to the Dead Sea to the east and to the "great sea," the "sea of the Philistines," the Mediterranean Sea, to the west the life-giving waters from Jehovah's temple would go after he and his Messenger of the covenant came to the temple.

⁸ Ezekiel prophesied of the destruction of the temple built by Solomon. When he got a vision of Jehovah's temple rebuilt, he said this of it: "And

---

7. To what were the life-giving benefits flowing from the temple likened at Joel 3:18 and at Zechariah 14:8, 9?
8. In his vision, what did Ezekiel see flowing from the rebuilt temple, and in what direction and with what increasing depths?

he [a glorious man with a measuring reed in his hand] brought me back to the door of the house; and behold, waters issued out from under the threshold of the house eastward: for the front of the house was eastward. And the waters came down from under, from the right side of the house, south of the altar. And he brought me out by the way of the gate northward, and led me round outside unto the outer gate towards [the gate] that looketh eastward; and behold, waters ran out on the right side. When the man went forth eastward, a line was in his hand; and he measured a thousand cubits, and he caused me to pass through the waters: the waters were to the ankles. And he measured a thousand [cubits], and caused me to pass through the waters: the waters were to the knees. And he measured a thousand and caused me to pass through: the waters were to the loins. And he measured a thousand: it was a river that I could not pass through, for the waters were risen, waters to swim in, a river that could not be passed through."—Ezekiel 40:3; 47:1-5, *Da.*

⁹ This stream had its source in Jehovah's restored temple and as it moved eastward did not dry up but grew deeper every fifteen hundred feet until it became a river a man could not ford. This pictures the flow of truth by publishers, beginning from the temple in 1919. At the beginning it flowed to only a small restored remnant. But as time moved on and the remnant, like Ezekiel, moved forward toward the light, the flow of truth by its publication through the spoken word and on the printed page increased. By 1931 it became a deep river that even the rise to power of Fascists and Nazis and Communists and Catholic Action could not check, no, not even World War II. That meant that not only more Bible literature was published by the Watch Tower Society and its foreign

9. What was pictured by this river and by its increasing depths?

branches but there were more publishers of the Kingdom news to distribute it and to preach by word of mouth. The full number of the remnant came in to do the publication as Jehovah's witnesses.

[10] The prophet Ezekiel now tells how his guide led him back to the riverbank. "When I returned, behold, on the bank of the river were very many trees on the one side and on the other. And he said unto me, These waters issue out toward the east district, and go down into the plain, and go into the sea; when they are brought forth into the [Salt] sea, the waters [thereof] shall be healed. And it shall come to pass that every living thing which moveth, whithersoever the double river shall come, shall live. And there shall be a very great multitude of fish; for these waters shall come thither, and [the waters of the sea] shall be healed; and everything shall live whither the river cometh. And it shall come to pass, that fishers shall stand upon it; from En-gedi even unto En-eglaim shall be [a place] to spread forth nets: their fish shall be according to their kinds, as the fish of the great sea, exceeding many. But its marshes and its pools shall not be healed; they shall be given up to salt. And by the river, upon its bank, on the one side and on the other, shall grow all trees for food, whose leaf shall not fade, nor their fruit fail: it shall bring forth new fruit every month, for its waters issue out of the sanctuary [Jehovah's temple]; and the fruit thereof shall be for food, and the leaf thereof for medicine."—Ezekiel 47:6-12, Da.

[11] This river of life-giving water from Jehovah's

10. Into what did the river empty, what was the effect upon its waters, who took up activity along it, and what grew on each bank of the river?
11. Who are pictured by the trees on the river banks, and what does this river figuratively do that the Jordan River never has done?

temple with symbolic trees lining its banks would be unlike any literal river on earth. Like shore-lining trees it has the fruitful members of the remnant of spiritual Israelites, "the planting of Jehovah." As the river of Ezekiel's vision emptied

into the Salt Sea, or Dead Sea, it produced a miracle. The Jordan River pouring into that Dead Sea had never sweetened it or made it suitable for fish. But the river from Jehovah's temple did heal those waters. It turned them sweet, so that fish came to life in those waters.

[12] Because of the abundance of fish that grew in the no more dead or salt sea, a fishing industry grows up and fishers spread their nets to haul in great catches of fish. What a prophetic picture this is of how the waters of Kingdom truth from Jehovah's temple being borne by the remnant of the temple class to the circumstances in which the "great crowd" or numberless "other sheep" are found heals those circumstances, makes those circumstances livable! Before the Kingdom truth from the temple reached them, they were living in the "shadow of death," in a dead world under doom of destruction at Armageddon. But when they received and drank up the waters of Kingdom truth, the circumstances changed for them. They came out from a lifeless element, a world dead in its sins, out from under the threat of destruction at Armageddon, and became alive to God. They are becoming like the fish of the "great sea," whom no man is "able to number." Noting their presence, the remnant of spiritual Israelites have become "fishers of men" and they unitedly set out their nets for them and haul them in, bringing them into the New World society. There they feed on the spiritual food that the "faithful and discreet slave" class, like ever-fruitful trees along the temple river banks, serve to them.—Matthew 4:19.

[13] In its antitypical meaning this resembles the

---

12. What is pictured by the growth of a fishing industry on the shores of the former dead or salt sea, and on what do those fished in feed?
13. In its antitypical meaning, whose healing does this resemble, and how did this non-Israelite come to be healed of his affliction?

healing that came to Naaman the Syrian general who had fought against Israel. His life was marred by the fact that he was a leper, unclean to the society of Jehovah's people. His wife had a little Israelite girl that had been captured. As a witness of Jehovah this girl expressed faith in Jehovah's prophet Elisha as able to cure the husband of her mistress. The faith of this little witness led at last to General Naaman's being sent to Elisha in Israel and riding up to his house in Samaria. Elisha sent out word to him to bathe seven times, not in any of Syria's clear rivers, but in Jordan's muddy waters. At first offended and unwilling, Naaman was persuaded to humble himself in faith and be obedient. "At that he went down and began to plunge into the Jordan seven times according to the word of the man of God, after which his flesh came back like the flesh of a little boy and he became clean."

[14] At this miracle Naaman became convinced that Elisha's God Jehovah is the only God: "Here, now, I certainly know that there is no God anywhere in the earth but in Israel." When Elisha refused any financial reward for God's gift through him, Naaman said: "If not, please, let there be given to your servant some ground, the load of a pair of mules, because your servant will no more render up a burnt offering or a sacrifice to any other gods but to Jehovah. In this thing may Jehovah forgive your servant: When my lord [the king of Syria] comes into the house of Rim'-mon to bow down there and he is supporting himself upon my hand and I have to bow down at the house of Rim'mon, when I bow down at the house of Rim'mon may Jehovah, please, forgive your servant in this respect." Elisha replied: "Go in peace."—2 Kings 5:1-19, *NW*.

---

14. Of whose godship did Naaman become convinced, and what requests did he make regarding future worship?

[15] Because he could not remain in Israel to worship Jehovah there, Naaman took two mule loads of Israelite earth that even in the midst of Syria he might worship Jehovah on Israelite soil. On that transplanted soil Naaman doubtless worshiped toward Jehovah's temple in Jerusalem, praying toward it as King Solomon described in his prayer. (1 Kings 8:41-43) His bowing in the house of the false god Rimmon in Damascus was only a formal convenience to his lord, the king of Syria, who, leaning upon Naaman then, would have to have him bow to make his own bow to Rimmon. But Naaman showed this was only a formal convenience, because he refused to offer any sacrifice to Rimmon or any other false gods.

[16] Naaman, too, typifies those of the "great crowd" who worship Jehovah today at his spiritual temple. Once condemned with this world, doomed to death like a leper, they seek the assistance of the remnant class, confess their sins, ask Jehovah's forgiveness through Christ, obediently bathe a complete number of times in the life-giving, cleansing water of Kingdom truth now flowing from Jehovah's temple, and are cleansed and made fit for the New World society. They take up the exclusive worship of Jehovah, who can cure believers in him spiritually for eternal life in the new world.

[17] Through the apostle John, the exalted Jesus Christ revealed the happy privilege of those who partake of the lifesaving benefit of the river of truth that flows forth from Jehovah's temple. Seeing a vision quite like Ezekiel's, John says: "And he showed me a river of water of life, clear as crystal, flowing out from the throne of God and of

---

15. How did Naaman worship after that, and how was his bowing in the house of Rimmon only a formal convenience?
16. Whom does Naaman typify, and in what respects?
17. What vision of a river did the apostle John see, and out from where does this river now flow?

the Lamb down the middle of its [the New Jerusalem's] broad way. And on this side of the river and on that side there were trees of life producing twelve crops of fruit, yielding their fruits each month. And the leaves of the trees were for the curing of the nations. And no more will there be any curse. But the throne of God and of the Lamb will be in it, and his slaves [the 144,000] will render him sacred service, and they will see his face, and his name will be on their foreheads." (Revelation 22:1-5; 14:1, *NW*) A·do·nay' Jehovah has come to his temple and sits enthroned there for judgment, as seen in Isaiah's vision. (Isaiah 6:1-5) Jesus Christ as Messenger of the covenant has come with him to the temple and also sits enthroned there. It is out from under their throne that the "river of water of life" flows.

[18] Since the New Jerusalem seen in the vision symbolizes the "bride, the Lamb's wife," and the river of water of life courses down through the broad way of the New Jerusalem, it pictures that the life-giving waters of Kingdom truth flow through the "bride" class, represented on earth by the present-day remnant. Also the ever-productive fruit trees on both sides of the river symbolize the members of the remnant, who must continually produce the 'fruits of the Kingdom,' especially for the food and curing of the "other sheep." (Matthew 21:43, *NW*) Their responsibility toward this "great crowd" is further shown in what the apostle John saw and heard after beholding the river of water of life: "And the spirit and the bride keep on saying, 'Come!' And let anyone hearing say, 'Come!' And let anyone thirsting come; let anyone that wishes take life's water free." (Revelation 22:17, *NW*) The remnant of the "bride" class must

---

[18]. (a) What does the river's flowing down the city's broad way picture, and who are pictured by the fruit trees on both sides? (b) How do the spirit and the bride now say to come to the water?

extend the gracious invitation* to the thirsty other sheep to come to the stream of life-imparting Kingdom truth that now flows like an irresistible river. The remnant must do the inviting in full harmony with the spirit of the prophecies of God's Word, including Ezekiel's vision. Not only the spirit of God's prophecies that apply now says, "Come!" but God's active force or spirit is operating upon the remnant of the "bride" toward having the invitation extended to people of all nations.

[19] Anyone hearing the invitation should come, if he is really thirsty through a consciousness of his spiritual need. But he should not enjoy the water only to himself. Realizing its benefit, he should want to share it with others and should tell others to come. Otherwise he would be selfish, grossly so, especially when there is plenty of water and it is free to all and all others need it. No one may make money off this water of life, like water vendors over in the Orient who sell water for so much a drink.† The remnant of the "bride" must instruct the thirst quenchers to join in inviting others to come, and must train them to do so by teaching them to be preachers of the Kingdom message. The "great crowd" must therefore take up the invitation and extend it to still other thirsty ones. It must not be withheld from anyone because of race, color, family or language. God's spirit or active force will work with the obedient ones in passing along the invitation and helping and directing others to the river of water of life from the heavenly throne. It is the drinking of this water and inviting others that lead to survival during Armageddon into God's new world.

---

* See the article "Gracious Invitation" in *The Watch Tower* of March 15, 1929.

† See Lamentations 5:4, *RS.*

---

19. (a) Who should come, but what should those coming also do? (b) What should the remnant of the "bride" class do, and what will God's spirit do?

CHAPTER XX

Awaiting the Attack by Gog of Magog

THE "time of the end" is fast nearing its close. Toward its close a total attack is to be expected upon the New World society. It will be the attack by the symbolic Gog of the land of Magog, which was long ago prophesied to take place "in the end of the days" or "in the latter days." (*AT; AS*) The direct object of Gog's attack is plainly stated to be the restored remnant of Jehovah's people, who, in their turn, are commanded to notify Gog that Jehovah God is against him and will bring about his destruction before their eyes. "Son of man, set thy face toward Gog, of the land of Magog, the prince of Rosh, Meshech, and Tubal, and prophesy against him, and say, Thus saith the Lord Jehovah: Behold, I am against thee, O Gog, prince of Rosh, Meshech, and Tubal; and I will turn thee about, and put hooks into thy jaws, and I will bring thee forth, and all thine army, horses and horsemen, all of them clothed in full armor, a great company with buckler and shield, all of them handling swords: Persia, Cush, and Put with them, all of them with shield and helmet; Gomer, and all his hordes; the house of Togarmah in the uttermost parts of the north, and all his hordes; even many peoples with thee."—Ezekiel 38:1-6, *AS*.

---

1. What attack is to be expected toward the close of the time of the end, and of what are the ones under attack to notify the leader of the attack?

[2] The exact meaning of the name "Gog" is not known, but since 1953 the bearer of that name has been exposed as being Satan the Devil himself, now that he has been hurled down from heaven to the earth. Gog is thus Satan the Dragon in his abased condition, and his land of Magog is his abased invisible location with his demons in the vicinity of this earth. It is in this symbolic land of Magog that he is wrathful at God's "woman" and goes to "wage war with the remaining ones of her seed, who observe the commandments of God and have the work of bearing witness to Jesus." (Revelation 12:13, 17, *NW*) He is still the "ruler of this world" or "the god of this system of things," for which reason he is able to assemble all the nations to a simultaneous, full-scale, final attack from all sides, hemming the remnant or "remaining ones" in, just as the nations in the prophecy hemmed in Israel from the north and south.

[3] Because God's time for the war of Armageddon approaches, God tells Gog of Magog to come on: "Be ready and keep ready, you and all the hosts that are assembled about you, and be a guard [a commander] for them. After many days you will be mustered; in the latter years you will go against the land that is restored from war, the land where people were gathered from many nations upon the mountains of Israel, which had been a continual waste; its people were brought out from the nations and now dwell securely, all of them. You will advance, coming on like a storm, you will be like a cloud covering the land, you and all your hordes, and many peoples with you."—Ezekiel 38:7-9, *RS*.

---

2. Who is the real Gog, what is his land of Magog, and why is he able to assemble all nations to the attack?
3. Why does God tell Gog of Magog to come on, and against whom?

⁴ Since A.D. 1919 the remnant of spiritual Israelites have been restored from Babylonish captivity and been regathered to Jehovah's theocratic
organization. They have not, like the postwar nations, tried to make money and build up material
prosperity but have specialized on preaching "this
good news of the kingdom" in all the inhabited
earth. Why, then, should the symbolic Gog want
to attack them in full force? It is because he be-
grudges them their spiritual prosperity, their spiritually powerful position in the earth. Jehovah exposes Gog's envious greed, saying to him: "On that
day thoughts will come into your mind, and you
will devise an evil scheme and say, 'I will go up
against the land of unwalled villages; I will fall
upon the quiet people who dwell securely, all of
them dwelling without walls, and having no bars
or gates'; to seize spoil and carry off plunder; to
assail the waste places which are now inhabited,
and the people who were gathered from the nations, who have gotten cattle and goods, who
dwell at the center of the earth. Sheba and Dedan
and the merchants of Tarshish and all its villages
will say to you, 'Have you come to seize spoil? Have
you assembled your hosts to carry off plunder, to
carry away silver and gold, to take away cattle and
goods, to seize great spoil?' "—Ezekiel 38:10-13,
RS.

⁵ The restored remnant of spiritual Israelites
dwell at the center or navel of the earth, that is,
they are at the center of the New World society.
Out from them this society radiates to the four
quarters of the earth; around them this society

---

4. In what have the remnant specialized since 1919,
and so why should the symbolic Gog want to attack
them?
5. (a) How do the restored remnant dwell at the center
of the earth? (b) Their transformation is like that of
what ancient man of integrity, and how was his
prosperity previously interrupted?

revolves. Since their deliverance after World War I the spiritual prosperity with which their God has blessed them has excited the comment of all the world. In their case it is true that "he raiseth up the poor out of the dust; from the dung-hill he lifteth up the needy, to set [him] among nobles, among the nobles of his people. He maketh the barren woman to keep house, [as] a joyful mother of sons." (Psalm 113:7-9, Da) The transformation is as remarkable as Job's; in fact, was typified by Job's experience. Job was not an Israelite but was distantly related to Abraham. He was a man of integrity toward Jehovah as God. For this Jehovah blessed him as he had blessed Abraham, with ten children (seven sons and three daughters) and with many servants and much livestock. Jehovah trusted in Job's integrity, but Satan the Devil did not. He accused Job of worshiping Jehovah for the material prosperity that he enjoyed from it. So Jehovah let Satan take away all Job's children and livestock. Still Job refused to curse God and accuse him of wrongdoing.

⁶ Unsatisfied, Satan now argued that if Job himself were personally afflicted in body he would fail in his integrity. To prove Satan a liar, Jehovah let him afflict Job with a loathsome, sleep-robbing nightmare-causing disease that covered him with itching boils from head to foot. Job's wife broke down and foolishly told him: "Curse God and die." But he did not curse God and did not die. Then three so-called "friends," who had no more confidence in Job's integrity than Satan did, visited him, presumably to comfort him but really to accuse him of a religious hypocrisy that his bodily affliction had at last made public. With argument after argument they tried to make Job admit that it was God who was punishing him for a lack of

6. What final trials did Satan bring to break Job's integrity, but how did Job keep his integrity?

integrity. Finally Job laid bare his own life pattern before them and silenced them. He kept his integrity toward God.

⁷ Here a young man listening, named E·li′hu, spoke up against Job's unfriendly accusers and in justification of God and for Job's enlightenment. Then he set forth the hope for Job's restoration and for the restoration of those typified by Job in these words:

⁸ "Man is also chastened with pain upon his bed, and with continual strife in his bones; so that his life loathes bread, and his appetite dainty food. His flesh is so wasted away that it cannot be seen; and his bones which were not seen stick out. His soul draws near the Pit, and his life to those who bring death. If there be for him an angel, a mediator, one of the thousand, to declare to man what is right for him; and he is gracious to him, and says, 'Deliver him from going down into the Pit, I have found a ransom; let his flesh become fresh with youth; let him return to the days of his youthful vigor.' Then man prays to God, and he accepts him, he comes into his presence with joy. He recounts to men his salvation, and he sings before men, and says: 'I sinned, and perverted what was right, and it was not requited to me. He has redeemed my soul from going down into the Pit, and my life shall see the light.' Behold, God does all these things, twice, three times, with a man, to bring back his soul from the Pit, that he may see the light of life."—Job 33:19-30, RS.

⁹ The remnant of spiritual Israelites came into such a condition as described. They were apparently smitten by God with a repulsive spiritual disease, like Job's, and were evidently marked for

---

7, 8. Who was E·li′hu, and with what words did he set forth the hope for Job's restoration and for the restoration of those whom Job typed?
9. How did the remnant come into a condition like that described above, and how were they likewise restored?

death, especially with religious clergy and leaders combining against them to accuse them falsely and make them renounce Jehovah. Christians as spiritually close to them as a wife to a man turned against them or even betrayed them to foes. Childless they seemed, with no ability to grow in numbers under the hatred and persecution in all nations. They were fulfilling Ezekiel's vision of the valley of dry bones and John's vision of God's two witnesses lying dead in the street three and a half days. Then Jehovah sent his Angel or Messenger, who is the Mediator of the new covenant under which the remnant have spiritual relationship with God and which provides for the removal of sins. Jehovah also shortened the days of tribulation for the sake of his chosen ones, the remnant, and thus kept them from going down into the pit or perishing by the swords of His executioners. By his Messenger Jehovah cleansed the remnant of their uncleanness and brought them back to spiritual health. As it were, their flesh became like that of a child's and their strength like that of youth, as in the days of the primitive apostolic congregation of the first century. Then they began recounting their salvation to the scattered "other sheep," the "great crowd."

¹⁰ What has resulted? Look back at Job. Jehovah God followed Elihu and gave the crowning answer to Job in perfect justification of Almighty God,

10. What did God show by his answer to Job, what did Job then do, and how was he rewarded for keeping his integrity?

showing God was justified in putting his servants to a test, to make their integrity show up and to perfect them in obedience to God. (Job, chapters 38-41) Job accepted the divine instruction and humbled himself repentantly. God then told Job to pray for his erring friends. "And Jehovah turned the captivity of Job, when he had prayed for his friends; and Jehovah gave Job twice as much as he had before." His brothers and sisters all came to him and comforted him. "And Jehovah blessed the latter end of Job more than his beginning; and he had fourteen thousand sheep, and six thousand camels, and a thousand yoke of oxen, and a thousand she-asses. And he had seven sons and three daughters. . . . And in all the land were no women found [so] fair as the daughters of Job; and their father gave them inheritance among their brethren. And Job lived after this a hundred and forty years, and saw his sons, and his sons'

sons, four generations." (Job 42:1-16, *Da*) Into a like prosperity the remnant of today have come spiritually.

¹¹ Beginning in 1919, Jehovah turned the captivity of the remnant, although the Dragon Satan has been permitted to continue to persecute them. In proof of this their prosperity has steadily grown in spite of all Satan does. Jehovah has given them youthful strength and courage by his outpoured spirit to preach the good news of the established Kingdom world-wide. By this means God has caused them to become father to a complete number of children, ten, as it were, to correspond with Job's seven sons and three daughters. They are the "great crowd" of fellow worshipers out of all nations; they correspond with the "ten men" out of all languages of the nations who take hold on the skirt of him that is a Jew, to go along with him to worship Jehovah. (Zechariah 8:23, *Da*) In all the religious realm there is no fruitage from Bible preaching to compare with these children for beauty of true godly devotion. The antitypical Job class continue to live on in spiritual youth as Job did; they have the Scriptural hope of living through Armageddon into the new world. The antitypical ten children, the "great crowd," will live through with them. After Armageddon the Job class will see these children be very fruitful toward others' gaining eternal life in the new world. They already produce fruit in preaching good news.

¹² In enjoying the God-given spiritual prosperity through the "good news of the kingdom" the remnant of spiritual Israelites have expanded. They

---

11. Beginning in 1919, how did Jehovah turn the captivity of the remnant, and how are they, like Job, blessed with children?

12, 13. Due to expansion, how have the remnant come into a fight like that of Jephthah with the Ammonites, and to what grievous experience did Jephthah's vow bring him?

have had to push back the enemy to do so, for the enemy have wrongly claimed that the remnant have crowded in upon their territory. It has been as in the days of Jephthah the Israelite of Gilead. He was rejected for a while, the same as the remnant of spiritual Israelites were. But God showed he was using Jephthah, and the Israelites saw in him the judge whom Jehovah had raised up to deliver them from the Ammonites.

¹³ Jephthah set the facts before the Ammonites to prove that God had given the Israelites the land and that they had taken nothing from Ammon and were not encroaching upon them. When the Ammonites refused to agree and still showed fight, Jephthah moved against them. He vowed that if Jehovah gave him the victory the first one to come out of his house to welcome him as victor should "become Jehovah's and I must offer that one up as a burnt offering." Jehovah did bless Jephthah's theocratic warfare with victory. But when he reached home his only child, a daughter, was the first to come out to greet him with music and dancing. He was grieved at what the paying of his vow would mean for her: she would have to remain virgin and not carry forward her father's family and name, for she could not become a man's wife now that she was Jehovah's exclusive property.

¹⁴ Jephthah's daughter theocratically told him to proceed with his vow, no matter what it cost her, "since Jehovah has executed acts of vengeance for you upon your enemies, the sons of Ammon." The vindication of Jehovah's universal sovereignty was more important to her than selfish personal considerations. So after two months of bewailing her virginity, which was to be perpetual, she yielded herself to her father. He did

14. How did Jephthah's daughter meet the situation, how did her father offer her up, and of what did she become a living testimonial?

not make a human sacrifice of her, like a literal burnt offering. Jehovah's law to Israel forbade that; his altar at the sacred tabernacle was not permitted to receive such a human sacrifice. Jephthah merely surrendered her to God at his tabernacle that she might continually serve God there. "As for her, she never had relations with a man," she being untouchable as God's devoted property. "And it came to be a regulation in Israel: From year to year the daughters of Israel would go to give commendation to the daughter of Jeph'thah the Gil'e·ad·ite, four days in the year." (Judges 10:17 to 11:40, *NW*) Jephthah's daughter was thus a living testimonial to Jehovah's vindicated sovereignty.

[15] Likewise the remnant of spiritual Israelites, after their restoration by God in 1919, have had to contest with antitypical Ammonites who have disputed the right of Jehovah's people to expand and have complained of having their religious pastures encroached upon. They have put up a fight through police, court, political, commercial and mob action to stop Jehovah's remnant under Christ. In desire for victory Jesus Christ, the Greater Jephthah, has promised to Jehovah God that those who would be first to hail his victory through the remnant should belong to Jehovah. The fight was for no selfish reason, for no creature's glory and the perpetuation of his name. The foremost issue was Jehovah's universal sovereignty, and this was the thing to be vindicated. So the fruits of victory belonged to Jehovah, and to Jehovah Jesus Christ determined they must go. The "other sheep" or the "great crowd" whom Jesus Christ had used his remnant to father through the preaching of the life-giving "good news" were the ones that were first to take sym-

---

15. How have the remnant had a contest like that of Jephthah's, and who have proved to be the antitype of Jephthah's daughter, and in what way?

bolic "palm branches" and hail his victory. They saw the issue; they saw that Jesus Christ was Jehovah's Chief Vindicator on the issue, and they rejoiced and came out on his side, doing good to his remnant of brothers and associating loyally with them. They are therefore the antitypical daughter of Jephthah.

[16] The Greater Jephthah has accordingly brought them under the theocratic organization and has turned them over to Jehovah at his temple that they might serve him there day and night forever. There they have become like the Gibeonite "gatherers of wood and drawers of water for the house of my God"; they have become temple slaves like the typical Nethinim. They must keep a perpetual spiritual virginity, not letting themselves be defiled by compromising unions with this world and its institutions. They are the fellow workers with the remnant of the "bride, the Lamb's wife," and as such they must be the "virgins her companions" that follow her to her union with the Bridegroom Jesus Christ. If ever coming into this relationship to Jehovah's temple cost them tears and bewailing, they have put that in the past and they are thankful to serve God in this fully dedicated and devoted condition for the sake of seeing his prosperity upon his witnesses continue.

[17] While the New World society of Jehovah's witnesses flourishes spiritually, the world under its god Satan suffers from extreme spiritual famine. These two opposites in spiritual conditions were foreshadowed by Egypt and the rest of the world in the days of Joseph the prime minister of Phar-

---

16. How has the Greater Jephthah offered up the antitypical daughter of Jephthah, and so what have become their responsibilities without further tears and bewailing?

17. When were the two opposites in spiritual conditions of the New World society and Satan's world once foreshadowed in Egypt, and how did Joseph happen to get down there and into prison?

aoh. Joseph was one of the ancient witnesses of Jehovah. (Hebrews 11:22; 12:1, 2, *NW*) He was the specially loved son of Jacob or Israel. Out of jealousy his ten half brothers sold him to traveling merchants. He disappeared to his family down in Egypt, his father being given to understand that his beloved boy was dead. In Egypt Joseph as a slave was thrown into prison under a false charge. There Jehovah made him prominent as a reliable interpreter of dreams.

[18] How, now, would Jehovah bring his witness Joseph out into a deserved prosperity for his faithfulness? Jehovah sent two troublesome dreams to Pharaoh the king. None of his magic-practicing priests or his wise men could quiet Pharaoh's mind with an interpretation. Then Pharaoh's cupbearer whose dream in prison Joseph had correctly interpreted called him to mind and recommended him to Pharaoh. Joseph was brought before Pharaoh. The king told Joseph the dreams. Joseph explained them both to be confirmatory of each other, that it was firmly established on God's part that there would be seven years of overflowing plenty upon Egypt followed by seven years of unproductiveness. He proposed to Pharaoh that a food administrator be appointed to store up all the excess during the seven plenteous years to counterbalance the food shortage during the lean years, so as to save human lives. Pharaoh at once appointed Joseph the prime minister. The seven years of plenty came and went and Joseph had all the surplus stored safely away for the famine. The seven lean years came. Joseph had food to sell.

[19] Up north his father Jacob was finally obliged

---

18. How did Joseph come to be Egypt's prime minister, and when famine came how was he prepared for it?
19. How was Joseph finally privileged to identify himself to all his brothers down in Egypt and to have all his family relationship come down to live with him there?

to send Joseph's ten half brothers down to Egypt
for food. Joseph identified them in the throng of
buyers, but they did not recognize him in his position, as he spoke through an interpreter. He skillfully arranged for them to come back, bringing
his full brother, young Benjamin, back with them.
In due time Jacob was obliged to send young Benjamin down with them to Egypt for more food.
Joseph put them to a test and proved they had repented of their past mistreatment of him and his
father. So, alone in their presence, he identified
himself to them. He calmed their fears, showed
affection for them, especially for his full brother
Benjamin, and sent them home with food and with
instructions to bring their father down, with all
their families, to live by him in Egypt. This was
done.

[20] In this prophetic drama Joseph typifies primarily Jesus Christ, Jehovah's beloved Son and
his Interpreter. But in the latter part of the drama
he is represented in a subordinate way by the
original remnant of his body members who faithfully endured the tests from 1914 to his coming
to the temple in 1918 for judgment work. Benjamin, Joseph's young full brother, typified the part
of the remnant that was added from 1919 onward
to 1931. Here there is a correspondency with Mordecai the Jew and his young cousin Queen Esther.
In 1931 the Benjamin class, that is, the younger
part of the remnant, was recognized in its relation
to the older part.*

[21] Joseph and Benjamin's ten half brothers typi-

---

* See the serial article "Esther and Mordecai," in six parts, in
The Watch Tower of May 15 to August 1, 1931. See also the book
Preservation, published in 1932.

---

20. Whom did Joseph typify primarily and in a subordinate way, and when was Benjamin's antitype recognized in its relationship to the antitypical Joseph?
21. Whom do Joseph's ten half brothers typify, and
when did the antitypical Joseph disclose his relationship
to them, and how?

fied those who become "other sheep," the "great crowd" out of all nations. Many of these had opposed and persecuted the Joseph and Benjamin classes or had given moral support to their persecutors. In 1935 the antitypical Joseph disclosed his identity to his brothers by the publication of the explanation of Revelation 7:9-17, revealing that the "great crowd" of worshipers from all nations were Christ's "other sheep" whom he had now united in "one flock" with the remnant of the "body of Christ." What rejoicing there was at this identification! To keep from perishing this "great crowd" has had to come to the Greater Joseph, Jesus Christ, Jehovah's Prime Minister and Food Administrator, for spiritual food and to be reconciled.

²² Not only ancient Egypt but other parts of the world had to come to Joseph for needed food supplies. To procure food the Egyptians themselves first gave their money till it was all spent, and then all their livestock they sold for foodstuffs. Finally, in need of further food they proposed to Joseph: "Buy us and our land for bread and we together with our land will become slaves to Phar'aoh, and give us seed that we may live and not die and our land not be laid desolate." To save their lives "Joseph bought all the land of the Egyptians for Phar'aoh, because the Egyptians sold each one his field, for the famine had got a strong grip on them, and the land came to be Phar'aoh's." Joseph then provided for their prosperous future, and the Egyptians said: "You have preserved our lives. Let us find favor in the eyes of my lord and we will become slaves to Phar'aoh."—Genesis 47:14-25, *NW*.

²³ The famine-stricken people of Egypt typified

---

22. What were the famine-stricken Egyptians themselves finally obliged to do to have their lives preserved?
23. What did Egypt's seven years of plenty and seven years of famine typify, and what did the Egyptians and their life-preserving action typify?

the people today who become conscious of their spiritual need and who come out of this world to the Greater Joseph, Jesus Christ, and become the "great crowd" of Jehovah's worshipers. (Revelation 11:8; 7:9) Back in ancient Egypt the seven years of famine followed the seven years of plenty, making fourteen years. But in the modern anti-type, the famine period and the plentiful period run concurrently, in this "time of the end" during the rule of Jesus Christ in the midst of his enemies. That is, to his enemies Jehovah sends a "famine in the land; not a famine of bread, nor a thirst for water, but of hearing the words of Jehovah." (Amos 8:11, *Da*) But to his faithful remnant under Jesus Christ Jehovah sends a great spiritual abundance of truth and service. So they have more than enough, enough for themselves and plenty to share with others who are spiritually hungry and seeking life in relationship with God. To gain life-sustaining Kingdom food the antitypical Egyptians have to come to Jehovah's abundantly provided organization under Jesus Christ. They must part with their all. They must make a full surrender or dedication of themselves to the Greater Pharaoh, Jehovah God, through Jesus Christ his Prime Minister, and they must become his slaves for all time, now and in the new world. In that way they become members of his New World society. In that way they gain hope of everlasting happiness in the new world and the prospect of surviving Armageddon to enter into it. They never hunger again in this old world, always receiving food convenient through God's well-fed organization.

²⁴ With death-dealing spiritual famine raging in

24, 25. (a) Why is it no wonder that Gog of Magog is moved with greed to despoil the remnant of spiritual Israelites? (b) What do the remnant and the "great crowd" await, and what notice do they obediently serve upon Gog?

Gog's organization and with such spiritual abundance obtaining among the remnant of spiritual Israelites, with their possession of the truth and of preaching privileges which are more precious than gold and silver; with their possession of Jehovah's name and being vindicators of it, with all the "great crowd" from all nations being dependent upon them for food at the proper time, and with the desirable, precious things of all nations coming in and filling Jehovah's house with glory, it is no wonder that Gog of Magog feels envious and is moved with greed to despoil them of every truly valuable thing that they have, yes, to blot them out of existence, to the reproach of Jehovah's name. The remnant and the "great crowd" of fellow worshipers know that Gog of Magog, or Satan the Devil, is envious and is gathering all nations against them, and together the remnant and the "great crowd" in Jehovah's land of spiritual prosperity await the sure-to-come attack by Gog and all his hordes. So they put him on notice by obeying this command:

[25] "Therefore prophesy, son of man, and say unto Gog, Thus saith the Lord Jehovah: In that day when my people Israel dwelleth in safety, shalt thou not know [it]? And thou shalt come from thy place out of the uttermost north, thou and many peoples with thee, all of them riding upon horses, a great assemblage and a mighty army. And thou shalt come up against my people Israel as a cloud to cover the land—it shall be at the end of days —and I will bring thee against my land, that the nations may know me, when I shall be hallowed in thee, O Gog, before their eyes."—Ezekiel 38:14-16, Da.

CHAPTER XXI

The Universal War of Armageddon Breaks Out

IN THE light of the fulfillment of Bible prophecy it is becoming clear that the war of Armageddon is nearing its breaking-out point. Global is the total extent to which war between nations of men can become. Universal, involving the visible earth and the invisible heavens, will be the war of Armageddon, which the Lord God Almighty will fight. The selfish wars of men have never settled anything permanently. The war of Armageddon will settle forever the leading issue before all heaven and earth, the universal sovereignty of Jehovah the Most High God. Ever afterward he will dominate the universe without question as to his right and ability and worthiness. The war of Armageddon, named after the ancient battlefield, spells victory for Jehovah, defeat for his foes.

[2] Bent on continued world domination, either by having the strongest nation conquer the globe or by an alliance of nations with an attempted "peaceful coexistence" of opposed blocs of nations, the worldly nations are fighting against Jehovah God and his Christ. Their god, Satan the Devil or Gog, is preparing for a final fight against Jehovah and

---

1. What will be the extent of the war of Armageddon, what will it settle forever, and what will it spell for Jehovah and for his foes?
2. What is the touchstone by means of which hostility to Jehovah and his Christ are exposed, and so against what is Gog's attack with all the nations really an attack?

331

his Anointed, and so are the nations, under Satan's undercover leadership. The nations of Christendom, claiming to be Christian, may deny this, but God's revealing Word exposes them as taking part in the fight against Him. The touchstone by contact with which their hostility to Jehovah and his Christ is laid bare is the remnant of Christ's kingdom heirs together with the Kingdom message that they preach everywhere. Jehovah's witnesses, the remnant and their companions, may be comparatively few and greatly despised and underestimated, but they are the key to understanding the true meaning of the aims and conduct of nations. As the nations do to Jehovah's witnesses, so they do to Jehovah and to his kingdom by Christ, for his witnesses uphold his side of the long-standing controversy. Therefore Gog's attack with all the nations upon Jehovah's witnesses is really an attack upon God's kingdom.

[3] The terrifying fight that follows Gog's attack and the battle of Armageddon described in The Revelation are one and the same thing. Both the prophecy concerning Gog of Magog and The Revelation disclose that all the nations are invisibly led by Satan and his demons to the attack against God's side, hence against his remnant and their sheeplike companions. Since Satan and his demon angels lost the war in heaven and were hurled down to the earth, they have been allowed to remain a "short period of time" to prepare for this very war of Armageddon. The abased, invisible realm near this earth where they have been confined and are held in reserve for Armageddon is the symbolic "land of Magog," out from which Gog the Devil operates. He uses his visible political agencies, the symbolic "wild beast" and the "false prophet," in the gathering of all the nations

3. How are the nations led to the universal fight, and what visible political agencies does Gog of Magog use for the gathering of them?

against Jehovah's enthroned King, represented on earth by the remnant of his royal joint heirs. These Gog uses as mouthpieces for demon-inspired propaganda to men. The Revelation pulls back the curtain to show us his operations:

4 "And I saw three unclean inspired expressions that looked like frogs come out of the mouth of the dragon and out of the mouth of the wild beast and out of the mouth of the false prophet. They are, in fact, expressions inspired by demons and perform signs, and they go forth to the kings of the entire inhabited earth, to gather them together to the war of the great day of God the Almighty. . . . And they gathered them together to the place that is called in Hebrew Har–Magedon."—Revelation 16:13-16, *NW*.

5 Since the nations, even so-called "Christian" ones, refuse to "live . . . on every utterance coming forth through Jehovah's mouth," they are led by what comes out of the Dragon's mouth to Har–Magedon or Armageddon. It is not to a fight among themselves that the demons under Gog lead them there. They do not go there to fight against a mere theory, a mere political ideology, a mere religious doctrine. They go to fight against something real, something actually in operation, namely, God's kingdom by his Anointed Jesus. It was really against this kingdom that the nations became wrathful at its establishment in the heavens in 1914, not ceasing then from World War I nor peacefully handing over their sovereignty to it. (Revelation 11:15-18) Against this everlasting kingdom the demons lead the power-greedy nations at Armageddon. They will therefore lead them against something visibly tangible that rep-

---

4. How does Revelation 16:13-16 unveil these facts to us?
5. To what fight do the demons under Gog lead the nations to Armageddon, and what will be the purpose of the nations under Gog?

resents that kingdom, the remnant of Christ's joint heirs and their companions in the New World society. (Revelation 12:17) The purpose will be the same as that described as moving Gog of Magog to action against the restored remnant of spiritual Israel, to strip them of their spiritual prosperity, to drive them out of Jehovah's favor, to destroy them as the foundation of the "new earth," to stifle their voice as Jehovah's witnesses, his Kingdom preachers.

⁶ Gog's attack therefore forces the issue and provokes action by Almighty God and his King. Jehovah God welcomes the fight; he wants the issue to be settled forever. He has waited long enough and now his time for the vindication of his universal sovereignty comes. For Him man's invention of the hydrogen bomb has not canceled out the war of Armageddon. The possession at that time of stockpiles of the hydrogen bomb by America, Great Britain, Communist Russia and any other nations will not act as any deterrent to the "war of the great day of God the Almighty," any more than the proclamation of God's prophecies concerning Armageddon have acted as a deterrent to the nations in their fight against him and his kingdom. He is not terrified or afraid of the consequences. For this reason he challenges the enemy to prepare and to come down to this modern "valley of Jehoshaphat." Although allowing the demons their full play with the nations under their control, yet he maneuvers them all, demons and nations, to gather them to the destruction that these criminals deserve and that he has decreed. Thus he leads Gog as by hooks in his jaws to the place of execution, before his remnant of spiritual Israel. To the remnant he says:

---

6. Why does Jehovah let nothing act as a deterrent to the war of Armageddon, and how does he get the demons and the nations down to the modern "valley of Jehoshaphat"?

⁷ "And thou, son of man, prophesy against Gog, and say, Thus saith the Lord Jehovah: Behold, I am against thee, O Gog, prince of Rosh, Meshech, and Tubal; and I will turn thee back, and lead thee, and will cause thee to come up from the uttermost north, and will bring thee upon the mountains of Israel. And I will smite thy bow out of thy left hand, and will cause thine arrows to fall out of thy right hand. Thou shalt fall upon the mountains of Israel, thou, and all thy bands, and the peoples that are with thee: I have given thee to be meat for the birds of prey of every wing, and to the beasts of the field. Thou shalt fall on the open field; for I have spoken [it], saith the Lord Jehovah."—Ezekiel 39:1-5, *Da.*

⁸ The time will now have come when "this good news of the kingdom" has been fully preached in all the inhabited earth for a witness to all the nations under Gog. The time will have now come when the last lost and strayed sheep has been found and gathered by the Right Shepherd and been made part of the "one flock" under the One Shepherd. All the "great crowd" of such worshipers of Jehovah will have assembled at his temple in response to the great Kingdom Signal raised up on the heavenly Mount Zion. The spiritual prosperity of the spiritual Israelites regathered to Jehovah's theocratic organization will have reached its pre-Armageddon peak. The time will have come for the "time of the end" to close, for the days of "great tribulation" upon Satan's or Gog's world to be shortened no longer for the sake of God's chosen ones. The time will have come for the "accomplished end" of this present wicked system of things, visible and invisible. The time will have come for the Kingdom Stone, which God's hands

---

7. What does Jehovah have the remnant say to Gog respecting his being led to his fall in battle?
8. For what climactic things will the time then have come?

have cut out, to crash into the symbolic image of Satan's creation and "break in pieces and consume all these kingdoms" and then itself stand forever afterward. The time will have come for the great Seed of God's "woman" to bruise the original Serpent in the head, dashing his nations in pieces like a potter's vessel struck with an iron scepter.—Matthew 24:21, 22, 14; Daniel 2:44, 45; Genesis 3:15; Romans 16:20; Psalm 2:8, 9.

⁹ What, then, as the remnant and the "other sheep," apparently defenseless, see the encircling hordes of Gog of Magog approaching from all sides like a growling, gruesome war cloud that, because of its multitude of over two billion regimented creatures, darkens the surface of the earth? Should they be paralyzed with fear? No; no more than was Elisha when surrounded by Syrian armies in Dothan. As Elisha then said to his terrified attendant, they should say to one another: "Fear not; for they that are with us are more than they that are with them." (2 Kings 6:16, *AS*) By faith their eyes should see the vision that the apostle John saw of the heavenly hosts under the great Seed of God's "woman" plunging forward to the battle against Gog's hordes:

¹⁰ "And I saw the heaven opened, and, look! a white horse. And one seated upon it is called Faithful and True, and he judges and carries on war in righteousness. His eyes are a fiery flame, and upon his head are many diadems. He has a name written that no one knows but he himself, and he is arrayed with an outer garment sprinkled with blood, and the name he is called is The Word of God. Also the armies that were in heaven were following him on white horses, and they were clothed in

---

9, 10. (a) Seeing the hordes of Gog closing in on them, how should the remnant and the "other sheep" take the situation as Elisha did at Dothan? (b) By faith what vision of the apostle John should their eyes see?

white, clean, fine linen. And out of his mouth there protrudes a sharp long sword, that he may smite the nations with it, and he will shepherd them with a rod of iron. He treads, too, the press of the wine of the anger of the wrath of God the Almighty. And upon his outer garment, even upon his thigh, he has a name written, King of kings and Lord of lords."—Revelation 19:11-16, *NW*.

[11] Seeing by faith this invincible host of heavenly executioners, Jehovah's witnesses will know they do not have to fight or strike a violent blow at Armageddon. No, for it is Jehovah's fight!

[12] In Ezekiel's vision Jehovah leads Gog of Magog as by hooks in his jaws south through mountainous Gilead and down the east side of the Jordan River and to the plateau of Moab east of the Dead Sea, and not to the place called the Mount of Megiddo. In the Revelation vision the invisible demons lead the assembled kings of the entire inhabited earth to the place called in Hebrew Har-Magedon or Armageddon. There is no conflict here regarding the battleground. It is not to the site of literal Megiddo in ancient Palestine that the enemy hosts are gathered; the place could not accommodate them with all their military, naval and air equipment. Though the battle will be fought in all quarters of the globe, still the battlefield will be Armageddon symbolically, because the ancient field of Megiddo was a symbol of gory warfare, of resounding victory for the winners and of calamitous defeat for the losers. Such will be the symbolic Armageddon with its head-on clash of opposing forces, those of the old world and those of the new world, and the crushing defeat for the

---

11. What will Jehovah's witnesses then know as to participation in the fight?
12. Where is Gog led for the fight, and to where do the demons lead the kings of the entire inhabited earth, and yet why is there no conflict here regarding the battleground?

former and the all-decisive victory for the latter.
—Ezekiel 39:11.

¹³ The battle lines will then be sharply drawn,
for and against Jehovah's universal sovereignty,
for and against his kingdom established in 1914.
On the one side will be Gog's hordes, invisible and
visible, embracing all the selfish, greedy nations.
On his visible side The Revelation shows the "wild
beast" (pictorial of all of Satan's earthly organization) and the political "false prophet" (pictorial
of the Anglo-American dual world power), which
takes in all worldly rulers and their armies. (Revelation 19:19, 20) The members of the United Nations (proposed by the "false prophet" system)
are there, like the ten horns on the seven heads of
the scarlet-colored "wild beast" of international alliance. "The ten horns that you saw mean ten
kings, who have not yet received a kingdom, but
they do receive authority as kings one hour with
the wild beast. These have one purpose, and so
they give their power and authority to the wild
beast. These will battle with the Lamb, but, because he is Lord of lords and King of kings, the
Lamb will conquer them. Also those called and
chosen and faithful with him will do so." The
Babylonish religious "woman" that rides seated
upon this "scarlet-colored wild beast" is there, but
now ready to be horned off and devastated and de-
nuded and devoured of all her flesh and then
burned with fire. (Revelation 17:1-18, *NW*) All
the modern worshipers of Baal, rulers and subjects alike, will be there in their fully donned robes
of identification. (2 Kings 10:18-23) And the goats
will have been separated from the sheep and be to
the left side of the King.—Matthew 25:31-33, 41.

¹⁴ On the other side will visibly be seen the remnant of spiritual Israel and an unnumbered crowd

---

13. As to the battle lines, who will be on Gog's side?
14. Who will be on the other side, visibly and invisibly?

of "other sheep," their companions, all backed up by the unseen hosts of heaven under Jesus Christ, the King of kings and Lord of lords, together with those of his anointed followers already resurrected. —Ezekiel 38:8-12; Revelation 2:26-29.

¹⁵ The hordes of Gog now invade the theocratic realm of spiritual Israel and violently attempt to despoil them. The provocative act thus occurs against these outwardly undefended witnesses of Jehovah, members of the New World society. Thieflike the unannounced day and hour of God's fixed time schedule then arrives for him to go forth and fight against the enemy as when he fought in ancient times in the day of battle. (Matthew 24:36; Revelation 16:15; 1 Thessalonians 5:2; Zechariah 14:3, *AS*) With the indignation of a taunted warrior he moves in and uses his battle weapons and strategy.

¹⁶ "And it shall come to pass in that day, in the day when Gog shall come against the land of Israel, saith the Lord Jehovah, [that] my fury shall come up in my face; for in my jealousy, in the fire of my wrath have I spoken, Verily in that day there shall be a great shaking in the land of Israel; so that the fish of the sea, and the fowl of the heavens, and the beasts of the field, and all creeping things which creep upon the earth, and all mankind that are upon the face of the earth shall shake at my presence; and the mountains shall be thrown down, and the steep places shall fall, and every wall shall fall to the ground. And I will call for a sword against him throughout all my mountains, saith the Lord Jehovah: every man's sword shall be against his brother. And I will enter into judgment with him with pestilence and with blood; and I will rain upon him, and upon his bands, and

15. As the provocative act by Gog occurs, what day and hour then arrives?
16. How does Ezekiel then describe the battle weapons and the strategy that Jehovah uses against Gog?

upon the many peoples that are with him, over-flowing rain and great hailstones, fire and brim-stone. And I will magnify myself, and sanctify my-self, and I will be known in the eyes of many na-tions, and they shall know that I [am] Jehovah."
—Ezekiel 38:18-23, *Da.*

[17] Release of all the nations' atomic bombs and hydrogen bombs, disease germ bombs and chem-ical gas bombs will not compare in magnitude, powerfulness and devastating effect with this "un-wonted act" of the Almighty God, Jehovah. Be-sides panic-striking physical phenomena in the literal earth and atmosphere, there will be tum-bling to ruin of human institutions political, social, commercial and religious that have long stood like mountainous backbones of human society. In the world-wide confusion, when "every man's sword shall be against his brother," the Babylonish, re-ligious, womanlike rider of the "wild beast" of in-ternational alliance will have its complete number of deadly horns turn upon her and make her perish with the sword of the state, which she all too often wielded against Jehovah's holy ones and the witnesses of Jesus. Every defensive wall will crash to the ground; and the wild beast of international alliance will be destroyed by the flying apart of the United Nations, despite all the cement applied by the political "false prophet." While still oper-ating, those institutions will be flung into a sym-bolic fiery lake of endless destruction:

[18] "And I saw the wild beast and the kings of the earth and their armies gathered together to wage the war with the one seated on the horse and with his army. And the wild beast was caught, and along with it the false prophet that performed in front of it the signs with which he misled those

---

17, 18. (a) What will the fulfillment of that prophecy at Armageddon mean? (b) What will happen to the visible ruling organization of Satan and the political "false prophet"?

who received the mark of the wild beast and those who render worship to its image [the United Nations]. While still alive, they both were hurled into the fiery lake that burns with sulphur. But the rest were killed off with the long sword of the one seated on the horse and which proceeded out of his mouth. And all the birds were filled from the fleshy parts of them."—Revelation 19:19-21; 20: 14, *NW*.

¹⁹ Blood will run deep as the royal Avenger of blood on the white horse and his heavenly hosts ride their white horses of righteous, theocratic warfare into the symbolic "great winepress of the anger of God," where the "vine of the earth," the visible, earthly system weighted down with wicked offspring, has been hurled. "And the winepress was trodden outside the city [the New Jerusalem], and blood came out of the winepress as high up as the bridles of the horses, for a distance of a thousand six hundred furlongs [two hundred miles]." —Revelation 14:18-20, *NW*.

²⁰ Why should not blood run deep and far with over two billion dead? Was there ever a war of the length of Armageddon's duration that left even a billion dead? Have all the wars of mankind's existence killed directly a total of two billion warriors? The global flood of Noah's day, which the Bible uses as a prophetic type of Armageddon, drowned all humans except the eight in the ark, and the human population must then have numbered many millions. But Armageddon will be a "tribulation such as has not occurred from the beginning of the creation which God created until that time and will not occur again." (Mark 13:19, *NW;* Matthew 24:21; Daniel 12:1) With the members of this generation that will not pass away be-

---

19. How does Revelation 14:18-20 picture that blood will run deep at Armageddon?
20. In view of what facts should blood then run deep and far?

fore Armageddon breaks out numbering now two billion five hundred million and with only the remnant and a larger group of "other sheep" inside the Greater Noah's "ark" surviving, the death toll of the "war of the great day of God the Almighty" will be appallingly all-surpassing, too many for the Armageddon survivors to bury.

²¹ Come on, birds and beasts! Have your fill then from the human corpses in retribution for the wanton slaughter of animal and birdlife of which the human race has been guilty! Jehovah the great Avenger will give you mistreated creatures your day: "And thou, son of man, thus saith the Lord Jehovah: Speak unto the birds of every wing, and to every beast of the field, Gather yourselves together, and come, assemble yourselves on every side to my sacrifice which I sacrifice for you, a great sacrifice upon the mountains of Israel, that ye may eat flesh, and drink blood. Ye shall eat the flesh of the mighty, and drink the blood of the princes of the earth, of rams, of lambs, and of goats, [and] of bullocks, all of them fatted beasts of Bashan. And ye shall eat fat till ye are full, and drink blood till ye are drunken, of my sacrifice which I sacrifice for you. And ye shall be filled at my table with horses and charioteers, with mighty men, and with all men of war, saith the Lord Jehovah. And I will set my glory among the nations, and all the nations shall see my judgment which I [not Israel] have executed, and my hand which I have laid upon them. And the house of Israel shall know that I [am] Jehovah their God from that day and forward."—Ezekiel 39:17-22, Da.

²² Not a human on the side against Jehovah's theocratic organization will survive. None of their dead will be given a decent burial in memorial

---

21. What invitation will then be given to the birds and beasts, and why justly?
22. How may the extent of the slaughter be measured, and what will befall the would-be despoilers?

tombs. The extent of the slaughter may be measured by the number of the enemy taking part in the war and being annihilated. The wood of the weapons of Gog's hordes, the shields, targets, bows and arrows, handstaves and spears, will be so immense a pile that it will take seven years to use it up as fuel, without collecting any wood from the forests. What wealth the exterminated ones will leave behind! The would-be despoilers of Jehovah's people will themselves be despoiled.—Ezekiel 39:8-10.

²³ Some time after the war has killed off all the visible, earthly enemy the land will be cleansed of flesh-stripped, sun-bleached bones, by their being collected and put out of sight. Jehovah's decree is: "And it shall come to pass in that day, [that] I will give unto Gog a place there for burial in Israel, the valley of the passers-by to the east of the sea; and it shall stop [the way] of the passers-by; and there shall they bury Gog and all the multitude; and they shall call it, Valley of Hamon-Gog [meaning Multitude of Gog]. And seven months shall the house of Israel be burying them [so many will be the slain], that they may cleanse the land; and all the people of the land shall bury [them]; and it shall be to them for renown in the day that I shall be glorified, saith the Lord Jehovah. And they shall sever out men of continual employment to go through the land, who, with the passers-by, shall bury those that remain upon the face of the land, to cleanse it: at the end of seven months shall they make a search. And the passers-by shall pass through the land, and when [any] seeth a man's bone, he shall set up a sign by it, till the buriers have buried it in the Valley of Hamon-Gog. And also the name of the city shall be Hamonah [meaning Multitude]. Thus shall they cleanse the land."

23. How does Ezekiel describe the cleansing of the land of bones?

²⁴ There will be a total cleansing of the land of unclean enemy bones. No memorial tombs symbolizing hope of a resurrection will be built for these nameless, unidentifiable bones. The name of the citylike organization for bone disposal will celebrate Jehovah's victory over so tremendous a multitude.—Ezekiel 39:11-16, *Da.*

²⁵ Thus the tongue of the royal Avenger of blood astride the white horse will be like a sharp long sword proceeding out of his mouth in decreeing execution, destruction, to the visible hordes of Gog of Magog. But what of Gog himself and his invisible demon hosts? They dwell in the symbolic "land of Magog," the abased spiritual realm near the earthly footstool of Jehovah, but figuratively far off to the north through being in the realm of invisibility. After they have been made to see the full evidence of Jehovah's almightiness and universal sovereignty by the destruction of their human dupes and the preservation of Jehovah's witnesses, then will come their turn for more personal instruction in these respects. After informing Gog that he will fall in open defeat, Jehovah notifies him: "And I will send a fire on Magog, and among them that dwell at ease in the isles: and they shall know that I [am] Jehovah. And my holy name will I make known in the midst of my people Israel; and I will not suffer my holy name to be profaned any more: and the nations shall know that I [am] Jehovah, the Holy One in Israel." (Ezekiel 39:6, 7, *Da*) So the symbolic land of Magog, which is the real instigator and the invisible moving power behind the visible attack on the seemingly vulnerable part of Jehovah's organization, will have fire

24. Does burial of those bones indicate a resurrection for those enemies, and what will the name of the bone-disposal organization celebrate?
25. (a) How will the horse rider's tongue be like a long sword protruding out of his mouth? (b) What will the land of Magog have sent upon it?

sent upon it, an illustration of which is given in the fire that Jehovah rained down from heaven upon the cities of Sodom, Gomorrah, Admah and Zeboiim in righteous Lot's day. (Deuteronomy 29:23, *NW;* Genesis 19:23-26) Destruction will come on Magog as by fire.

²⁶ At first this fire will mean a further abasement of Gog or Satan and his demon angels. By the war in heaven from 1914 to 1918 they were ousted from heaven and hurled down to earth's vicinity, to occupy the symbolic land of Magog during this time of the end. But now the sending of fire upon symbolic Magog will mean the bruising of the original Serpent in the head and the plunging of him and his demon legions from abased Magog into the depths of the abyss. This further demonstration of Jehovah's universal sovereignty in the spirit realm was symbolically pictured to John.

²⁷ Previewing *A·do·nay'* Jehovah's Angel of the covenant going into action against Magog, John wrote: "And I saw an angel coming down out of heaven [from which Satan and his demons had been hurled] with the key of the abyss and a great chain in his hand. And he seized the dragon, the original serpent, who is the Devil and Satan, and bound him for a thousand years. And he hurled him into the abyss and shut it and sealed it over him, that he might not mislead the nations any more until the thousand years were ended. After these things he must be let loose for a little while. And I saw thrones, and there were those who sat down on them, and power of judging was given them. Yes, I saw the souls of those executed with the ax for the witness they bore to Jesus and for speaking about God, and those who had worshiped neither the wild beast nor its image and who had

---

26. What will this mean for the inhabitants of symbolic Magog?
27. How was this symbolically pictured to John?

not received the mark upon their forehead and upon their hand. And they came to life and ruled as kings with the Christ for a thousand years. . . . This is the first resurrection. Happy and holy is anyone having part in the first resurrection; over these the second death has no authority, but they will be priests of God and of the Christ, and will rule as kings with him for the thousand years." —Revelation 20:1-6, *NW*.

²⁸ This means that unending destruction, the "second death," will first be executed upon Satan and his demons at the end of Christ's thousand-year reign. Jesus Christ, the Word of God, was once in the abyss and was brought up out of it on the third day. For him his being in the abyss meant being in the depths of death, his bringing up out of it, resurrection. (Romans 10:6, 7; Deuteronomy 30:11-13) For Satan and his demons a thousand years in the abyss will mean a millennial deathlike powerlessness and inactivity. (Luke 8:31, *NW*) With their abyssing the war of Armageddon ends.

²⁹ Thus Satan's entire world or system of things, its invisible demonic heavens and its visible wicked human earth, will be destroyed as by fire. The apostle Peter symbolically describes its destruction in the great day of Jehovah in these words: "But by the same word [of God] the heavens and the earth that are now are stored up for fire and are being reserved to the day of judgment and of destruction of the ungodly men. Yet Jehovah's day will come as a thief, in which the heavens will pass away with a hissing noise, but the elements being intensely hot will be dissolved, and earth

---

28. (a) When will "second death" be executed upon Satan and his demons? (b) So what will their thousand years in the abyss mean?
29. Thus Satan's entire world will be destroyed as by what element, and how does Peter symbolically describe it?

and the works in it will be discovered [to be in the same condition, dissolved]. Since all these things are thus to be dissolved, what sort of persons ought you to be in holy acts of conduct and deeds of godly devotion, awaiting and keeping close in mind the presence of the day of Jehovah, through which the heavens being on fire will be dissolved and the elements being intensely hot will melt!" —2 Peter 3:7, 10-12, *NW*.

[30] Will there then be nothing to survive for? Yes indeed. The destruction of Satan's worldly heavens and earth will not leave a void, a vacuum. It will be replaced by a new world with righteous heavens and earth. For Peter continues on to say: "But there are new heavens and a new earth that we are awaiting according to his promise, and in these righteousness is to dwell." (2 Peter 3:13, *NW*) For this righteous new world Jehovah God Almighty will preserve survivors, the remnant who are destined for the new heavens and the "other sheep" who are to be permanent inhabitants of the new earth. Despite being under furious attack by prince Gog and all his hordes, demon and human, they will not be dislodged from this earth. Without taking any violent part in the combat they will stand and see the salvation of Jehovah for them. They will be eyewitnesses of his incomparable victory over the combined enemy world, and will sing of it then and throughout endless time.

---

30. (a) Does Peter indicate there will be anything to survive for? (b) Will there be any survivors without their fighting for survival, and of what will there be eyewitnesses and singers?

CHAPTER XXII

God's New World After the Battle

THE new world will start out under the most promising conditions, with an overflow of joy in heaven and on earth. The universal troublemaker, Satan the Devil, together with his demons, will have been abyssed, not free and active to corrupt human society as he did after the flood of Noah's day. His oppressive, wicked earthly organization will have gone down in destruction before his eyes. Jehovah's universal sovereignty will have been vindicated for all time by his glorious victory through his Warrior King Jesus Christ. The winners in the war of Armageddon will not come out losers, terribly crippled, as by the forevisioned dreaded results of a nuclear-weapons war between nations of this world. The heavenly Victors will be gainers, and Jehovah God will have made a name for himself that will never be forgotten or profaned again anywhere in the boundless, everlasting universe. (Isaiah 63:12, 14; 2 Samuel 7:23) The victory will bind the triumphant creatures of heaven forever to Jehovah as God and universal Sovereign, and on earth the Armageddon survivors will celebrate his triumph more jubilantly than the Israelites did safe on the eastern side of the Red Sea after Jehovah had brought back the parted sea waters upon the trapped pursuing Egyptian military forces. Many will be the days that they will be collecting the

---

1. How will the new world start out under the most promising conditions for those on the winning side?

348

material spoils of the Armageddon victory, as the Jews under King Jehoshaphat did after Jehovah won the battle for them against the oncoming combined forces of Moab, Ammon and Mount Seir. —Exodus 15:1-21; 2 Chronicles 20:1-25.

[2] The desolations that Jehovah of armies will have wreaked on the enemy's visible organization may be everywhere visible on the earth, yet the Armageddon survivors will start out with a spiritual paradise in the fullest sense. The attack by the abased Satan or Gog of Magog will have failed to gain its objective, to strip them of Jehovah's name, favor, service and protection. He and his demons in the abyss will be unable to interfere with their service and worship of Jehovah and require them to fight spiritually against superhuman governments, authorities and world rulers of this darkness, and "wicked spirit forces in the heavenly places." The "wicked day" will have passed, and they will have stood firm in God's complete suit of armor" and come off completely victorious through God who has loved them.—Ephesians 6:11-18 and Romans 8:37, *NW*.

[3] As for Satan's wicked servants on earth, "the wicked will be no more; though you look well at his place, he will not be there. But the meek shall possess the land, and delight themselves in abundant prosperity." (Psalm 37:10, 11, *RS*) The religious buildings of hypocritical Christendom and the pagan temples of false gods will have been reduced to loathsome ruins like ancient Jerusalem's polluted temple and Samaria's temple of Baal, and the temple of Jehovah's pure worship will remain standing filled with unsurpassed glory. The remnant of "living stones" will be ministering there as Jehovah's anointed priests, and the "great crowd"

2, 3. Though the desolations of the enemy organization may yet be visible, how will Armageddon survivors yet start out with a spiritual paradise?

of faithful worshipers from all the destroyed nations will keep on serving him day and night in true worship. "For the earth shall be filled with the knowledge of the glory of Jehovah, as the waters cover the sea." (Habakkuk 2:14, *AS*) That spiritual paradise will never disappear from the "new earth."

⁴ In time, however, the literal earth will be cleared of the desolations upon the enemy and be transformed into a natural paradise of which the original paradise garden of Eden was but a sample. The beloved Son of God, Jehovah's fellow worker in planting that original paradise for Adam and Eve's home, gave a reliable promise that paradise would be re-established on earth and that he would be invisibly present in it. (Luke 23:43, *NW*) The Armageddon survivors, especially the "other sheep," will have the privilege and obligation of working at the restoring of this natural paradise and maintaining it, Jehovah's all-necessary blessings upon the soil and climate favoring the regrowth of it. Not only the war survivors, but also their children that will be born in the "new earth," will enjoy that delightful service. The war of Armageddon will not annul the marriage ties of couples that live through, nor will the bringing in of the new world with a "new earth" prohibit the marriage of survivors who are single. The original paradise of Eden witnessed the first human marriage; the paradise of the "new earth" will witness many marriages of the war survivors. The original paradise did not witness the birth of a baby in righteousness; the paradise of the "new earth" will witness the birth of babies in righteousness, to demonstrate actually God's ability to produce

---

4. However, what assurance have we that there will also be a natural paradise on earth? who will work at restoring and maintaining it, and what may be said of marriage and childbirth in it?

babies in an earthly paradise. Jesus, in prophesying on the "time of the end," said: "Just as the
days of Noah were, so the presence of the Son of
man will be."—Matthew 24:37, *NW*.

⁵ Since the flood was a type of the war of Armageddon, it is reasonable that Noah's experience
immediately after the flood when he came out of
the ark of survival with his family should also be
a type. "And God went on to bless Noah and his
sons and to say to them: 'Be fruitful and become
many and fill the earth.'" (Genesis 9:1, *NW*)
Noah's sons and their wives proceeded to carry
out this procreation mandate that corresponded
with that given to Adam and Eve in the paradise
of Eden. (Genesis 1:27, 28) Just what instructions
Jehovah will issue to the antitypical sons and
daughters-in-law of the Greater Noah to correspond with that, we do not know. He will, however,
bless them with the fruit of the womb just as abundantly as he did the Israelites down in Egypt
under less favorable conditions. (Exodus 1:7) He
will allow them and their offspring to produce
children to the extent that he wants them to people
the earth with children righteously conceived. He
will regulate this, by his controlling power, that a
satisfying demonstration may be given on a sufficient scale of the fulfillment of the initial procreation mandate to perfect man and woman in
Eden. This will be for the vindication of his original purpose, which may not fail to his reproach.
—Isaiah 45:12, 18; 46:9, 10.

⁶ Although mortal, those children conceived in
righteousness will not then be born to die, inherit-

---

5. What mandate was issued to Noah and his sons
after coming out of the ark, and what may we expect
to correspond with this after Armageddon, and to give
a demonstration of what?
6. Why will the surviving remnant die after Armageddon, but what will be opened up for the earthly "great
crowd" of survivors and their children?

ing a condemnation to death. The earthly "great crowd" of Jehovah's worshipers will not be spared to survive Armageddon just to die some time later. True, the remnant of the "little flock" of Christ's joint heirs must follow his steps down into death, proving faithful until death in vindication of Jehovah's sovereign will. They must lay aside blood, flesh and bone, in order to be resurrected a "spiritual body" and be "conformed to his glorious body," for a "spirit does not have flesh and bones" and "flesh and blood cannot inherit God's kingdom." (Philippians 3:20, 21; Luke 24:39 and 1 Corinthians 15:44, 50, *NW*) How Jehovah by his Greater Solomon, Jesus Christ, will accomplish the transfer of these "living stones" from their earthly situation to their place in the heavenly temple of which he is the Foundation Cornerstone is not yet discerned. (Revelation 14:13) But for the earthly "great crowd" of survivors the way will be opened up for uninterrupted, everlasting life in the new world. There will not, as a result of Armageddon, be any death-dealing clouds of radioactive particles or contaminated atmosphere floating around the globe for a thousand years, making life impossible or affecting the survivors' powers to bring forth normal children.

⁷ Humankind then will correspond with the twelve non-Levite tribes of Israel on the typical day of atonement. In the Most Holy of God's presence Jehovah's High Priest, the glorified Jesus Christ, will then apply the value of his human sacrifice in favor of his "other sheep," beginning with these Armageddon survivors. These will not receive a justification "by faith" in consequence of this, but will begin to receive actual physical

7. To whom will humankind then correspond on the day of atonement, and what will be the benefits of the application of the value of the atoning sacrifice in their behalf?

health benefits and healing in proof of the forgiveness of their sins. (Matthew 9:2-7) This will also be true of their natural offspring who, though born in righteousness after Armageddon, will be born of imperfect parents and hence themselves be still imperfect and in need of the life benefits of Jesus' atoning sacrifice. Hence, instead of growing older, weaker and impaired with age, they will grow young, strong and gradually freed from all blemishes and marks of imperfection. The ministry of the heavenly High Priest together with the 144,000 who will be his underpriests and "priests of God" will lift up the antitypical twelve tribes of Israel to human perfection by the end of the thousand years of Christ's reign.—Matthew 19:28, *NW*.

[8] It follows that a "great crowd" of sheeplike worshipers of Jehovah now living before Armageddon will never die, not by a bodily rapture of them to the skies, but by the curative, perfecting powers of Christ's kingdom. (John 11:25, 26) They will not perpetuate old nations after Armageddon, nor will their offspring then born produce new nations as was true long after the Flood. No, but all will receive life through the one High Priest of Jehovah and will become his everlasting children. Thus he will acquire the title "Everlasting Father." "The government shall be upon his shoulder: and his name shall be called Wonderful, Counsellor, Mighty God, Everlasting Father, Prince of Peace." (Isaiah 9:6, *AS*) There will be no national or patriarchal governments of men. They will all have but the one Everlasting Father, who will be their one Royal Governor without a successor. Thus they will all be one undivided human family, all brothers.

---

8. How will a "great crowd" now living before Armageddon never die off earth, but all be one undivided human family, all brothers?

⁹ One other astonishing benefit of the High Priest's atoning sacrifice will be the resurrection of the dead. The King Jesus Christ will not only be High Priest, a royal priest like Melchizedek, but also be judge. He will judge who deserve to be raised from death to human life or who could profit from a resurrection of judgment. "For the Father judges no one at all, but he has committed all the judging to the Son. And he has given him authority to do judging, because Son of man he is. Do not marvel at this, because the hour is coming in which all those in the memorial tombs will hear his voice and come out, those who did good things to a resurrection of life, those who practiced vile things to a resurrection of judgment." (John 5:22, 27-29, *NW*) The Judge knows the divine rule: "The memory of the righteous [man] shall be blessed; but the name of the wicked shall rot." (Proverbs 10:7, *Da*) Those "wicked" ones will include such rebellious ones as Adam and Eve, Cain, Judas Iscariot the betrayer of Jesus Christ, and the religious hypocrites to whom Jesus said: "Serpents, offspring of vipers, how are you to flee from the judgment of Ge·hen′na?" (Matthew 23:33, *NW;* John 6:70, 71; 17:12; 1 John 3:10-12) Gehenna was no place of memorial tombs, but was a place of destruction of refuse. For such wicked ones who go to the symbolic Gehenna there will be no "resurrection of judgment." (Matthew 10:28, *NW*) They perished.

¹⁰ The "resurrection of life" includes the "first resurrection," which is the resurrection to instantaneous perfection of life, spirit life, in which Jesus

---

9. What other astonishing benefit will there be from the atoning sacrifice, and who will judge as to the ones to enjoy that benefit or not? And who will not Scripturally enjoy it?

10. What is the "first resurrection," and, besides participants in that resurrection, whom will the "resurrection of life" also include?

himself participated and in which only the 144,000 joint heirs participate with him. (Revelation 20:5, 6; Colossians 1:18) Others who "did good things" in God's sight and who will share in the "resurrection of life" will be those of the "great crowd" of sheeplike persons who may die before Armageddon; also the faithful witnesses of Jehovah who died before Pentecost A.D. 33 when the holy spirit was poured out, namely, the pre-Christian witnesses from martyred Abel up to John the Baptist.

[11] Reasonably their resurrection will be early after Armageddon, because many of these will be made theocratic princes in all parts of the earth. They will all become children of the Everlasting Father Jesus Christ, who laid down his human life for them. These will include many of the earthly forefathers of Jesus Christ, such as Enoch, Noah, Abraham, Isaac, Jacob and David. In the psalm addressed to him as the Bridegroom King it is said: "Instead of thy fathers shall be thy sons; princes shalt thou make them in all the earth." (Psalm 45:16, Da) When these pre-Christian witnesses of Jehovah receive their resurrection of life on earth they, too, will become "other sheep" of the Right Shepherd, who surrendered his soul for the life of all his sheep. (John 10:11, 15, 16, NW) Because these men did good as faithful witnesses of Jehovah they will be entrusted with princely or leading positions in the "new earth" as the visible representatives of their Everlasting Father, the King Jesus Christ. Even now before Armageddon and since Christ's enthronement A.D. 1914 many of the other sheep are occupying positions as theocratic princes with those of the remnant in the New World society; as it is written: "Behold, a king will reign in

---

11. (a) When will the resurrection of these latter ones take place, and why? (b) Will princely responsibilities carry through Armageddon with any survivors, and why?

righteousness, and princes will rule in justice. Each will be like a hiding-place from the wind, a covert from the tempest." (Isaiah 32:1, 2, *RS*) The Armageddon survivors will doubtless have these princely responsibilities carry through Armageddon with them.

[12] As "there is going to be a resurrection of both the righteous and the unrighteous," those in the memorial tombs who "practiced vile things" will come forth to a "resurrection of judgment." (Acts 24:15, *NW*) This will include the friendlily disposed evildoer on the tree to whom Jesus, also on a tree, said: "Truly I tell you today, You will be with me in Paradise." (Luke 23:43, *NW; Ro; Cureton; Lamsa; Reinhardt*) Jesus Christ the Right Shepherd died for them, not to put them on judgment for their past vile lives, but to provide for them a period of judgment in the new world in hope of their reforming and practicing good things and deserving to be lifted up to human perfection, thus to be judged according to their future works under the Kingdom. They will have the opportunity to become "other sheep" by listening to the voice of the Shepherd King and obediently following him, that he may gather them into the "one flock." As Jehovah's High Priest, the Shepherd King will be able to apply the merit of his atoning sacrifice (typified by the blood of Jehovah's goat) in behalf of their sins. In that way their sins may be forgiven and canceled and they may be cured of their imperfections and brought to the image and likeness of God by the end of Christ's thousand-year reign. (Mark 2:5-12) If any resurrected ones then under judgment prove unreformable or turn rebellious after a sufficient period of trial, they may be executed, destroyed in the sec-

---

12. (a) For whom will there be a "resurrection of judgment," and what evildoer did Jesus include among them? (b) According to what will they be judged, and how will the unreformable and rebellious be dealt with?

ond death, without further delay, their names never getting to be written in the book of life.

[13] The resurrection of all in the memorial tombs to earthly life is pictured at Revelation 20:11-15. By the resurrection of all such mankind's common grave, which the Hebrew, Greek and English Scriptures call She'ol, Ha'des and hell, will be wiped out, pictured as being "hurled into the lake of fire. This means the second death, the lake of fire." (*NW*) Not only will She'ol, Ha'des or hell die, but the death that mankind inherited from Adam and that put dying mankind in She'ol, Ha'des or hell will also be hurled into the same symbolic lake and die out. That will be by the end of Christ's thousand-year reign as King when he finishes applying the merit of his human sacrifice as High Priest of God.

[14] Then all those who have been cleansed and cured of every trace of condemnable sin and imperfection inherited from sinner Adam will be free of the death due to him. That death will thus itself have been put to death, in the second kind of death. After that, if any lifted up to a perfect human image and likeness of God die, it will not be a death traceable to Adam but a death due to the perfect sinner's own willfulness and rebellion. It will be punished with that second kind of death from which there will be no resurrection from a memorial tomb, "second death." So at the end of Christ's millennial reign he turns over the perfected human race to stand trial before God, for only God is the one who can justify creatures to everlasting life.—Romans 8:33.

---

13. The resurrection of all in the memorial tombs will result in the death of what things, and when will this be fully accomplished?
14. After the death of the death due to Adam, for what will any die after that and with what kind of death? Hence before whom must perfected mankind finally be put on trial?

¹⁵ How will perfect mankind in the earth-wide paradise then be put to the proof? In the original garden of Eden it was not necessary for a devil to come into existence to put Adam and Eve to the test; the prohibition upon the "tree of the knowledge of good and bad" was means enough for God to prove their integrity to him. But Satan the Devil put in question God's ability to enable any of Adam's descendants to keep integrity to him as universal Sovereign. Since Satan the Devil raised the question, he has injected himself into the testing process. Inasmuch as perfected mankind in the paradise of the "new earth" will know also what good and bad are, it will not be fitting to replant the tree of knowledge of good and bad and test mankind by a prohibition upon it. Satan the Devil is the proper one, with his demons, to be used as God's instrument to test the enduring quality of man's integrity to God.

¹⁶ Hence at the end of the thousand years Satan and his demons will be let loose from the abyss, but not admitted back to heaven. His spiritual "land of Magog" was destroyed, burned up, a thousand years before then. He is no longer god and ruler of the world, hence no longer "prince of Rosh, Meshech and Tubal." Letting them loose will lead, not to the restoration of the "wild beast" and the "false prophet" and to a new battle of Armageddon, but to an attack upon the "new earth." This will be at the same time an attack upon the "new heavens," the New Jerusalem, which that "new earth" represents visibly. By then perfected mankind will have been sanctified by the

---

15. Why will perfected mankind in paradise properly be put to the proof, not by means of a tree of knowledge of good and bad, but by means of Satan and his demons?
16. The loosing of Satan and his demons from the abyss will lead to what attack, and for what reason will any on earth get misled by them, and how many?

atoning blood of the King Priest Jesus and will be holy ones. (Hebrews 13:12, *NW*) Satan and his demons will want to have earthly allies in this attempt to overthrow Jehovah's universal sovereignty as regards the earth, to turn all mankind to Satan. He will go out to mislead as many as he can and thus try to prove God a liar as to man's integrity. The Revelation foresees that he will mislead many, who will yield to Satan for selfish reasons just as perfect Adam did in Eden. These many misled ones from the four quarters of the earth are likened to the nations that assaulted the New World society at Armageddon and are therefore also called "Gog and Magog." They are as indefinite in number as the "sand of the sea," though they might not be over 144,000.

[17] The Revelation's advance report of this tells what follows: "And they advanced over the breadth of the earth and encircled the camp of the holy ones and the beloved city. But fire came down out of heaven and devoured them. And the Devil who was misleading them was hurled into the lake of fire and sulphur, where both the wild beast and the false prophet already were [for a thousand years]; and they will be tormented day and night for ever and ever [by being restrained as an odious, condemnable example there forever]. . . . This means the second death, the lake of fire. Furthermore, whoever was not found written in the book of life was hurled into the lake of fire." (Revelation 20:7-10, 14, 15, *NW*) Satan and his demons are not hurled back into the abyss to a deathlike inactivity, but are plunged into the symbolic lake of fire of second death, absolute destruction from which there is no release. (Hebrews 2:14) Those perfected humans who selfishly let

---

17. What happens to the spirit attackers and to the human attackers against the "new earth" and the heavenly government?

themselves be misled by Satan and his demons and who attack the camp of the holy ones and the beloved city are not "found written in the book of life." So they are hurled into the same symbolic fiery lake of second death where Satan and his demons are hurled. These particular ones who are misled into the attack upon the "new earth" and the heavenly government are also pictured as having fire come down from heaven and devour them. The wicked souls are destroyed, being condemned, not justified by God.

[18] The holy ones, camped on the side of Jehovah's universal sovereignty, will not be misled or be regimented into Satan's earthly forces. The holy ones will resist and remain firm for Jehovah as God and Universal Sovereign and for his "beloved city," the New Jerusalem, as the new world's rightful government. They will hold fast their integrity and show unchangeable decision for righteousness until Satan's loosing for a little while ends in his own destruction and in the destruction of all his demons and misled human dupes. God will be vindicated as true by their unbreakable steadfastness and he will judge them worthy of the right to everlasting life in the earthly paradise. He will accordingly justify them, and the names of these unchangeably righteous ones will be "written in the book of life." The prophecy of long ago will then stand vindicated: "He hath swallowed up death for ever; and the Lord Jehovah will wipe away tears from off all faces; and the reproach of his people will he take away from off all the earth: for Jehovah hath spoken it." (Isaiah 25:8, *AS;* Romans 8:33) The "new earth" will thus remain forever, uncorrupted, irreproachable.

---

18. What will the holy ones camped on God's side do, and what will God do to them in reward, completely fulfilling Isaiah 25:8?

[19] The apostle John had unveiled to him in symbolic signs the heart-enrapturing state that will then obtain. He describes it in these words: "I saw a new heaven and a new earth, for the former heaven and the former earth had passed away, and the sea [that produced the wild beast of Satan's visible organization] is no more. I saw also the holy city, New Jerusalem, coming down out of heaven from God and prepared as a bride adorned for her husband. With that I heard a loud voice from the throne say: 'Look! the tent of God is with humankind, and he will reside with them, and they will be his peoples. And God himself will be with them. And he will wipe out every tear from their eyes, and death will be no more, neither will mourning nor outcry nor pain be any more. The former things have passed away.' And [God] the one seated on the throne said: 'Look! I am making all things new.'"—Revelation 21:1-5, *NW*.

[20] With all the former things gone, including death inherited from Adam, mourning, outcry and pain traceable to Adam's rebellion and Satan's misrule, tear-filled eyes, the Devil's world and its lusts and ungodliness, the Revelation vision leaves the righteous world of all things new before our gaze. Endlessly, changelessly it will continue in that blessed state. Jehovah's spirit will permeate the whole new world. The fruitage of his spirit, which is love with all its attendant amiable qualities, will prevail, love first to God with all one's heart, mind, soul and strength, and love for one's perfect, godly neighbor as for oneself. In that new world "love never fails." It will be as immortal as God. "God is love."—Galatians 5:22, 23; Mark 12:28-31; 1 Corinthians 13:8, *NW;* 1 John 4:8, 16.

---

19. In what words does John describe the state that will then obtain?
20. Thus the Revelation leaves the new world in what state before our gaze, how long will it continue thus, and what will never fail in it?

CHAPTER XXIII

Individual Decision Now for Surviving Armageddon

EACH informed individual is now faced with the need to make the decision upon which depends his fate at Armageddon. He cannot look to Christendom for guidance, for her fruits make her known as not Christian. She is a light that has failed amid the deepening world darkness, and her appeals for a great spiritual revival will continue to prove vain. In this "time of the end" she has shown herself to be like unfaithful Israel of old, a shameless nation, refusing divine discipline, making no spiritual improvement and displaying no religious cohesion. She is doomed and her silver and gold will not be able to deliver her from her foretold end. Do not try to hide in her. In the face of the approaching day of the Lord Jehovah's wrath upon her it is now the time for individual decision and action. Amid a situation that typed ours of today the prophet Zephaniah, whose name means "Concealed by Jehovah," advised the only course to take that leads to concealment from harm:

[2] "Gather yourselves together, yea, gather together, O shameless nation: before the decree bring forth the day when one passeth as the chaff, before the fierce anger of the LORD [Jehovah]

1, 2. (a) Why is each informed individual now faced with the need to make a decision, and why may he not try to hide in Christendom? (b) What did Zephaniah, amid a situation like ours today, say in advice on the only course leading to shelter?

come upon you, before the day of the LORD's anger come upon you. Seek ye the LORD [Jehovah], all ye humble of the earth, that have executed His ordinance; seek righteousness, seek humility. It may be ye shall be hid in the day of the LORD's anger."—Zephaniah 2:1-3, So.

[3] The humble are the ones that the Lord Jehovah has promised to save. He has anointed his faithful remnant to preach the good news to the humble. His proverb says: "Before destruction the heart of man is haughty; and before honor goeth humility." If you do not want destruction at Armageddon, be humble, seek humility in the fear of Jehovah. You stand to gain by it. "The reward of humility and the fear of Jehovah is riches, and honor, and life." (Proverbs 18:12; 22:4, AS) As it is Jehovah's anger that is to be expressed at Armageddon, it is Jehovah whom we should seek now while he may be found and his favor may be won. What he has ordained for the humble to do in this critical day is what we should execute. All self-righteousness we should abandon, and his righteousness we should seek through Christ. Sheeplike humility under Jehovah's hand we should seek. Only by that course may you hope to be "hid in the day of Jehovah's anger" and survive.—AS.

[4] This is no occasion for gambling with time. In the past you may have squandered your opportunities to enjoy the love, care and provision of the heavenly Father like the prodigal son of Jesus' parable. If you now appreciate the spiritual famine that is ruining Christendom and all the na-

---

3. To be hidden in the day of Jehovah's anger, why is humility important, and what kind of righteousness, and what is the ordinance that we should execute?
4. Those who have been squandering their opportunities to enjoy the heavenly Father's provision should now act like whom, in full assurance of what joyful outcome?

tions, come to your senses like the impoverished prodigal son, leave the doomed, spiritually starving world, repentantly return to the Father, Jehovah God, and humbly confess your sin against him. He will come out to meet you as you draw near and will be lovingly forgiving. He will make a great rejoicing over you within his theocratic organization and will treat you as a son. Any who object to this he will rebuke. (Luke 15:11-32) You will enjoy living in his New World society.

⁵ Make time count now for your deliverance. Accept the help of Jehovah's witnesses to speed your getting out of this doomed modern Sodom. If you are greatly distressed by the lawless, loose people of this world, then remember Lot and his daughters in Sodom, for ancient Sodom is prophetically used as a type of this world in its "time of the end." (2 Peter 2:6-10; Jude 7; Luke 17:28-30) After Lot warned his sons-in-law in vain of the impending fiery destruction, Jehovah's two angels seized hold

5. Whose help should you now accept to speed your escape, and how were Lot and his family an example?

of the hands of Lot, his wife and two daughters and hastened their getting out of doomed Sodom. Outside they were told to move quickly out of the danger zone: "Escape for your soul! Do not look behind you and do not stand still in all the District! Escape to the mountainous region for fear you may be swept away!" By the speediest movement out of the doomed area their lives were spared, except that of Lot's wife, who stopped, turned and looked back selfishly and disobediently.—Genesis 19:1-29; Luke 17:32, *NW*.

⁶ Show faith like Lot, sound the warning to others in modern Sodom, and get out from being any part of this doomed, iniquitous system. Move without delay. Never slow up for any regrets and look back. "Remember the wife of Lot." God does not send two angels to you visibly, but he does send His witnesses under angelic guidance. Entertain them and try to shield and protect them from harm and interference. Act humbly, wisely, on their advice.

⁷ Imitate Jesus' ancestress, Rahab. In ancient Jericho she showed faith in Jehovah by receiving the Israelite spies, hiding them, aiding their escape and acting on their advice. When Jehovah's miracle collapsed Jericho's walls, the part on which her house stood remained standing. When Jehovah's Israelite executioners moved in for the kill, Rahab and her relatives in her house were spared. Rahab is set as an example for you now before Jehovah wrecks this modern Jericho and his executioners under Christ move in for the destruction of all the faithless worldlings. Be like Rahab and be hidden and spared at Armageddon.—Joshua 2:1-24; 6:1-25; James 2:25; Hebrews 11:30, 31; Matthew 1:1-6.

---

6. How may you show faith like Lot, acting on advice of those who are under angelic guidance?
7. How may you imitate Rahab of Jericho, and with what assurance?

⁸ In view of all the other ancient types and prophecies the safe course is clearly marked out before you. You are not left alone, with no place to go, with nothing tangible with which to associate. Jehovah God has built up his New World society on earth, and it teems with happy, fear-free, faith-practicing members and overflows with spiritual prosperity. He keeps it covered under the shadow of his protective hand, to preserve it for his righteous new world. He gives it his guarantee of survival through the "war of the great day of God the Almighty."

⁹ Those dwelling in the New World society live not on material bread alone, but on the utterances out of Jehovah's mouth. Regularly they study his Word, the Bible, and faithfully endeavor to live by it. You are welcomed to study it with them. Learn of Jehovah's provisions for your everlasting life in his new world through Jesus Christ. In humility and loving appreciation, in imitation of Jesus Christ himself, dedicate your life to the One who is the Source of all life and goodness, Jehovah God, and symbolize your dedication as Jesus did, by immersion in water. Then prove your dedication by undertaking His service as prescribed in His Word, preaching "this good news of the kingdom" and declaring the "day of vengeance of our God." Do this in unbreakable unity with the New World society, keeping your personal integrity toward the Universal Sovereign under all tests that may come and enduring them to the finish. Joyfully following this Scripturally outlined course, then "YOU MAY SURVIVE ARMAGEDDON INTO GOD'S NEW WORLD."

---

8. Why are you not left alone, with no place to which to go in hope of survival?
9. What course is recommended to you as regards God's Word, Christ's example, Jehovah's service and his New World society, so as to apply to yourself the theme of this book?

LIST OF 42 TYPES AND PROPHECIES
OF THE EARTHLY HEIRS OF THE NEW WORLD

(In the order of their occurrence herein)

1. The twelve non-Levitic tribes of Israel on the annual day of atonement.—Pages 39, ¶12; 45, ¶20–46, ¶21; 50, ¶26; 352, ¶7.

2. Those who with the meek spiritual Israelites seek Jehovah and righteousness and meekness.—Pages 58, ¶12, 13; 362, ¶2–363, ¶3.

3. Ebed-melech the Ethiopian.—Pages 62, ¶17–63, ¶20.

4. The Rechabites.—Pages 64, ¶21–67, ¶26.

5. The "mixed company" that left Egypt with Israel.—Pages 122, ¶23–125, ¶27.

6. The Nethinim (temple slaves), the non-Israelite slaves and singers and the descendants of the servants of King Solomon.—Pages 142, ¶26–147, ¶33; 300, ¶19.

7. The Gibeonites.—Pages 145, ¶30; 239, ¶14–243, ¶21; 300, ¶19.

8. The mariners with whom the prophet Jonah shipped.—Pages 149, ¶35–150, ¶37.

9. The repentant Ninevites.—Pages 152, ¶40–158, ¶48.

10. The sheep gathered to the King's right.—Pages 164, ¶7–167, ¶12.

11. The "other sheep."—Pages 167, ¶12–169, ¶14.

12. The "great crowd" in white robes, with palm branches. —Pages 176, ¶10–182, ¶19; 305, ¶6.

13. King Hiram's woodcutters and stone quarriers and King Solomon's conscripted laborers for doing work before and after the temple's construction.—Pages 182, ¶20–185, ¶23.

14. The gathered, fed, guided and protected ones of Isaiah 49: 9-13.—Pages 185, ¶24–189, ¶29.

15. The men in Jerusalem that sigh and cry over the abominations.—Pages 211, ¶14–217, ¶22.

16. Rebekah's nurse Deborah and other lady attendants.—Pages 224, ¶8; 226, ¶10; 229, ¶14.

17. The bride's "virgins her companions."—Pages 227, ¶12; 229, ¶14–230, ¶16.

18. The temporary resident and the settler who flee to the city of refuge for unintentional manslaughter.—Pages 233, ¶4–238, ¶12.

19. Jonathan the son of King Saul.—Pages 246, ¶3–248, ¶6.

20. Foreigners who fought along with King David.—Pages 251, ¶10–252, ¶12.

21. Those in the Persian empire who Judaized in favor of Mordecai and Esther.—Pages 258, ¶22–259, ¶23.

22. The "desire of all nations" that comes into the temple.—Pages 263, ¶6–269, ¶16.

23. The "abundance of the sea" and those who fly like clouds of doves to their dovecotes.—Pages 266, ¶12–268, ¶14.

24. The queen of Sheba who visited King Solomon.—Pages 268, ¶14–269, ¶15.

25. The nations and peoples that flow to the mountain of Jehovah's house to be taught his ways.—Pages 270, ¶17–272, ¶20.

26. Jehonadab the son of Rechab.—Pages 276, ¶6–281, ¶13.

27. Midianite Hobab, the kinsman of Moses.—Pages 281, ¶14–283, ¶16.

28. Jael the wife of Heber the Kenite.—Pages 283, ¶16–287, ¶22.

29. Noah's sons and daughters-in-law.—Pages 290, ¶5–293, ¶9; 350, ¶4–351, ¶5.

30. The strangers and sons of the alien who serve as feeders of Israel's flocks and as plowmen and vinedressers.—Pages 296, ¶14–298, ¶16.

31. The foreigner who comes from afar and prays toward the temple.—Pages 297, ¶15–298, ¶16.

32. The "ten men" that "take hold of the skirt of him that is a Jew."—Page 299, ¶17.

33. The very great multitude of fish that come to life in the healed waters of the Salt Sea.—Pages 308, ¶10–309, ¶12.

34. Naaman the Syrian healed by Elisha's prescription.—Pages 310, ¶13–312, ¶16.

35. Any thirsty one who hears the invitation and himself says, "Come!"—Pages 313, ¶18–314, ¶19.

36. The second set of ten children born to Job after his recovery.—Pages 319, ¶9–322, ¶11.

37. Jephthah's daughter.—Pages 323, ¶13–325, ¶16.

38. Joseph's ten repentant half brothers.—Pages 326, ¶19–327, ¶21.

39. The famine-stricken Egyptians who sold themselves to Joseph.—Page 328, ¶22, 23.

40. The prodigal son of Jesus' parable.—Page 363, ¶4.

41. Lot and his daughters.—Page 364, ¶5, 6.

42. Rahab of Jericho.—Page 365, ¶7.

Subject Index

A

Aaron ('s), anointed, 41, ¶15
  burned incense; why, 43, ¶18
  foreshadowed Christ, 41, ¶15; 71, ¶6
  made atonement, 43, ¶17
  offered goat, 45, ¶20
  treatment of live goat, 46, ¶22
Abraham, 225, ¶9
Adam, son of God, 32, ¶2
Adon, 87, ¶6
"Adonay," 21, ¶6
  came to temple, 95, ¶17; 100, ¶24; 102, ¶27–103, ¶28; 106, ¶32; 117, ¶15; 134, ¶13; 160, ¶2, 3; 170, ¶1; 175, ¶7; 179, ¶15; 206, ¶8; 260, ¶1; 302, ¶12; 317, ¶17
  Jews did not seek, 95, ¶16
  John identifies, 92, ¶14
  judged Messenger, 95, ¶16
  Malachi foretells, 85, ¶1, 2
  means Jehovah, 89, ¶8; 91, ¶11
  origin of word, 88, ¶7
  use of word in Scriptures, 89, ¶8
  visitation of, 95, ¶16
Altar in Jerusalem, 132, ¶9
Angel of the covenant, accompanies "Adonay," 100, ¶24; 172, ¶3
  identified, 89, ¶9–91, ¶12; 111, ¶8
  rejected, 94, ¶15
  seals remnant, 181, ¶17
Angel(s), associated with Jesus Christ, 23, ¶9; 25, ¶11; 27, ¶13
  vision of sixth, 198, ¶14–199, ¶15
Anglo-American world power, 338, ¶13
"Appointed times of the nations," 102, ¶26; 111, ¶8
  began 607 B.C., 134, ¶13
  ended 1914, 134, ¶13
  See Times of the Gentiles
Ark of the covenant, contained law, 42, ¶16
  symbolized divine presence, 100, ¶24; 102, ¶27
Armageddon, a universal war, 23, ¶9
  battle line of, 338, ¶13–342, ¶22
  battle of gods, 19, ¶4–20, ¶5
  calamitous catastrophe, 14, ¶12
  "Congressional Record" on, 12, ¶9
  David's warfare, picture of, 204, ¶5
  death-dealing windstorm, 170, ¶1
  extent of slaughter, 342, ¶22–343, ¶23
  how named, 12, ¶10
  human bomb to go off at, 272, ¶20
  meaning of prophecy of, 340, ¶17, 18
  no neutrals in, 14, ¶13
  not far off, 13, ¶11
  not to be flood, 290, ¶5
  pictured by Megiddo battle, 286, ¶21
  Scripturally called war, 18, ¶1
  to outrank all previous battles, 21, ¶7
  universal conflict, 57, ¶11; 331, ¶1
  urgency of proclaiming, 12, ¶8
  warning, not calamity-howling, 14, ¶12
  why windstorm held back, 171, ¶2–172, ¶3; 175, ¶7; 176, ¶10
  worst thing to hit earth, 10, ¶6

B

Babylon, fall of, 129, ¶5
  remnant streamed out of antitypical, 137, ¶17
  thousands fled antitypical, 175, ¶8
  type of Satan's organization, 132, ¶11
Babylonians, 134, ¶14
Barak (and Deborah), 283, ¶17; 286, ¶21
  Jesus Christ Greater, 287, ¶22
Beelzebub, 18, ¶2
Bible, not old-fashioned, 15, ¶14
  only book telling of Armageddon, 15, ¶14
  writers of, inspired, 16, ¶15
Blood at Armageddon, 341, ¶19–342, ¶21
Blood avenger, 232, ¶3–234, ¶5; 238, ¶11; 239, ¶13; 341, ¶19; 344, ¶25
Bride, Christ's love for, 221, ¶5
  how a suitable marriage mate, 221, ¶5–222, ¶6
  Lamb's wife, 313, ¶18
  like Rebekah, 223, ¶8
  religious churches claim to be, 223, ¶7
Bridegroom, announced by John, 219, ¶3
  at temple, 223, ¶7
  bride glorified with, 221, ¶5–223, ¶7

C

Captivity, 162, ¶5
Choice, between life and destruction, 159, ¶1
Chosen ones, 252, ¶12
  days of tribulation cut short for, 111, ¶7, 8; 114, ¶11; 120, ¶20; 170, ¶1
  gathering of, 142, ¶26
Christendom('s), a failing light, 362, ¶1
  apostate, foreshadowed, 52, ¶13
  armies fought for world domination, 29, ¶16
  asks for a "sign," 155, ¶44
  attempt to destroy remnant, 110, ¶5
  bloodguilty, 232, ¶2–233, ¶4; 236, ¶9; 239, ¶13
  destruction of, 53, ¶5; 55, ¶8; 84, ¶26; 215, ¶19; 216, ¶21
  end of, not different from Jerusalem's, 209, ¶12
  first to go down, 55, ¶8; 84, ¶26
  hypocritical, 51, ¶2; 55, ¶8
  ignores sign, 157, ¶47
  included among goats, 165, ¶8, 9
  Jesus foretold end of, 94, ¶15
  judgment of, 208, ¶10
  nations of, to perish, 51, ¶2
  not to escape, 25, ¶11
  proved to be a shameless nation, 58, ¶13
  refuses to take witnesses seriously, 66, ¶25
  rejects Jesus' followers, 107, ¶1
  temple typified by Jerusalem's, 109, ¶4
Cities of refuge, 233, ¶4–235, ¶8
  unintentional manslayer not to leave, 238, ¶11
Cleansing of the land, 344, ¶24
Clergy, approve United Nations, 245, ¶1
Communism, nations make common cause with, 200, ¶16

Congregations, growth of, 296, ¶13
Conventions, Cedar Point, 119, ¶18; 140, ¶22
  Columbus, Ohio, 211, ¶14
  Washington, D.C., 179, ¶15
Cyrus, decree of, 130, ¶6; 262, ¶4, 5
  fulfilled purpose of Jehovah, 130, ¶6
  Jesus Christ Greater, 186, ¶25

D

Dates, 1513 B.C., 69, ¶4; 121, ¶22; 128, ¶4
  1512 B.C., 73, ¶9
  1070 B.C., 202, ¶2
  1038 B.C., 105, ¶31
  1037 B.C., 74, ¶12
  1034 B.C., 73, ¶11–74, ¶12; 105, ¶31
  852 B.C., 149, ¶35
  632 B.C., 128, ¶4
  607 B.C., 55, ¶8; 59, ¶14; 61, ¶16; 66, ¶24; 68, ¶1; 73, ¶10; 99, ¶23; 102, ¶27; 128, ¶4–129, ¶5; 134, ¶13; 208, ¶11; 215, ¶19; 231, ¶1
  539 B.C., 129, ¶5
  537 B.C., 130, ¶6; 132, ¶9; 135, ¶15; 137, ¶17, 18; 140, ¶22; 262, ¶4; 300, ¶19
  520 B.C., 262, ¶4
  468 B.C., 144, ¶28
  A.D. 29, 40, ¶14; 101, ¶25
  A.D. 30, 91, ¶12
  A.D. 33, 40, ¶14; 45, ¶19; 92, ¶13; 101, ¶25; 172, ¶4; 223, ¶7; 354, ¶10
  A.D. 70, 49, ¶25; 68, ¶1; 83, ¶25; 84, ¶26; 171, ¶2; 215, ¶19; 231, ¶1; 239, ¶13
  A.D. 96, 13, ¶11; 98, ¶21
  A.D. 1914, 58, ¶13; 99, ¶23; 102, ¶26, 27; 109, ¶4; 111, ¶8; 113, ¶10; 133, ¶12; 134, ¶13–135, ¶15; 155, ¶44–156, ¶46; 177, ¶12; 191, ¶3; 195, ¶9; 202, ¶1; 204, ¶5; 232, ¶2; 245, ¶1–246, ¶2; 260, ¶1; 265, ¶10; 289, ¶3; 292, ¶7; 338, 13; 355, ¶11
  A.D. 1914-1918, 110, ¶6; 267, ¶13; 345, ¶26
  A.D. 1918, 102, ¶27–103, ¶28; 104, ¶29; 106, ¶32; 117, ¶15; 134, ¶13; 156, ¶46; 160, ¶3; 162, ¶5; 170, ¶1; 172, ¶3; 206, ¶8; 218, ¶1; 223, ¶7; 260, ¶1; 266, ¶11; 302, ¶1; 304, ¶3
  A.D. 1919, 66, ¶25; 118, ¶16; 135, ¶15; 136, ¶16; 137, ¶18; 140, ¶22; 156, ¶46; 162, ¶5; 168, ¶13; 192, ¶5; 249, ¶8; 266, ¶11; 267, ¶13; 296, ¶13; 307, ¶9; 317, ¶4; 324, ¶15
  A.D. 1922, 140, ¶22
  A.D. 1931, 181, ¶17; 188, ¶27; 211, ¶14; 263, ¶7, 8; 267, ¶13–268, ¶14; 271, ¶19; 296, ¶13; 307, ¶9
  A.D. 1932, 141, ¶24; 175, ¶8
  A.D. 1935, 176, ¶10; 179, ¶15
  A.D. 1945, 245, ¶1
  A.D. 1950, 273, ¶1
  A.D. 1953, 7, ¶1; 264, ¶9–265, ¶10; 316, ¶2
David('s), conquests, 204, ¶5
  made Zion capital, 202, ¶2
  persecutions of, picture, 247, ¶4

  prefigured King Christ Jesus, 202, ¶2; 204, ¶5
  theocratic warfare, 203, ¶3–204, ¶4; 216, ¶2–247, ¶4; 249, ¶8
  warfare against Philistines, 203, ¶3; 204, ¶5
Day of atonement, 38, ¶11
  defined, 38, ¶11
  what it was, 40, ¶14
  who typified by tribe of Levi on, 39, ¶12
  who typified by twelve tribes of Israel on, 39, ¶12
Day of salvation, 186, ¶25–187, ¶26; 189, ¶29
Days of tribulation, culmination of, 170, ¶1
  cut short, 114, ¶11–115, ¶12; 120, ¶20; 162, ¶5; 170, ¶1; 172, ¶3; 206, ¶8; 218, ¶1
Death, of death due to Adam, 357, ¶14
  three rebels sentenced to, 32, ¶3
Deborah and other lady attendants, typify whom, 226, ¶10
Decision, for all informed, 362, ¶1, 2
Dedication, of many thousands during postwar period, 175, ¶8
  prove, 366, ¶9
  to Greater Pharaoh, 328, ¶23
Deliverance, humility necessary for, 363, ¶3, 4; 365, ¶6
Demon(s), abasement of, 345, ¶26; 349, ¶2
  challenge Jehovah's sovereignty, 29, ¶16
  channel unclean expressions, 199, ¶15
  defeated, 113, ¶10
  destruction of, 165, ¶8; 346, ¶28, 29; 359, ¶17
  gods, 19, ¶4
  hurled to earth, 134, ¶13
  invisible, 18, ¶2
  ruler of, 18, ¶2
  sent out by Satan, 115, ¶12
"Desire of all nations," fill house with glory, 269, ¶16
  plural in number, 260, ¶1–261, ¶3
  revealed to be great multitude, 264, ¶9
Desolation(s), 132, ¶9, 10; 349, ¶2–350, ¶4
Devil, called "Azazel," 34, ¶5; 45, ¶20
  meaning of title, 32, ¶3
  See Satan
Disciples, carried forward the fulfillment of Jonah in witnessing, 152, ¶40
  entered into deathlike inactivity, 152, ¶40
Doves, flight of "great crowd" like, 267, ¶13

E

Earth, battle with reference to, 21, ¶6
  literal meaning, 31 ¶1
Ebed-melech, an Ethiopian eunuch, 62, ¶17
  came to Jeremiah's aid, 62, ¶17
  meaning of name, 63, ¶20
  modern, preserved, 66, ¶25–67, ¶26
  sought Jehovah, 62, ¶18
Egypt(ians), ancient, symbol of world, 126, ¶1
  Jehovah destroyed, 125, ¶26
Elect ones, 107, ¶1
Elisha, not fearful, 336, ¶9
End of the world, 51, ¶1

See **Armageddon; Date 1914**
Evil, permitted, 127, ¶2
"Evil slave" class, 304, ¶4
Executional forces, begin at profane sanctuary, 215, ¶20
  destroy all unmarked, 215, ¶19; 216, ¶21
  pictured, 210, ¶13
Ezekiel('s), pictured remnant's coming to life, 136, ¶16
  seven men in vision of, 210, ¶13
  six men in vision of, 210, ¶13
  vision of, 208, ¶11–211, ¶14; 306, ¶8–309, ¶12
  vision of many spared, 208, ¶11

F

"Faithful and discreet slave," appointed, 207, ¶9
  entrusted with belongings, 207, ¶9
  linen-clad writer pictured, 210, ¶13
  trusted with Kingdom interests, 304, ¶4–306, ¶7
  work of, 211, ¶14; 217, ¶22
"False prophet," 338, ¶13
Fishers of men, 310, ¶12
Flood, type of Armageddon, 351, ¶5
Foreigners, in David's army, 251, ¶10, 11

G

Gibeonites, 239, ¶14–242, ¶19; 300, ¶19
  deliverance of, 243, ¶20, 21
Glory of Jehovah, 268, ¶14
Goatlike ones, destruction of, 165, ¶8, 9
  everlasting cutting-off for, 166, ¶10
  no blessings for, 165, ¶8
  refuse to be marked, 214, ¶17
Gods, invisible and human, 19, ¶4
Gog, abasement of, 345, ¶26
  burial of, 343, ¶23
  God's order to, 316, ¶3
  hordes of, invade, 339, ¶15, 16
  notified of destruction, 315, ¶1
  object of his attack, 315, ¶1; 329, ¶24; 331, ¶2–334, ¶6
  Satan the Devil, 316, ¶2
  uses symbolic "wild beast" and "false prophet," 332, ¶3
  where led, 337, ¶12
"Golden Age, The," 119, ¶18
Good news, 206, ¶8
  many thousands heard, 175, ¶8
  other sheep join in preaching, 188, ¶27
  preaching of, by remnant, 207, ¶9; 249, ¶8; 266, ¶12; 335, ¶8
  proclaimed at stadium, 10, ¶6
  proclamation of, carried forward by this book, 17, ¶17
Grave (She'ol, Ha'des, hell), wiped out, 357, ¶13
"Great crowd," accompany remnant of bride class, 226, ¶10; 229, ¶14–230, ¶16
  assembled to the Signal, 179, ¶15; 335, ¶8
  carry on unified worship, 302, ¶1
  come out of antitypical Babylon, 182, ¶19
  "come out of the great tribulation," 180, ¶16–181, ¶17
  "desire of all nations," 264, ¶9
  enjoy benefits of Jesus' blood, 46, ¶21

"eyes" to remnant, 282, ¶15
flee to refuge city, 237, ¶10–238, ¶12
gathered by King, 201, ¶18
identified, 180, ¶16; 212, ¶15
invite others, 314, ¶19
in white robes, 178, ¶13; 179, ¶15
Jesus' parable speaks of, 181, ¶18
life in new world for, 351, ¶6
never die, 353, ¶8
not "living stones," 182, ¶19
not sealed, 181, ¶18
not to leave city of refuge, 238, ¶11, 12
obey command to "go forth," 186, ¶25
one flock with remnant, 229, ¶15
palm branches in their hands, 178, ¶13; 185, ¶23; 188, ¶27; 229, ¶15
pictured by Ebed-melech, 63, ¶19, 20
pictured by foreigners, 251, ¶11
pictured by Gibeonites, 241, ¶17
pictured by Nethinim, 182, ¶19
prisoners, 185, ¶25
question as to identity, 179, ¶15
result of holding back of winds, 176, ¶10–177, ¶11
saved, pictured by saving of mixed multitude, 125, ¶27
serve at temple day and night, 182, ¶20; 185, ¶23; 188, ¶27
sheep of the Lamb, 180, ¶16; 185, ¶24–186, ¶25
typified by Naaman, 312, ¶16
wash robes, 181, ¶18; 188, ¶27
worship with remnant, 182, ¶19; 185, ¶23
Zechariah foretells of, 299, ¶17
Greater Moses, 118, ¶16; 132, ¶11
Great tribulation, 181, ¶17

H

"Hades," 81, ¶22; 357, ¶13
Haggai, "Watchtower" (1935) on, 264, ¶8
Healing, for "great crowd," 352, ¶7
  Naaman's, 310, ¶13–312, ¶16
High priest, Aaron the first, 36, ¶8
  Jesus Christ the antitypical, 71, ¶6
Hiram, 182, ¶20, 21
Hobab, 281, ¶14–283, ¶16
Holy ones, 360, ¶18–361, ¶19
Holy spirit, Jehovah poured out, 96, ¶18; 104, ¶29; 190, ¶2
  pictured by man who led goat away, 46, ¶22
Hope, Scripturally based, dispels fear, 51, ¶1
Hypocrites, God hates, 51, ¶2
  Israelites became, 53, ¶4

I

Idol worship, 82, ¶23
Integrity, personal, to Sovereign, 366, ¶9
  remnant's tested, 127, ¶3
Isaac, type of Jesus, 224, ¶9
Isaiah, words of, how applied at Yankee Stadium, 8, ¶3
Israel(ites), deliverance of spiritual, 118, ¶16
  nation of, fell, 52, ¶3–53, ¶4
  rejected priest of God, 107, ¶1
  spiritual taken captive, 133, ¶12
  typified spiritual, 132, ¶11
Issue (chief), 21, ¶6
  before all creation, 26, ¶12

of world domination, 99, ¶23
settled, 21, ¶7; 26, ¶12; 29, ¶16;
    331, ¶1; 334, ¶6

J

Jael, 284, ¶18–286, ¶20
type of "other sheep," 287, ¶22
Jehonadab, 276, ¶5–281, ¶13
Jehoshaphat, 348, ¶1
meaning of name, 193, ¶7
See Valley of Jehoshaphat
Jehovah('s), "Adonay," 88, ¶7–89, ¶3
Almighty God, 20, ¶5
called "tribal God" by religionists, 28,
    ¶15
chooses wife for Son, 219, ¶2
claimed fat of sacrifices, 47, ¶23
Great Shepherd, 168, ¶13
Great Sovereign, 21, ¶6; 25, ¶11
love great for world, 27, ¶14
manifested himself in Zion, 131, ¶7, 8
name to be known, 19, ¶3
Supreme Judge, 196, ¶10
"the Lord" who came to temple, 87,
    ¶5–88, ¶7
typed by Darius, 134, ¶13
Jehovah's witnesses, bear reproaches, 49,
    ¶25
engaged in lifesaving activity, 292, ¶8
new name received, 211, ¶14
serve notice on nations, 194, ¶8
stand for lives (pictured), 253, ¶13–
    259, ¶24
Jeremiah, called attention to Jerusalem's
    bloodguilt, 231, ¶1
imprisoned, 59, ¶14
lowered into pit, 62, ¶17
meaning of name, 60, ¶15
prophesied, 59, ¶14; 65, ¶23
prophetically passed cup to nations, 56,
    ¶9
typified Jehovah's remnant of today, 60,
    ¶15
Jerusalem, a nation without shame, 58,
    ¶13
bloodguilty, 231, ¶1
destruction of, 49, ¶25; 54, ¶6, 7;
    56, ¶9; 191, ¶3; 231, ¶1
Jeshua, 132, ¶9
Jesus (Christ), anointed, 40, ¶14; 97,
    ¶19, 20; 105, ¶31
ascension of, 95, ¶17
as "the Son of man," 23, ¶9; 160, ¶3;
    292, ¶7
as "The Word of God," 23, ¶9
Avenger of human blood, 239, ¶13
baptism of, 101, ¶25; 102, ¶27
begotten by spirit, 41, ¶15; 97, ¶20
born a Jew, 36, ¶8
born as perfect baby, 33, ¶4
bruised at the heel, 33, ¶4; 48, ¶24;
    113, ¶10
builder of real temple, 80, ¶18
came to literal temple, 91, ¶12–92, ¶13
Chief Executioner, 202, ¶1, 2; 205, ¶6,
    7; 210, ¶13; 218, ¶1; 241, ¶17
Chosen One, 107, ¶1
cleansed temple, 92, ¶14; 97, ¶19
comes as fighter, 25, ¶11; 27, ¶13
correspondency of spirit-begettal and
    anointing, 102, ¶26
death of, 101, ¶25
Everlasting Father, 355, ¶11
expression of God's love, 202, ¶1

foretold gathering of remnant, 142, ¶25
foretold his resurrection, 80, ¶19
Foundation Cornerstone, 80, ¶18; 82,
    ¶23; 95, ¶17–97, ¶19; 101, ¶25;
    103, ¶28; 107, ¶1–108, ¶2; 118,
    ¶16; 303, ¶2
given kingship, 100, ¶24
Greater Cyrus, 186, ¶25
Greater David, 251, ¶11
Greater Jephthah, 324, ¶15–325, ¶16
Greater Joshua, 244, ¶22
Greater Noah, 351, ¶5
High Priest, 133, ¶12; 202, ¶1
how like Jonah, 150, ¶37
hurled Satan down to earth, 134, ¶13
immortal priest, 71, ¶6
Jehovah's Chief Agent, 161, ¶4
Judge, 207, ¶9
kept integrity, 24, ¶10; 43, ¶18; 107,
    ¶1
King, 36, ¶8; 92, ¶13, 14; 101, ¶25–
    102, ¶27; 134, ¶13; 245, ¶1
King-Priest, 102, ¶26, 27; 105, ¶31
Lamb, 188, ¶27, 28
loyal to Jehovah's sovereignty, 22, ¶8;
    24, ¶10
made High Priest, 35, ¶6; 36, ¶8; 50,
    ¶26
materialized, 95, ¶17
messenger, 86, ¶4; 89, ¶9–91, 12;
    303, ¶2–304, ¶3; 312, ¶17
ministry of, 101, ¶25
persecuted, 48, ¶24
pictured by live goat, 46, ¶22
prefigured by King David, 202, ¶2
resurrected, 33, ¶4; 80, ¶19; 81, ¶22;
    97, ¶19; 101, ¶25
Right Shepherd, 180, ¶16; 188, ¶28;
    213, ¶16; 335, ¶8
rules in midst of enemies, 111, ¶8
sacrificed perfect humanity, 34, ¶5; 37,
    ¶10; 107, ¶1
sacrifice typified on day of atonement,
    38, ¶11
Servant at temple, 187, ¶26–188, ¶28
Son of David, 138, ¶20; 205, ¶6–
    206, ¶8; 246, ¶2; 269, ¶15
"Son of God," 101, ¶25
typed by Cyrus, 134, ¶13–138, ¶20
typified by high priest Aaron, 37, ¶9;
    41, ¶15; 71, ¶6
value of human life taken into heaven,
    48, ¶24
will bruise serpent's head, 22, ¶8; 27,
    ¶13; 33, ¶4–34, ¶5
witness of Jehovah, 101, ¶25
Jews, religious, killed Jesus, 163, ¶6
time of judgment, 95, ¶16
Job, typified transformation of remnant,
    317, ¶5–321, ¶11
Joel's prophecy, 190, ¶2–192, ¶4; 194,
    ¶8–195, ¶9
John's vision of river, 312, ¶17–314,
    ¶19
John the Baptist announced Bridegroom,
    219, ¶3
Jonah, 149, ¶35–150, ¶38; 152, ¶40–
    154, ¶43
Jonathan, 246, ¶3–249, ¶7
pictured witnesses before Christ, 247, ¶4
Joseph, prime minister, 325, ¶17–328,
    ¶23

Joshua, pictured Jesus Christ, 241, ¶17
took enemy by surprise, 243, ¶20
Judah, Jehovah's miracle toward, 129, ¶5
land of, left desolate, 128, ¶4
Judges, 283, ¶17–287, ¶22
Jephthah, 322, ¶12–325, ¶16
Judgment, of sheep and goats, 269, ¶15
of sheeplike ones, 167, ¶11, 12
started at house of God, 117, ¶15–118,
¶16; 160, ¶2, 3; 207, ¶9; 215, ¶20
time for, 164, ¶7
work of, described, 302, ¶1
Justice, foremost act of, 26, ¶12
God's, required ransom, 35, ¶7

K

Kingdom (of God), advertised, 141, ¶23,
24
birth of, 99, ¶23–100, ¶24; 102, ¶26
"city" to come, 50, ¶26
due to begin, 99, ¶23
heavenly, 249, ¶8
preached by Jesus, 148, ¶34
separating work over question of, 159,
¶1–160, ¶2
set up 1914, 109, ¶4
Kings, of earth march, 199, ¶15
"Kolasis," 166, ¶10

L

League of Nations, 18, ¶2; 127, ¶3
Light of world, remnant only, 266, ¶12
Literature banned, 116, ¶13
"Little flock," 167, ¶12
Living stone(s), 103, ¶28; 263, ¶7
chief, 107, ¶1
days of tribulation cut short for, 170,
¶1
freed from antitypical Babylon, 135, ¶15
great crowd co-operate with, 188, ¶28
transferred, 351, ¶6
Lord, came to temple, 87, ¶5–88, ¶7
"the," not angel, 89, ¶9–91, ¶11
Lost sheep, 189, ¶29
Lot and family, example, 364, ¶5, 6
Love required to survive Armageddon, 30,
¶17

M

Magog (land of), 316, ¶2, 3; 332, ¶3;
344, ¶25–345, ¶27
Man created to live forever, 32, ¶2
Mandate, issued to Noah and sons, 351,
¶5
Man in linen, 212, ¶15–213, ¶16; 214,
¶18
Mankind, perfect, put to proof, 358, ¶16
test of perfect submission, 32, ¶2
Mark on forehead, 213, ¶16–214, ¶18
Marriage of God's Son, 218, ¶1
beginning, 226, ¶11
Bridegroom not ashamed, 228, ¶13
espousal, 219, ¶3
how bride treats invitation, 228, ¶13
Psalm 45 associates with war, 227, ¶12
Megiddo, 199, ¶15
Melchizedek, priest, 69, ¶3
Son of God like, 107, ¶1
Mercy, for remnant, 115, ¶12–116, ¶13;
117, ¶15; 121, ¶21
Messenger, came to temple, 96, ¶18–97,
¶19; 102, ¶27–103, ¶28; 105, ¶31;
117, ¶15–118, ¶16; 134, ¶13

Jews did not seek, 95, ¶16
judgment of, separates, 160, ¶2
materialized, 95, ¶17
sent to prepare way, 86, ¶4
Michael's fight with Serpent, 112, ¶9
Mixed company, 122, ¶23–123, ¶25
saved, 125, ¶27
Moses, mediator, 70, ¶5
Most Holy, 73, ¶11
blood of two animals presented in, 42,
¶16
incense burned in; why, 43, ¶18
law kept in, 70, ¶5
Shekinah light in, 70, ¶5
symbolized heaven, 42, ¶16; 70, ¶5
type of God's residence, 71, ¶6

N

Naaman, healing of, 310, ¶13–312, ¶16
worshiped on Israelite soil, 312, ¶15
Nation, new, brought forth, 131, ¶7, 8;
265, ¶10
Nations, became wrathful, 99, ¶23–100,
¶24
Jehovah challenges, 197, ¶13
make common cause with communism,
200, ¶16
of world to perish, 51, ¶2
outside Christendom to be destroyed, 56,
¶10
sanctify their warfare, 195, ¶9
time of their judgment, 196, ¶10
unite against Kingdom, 195, ¶9
Nethinim, 297, ¶15
Artaxerxes respected, 144, ¶28
great crowd pictured by, 182, ¶19
meaning of name, 142, ¶26
returned with Israelites, 142, ¶26–146,
¶32
support restored remnant, 145, ¶31–
147, ¶33
New earth, founded, 293, ¶10
"other sheep," to be permanent inhabitants of, 347, ¶30
New Jerusalem, 313, ¶18
New world, 29, ¶16; 347, ¶30; 361,
¶20
New World society, attack on, 315, ¶1
great crowd invited into, 282, ¶15
greatest optimists, 275, ¶4
growth of, 300, ¶18; 301, ¶20
how formed, 273, ¶1; 293, ¶10
Isaiah's words applied to, 8, ¶3; 274,
¶2
Jehovah's promise power to, 274, ¶2, 3
marked by worship, 276, ¶5
members baptized, 291, ¶6
Noah's activities picture those of, 289,
¶2–293, ¶9
prosperity of, 325, ¶17
realistic people, 288, ¶1
remnant dwells at center of, 317, ¶5
studies of, 366, ¶9
Nineveh, 154, ¶43–155, ¶44; 158, ¶48
Ninevites, believed Jonah, 154, ¶43
destined to afflict Israelites, 149, ¶35
modern, repent, 157, ¶47–158, ¶48
Noah, 289, ¶2–293, ¶9
experiences of, type, 351, ¶5
mandate issued to, a type, 351, ¶5, 6
three sons typified "other sheep," 292,
¶7
typed exalted Jesus, 292, ¶7

wife of, typed "bride," 292, ¶7
Non-Israelites, 142, ¶26
sided with Israelites, 122, ¶23, 24

O

One hundred and forty-four thousand, 39,
¶12–40, ¶13; 60, ¶15–61, ¶16; 63,
¶19; 66, ¶25; 103, ¶28; 180, ¶16;
190, ¶1
foreordained number, 221, ¶5
Jesus' blood applied first for, 45, ¶19;
46, ¶21
"living stones," 108, ¶2
postwar additions to, 175, ¶8
remnant, 207, ¶9
return from captivity, 192, ¶5
"saints," 160, ¶3–161, ¶4
sealed, 171, ¶2–172, ¶4; 174, ¶6–175,
¶7
seek "city" to come, 50, ¶26
wife of Jesus Christ, 219, ¶2
Organization (spiritual), God's woman,
22, ¶8; 33, ¶4
Jehovah brough forth Kingdom from,
100, ¶24
Original serpent, 22, ¶8, 9
"Other sheep," aid remnant, 229, ¶14–
230, ¶16
gathered in, 167, ¶12–169, ¶14
go forth, 188, ¶27
great crowd identified as, 180, ¶16
pictured, 287, ¶22
sighing and crying of, 213, ¶16

P

Paradise, 296, ¶14; 349, ¶2–350, ¶4
"Parousia," 160, ¶2
Passover, 102, ¶27; 118, ¶16; 122, ¶23
Paul, described relationship between Christ
and congregation, 220, ¶4
Pentecost, 66, ¶24; 101, ¶25; 151,
¶39–152, ¶40; 172, ¶4; 174, ¶6;
190, ¶2; 223, ¶7; 354, ¶10
Pharaoh, 325, ¶17–326, ¶18; 328, ¶22,
23
symbol of Satan, 126, ¶1
why antitypical kept in existence, 126,
¶1
Prophetic patterns, of city of Jerusalem,
191, ¶3
Punishment, upon those who know not
God, 27, ¶13
Pure worship, carried on forever, 84, ¶26
remnant engage in, 186, ¶25; 271, ¶19
See **True Worship**

Q

Queen of Sheba, 268, ¶14–269, ¶15

R

Rahab, 365, ¶7
Ransom, God's justice required, 35, ¶7
typified, 38, ¶11
Rechabites, descended from Jonadab, 64,
¶21
feared Jehovah, 64, ¶21
God gave promise to, 66, ¶24
modern, preserved, 66, ¶25–67, ¶26
not to drink wine, 64, ¶21
not to live in houses, 64, ¶21
tested, 64, ¶22
Regnal years, 105, ¶30
Religionists (Christian), blaspheme God,
28, ¶15

pray for God's blessing on armies, 28,
¶15
Remnant, anointed congregation, 60, ¶15
as in belly of fish, 156, ¶45, 46
assembled at Signal, 141, ¶24
at battle lines, 338, ¶14
carry on unified worship, 302, ¶1
cast off fear, 135, ¶15
do not fear Gog, 336, ¶9–337, ¶11
flee to antitypical refuge city, 237, ¶10–
238, ¶12
gather to Signal, 139, ¶21; 142, ¶25;
177, ¶12
God's spirit poured out on Jewish, 104,
¶29
imitate Jeremiah's course, 61, ¶16
in death state, 116, ¶14; 118, ¶16;
266, ¶11
in God's disfavor, 110, ¶6; 116, ¶13
integrity tested, 127, ¶3; 161, ¶4–162,
¶5
in union with Lord Jesus, 108, ¶3
Jehovah's mercy for, 115, ¶12–116,
¶13; 117, ¶15
keep virgin's chastity, 229, ¶14
persecuted, 250, ¶9
preserved through Armageddon, 61, ¶16;
106, ¶32
priests of Jehovah, 298, ¶16
prosperity of, 322, ¶12; 335, ¶8
raise Signal, 138, ¶20
raising of those asleep, 108, ¶2; 118,
¶16
restored, 317, ¶4, 5
return to Jerusalem, 132, ¶9
revived, respond to call, 120, ¶19
view great crowd, 176, ¶10–179, ¶14
Restoration work, 293, ¶14–298, ¶14;
304, ¶4–306, ¶7
Resurrection, benefit of atoning sacrifice,
354, ¶9
bride joined to Christ Jesus by, 219, ¶2
first, 229, ¶14; 354, ¶10
Jesus foretold own, 80, ¶19
of dead to be judged, 100, ¶24; 103,
¶28
of Jesus by Jehovah, 81, ¶22
of judgment, 356, ¶12–357, ¶13
of life, 354, ¶10–355, ¶11
Royal priesthood, great crowd assist, 182,
¶19

S

Sacrifice(s), Aaron offered, 36, ¶8
benefits of atoning, 352, ¶7–357, ¶14
Jesus' perfect, necessary, 37, ¶10
what the bull pictured, 43, ¶17; 45,
¶19
Saints, great crowd not, 181, ¶18; 252,
¶12
reign with Christ, 160, ¶3
spiritual brothers of Christ, 161, ¶4
Sanctuary, opened up, 100, ¶24; 102,
¶27
Satan, abyssed, 348, ¶1–349, ¶2
began treason on earth, 21, ¶7
bruised in head, 126, ¶1; 345, ¶26
destruction of, 165, ¶8; 359, ¶17
god of this system of things, 19, ¶4;
201, ¶17
hurled to earth, 114, ¶11; 172, ¶3;
206, ¶8; 250, ¶9
pictured by King Jabin, 286, ¶21

reproached God, 32, ¶3
ruler of this world, 18, ¶2; 113, ¶10;
133, ¶12–134, ¶13; 316, ¶2
sentenced to death, 33, ¶4
wars with remnant, 121, ¶21
Satan's organization, pictured as wild
beast, 127, ¶3
Saul of Tarsus, Paul, 220, ¶4
Seal(ed, ing), natural Gentiles, 174, ¶6
of disciples, 173, ¶5
of 144,000, 171, ¶2–172, ¶4; 176,
¶9, 10; 181, ¶17; 212, ¶15; 248, ¶5
remnant sent out to seek sheep, 189, ¶29
symbol of holy spirit, 172, ¶4
Second death, 166, ¶10; 346, ¶28, 29;
359, ¶17
Seed of serpent, 166, ¶10
Seed of woman, bruises Satan's head,
126, ¶1
Separating work, according to conduct,
163, ¶6
blessed time, 168, ¶13
how determined, 166, ¶10; 190, ¶1
Jesus emphasizes fact of completion of,
164, ¶7
now in progress, 160, ¶2; 163, ¶6
Seven men, 210, ¶13
Seventieth week, 97, ¶20
Shaking of the nations, 269, ¶16
Sigh and cry, 208, ¶11; 212, ¶15–213,
¶16; 217, ¶22
Signal, exhortation to raise, 141, ¶23
identified, 139, ¶21
many thousands caught sight of, 175,
¶8
raised, 138, ¶20; 140, ¶22; 141, ¶24;
146, ¶32–147, ¶33; 162, ¶5; 177,
¶12
spiritual remnant came to, 137, ¶18
Sign of Jonah, 148, ¶34; 151, ¶39–
152, ¶40; 155, ¶44; 156, ¶46
Sin offering, applying of benefits of, 40,
¶14
disposition of carcasses of, 47, ¶23–48,
¶24
only basis for survival, 50, ¶26
type of bull, 41, ¶15
type of goat, 41, ¶15; 46, ¶21
Sins, mankind's inherited, borne away by
Christ Jesus, 46, ¶22
Six armed men, 210, ¶13
Slaves, serve in building program, 184,
¶22
Solomon, antitypical, began building, 83,
¶25
built temple, 74, ¶12; 105; ¶31; 182,
¶20–185, ¶23
correspondency in temple-building, 105,
¶30
dedicated temple, 75, ¶13–79, ¶17
temple prayer of, 297, ¶15–298, ¶16
type of Jesus Christ, 182, ¶20; 269,
¶15
"Sons of Levi," 305, ¶6
antitypical, tested, 304, ¶3, 4
"Sons of the alien," 300, ¶19
Sovereignty, defined, 21, ¶6
Strangers, 297, ¶15–298, ¶16; 300, ¶18
Survival of Armageddon,
choose the way of, 14, ¶13
Jehovah guarantees, 366, ¶8
knowledge necessary for, 159, ¶1
love required for, 30, ¶17

possibility of, 16, ¶16; 121, ¶22
remnant's, made sure, 106, ¶32
Survivors, Ebed-melech one of Jerusalem's,
62, ¶17
Jehovah's purpose to have, 115, ¶12
many of this generation may be, 31,
¶1
of today pictured, 58, ¶13; 63, ¶20;
66, ¶25
Peter's prophecy concerning, 347, ¶30
princely responsibilities of, 355, ¶11
proof there will be, 197, ¶12
restore natural paradise, 350, ¶4
spiritual paradise of, 349, ¶2
Zephaniah prophesies of, 58, ¶12

T

Tabernacle, Israelites built, 70, ¶5–71,
¶6; 73, ¶9
its typicalness, 71, ¶7–73, ¶10
replaced by temple, 73, ¶10
Temple(s), "Adonay" came to, 102, ¶27
antitypical, 80, ¶18; 83, ¶25–84, ¶26;
97, ¶20
demolished 607 B.C.; A.D. 70, 68, ¶1
did not survive, 79, ¶17
Ezekiel's vision of, 208, ¶11–211, ¶14
heavenly, completed, 106, ¶32
house of Jehovah, 262, ¶4–263, ¶6
inspection of spiritual, 98, ¶21, 22
Jehovah's temple, 81, ¶20, 21; 84, ¶26
Jesus builds spiritual, 96, ¶18
none on earth down to Flood, 69, ¶3
rebuilding began, 132, ¶9
Solomon's, 73, ¶10–79, ¶17
twelve apostles serve in spiritual, 82,
¶23
typical abandoned, 97, ¶20
Temple-building, antitypical, 263, ¶7
by zealous remnant, 131, ¶7
Temple of God, Christendom claims to be,
53, ¶5
"Time of the end," 245, ¶1; 269, ¶16;
293, ¶10; 335, ¶8
of Christendom, 109, ¶4; 166, ¶10;
273, ¶1
remnant, prisoners at beginning of, 186,
¶25
total attack at, 315, ¶1
Times of Gentiles, 99, ¶23
Trailer City, record crowd at, 10, ¶5
Tribulation, greatest, 27, ¶13
True worship, not destroyed, 68, ¶2; 83,
¶25
restoration of, foreshadowed, 132, ¶11
restored, 131, ¶7; 145, ¶31–147, ¶33
Truth, flow of, 307, ¶9–309, ¶12
Twelve apostles, secondary foundation, 82,
¶23
Twelve tribes of Israel, antitypical, lifted
to perfection, 352, ¶7
delivered from Egypt, 69, ¶4
first beast takes captive, 128, ¶4
humankind to correspond with, 352, ¶7
Moses mediator of, 70, ¶5
organized as a nation, 69, ¶4
origin, 69, ¶4
proved to be no longer chosen, 173, ¶5
Type, Aaron was a, 37, ¶10; 71, ¶6
antitype, fulfillment of, 37, ¶9, 10; 71,
¶6

defined, 37, ¶9
of two animal sacrifices, 41, ¶15
Typical pictures and prophecies, forty-two considered, 17, ¶17

U

Underpriests, 352, ¶7
sons of Aaron, 36, ¶8
spiritual sons, 45, ¶19
United Nations, against Jehovah, 195, ¶9
at the battle lines, 338, ¶13
eighth world power, 18, ¶2
failure of, 270, ¶18
fight among themselves, 272, ¶20
formed in 1945, 245, ¶1
Isaiah's words carved on wall of, 7, ¶1, 2; 270, ¶18
not proclaimer of good news, 7, ¶2
perpetuate doomed earth, 273, ¶1
political expression, 195, ¶9
sign, 199, ¶15
Universal sovereignty (Jehovah's),
chief issue, 21, ¶6; 26, ¶12; 159, ¶1
great crowd ascribe salvation to, 178, ¶13–179, ¶14
lines drawn for and against, 338, ¶13–343, ¶23
upheld by remnant, 61, ¶16
vindicated, 21, ¶7; 24, ¶10; 26, ¶12; 111, ¶8; 348, ¶1

V

Valley of Jehoshaphat, symbolic, 192, ¶5–195, ¶9; 334, ¶6
Vengeance, remnant declare God's, 61, ¶16
Vindication, 26, ¶12
Jesus Chief One in carrying out, 26, ¶12
Jesus' death served as, 24, ¶10
of universal sovereignty, 111, ¶8; 159, ¶1; 161, ¶4
Vindicator, Chief, 218, ¶1

Vine of the earth, 196, ¶10, 11; 341, ¶19

W

War in heaven, Satan defeated, 113, ¶10
WBBR, broadcast convention features, 10, ¶5
White horses, at battle of Armageddon, 341, ¶19
White robes, 178, ¶13; 185, ¶23; 188, 27; 226, ¶10; 264, ¶8
other sheep enter King's palace with, 229, ¶15
Wild beast, at battle lines, 338, ¶13
Devil's visible organization, 199, ¶15
first head of, took twelve tribes into captivity, 128, ¶4
fourth head of, 129, ¶5
Gog uses, 332, ¶3
pictures Satan's organization, 127, ¶3
second head of, 128, ¶4
seven heads of, 127, ¶3
third head of, 128, ¶4
Winepress, 341, ¶19
Jehovah's, 196, ¶10, 11
Witness(es, ing), in sackcloth, 116, ¶13, 14
remnant, 162, ¶5; 207, ¶9
revived, 118, ¶16; 119, ¶18–120, ¶20
World powers, Babylon the third of the, 132, ¶11
seven great, 18, ¶2; 127, ¶2, 3
World War I, broke out, 99, ¶23
effect on remnant, 116, ¶13; 137, ¶17; 162, ¶5; 175, ¶7; 295, ¶12
"time of the end," 109, ¶4

Y

Yankee Stadium, how filled, 9, ¶4

Z

Zerubbabel, 132, ¶9; 142, ¶26

Index to Scriptures Cited

GENESIS		22:1-18	224	15:3-18	125	24:10	123
Chap. 1	21	22:15-18	92	17:8-15	254		
1:26-28	32	22:17, 18	189	19:5	173	NUMBERS	
1:27, 28	351	22:18	36, 176	21:23-25	36	3:40-51	304
2:15-17	32	24:59-61	224	23:17	88	10:29-33	282
2:18-25	32	24:62-67	224	33:20	91	11:4, 5	123
3:1-5	33	35:8-19	226	34:23	88	35:9-15	233
3:14, 15	34	46:2-27	70			35:16-21,	
3:15	23, 112,	47:14-25	328	LEVITICUS		30, 31	234
	336	49:28	70	3:16	48	35:22-25	234
3:22	32			4:31	48	35:26-28	238
5:1-5	33	EXODUS		16:2	42		
9:1	351	1:7	351	16:6, 11	43	DEUTERONOMY	
9:1-6, 12-16	232	2:15-22	282	16:8, 10, 26	35	6:5	26, 48
9:22-25	240	9:15, 16	126	16:12, 13	43	21:1-9	237
10:15-19	240	Chaps. 12,		16:15	46	22:23, 24	223
12:2, 3	36, 90	13	118	16:20-22	47	29:23	345
12:3	176	12:37, 38	123	16:25	47	30:11-13	346
14:18-20	69	12:43, 44,		16:27	49	30:13	117
15:18-21	203	48, 49	122	19:18	26		
19:1-29	365	12:49	301	21:10-15	222	JOSHUA	
19:23-26	345	15:1-21	349	23:26-32	38	2:1-24	**365**

6:1-25	365	10:15-17	277	8:17	258	8:13-15	303
9:1-15	241	10:18-23	338	9:1-3	258	9:6	353
9:16-27	241	10:18-28	281			9:6, 7	292
9:22-27	145	14:23-25	149	**JOB**		10:16, 33	88
10:1-15	243	25:18-21	216	1:6-2:7	114	11:1, 2, 10-12,	
10:42	28			23:28	89	15, 16	139
20:1-7	283	**1 CHRONICLES**		33:19-30	319	11:10	147
20:1-9	234	2:55	283	Chaps. 38–		11:16	121
		8:34-40	249	41	320, 321	12:1-3	121
JUDGES		9:1, 2	143	42:1-16	322	13:1-4	252
1:16	283	11:10–12:39	249			19:4	88
4:8, 9	284	11:26, 46	251	**PSALMS**		25:8	360
4:11	283	14:8-17	204	2:1-9	102, 205	26:21	239
4:17-21	285	18:17	251	2:8, 9	336	28:16	96, 104
4:22	286	29:22	105	2:10-12	201, 259	28:21	205
5:1, 24-27	286	29:23	206	3:8	178	28:21, 22	244
5:19-23	284			11:4	88	32:1, 2	356
9:13	197	**2 CHRONICLES**		23:1	168	34:1-4	52
10:17–11:40	324	2:8-18	183	37:10, 11	349	40:3	87
		3:1-3, 8	74	Ps. 45	227	43:10-12	212
RUTH		3:2	105	45:1-5	227	43:27	36
2:20	235	5:1-10	77	45:10-15	228	44:24-45:4	135
3:12, 13	235	5:11-14	79	45:16	355	45:12, 18	351
4:1-10	235	6:18, 32, 33	79	46:1-3	51	46:9, 10	351
		6:32, 33	298	82:6, 7	20	49:3, 5,	
1 SAMUEL		7:1-3	79	83:17, 18	19	8, 9	187
17:34-54	246	7:7-10	78	94:20	264	49:9-13	186
18:1-3	247	8:7-9	185	102:13-20	118	51:14-16	294
23:16-18	247	20:1-25	349	102:15-22	131	54:1-6	219
25:28	246	20:1-29	193	104:15	197	55:4	274
		20:29	28	107:23-31	150	56:7	87
2 SAMUEL		26:16	87	110:1, 2	112, 245	60:1, 2	266
5:4, 5	105	33:7	84	110:1-6	206	60:1-14	268
5:4-10	203	36:17	215	110:4	37, 41	60:10	300
7:23	348	36:20-23	130	110:5	23	61:1, 2	157
8:1-15	204			112:7	51	61:1-3	294
8:18	251	**EZRA**		113:7-9	318	61:4	295
9:7, 8	249	1:1-4	130	137:8, 9	215	61:4-9	297
11:6-17	251	1:7	87	141:2	43	62:10-12	138
14:7-11	235	2:43, 55, 58,				63:12, 14	348
15:18, 19	251	64, 65, 70	143	**PROVERBS**		65:17, 18	274
19:27-30	249	2:43, 58	145	1:22	15	66:1	114
20:7, 23	251	2:64	132	6:12-19	52	66:7-14	266
21:1-9	242	3:1	143	10:7	354	66:8	131
21:2	240	3:1-13	132	18:10	59		
23:2, 3	16	3:6, 7	184	18:12	363	**JEREMIAH**	
23:37-39	251	4:1-6:15	263	19:2	15	1:9, 10	81
		6:11, 12	110	21:11	15	2:34, 35	231
1 KINGS		6:21, 22	143	22:3	15	7:10, 4	87
1:38, 44	251	7:7, 24	144, 145	22:4	363	23:19	170
5:6-18	183	8:17-20	144	29:25	111	25:8-12	129
6:1	105	8:20	145			25:15-26	56
6:1, 2, 19,				**ECCLESIASTES**		25:27-29	57
20, 7	74	**NEHEMIAH**		1:4	31	25:31-36	58
6:37, 38	75	3:7	301			25:32	170
8:1-9	77	7:25, 46-56,		**ISAIAH**		29:10-14	129
8:29	84	60	301	1:24	88	35:1-11	277
8:41-43	298, 312	9:38	146	2:1-5	270	35:1-18	66
8:64-66	78	10:1, 9, 14,		2:4	8	35:18, 19	66
9:3, 7	87	28-30	146	3:1	88	38:1-23	62
9:6-9	129	11:3, 21	146	6:1	89	39:15-18	63
10:1-9	269			6:1-5	89, 313	51:27-29	252
		ESTHER		6:8	91	52:1-29	129
2 KINGS		3:8	255	6:8-10	91	52:24-27	216
5:1-19	311	4:16	255	7:14	34	**LAMENTATIONS**	
6:16	336	7:6-10	256	8:5-7	89	5:4	314

EZEKIEL

8:1-18	209
9:1, 2	210
9:1-4	276, 298
9:3, 4	211
9:5, 6	215
9:6, 7	216
9:8-10	217
9:11	217
34:11, 12, 23, 24, 31	169
36:21-24	175
36:34, 35	296
37:1-14	137, 156
38:1-6	315
38:7-9	316
38:8-12	339
38:10-13	317
38:14-16	330
38:18-23	340
39:1-5	335
39:6, 7	344
39:8-10	343
39:11	338
39:11-16	344
39:17-22	342
40:3	307
43:3	81
47:1-5	307
47:6-12	308

DANIEL

2:44, 45	336
7:9, 13, 14, 27	161
7:13, 14	148, 205
9:24-27	97
11:40	109
12:1	112, 341
12:4	109

HOSEA

10:14	215
13:16	215

JOEL

2:28, 29	173
2:28, 29, 32	176
2:28-32	191
3:1-3	192
3:9	252
3:9-17	195
3:18	306

AMOS

8:11	329

JONAH

1:1-16	150
1:17	151
2:1-10	154
2:10	151
3:4, 10	155
4:11	154

NAHUM

Chaps. 1-3	155

HABAKKUK

2:14	350
2:20	88
3:19	89

ZEPHANIAH

1:1-18	55
2:1-3	58, 363
2:4-15	56

HAGGAI

1:1-15	263
2:6, 7	260
2:7	8, 261, 265
2:7-9	270
2:8, 9	263
2:15-19	263

ZECHARIAH

8:18-23	299
8:23	322
14:3	339
14:3, 9	30
14:8, 9	306

MALACHI

1:6-2:9	305
3:1	85, 87, 88, 89, 97, 98, 207, 260
3:2-5	303
3:10-12	306

MATTHEW

1:1-6	365
1:1-18	134
1:22, 23	34
3:13-17	101
4:17	141
4:19	310
6:9, 10	100
7:21-23	166
9:2-7	353
9:34	19
10:6	189
10:28	354
10:40	163
11:10-15	87
11:11	248
12:24-28	19
12:38-41	148
12:42	80, 182
16:1-4	148
16:18	81
19:28	50, 353
21:7-9	92
21:43	313
22:1-3	220
22:8-14	176
22:21	288
22:35-40	26
22:41, 42	134
22:41-45	206
23:1-24:22	95
23:33	354
23:33-38	239

23:34-37	231
24:1-3, 15, 16	80
24:9	237
24:14	142, 157, 246
24:14, 21, 22	207, 336
24:21	27, 341
24:21, 22	112, 162, 181
24:30, 31	142
24:35-39, 42	289
24:36	339
24:37	351
24:45-47	208
24:45-51	305
25:1-13	220
25:14-30	305
25:31	24
25:31, 32	160
25:31-33, 41	338
25:31-46	167
25:37, 46	182
26:31, 32	152
26:48-54	25
27:50, 51	95

MARK

1:1-4	87
2:5-12	356
7:6-8	52
11:9, 10	92
11:11-18	94
12:28-31	361
13:8	110
13:9-13	110
13:10	157, 301
13:19	341
13:19, 20	111, 218
13:20	171

LUKE

1:9, 10	43
1:59, 76-78	90
3:21-23	101
3:38	32
4:1, 2	47
4:5-7	19
7:27, 28	87
8:31	346
10:10, 11	101
11:29, 30, 32	152
11:29, 31	269
12:42-48	305
13:33, 34	231
15:3-7	189
15:11-32	364
17:20, 21	101
17:28-30	364
17:32	365
19:9, 10	189
19:11-27	305

19:38	92
19:44	95
23:43	350, 356
24:39	352

JOHN

1:12, 13	221
1:14	235
1:29, 36	177
2:13-16	92
2:13-22	80
2:16	87
3:16, 17	26
3:27-30	247
3:28, 29	219
5:22, 27-29	354
5:28, 29	168
6:70, 71	354
8:32	295
9:4	152
10:11, 15, 16	355
10:16	168, 292
10:34-36	20
11:25, 26	353
11:46-54	94
12:12-15	179
12:12-16	92
12:12-19, 36-43	94
12:31	19
12:39-41	91
14:1-3	220
14:30	19
14:31	27
15:18-20	196
16:2	237
17:12	354
17:17	16
17:24	220

ACTS

1:1-11	96
2:1-4, 14, 32, 33	173
2:1-42	175
2:1-3:1	83
2:16-21	191
2:32	152
2:32, 33	96
2:32-36	102
3:20-26	118
4:10-12	102
4:25-28	205
5:29-32	128
5:38, 39	200
7:47-50	79
7:48, 49	114
7:56	96
7:58	236
8:1	236
9:1-5	166
9:1-19	236
10:1-48	175
10:40-43	152
15:14	84
17:24-27	69

20:32 252
22:4-16 236
24:15 356
26:9-19 236
26:18 252

ROMANS
2:28, 29 174
5:12-14 36
6:5 229
6:9 95
6:16 20
8:15-17 173
8:15-18, 28-30 221
8:33 357, 360
8:37 349
9:22-26 171
9:33 96
10:6, 7 346
10:7 117
15:4 17
16:20 336

1 CORINTHIANS
1:2 252
3:16, 17 54, 110
4:15 292
5:7 118
6:9-11 174
8:4-6 20
10:1, 2 124, 291
10:6, 11 38, 132
10:20 20
12:12, 13, 27, 28 83
12:27 61
13:8 361
14:33 252
15:42-44 117
15:44, 50 352
15:44-54 40
15:50 49

2 CORINTHIANS
1:21, 22 174
4:4 20
5:20 163
6:1, 2 187
6:16 82
10:3-5 250
11:2 292
11:2-4 222

GALATIANS
3:8, 16 36
3:16, 29 176
4:4 235
4:26, 27 219
5:22, 23 361
6:15, 16 173

EPHESIANS
1:13, 14 174
1:22, 23 83
2:11-19 174
2:20-22 82
4:30 174
5:22-32 221
5:27 229
6:11, 12 250
6:11-18 349
6:13-17 258
6:13-18 251

PHILIPPIANS
3:20, 21 352
4:18 305

COLOSSIANS
1:18 61, 83, 355

1 THESSALONIANS
4:13-17 104
4:15-17 109
4:16, 17 120
5:2 339

2 THESSALONIANS
1:6-8 259
1:6-10 27
1:7-9 167, 202

1 TIMOTHY
1:13-16 236
2:5, 6 39
3:16 95, 221

2 TIMOTHY
2:13 26
4:8 104

HEBREWS
1:2 291
1:8, 9 227
2:10-12, 18 162
2:14 33, 359
2:14, 15 35
2:14-17 219
4:14 35
5:4-10 41
5:5, 6 35
5:7, 8 43
7:14-27 37
7:15-28 41
8:1-6 72
9:1-5, 23, 24 72
9:11-14 41
9:24 42
10:1 38, 72
10:13 206
11:1-12:2 247
11:7 290
11:22 326

11:30, 31 365
11:32-12:2 286
11:36 61
12:1, 2 326
12:23 304
13:11-15 50
13:12 359
13:15, 16 305

JAMES
2:25 365
4:4 155, 223

1 PETER
1:1, 2 252
1:8 223
1:10-12 247
2:4, 5 108
2:4-7 96
2:4-8 81, 303
2:5, 9 252
2:9 299
3:18 34, 95
3:20-22 291
4:17 207, 215
4:17, 18 117

2 PETER
1:4 239
1:19 17
1:20, 21 16
2:4-9 293
2:6-10 364
2:12 32
3:7, 10-12 347
3:9-14 275
3:13 347

1 JOHN
3:8 35
3:10-12 354
4:8, 16 361
5:19 19

JUDE
7 364
9 112

REVELATION
1:1 13
2:9 213
2:26-29 339
3:9 213
3:21 206
6:14-17 171
Chap. 7 213
7:1-4 276
7:1-8 172, 213
7:4-8 174
7:9 329
7:9-12 177
7:9-17 264, 328

7:13-17 180
8:3, 4 43
Chap. 11 266
11:1, 2, 15-19 99
11:3-13 137, 156
11:7-10 117
11:8 329
11:11-13 119
11:15-18 161, 333
12:1, 2, 5 99
12:5-17 113
12:7-13 172
12:9 19
12:9, 13-17 33
12:13, 17 316
12:17 251, 334
13:1 117
13:1-10 128
14:1 313
14:1-5 40, 219
14:13 352
14:18-20 341
16:12-16 199
16:13-16 13, 333
16:14, 16 18
16:15 339
17:1-18 338
17:3, 8-11 128
17:6 233
17:18 199
18:1-4 175
18:4, 5 186
19:6-21 227
19:7 292
19:8, 9 229
19:11-16 24, 196, 337
19:13, 14 205
19:19, 20 338
19:19-21 341
20:1-3 115
20:1-6 346
20:2 33
20:5, 6 355
20:6 229
20:7-10, 14, 15 359
20:7-11, 14, 15 33
20:10, 14 167
20:11-15 357
20:14 341
21:1, 5 274
21:1-5 361
21:2, 9-27 50
21:8 167
21:9 292
21:22 81
22:1-5 313
22:17 313

THE NEW WORLD BIBLE TRANSLATIONS

Why new translations? Languages keep changing; knowledge of the languages in which the Bible was originally written keeps increasing, and the light of truth on God's Word keeps on shining brighter and brighter, all of which makes better translations possible, yes, necessary.

NEW WORLD TRANSLATION OF THE HEBREW SCRIPTURES (Volume I)

This is an entirely new translation (published in 1953) of the first eight books of the Hebrew Scriptures, Genesis to Ruth, in modern English. It has more than 31,000 cross references and footnotes, maps, drawings and a helpful appendix. It contains 864 pages and measures only 7 5/16" x 5" x 7/8". Bound in green leatherette hard cover, embossed in gold, it is available for only $1.50. De luxe edition in green morocco, flexible leather cover, gilt edges, is $5.00.

NEW WORLD TRANSLATION OF THE HEBREW SCRIPTURES (Volume II)

The historical Bible books from 1 Samuel to Esther take on added force and meaning in the modern-day English used in this translation (published in 1955). Like Volume I described above, Volume II has valuable cross references, footnotes and maps. It also comes in two editions: green leatherette hard cover, title embossed in gold, postpaid, on a contribution of $1.50, and the de luxe edition, leather bound with gold-edged leaves, $5.00.

NEW WORLD TRANSLATION OF THE CHRISTIAN GREEK SCRIPTURES

First published in 1950, this translation is based on the best Greek text available, that of Westcott and Hort of 1881. It embodies the very latest findings regarding early Greek manuscripts. No effort has been spared to make this the most accurate translation available. It contains excellent information about manuscripts and versions, and has copious valuable marginal references and footnotes. Especially valuable is its 30-page appendix throwing the light of careful Bible research on many misunderstood texts. Printed on thin Bible paper, 800 pages, bound in green leatherette, it is sent, postpaid, on a contribution of $1.50. De luxe green leather edition is available for $5.00.

For ordering the above see addresses on the last page.

QUALIFIED TO BE MINISTERS

The ideal textbook for training the Christian witness of Jehovah for every part of his ministry, with the congregation and in the field, publicly and from house to house. Its valuable information is listed under the following headings: Speech Preparation; Delivery; Meetings; Composition; Private Study; Our Ministry; Congregational Activities; Worship—Clean and Unclean; Modern History of Jehovah's Witnesses, and Theocratic Society. Each of its 90 studies has comprehensive questions to facilitate personal study and for congregational or classroom use. It has 384 pages, is bound in olive-green cloth and is sent, postpaid, anywhere on a contribution of 50 cents.

"MAKE SURE OF ALL THINGS"

"Make Sure of All Things" is the Bible handbook for every Christian minister who wants handy proof from the Bible for all he believes and preaches. Seventy major Bible themes are comprehensively discussed, each of which is first defined and its origin noted. Then under subheadings dealing with various aspects of that subject Scripture texts are quoted or cited without comment, showing what the Bible teaches on the subject. It also has an alphabetical list of 287 religious subjects in its index. Bound in brown cloth it measures 6¾" x 4½" x ½", and is available on a contribution of 75 cents a copy, postpaid.

"EQUIPPED FOR EVERY GOOD WORK"

"Equipped for Every Good Work" helps the Christian minister to be just that. It gives facts regarding the origin, preservation and authenticity of the Bible, regarding the three Bible languages, Hebrew, Aramaic and Greek, and about Hebrew and Greek Scripture papyri and vellum manuscripts. It tells of the growth of the Bible canon and of the Bible's fight to live. Then it gives the facts regarding each of the sixty-six books of the Bible, when, where and by whom written, proof of authenticity and a brief summary of its contents. It has 384 pages, is bound in maroon cloth and is available on a contribution of 50 cents.

For ordering the above see addresses on the last page.

"LET GOD BE TRUE"

How will this volume help you? It will let God instead of men answer doctrinal questions that perplex people of all religions. Many feel the clergy have not satisfyingly answered such vital questions as: Who is Jehovah? Did God make a Devil? When will Satan be destroyed? What is man? Is the Bible hell hot? Is there a trinity? Who will return in the resurrection? What is "the end of the world"? There is no need for you to be uninformed and uncertain on these and other Bible doctrines. The foggy answers and conflicting views of many religions have obscured the truth from many people, because they let men determine what they believe instead of God's Word. The 320-page Bible study aid *"Let God Be True"* dispels man-made religious fog and enables right-hearted persons to have the assurance and understanding that can come only by letting God be true, by letting his Word speak for him. This 26-chapter volume is sent on a contribution of 50 cents.

"THIS MEANS EVERLASTING LIFE"

How long do you choose to live? You can choose to live "threescore and ten," or you can choose to live forever in a perfect new world of righteousness. Fantastic? No, for everlasting life is no wild dream; it is the hope God's Word validly offers those willing to obtain the right kind of knowledge. Most people scoff because they lack knowledge. Yet life-giving knowledge is available. The 30 chapters of *"This Means Everlasting Life"* not only prove that you can choose everlasting life but clearly point out the requirements for gaining life. They prove from the Scriptures that the enemy death is to be destroyed and that God's original purpose that all the earth be a paradise will be fulfilled. This 320-page volume may be had on a contribution of 50 cents.

For ordering the above see addresses on the last page.

"NEW HEAVENS AND A NEW EARTH"

"New Heavens and a New Earth" is new, inspiring, exciting—different! Millions of copies of this most remarkable book are already in the hands of the people. And no wonder! Its stimulating message is as sound and refreshing as the Bible. Twenty-two chapters of skillfully blended truths are simply and understandably written with powerful and thoughtful advice. Its compelling account reveals a fascinating story about earth's creation, the beginning of conscious life on it, the reasons for world woes and the incoming of a new world for mankind. Here, firsthand, the real problems confronting mankind are exposed, vital Bible doctrines are explained without sectarian coloring or influence. Its 384 pages overflow with warmth and wisdom that will renew faith, increase knowledge, build appreciation and aid the truth seeker to rise above present anxieties to achieve a richer, happier and more rewarding life. You owe it to yourself and your family to be treated with a copy of this most helpful and informative book. One will be mailed to you, anywhere, on a contribution of only 50 cents.

WHAT HAS RELIGION DONE FOR MANKIND?

Here is a volume that is frank, straightforward and refreshingly truthful in answering the question, "What has religion done for mankind?" Its powerful message is for the uninhibited thinker, a challenge to even the most broad-minded scholars of our time. The book is a monument of research and study, strikingly contrasting true and false religion. It rips the mask off the religion of communism, analyzes the major religions of the earth, laying bare their origins and beliefs, and shows how you can identify the ONE true religion in the earth today. The wisdom that it presents will be of helpful service to you, and its mature, thoughtful advice gives reassuring strength. This 352-page book, durably bound and stamped in gold, is illustrated and provided with convenient subject and Scripture indexes. Take advantage of its enlightening, hopeful message by mailing your order in now. A copy will be sent to you, anywhere, on a contribution of only 50 cents.

For ordering the above see addresses on the last page.

Chief Office and Official Address of

WATCH TOWER BIBLE & TRACT SOCIETY
WATCHTOWER BIBLE AND TRACT SOCIETY, INC.
INTERNATIONAL BIBLE STUDENTS ASSOCIATION

is

124 Columbia Heights, Brooklyn 1, New York, U. S. A.

Addresses of Branch offices:

America (U.S.), 117 Adams St., Brooklyn 1, N. Y. ****Australia,** 11 Beresford Road, Strathfield, N.S.W. ****Austria,** Liechtensteinstr. 24, Vienna IX. ****Bahamas,** Box 1247, Nassau, N.P. ****Belgium,** 28 Ave. Gen. Eisenhower, Schaerbeek-Brussels. ****Bolivia,** Casilla No. 1440, La Paz. ****Brazil,** Rua Licinio Cardoso 330, Rio de Janeiro. ****British Guiana,** 50 Brickdam, Georgetown. ****British Honduras,** Box 257, Belize. ****Burma,** P.O. Box 62, Rangoon. ****Canada,** 40 Irwin Ave., Toronto 5, Ontario. ****Ceylon,** 35 Beach Rd., Mount Lavinia. ****Chile,** Moneda 1710, Santiago. ****Colombia,** Apartado Nacional 147, Barranquilla. ****Costa Rica,** Apartado 2043, San José. ****Cuba,** Avenida 15 No. 4608, Almendares, Marianao, Havana. ****Cyprus,** Box 196, Famagusta. ****Denmark,** Sondre Fasanvej 54, Copenhagen-Valby. ****Ecuador,** Casilla 4512, Guayaquil. ****Egypt,** Post Box 387, Cairo. ****Eire,** 86 Lindsay Road, Glasnevin, Dublin. ****El Salvador,** Apartado 401, San Salvador. ****England,** 34 Craven Terrace, London, W. 2. ****Ethiopia,** Box 1781, Addis Ababa. ****Fiji,** Box 23, Suva. ****Finland,** Vainamoisenkatu 27, Helsinki. ****France,** 3 Villa Guibert, Paris 16°. ****Germany (Western),** Am Kohlheck, (16) Wiesbaden-Dotzheim. ****Gold Coast,** B.W.A., Box 760, Accra. ****Greece,** No. 6 Kartali St., Athens 6. ****Guadeloupe,** B. P. 239, Pointe-à-Pitre. ****Guatemala,** 11 Avenida Norte No. 5-67, Guatemala. ****Haiti,** Post Box 185, Port-au-Prince. ****Hawaii,** 1228 Pensacola St., Honolulu 14. ****Honduras,** Apartado 147, Tegucigalpa. ****Hong Kong,** 232 Tai Po Rd., 2d Floor, Kowloon. ****India,** 167 Love Lane, Bombay 27. ****Indonesia,** Postbox 2105, Djakarta. ****Israel,** P.O. Box 385, Jerusalem. ****Italy,** Via Monte Maloia 10, Monte Sacro, Rome 742. ****Jamaica,** 151 King St., Kingston. ****Japan,** 1 Toyooka-Cho, Shiba-Mita, Minato-Ku, Tokyo. ****Korea,** P.O. Box 7, Sodaemun-ku P.O., Seoul. ****Lebanon,** P.O. Box 1122, Beirut. ****Leeward Islands,** Box 119, St. John's, Antigua, B.W.I. ****Liberia,** P.O. Box 171, Monrovia. ****Luxembourg,** 66 Boulevard General Patton, Luxembourg. ****Mexico,** Calzada Melchor Ocampo 71, México 4, D.F. ****Netherlands,** Koningslaan 1, Amsterdam-Z. ****Netherlands West Indies,** Breedestraat 12, Otrabanda, Curaçao. ****Newfoundland, Canada,** 239 Pennywell Road, St. John's. ****New Zealand,** G.P.O. Box 30, Wellington, C. 1. ****Nicaragua,** Apartado 183, Managua, D.N. ****Nigeria, West Africa,** P.O. Box 695, Lagos. ****Northern Rhodesia,** 84 King George Ave., Luanshya. ****Norway,** Inkognitogaten 28 B., Oslo. ****Nyasaland,** Box 83, Blantyre. ****Pakistan,** Post Box 346, Lahore. ****Panama,** Box 274, Ancon, C.Z. ****Paraguay,** Ayolas 394, Asunción. ****Peru,** Pasaje Velarde 165, Lima. ****Philippine Republic,** 104 Roosevelt Rd., San Francisco del Monte, Quezon City. ****Puerto Rico,** 704 Calle Lafayette, Pda. 21, Urb. Hip., Santurce 34. ****Sierra Leone,** Box 136, Freetown. ****Singapore** 15, 33 Poole Road. ****South Africa,** Private Bag, P.O. Elandsfontein, Transvaal. ****Southern Rhodesia,** P.O. Box 1462, Salisbury. ****Surinam,** Zwartenhovenbrugstraat 181 Boven, Paramaribo. ****Sweden,** Jakobsberg. ****Switzerland,** Allmendstrasse 39, Berne 22. ****Thailand,** Box 67, Bangkok. ****Trinidad,** 21 Taylor St., Woodbrook, Port of Spain, B.W.I. ****Uruguay,** Joaquín de Salterain 1264, Montevideo. ****Venezuela,** Avda. Honduras, Quinta Luz, Urb. Las Acacias, Caracas, D.F.